Racial Indigestion

America and the Long 19th Century

GENERAL EDITORS
David Kazanjian, Elizabeth McHenry, and Priscilla Wald

Black Frankenstein: The Making of an American Metaphor
Elizabeth Young

Neither Fugitive nor Free: Atlantic Slavery, Freedom Suits, and the Legal Culture of Travel
Edlie L. Wong

Shadowing the White Man's Burden: U.S. Imperialism and the Problem of the Color Line
Gretchen Murphy

Bodies of Reform: The Rhetoric of Character in Gilded-Age America
James B. Salazar

Empire's Proxy: American Literature and U.S. Imperialism in the Philippines
Meg Wesling

Sites Unseen: Architecture, Race, and American Literature
William A. Gleason

Racial Innocence: Performing American Childhood from Slavery to Civil Rights
Robin Bernstein

American Arabesque: Arabs and Islam in the 19th-Century Imaginary
Jacob Rama Berman

Racial Indigestion: Eating Bodies in the 19th Century
Kyla Wazana Tompkins

Racial Indigestion

Eating Bodies in the 19th Century

Kyla Wazana Tompkins

NEW YORK UNIVERSITY PRESS
New York and London

NEW YORK UNIVERSITY PRESS
New York and London
www.nyupress.org

LIBRARY OF CONGRESS CATALOGING-IN-PUBLICATION DATA

Tompkins, Kyla Wazana.
Racial indigestion : eating bodies in the 19th century /
Kyla Wazana Tompkins.
p. cm. — (America and the long 19th century)
Includes bibliographical references and index.
ISBN 978-0-8147-7002-3 (cl : alk. paper)
ISBN 978-0-8147-7003-0 (pb : alk. paper)
ISBN 978-0-8147-7005-4 (ebook)
ISBN 978-0-8147-3837-5 (ebook)
1. Food habits—Social aspects—United States—History—19th century. 2. Diet—Social aspects—United States—History—19th century. 3. Cooking—Social aspects—United States—History—19th century. 4. Human body—Social aspects—United States—History—19th century. 5. United States—Race relations—History—19th century. 6. Graham, Sylvester, 1794–1851. 7. Alcott, Louisa May, 1832–1888—Criticism and interpretation. 8. Food in literature. I. Title.
GT2853.U5T66 2012
394.1'20973—dc23
2011051505

References to Internet Websites (URLs) were accurate at the time of writing. Neither the author nor New York University Press is responsible for URLs that may have expired or changed since the manuscript was prepared.

New York University Press books are printed on acid-free paper, and their binding materials are chosen for strength and durability. We strive to use environmentally responsible suppliers and materials to the greatest extent possible in publishing our books.

Manufactured in the United States of America
c 10 9 8 7 6 5 4 3 2 1
p 10 9 8 7 6 5 4 3 2 1

A book in the American Literatures Initiative (ALI), a collaborative publishing project of NYU Press, Fordham University Press, Rutgers University Press, Temple University Press, and the University of Virginia Press. The Initiative is supported by The Andrew W. Mellon Foundation. For more information, please visit www.americanliteratures.org.

I don't think you're ready for this jelly
My body's too bootylicious for you. —Destiny's Child

Contents

Acknowledgments

Though I will come quickly to the long list of people to whom I am indebted, I hope that I will be forgiven a quick digression so that I may acknowledge the many tables where I began to observe the politics of food and eating. Eating and cooking—at restaurants or at home—have always gone hand in hand with the world of ideas and art for me. I stumbled over many of the ideas in this book either talking and eating with family or, alternately, sitting alone in a café or bar with a cold cup of coffee, something small and delicious (and, while a student, cheap), and my laptop or a book.

To wit, let me start with my mother, Lydia Wazana, and her restaurant Miro—formerly La Pizzeria—which is to be found beachside in Cabarete, the Dominican Republic. Anyone whose parent runs a restaurant knows how lucky I have been to have Miro to retreat to. To Miro I would add Friday-night Shabbat French fries at my great-grandmother's; Saturday dafinas in my grandmother Margaret Reboh's home; breakfasts, lunches, and dinners with my aunts Kathy and Madeleine Wazana; and my aunt Nadine Reboh's excellent grilled cheese sandwiches.

For intellectual nourishment I owe many thanks to the professors and teachers who inspired and guided me along the way, including my high school teacher John Pendergrast, who, though he may not know it, changed everything with a few words. At York University I was lucky not only to learn literary theory from Marie-Christine Leps and postcolonial theory and literature from Arun Mukherjee but to be a part of a group of activist intellectual women who congregated around what is now the Centre for Women and Trans People. Almost everything I know about teaching I learned at a university where most of us were from the first generation in our family to attend a postsecondary school. During my master's degree at the University of Toronto I was aided along the way by Chelva Kanaganayakam and Garry Leonard. A few words—not enough, surely—must go to Linda Hutcheon: adored mentor, intellectual idol, and, now, friend. I am but one of a long list of Canadian-born scholars who were fortunate to be her student, receiving the benefits of her advice and role modeling.

At Stanford University I was guided along by the example and generous advice of David Palumbo-Liu, Sharon Holland, Paula Moya, Harry Elam, Michael Thompson, Oksana Bulgakowa, Jack Rakove, Akhil Gupta, Seth Lerer, and Yvonne Yarbro Bejarano. I was lucky to be able to participate in Sander Gilman's "Body Matters" seminar at Cornell's School for Criticism and Theory: many of the ideas shared in that classroom and over lunch and dinner in Ithaca found their way into this book. Similarly I must thank Ann Laura Stoler, whose seminar at Stanford introduced me to many of the key concepts I needed to work through my materials. A special mention to Jan Hafner and Monica Moore, proxy moms to us all in the Program in Modern Thought and Literature.

The project was conceived in Jeffrey Schnapp's "Food and Literature" seminar but born in Jay Fliegelman's "Eighteen-Forties" seminar, more specifically in his generous and brilliant feedback to my final paper for that class. I am particularly grateful to Scott Bukatman, whose example as a teacher and scholar showed me what it was like to live a joyful intellectual life, and to Hilton Obenzinger for giving me a job and also great, and blunt, advice when I needed it. And of course, one can never ever thank one's committee enough: to Arnold Rampersad for pushing me to see the relationship between good writing and clear ideas and for his reminder to love literature for what it is and aspires to be; to Estelle Freedman as an example of human kindness, intellectual integrity, and fierce feminist grace; and to Sianne Ngai for all of the above, plus the great gift of not only believing in the project but telling me to take what was already there and to *keep going* to the creative and intellectual edge. And of course, again, to Linda, for being my external reader and long-distance sounding board.

To this list I must add the fellow students with whom I was lucky enough to share the peaks and valleys of graduate education. Thanks and love to Lara Doan, Daniel Kim, Tim'm West, Lisa Arellano, Richard Benjamin, Mishuana Goeman, Shona Jackson, Gabrielle Moyer, Evelyn Alsultany, Nirvana Tanoukhi, Ebony Coletu, Allegra Mcleod, Rachel Poliquin, Vida Mia Garcia, Bakirathi Mani, Teresa Delfin, Julia Carpenter, Ericka Beckman, and Yael Ben-Zvi. I am grateful to Cindy Wu for reading a version of chapter 4. In Marcia Ochoa, Martha Kelly, Nicole Fleetwood, Amelia Glaser, and Raul Coronado I have been blessed to find fierce interlocutors, sometime roommates, fellow voyagers, and lifelong friends: thank you for being there and for being so fabulicious.

Along the way I was helped by those angels who walk amongst us: librarians, archivists, and curators. I must first thank Barbara Haber, Sarah Hutcheon, and Barbara K. Wheaton, whose patience with a very green graduate student who was very obviously lost in the stacks of the Julia Child collection at Radcliffe's Schlesinger Library helped yield many parts of this book. In particular, Barbara Ketchum Wheaton sent me over to the Baker Library at Harvard Business School to look at the trade cards in its advertising archives—for that, and because she is one of the godmothers of food studies, I will always owe her. At the American Antiquarian Society I was helped by Joanne Chaison and Marie Lamoureux and most kindly encouraged by John Hench. For their swift help while I was putting together the images and permissions for this book I must also thank Jaclyn Penny at the AAS, Melissa Murphy at the Baker, and Ben Crane of The Trade Card Place. I have appreciated being welcomed as a reader to the Huntington Library by Kadin Henningsen and Sarah N. Ash Georgi.

At the research stage I was supported by an Ontario Graduate Scholarship, the Mrs. Giles A. Whiting fellowship, and a fellowship at the Center for Comparative Studies in Race and Ethnicity. The Stanford University School of Humanities and Sciences kindly supported me for six years and gave me research and travel funds as well as support to travel to the School for Criticism and Theory. Pomona College has supported this project with generous research and travel funds, subventions, a Mellon faculty grant, and the Dorothy M. Steele leave for pretenured faculty.

I have been blessed with great friends and colleagues at Pomona College: in the English Department, Kevin Dettmar, superb chair, superfun office neighbor, and champion of junior faculty, as well as Dara Regaignon, Claudia Rankine, Valorie Thomas, Kathleen Fitzpatrick, Toni Clark, Paul Mann, Jonathan Lethem, Arden Reed, Helena Wall, and Verlyn Klinkenborg, defender of the sentence. It has been more than fun to keep vigil in the trenches of junior faculty life with Aaron Kunin, Sarah Raff, Colleen Rosenfeld, and Hillary Gravendyk. Moved on to other adventures but not forgotten are Cris Miller, Rena Fraden, Martha Andresen, and Paul Saint-Amour. And of course, to David Foster Wallace, fellow dog lover. Thank you for introducing me to the proper use of the word "pud." We loved you. You are missed.

In the Program in Gender and Women's Studies thank you to my mentors Deborah Burke, Peggy Waller, and Cecilia Conrad and to friends and colleagues Pardis Mahdavi, April Mayes, Erin Runions, Zayn Kassam, Jonathan Hall, and Chris Guzaitis. Thank you to my inspiring students at Pomona College, including but not limited to Lauren Rosenfeld, Andrew Ragni, Elizabeth Cobacho, Allison Feldman, Aakash Kishore, and Lindsay Jonasson. Thank you to Mary Buchner, who typed out the bibliography.

The field of food studies, in particular the good folks of the Association for the Study of Food and Society, heard pieces of this book early on and believed that the study of food and eating was more than just a hobby interest. For many great meals and conversations and for many more to come thank you to Fabio Parasecoli, Amy Bentley, Warren Belasco, Netta Davis, Charlotte Biltekoff, Rafia Zafar, and Carolyn de la Peña. Amy, Warren, and Carolyn in particular mentored and supported my project early in my career, for which I will always be grateful.

Deepest thanks to my anonymous readers: if I got anything right, it's because of you. Thank you to Eric Zinner, Priscilla Wald, Elizabeth McHenry, and Ciara Mclaughlin. To David Kazanjian, who invited me to submit my manuscript to NYU Press: thank you for championing the project when it was far from ready. Thank you too to anonymous readers at *Callaloo* and *Gastronomica*, where portions of earlier versions of chapters 2 and 3 were published.

This is an amazing moment in nineteenth-century studies: not only is the field flourishing intellectually; it seems to be filled with just plain good people. Thank you to Ivy Wilson for inviting me into conversation; Ivy, you will never know how important that was to me. I am grateful for the good humor and brilliance of Dana Luciano, Glenn Hendler, Jordan Stein, Robin Bernstein, Elizabeth Freeman, Lloyd Pratt, Sarah Mesle, Chris Looby, and Peter Coviello. Dana, Beth, and Glenn read this manuscript closely, incisively, and generously: thank you, all three, for everything. Next round's on me. Thank you too to Roger Gathman, David Lobenstine, Victoria Baker, and Andrew Katz.

I must also thank my expatriate Canadian Bay Area tribe, Sara Gillingham, Sara O'Hearn, and of course my Matthew Lawrence. Thank you to Buffy Summers and Barbra Streisand, they know why. And while I never wrote a word there, as a space of joy, abandon, creativity, fraternity, and sorority that could only have been born in the age of AIDS, that carried me forward spiritually with house music and continues to do so to this day, I am indebted to Toronto's late, great club The Twilight Zone, where I met and danced with my first urban tribe: Ann, Marla, Chantal, Ford, and everyone else who remembers that in the beginning there was Jack . . . and Jack had a groove.

To family lost along the way but who haunt these pages: my great-grandmother Mémé Dona Ohnona, Pépé Henri Wazana, my grandmother Margaret Tompkins, my grandfather Walter Tompkins, and my father, David Tompkins. Many, many, many thanks go to my mother, Lydia Wazana, for whom the word *fierce* was invented. This book would never have happened if I hadn't been the child of a single mother who saw nothing unusual about reading me Gertrude Stein's *Ida* at bedtime or taking me at age four, to meet Andy Warhol. How lucky I was. And last but not least: my son, Andualem David, and my best friend and husband, Tim. The word *love* just isn't big enough to describe it. But it'll do for a start.

Introduction

Eating Bodies in the 19th Century

In 1900, the Thomas Edison Company produced a silent gag film called *The Gator and the Pickaninny*, depicting a theatrical scene in which a black child is fishing on a water shore. An alligator crawls up behind him and eats the child up; soon after, a man runs up, cuts open the alligator, and pulls the child out whole. Celebration ensues. On one level, this film does not stray far from the features we can expect from the American popular entertainment of the era, with its broad racist humor—signaled by the very term "pickaninny"—and its vaudevillian gag and dance routines. However, if we approach the film on another level, asking about the eating motif around which the film turns, it presents us with a puzzle: how does a film of a black child being eaten become legible to audiences in the early twentieth century? More than solely an insight into racist images in the period, this idea—of the edible and delicious black subject—reveals something larger about the relationship between eating and racial identity, between bodies inscribed with the marks of race and food.

Through readings of material culture—novels, chapbooks, poetry, cookbooks, and visual culture—this book examines the social and symbolic practices through which eating and food cultures inform the production of racial difference and other forms of political inequality. This is not, however, entirely a project about food. Rather, in *Racial Indigestion* I contribute to the growing field of food studies by examining *eating*; I uncover and analyze cultural texts and moments during which acts of eating cultivate political subjects by fusing the social with the biological, by imaginatively shaping the matter we experience as body and self. In five separate case studies, I examine images of mouths and bodies, of eaters and the eaten, to produce a story about the consolidation of racist ideologies in the intimate workings of the body politic as refracted through what I term *eating culture*. That is, in *Racial Indigestion* I look beyond food itself to consider practices and representations of ingestion and edibility, including literary, dietetic, and visual texts in which objects, people, and political events are metaphorically and metonymically figured through the symbolic process of eating.

To date, most work in this vein has focused on the twentieth and twenty-first centuries.[1] In *Racial Indigestion*, however, I uncover eating as a trope and technology of racial formation during the first 130 years of the U.S. republic. Not unlike the current foodie moment, and perhaps original to it, eating culture in that period played a significant part in the privileging of whiteness during the nineteenth century. Such anxious girding of the boundaries of whiteness, however, could only happen where those boundaries were threatened, and it is exactly as a site of racial anxiety that eating is most productively read.

My goal in making this shift from food to eating—a shift to a framework we might call *critical eating studies*— implicitly entails the examination of the field of food studies' unconscious investments in the commodity itself. It is also a move that weds food studies to body theory, here with a particular focus on race in the context of the literary and cultural production of the nineteenth-century United States.[2] The emergence of the relatively young field of food studies in the late eighties and early nineties coincided with a national explosion in food culture and the growth of what has come to be known as urban "foodie" culture, a congruence that has led some critics to dismiss the field as "scholarship-lite."[3] Although I do not agree with this skeptical and lazy opinion, given my decade-long involvement in the field, I do have my own criticisms. As many food studies scholars in the social sciences have noted, foodie culture is founded on problematic racial politics in which white, bourgeois, urban subject positions are articulated, on the one hand, through the consumption and informational mastery of foreign, that is, non-Anglo-American food cultures and, on the other hand, performed through romanticized and insufficiently theorized attachments to "local" or organic foodways, attachments that at times suspiciously echo nativist ideological formations.[4] Using the readings in this book as a testing ground, I want to nudge food studies' interests and methods away from an unreflective collaboration in the object-based fetishism of the foodie world, a collaboration that has produced an unending stream of single-commodity histories and ideologically worrisome localist politics.[5] Instead, I hope to push us further toward a critique of the political beliefs and structures that underlie eating as a social practice.[6]

Part of my work in this project, then, is to more closely bind food studies to feminist, queer, and gender studies, as well as to critical race theory; in doing so I interrogate eating at various historical points in order to set in relief the (un)imaginative limits of normative notions of bodily being. My approach seeks to render discursive two kinds of matter toward which so much human appetitive energy is directed: food and flesh. As we will see, what is yielded by this new framework is a move beyond the concern with skin and boundary that has dominated body studies, and thus away from an investment in surfaces that I want to argue is the intellectually limited inheritance of the epidermal ontology of race.[7] By reading *orificially*, critical eating studies theorizes a flexible and circular relation between the self and the social world in order to imagine a dialogic in which we—reader and text, self and other, animal and human—recognize our bodies as vulnerable to each other in ways that are terrible—that is, full of terror—and, at other times, politically productive.

In the context of the nineteenth-century United States, the dialogical relations that underlie eating had particular consequences for a nation in the process of cultural, political, and ideological formation. Eating threatened the foundational fantasy of a contained autonomous self—the "free" Liberal self—because, as a function of its basic mechanics, eating transcended the gap between self and other, blurring the line between subject and object as food turned into tissue, muscle, and nerve and then provided the energy that drives them all. At the same time, images of food in the period often pointed to the fleshliness—the biological meatiness, even—of the body, seeming to imply a reassuring materiality of self that exists prior to, and as the condition of, discourse. As a simultaneously cultural and biological process, eating, and images thereof, were therefore often deployed in the service of fixing bodily fictions: "Tell me what you eat and I shall tell you what you are," the eighteenth-century gastronome Anthelme Brillat-Savarin most famously said, in what is now a chestnut of food studies scholarship.[8]

As is so often the case, it is exactly at the moment of their most anxious deployment that fictions of the self—the permanence and futurity of "what you *are*"—prove to be their most precarious. Understood in its Western context, by the nature of the act in which an organism yields and opens to the outer world, eating reveals the self to be reliant upon that which is beyond its epidermal limits. The very social and interdependent nature of eating, then—its *dependence* on the "what" of Brillat-Savarin's "what you eat"—also lends itself to the unraveling of bodily essentialisms.[9] But it is not simply the "what" of what one eats that matters. It is the "where" of where we eat and where food comes from; the "when" of historically specific economic conditions and political pressures; the "how" of how food is made; and the "who" of who makes and who gets to eat it. Finally, and most important, it is the many "whys" of eating—the differing imperatives of hunger, necessity, pleasure, nostalgia, and protest—that most determine its meaning. In reckoning with each of these interrogatives, by turning them *into* interrogatives, we can begin to get at the materialist conditions that determine how, and why, to borrow from Judith Butler, the matter of food comes to "matter."[10]

The insight that the act of eating dissolves the boundary between self and other, between subject and object is not mine alone,[11] nor is the idea that eating is also a social practice that confirms and delineates difference, demarcating social barriers and affirming group formations.[12] However this paradox, as it appears across the nineteenth century, makes eating an important case study in the production and consolidation of fictions of national unity *and* racial difference in the period. If in food culture the act of fleshly materialization is rendered visible as material culture, if, as we will see in chapter 2, the mythical virtues of a wheat-centered diet arise in connection to the body ideal that underlies the antebellum project of U.S. expansion and is in turn dependent on it, then we should recognize that the study of this problematic cannot ignore the materials and processes of eating culture. Eating intervenes as a determining moment in what I argue are paradoxical and historically specific attempts to regulate embodiment, which I define as living in and through the social experience of the matter we call flesh. Nationalist foodways—and the objects fetishized therein—in turn become allegories through which the expanding nation and its attendant anxieties play out. What we see in the nineteenth century—as indeed we do today in such racialized discourses as obesity, hunger, and diabetes—is the production of social inequality at the level of the quotidian functioning of the body. What also emerges, however, are fissures and openings in the body politic, spaces where political fictions are exposed, messy, and only semidigested.

One such site, at the obvious center of eating culture, is the mouth. I do not—I would not dare—offer a single model through which to understand the mouth in nineteenth-century U.S. literature and culture. At times the mouth reveals vulnerability; at other times it is a sign of aggression. Some mouths in *Racial Indigestion* are forced open; other mouths speak, eat, and laugh with the energy generated by suppressed political affect. Some mouths—the mouth of the reader or viewer in particular—are never visible in text or image but rather are assumed to exist, invited to engage with the page through various tropes of desire, disgust, laughter, and enjoyment. In *Racial Indigestion* the mouth is understood as a site *to which* and *within which* various political values unevenly adhere and *through which* food as mediated experience imperfectly bonds with the political to form the fictions that are too often understood within everyday life as racial truths.

mouth

The mouth is also a space with a cultural and erotic history of its own, one that, particularly in the overlapping of dietetic and sexual reform in the antebellum period, offers glimpses of a presexological mapping of desire, appetite, and vice. In many of the texts I investigate in this book, eating functions as a metalanguage for genital pleasure and sexual desire. But eating is often a site of erotic pleasure itself, what I call, as a means of signaling the alignment between oral pleasure and other forms of nonnormative desire, *queer alimentarity.*

At the end of the nineteenth century Freud theorized the "erotogenic significance of the labial region"—the mouth—as the second stage in the development of infantile sexuality, an autoerotic moment which, in "normal" sexual development, would later be surpassed by genital orientation toward the opposite sex.[13] The mouth certainly does surface as a site of autoerotic pleasure in the antimasturbation and dietetic reform tracts I read in this book. However, in the map of the nervous system that was promulgated by Sylvester Graham and William Alcott, which I discuss in chapter 2, and then reinterpreted by various of their cultural inheritors, including Louisa May Alcott, whom I discuss in chapter 4, the mouth and the genitals function as *coeval* sites of erotic intensity in adults as well as in children. In Graham's writing both can be overstimulated, and indeed sensual indulgence at one of those sites inevitably drives the appetitive needs of the other.[14]

This presexological mapping of erotic and alimentary pleasure in the antebellum period had its corollary in the literal, that is, geographic, mapping of the nation, and it was at the overlap between the two that the mouth, as a doorway into the consuming body, first became a site of biopolitical intensity in the United States. Biopolitics is understood in this book not as the project of state intervention into the well-being of its population in the classic Foucauldian sense.[15] Rather, I resituate biopolitics in the context of the United States as a collective ideological effort driven by various reform movements in the antebellum United States via a series of uneven, asynchronous, and local campaigns, each of them reworking republicanism to construe the ideal citizen as self-policing, temperate, and moral. In the context of reform dietetics, which was closely allied with the temperance movement and antimasturbation campaigns, the ideal citizen was to be made and remade via the quotidian practices of correct consumption, self-care, and sexual hygiene.

To be "correct" within these discourses, or, more precisely, to be "virtuous," meant to be identified with the nation-building project, both with and against the British past. The girding of these bodily ideologies became even more overdetermined as, over the course of a half century, the rapidly expanding national borders came to encompass the formerly French South and the formerly Spanish Southwest, as well as waves of new European immigration. Across that same period, the United States also propelled its borders over and decimated Native American cultures and peoples, reconstituting and relocating those First Nations, all the while grappling with the possibility of slave emancipation and black men's enfranchisement. In that context, the construction and defense of whiteness as a majoritarian demographic seemed all the more pressing to those unwilling to remake their nation in the image of its actual inhabitants. The particular contribution of the reform movement was to stitch nationalism to the individual white body, a shift that made the project of defending the white body against various (racializing) vices dependent on a citizenry that construed politics to be an individual matter.[16] Eating culture, tied as it was to economic and political matters of trade and expansion and thus commodity consumption, became one site of intimate political intensity, where "eating American," that is, eating foodstuffs tied to the transplanted ecological history and foodways of the Euro-American majority—what we might think of as an early and paradoxical iteration of the "local" foods idea—was one way to produce a moral body, unswayed by dangerous appetites for exotic and overstimulating, that is, "foreign," foods.

Within these local, national, and transnational discourses, the mouth became the focus of a disciplinary project within which the correct embodiment of the individual was understood to be of deep importance to the burgeoning nation. Such disciplinary models changed across the century, to be sure, as different cultural and political anxieties, as well as various transnational relations, occupied the cultural imagination. Each of these moments, further, took on its own allegorical relationship to both the individual body and the body politic; at each of the five moments that I discuss in this book eating played an important role, as a practice or representation. Following the evolution of eating culture across this period opens up new areas of inquiry into the alignment between bodies and bodies politic, revealing different forms of racial embodiment as they shifted with the political and economic contingencies of the period.

A central argument of this book, then, is that eating is central to the performative production of raced and gendered bodies in the nineteenth century. Consider for instance the following passage, written by Oliver Wendell Holmes and quoted by Catharine Beecher and Harriet Beecher Stowe in the nutrition chapter of the 1869 edition of *The American Woman's Home*:

> Every organized being always lives immersed in a strong solution of its own elements. . . . We are all chameleons in our diet, as we are all salamanders in our habitat, inasmuch as we live always in the fire of our own smoldering combustion. . . . We are perishing and being born again at every instant. . . . We do literally enter over and over again into the womb of that great mother from whom we get our bones and flesh, and blood, and marrow.[17]

Holmes's allegory of constant death and rebirth intersects directly with Butler's understanding of performativity as "ritualized repetition"—biological processes are here given a circular, iterative temporality linked to death and rebirth, making and unmaking.[18] But this sense of dietary immersion in one's own elements, of burning from within, of the self indistinguishable from the "strong solution" of its surroundings hints that from within the study of eating in the nineteenth century the production of bodily materiality looks a little different than it does within the bourgeois norms of the twenty-first century. This passage in fact points us to a messier idea of materialization, one in which, as William Ian Miller has written, we are soaking in "life soup, the roiling stuff of eating, defecation, fornication, generation, death, rot, and regeneration."[19]

Holmes's "womb of that great mother" entails an orifice out of which "our bones and flesh, and blood, and marrow" are delivered. Importantly, Holmes never specifies what orifice he means that we enter and exit, and indeed it is at the point—or perhaps more precisely from within the gorge—of the orifice that I wish to make my intervention. Reading fictions of bodily essence and materiality through the mouth points to the ways that food and eating culture provide a metalanguage through which we tell stories about the materials that constitute both object *and* subject, food and flesh.[20] More than that, examining these fictions offers new insights into the intersection of racial hierarchy with various forms of political citizenship across the period.

Because of the close link between eating, racial formation, and political culture in the period, the history of whiteness is at the center of this book. However, in *Racial Indigestion* eating culture is also understood as a privileged site for the representation of, and fascination with, those bodies that carry the burdens of difference and materiality, that are understood as less social, less intellectual, and, at times, less sentient: racially minoritized subjects, children, women, and, at times, animals. Often referred to as "hyperembodied" in this book, racially minoritized—mostly black and sometimes Asian—subjects are at times closely aligned with what we might think of as the bottom of the food chain.[21]

As the following five chapters attest, there are the eaters, and then there are the eaten; similarly, there are the eaters, and then there are the hungry. The image of the black body as an edible object is a strong and consistent trope in this book, and it is an image that carries the weight of many centuries of forced labor, of coercive and violent sexual desire, and of ongoing political struggle. As we will see, however, the fantasy of a body's edibility does not mean that body will always go down smoothly. Rather, the title of my book, *Racial Indigestion*, points to the idea that the constitution of whiteness via the most racist images and practices of eating culture is neither seamless nor easy. Although I trace the image of the black body as an edible object across the last half of the nineteenth century, at no point does my analysis understand the black body and therefore black subjects to be without agency. For as these images and the cultural logics that flow through them show, across the nineteenth century black bodies and subjects stick in the throat of the (white) body politic, refusing to be consumed as part of the capitalist logic of racism and slavery as well as the cultural and literary matter that they produced.

Whether impeding absorption—getting stuck in the craw or producing colicky white bodies and thereby disturbing the easy internalization of blackness—or whether testifying from the space of imminent death and expulsion from the bowels of a slave-dependent nation, black bodies and subjects in these encounters fight back, and bite back, both in the white imaginary and in domestic manuals and novels produced by black authors. Although excluded from the biopolitical, nation-building imperatives of a mostly white reform movement that nonetheless often aligned itself with abolition, black authors and citizens insisted on their relevance and centrality to national narratives of bodily belonging.

As we will see, particularly in chapters 3 and 5, black subjects often resist through the trope of excess—of affect, of aesthetic intensity, or, as the cook Chloe in *Uncle Tom's Cabin* tells us, through sheer "sauciness." In other words, black subjects resist via the aesthetic strategy that Daphne Brooks has termed *opacity*—by refusing to be reduced to a function of white well-being.[22] In refusing white instrumentalization black subjects in these texts interrupt the easy flow of white desire and entitlement, which appears in the desire to consume the black subject, a dialectic that, given the emphasis on texts directed at white women and children in this book, I read as the feminized inversion of the more common trope of nineteenth-century racism in which white men inhabit and impersonate blackness. What the texts examined in *Racial Indigestion* point to is that in many of those moments when racism appears to produce its most abject representations—through comic debasement, for instance—black characters and subjects inhabit the limits of language and aesthetic form, performing moments of spectacular visibility, at times despite and beyond the creator's intentions.

From within these images, it is not simply the white mouth that is of interest, in its voracious and cannibalistic desire to experience, enjoy, and destroy the other, what bell hooks called, in her foundational formulation of the phrase, "Eating the Other."[23] As I show, the black mouth is a site of political intensity itself, as it consistently occupies and preempts the domination of white desire, from the kitchen, from the back of the house and below the stairs, and then ultimately in the sphere of urban commodity culture. In *Racial Indigestion*, the black mouth speaks, laughs, and eats in the face of the violent desires of white supremacy; in fact, speech, laughter, and eating are conjoined as tropes of black cultural presence and resistance. Across this book eating is an act that is also symbolic of access to the sphere of public politics and citizenship and thus metonymic of the struggle for political agency.

As a foundation for this investigation of the conjoined tropes of laughter, politics, and eating, in chapter 1 I develop a literary history of eating culture via the intertwined histories of the colonial hearth and the kitchen in the United States. Developed out of many years of teaching Rabelais and Bakhtin in my "Eating the Other" course, *Racial Indigestion* also contains an argument about the association of comedy and vernacular speech—another form of orality, or voice, that exceeds or counters intextuation, in de Certeau's terminology—with the politically devalued and thus often hyperembodied populations that appear with food and in food spaces: immigrants, blacks, servants, and, in particular, cooks.[24]

Specifically, I put these discourses into conversation with theater history and performance studies to understand literary representations of hearths and kitchens and the subaltern bodies that work there as drawn from colonial, transatlantic, and early-American theater culture, in which travesty, cross-dressing, and racial and species inversion were mutually intertwined as carnivalesque traditions. In *Racial Indigestion*, I see the kitchen as a space whose politics and representations must be analyzed in terms of abjection and inversion. The kitchen in this formulation is a space of blood and guts, plucked chickens and cooked tongue, rancid and sweet butter, rising bread and fermenting beers, and other items only semi-formed on their way to the site of ingestion, be it dining room or kitchen table. Feminist critics have long viewed the kitchen as the space within the house where the politics of both the public sphere and the home are most contentious and visible. In *Racial Indigestion*, I read that clash in the violent confrontations between mistress and servant or slave, in the unavoidable economics of what is available and affordable, in the cultural politics of who eats what and when.

My move to consider literature from the back of the house is thus a move to think specifically about how food and kitchen imagery begins to account for the viscerality of regimes of inequity organized around mythologies of difference, as well as the ways that food metaphorizes fleshly experience as a "natural" limit of social, linguistic, and literary expression. Kitchens in *Racial Indigestion* are not only sites of utopic possibility, of the possible inversion of classes of people, and of the worlding dreams of early feminism, although they are all that: they are also dystopic spaces whose abjection in the internal economy of the home allows the repressed to be represented in the visceral commonplaces of kitchen work—cutting, scraping, peeling, and boiling.

Chapter 2 shifts to an examination of the queer racial erotics of Sylvester Graham's intimate and imperialist dietetic project, focusing specifically on the consolidation of whiteness as the racial formation at the heart of republican citizenship. In particular, I look at the politics of bread and wheat in the antebellum period, examining the transnational and imperial consequences of Sylvester Graham's "farinaceous" diet to reveal the homology between these prescriptive cures and an imperial politics of U.S. expansion.

In some ways, my work on Graham seems to belie one of the central ideas behind this book: to shift food studies attention away from the *what* of food to the *how* of eating. But in reading these antebellum reformer texts, I hope to point to the fact that the *what* of food was in part determined by the material and symbolic processes that brought food into contact with the mouth and the digestive system. Additionally, this chapter begins to lay the claim that the commodity citizen of the late twentieth and early twenty-first centuries is a direct descendant of Graham and other food reformers' ideal eaters. Much like today's locavores and food reformers, reform dietetics invited consumers to direct their desire toward virtuous objects, to substitute a hypervigilant digestive life for critical engagement with political and economic processes. Thus, while on the surface this chapter is interested in bread as a foodstuff, it is ultimately focused on reform dietetics as an early iteration and case study in the production of the consumer-citizen as a racially specific and politically limited eater-activist.

Chapter 3 looks at Harriet Beecher Stowe's, Nathaniel Hawthorne's, and Harriet Wilson's deployment of the trope of the black body as edible object during the 1850s. I use this deeply disturbing and at the same time pervasive image, written about so casually in this period, to further develop my theory of eating as a racially performative act, one through which we can unveil and ideally destabilize politically limited ideas of racial embodiment. Reversing the trope of blackface, in which blackness is *put on*, in these texts whiteness is consolidated through the metaphor of ingestion: blackness is *put in*. I begin by uncovering the allegorical effect of the edible black body as a Jim Crow cookie in Nathaniel Hawthorne's *House of Seven Gables* and then trace variations on the edible black body in two abolitionist and antiracist writers, Harriet Beecher Stowe and Harriet Wilson, as they seek to work out the place of the black subject in the white body politic.

What I hope to make clear in this chapter, however, is that those subjects pictured as edible hardly concede to that relationship. Even in *Uncle Tom's Cabin* and *The House of the Seven Gables*, two texts with problematic, racist representations, the consumable black body will not go down easily but rather pushes back against the body that seeks to consume and thereby obliterate it. In Harriet Wilson's *Our Nig*, Frado refuses consumption entirely, demanding a place at the table and documenting the middle-class kitchen and its visceral terrors as experiences at the edge of what may be represented and spoken. The black literary body here is put in service of the black subject and the black public sphere.

Chapter 4 returns to the reform movement's nutritional and erotic thematics via Louisa May Alcott's postbellum adoption of reform dietetics and antiaddiction discourse in two of her lesser-known novels, which are staged during the heart of the antebellum China trade. As the niece of William Alcott, and as Bronson Alcott's daughter, Louisa May Alcott was subject, when young, to the enthusiastic application of Grahamite principles at her own table and could observe their effects on her mother as well, who was ultimately the organizer and producer of the family meal. Louisa May Alcott, with her family connection to reformist politics, modifies and invests themes from it in her postbellum novels. In as much as these novels are explicitly didactic, they promote the reformist ideal of white femininity, even as they mitigate the harsher, republican virtue ethic with a more accepting view of consumer citizenship. Alcott produces an image of a progressive shopping subject—the consumer activist—who buys or refuses to buy in service of her political ideals, who seeks to reduce her dependence on commodity culture but succeeds only, in fact, in suppressing or redirecting it toward other objects. At the same time, the concretizing of racial hierarchy in Alcott's texts seems to work in tandem with the much-documented queer subtexts of her work.

I conclude the book with a discussion of race, eating, and representation in chromolithographic trade cards, an underexamined advertising medium of the late nineteenth century that, as I will argue, borrowed heavily from the theatrical model of racial impersonation in order to incite consumer desire and imagine new consuming publics. Flipping the image of the edible black body around, in chapter 5 trade cards depict people of color—African Americans and Asians—consuming commodities. Following Harriet Wilson's work in tracing the black subject coming into being, I argue that these images stand in for what we might call having a place at the political table. Eating in these advertisements is a replacement for (and thus, logically, analogous to) political power: I read these images as a sign of the presence and importance of nonwhite postbellum U.S. consumers and the booming transnational market economy.

This chapter also puts the past two decades of scholarly work on blackface into conversation with my larger argument about eating. Images of eating here illuminate the connection between desire and embodiment as it was imagined by advertisers in the period, when advertising was a disparate and ad hoc sector, not yet institutionally congealed into specialized "agencies." In a sense, at this time advertising was much nearer popular culture, which is to say that it was articulated in the heart of everyday life, by printers and owners of stores and the like rather than by advertising professionals. This gives the trading cards I examine an interesting status as products that have not yet been captured by any particular institution or business and that reflect the obsessions of everyday life. Often, they show a mode of looking that I will argue was borrowed from the theater, at that time one of the great venues of popular entertainment.

Ultimately, these cards stage encounters that show nineteenth-century commodity culture to have been an important sphere of racialization that was on the one hand mediated through the senses and on the other hand seen as always and already a theatrical space. As we will see, in the sphere of commodity consumption, the production of race ultimately undoes its own logic: for just as the cards often attach extreme commodity pleasure to nonwhite bodies, the consistent trope of interracial and intercultural encounter in the cards points to the existence of a shared eating culture that mediated between disparate and radically unequal demographics.

1

Kitchen Insurrections

We begin at the hearth. Here, at the mouth of the fireplace, at the bottom of the chimney's throat, lies the ground for what follows in chapters 2 through 5, a conversation about the literature and visual texts that flowed from nineteenth-century eating culture. Across this conversation the hearth—and its descendant, the kitchen—will become less and less the primary location of U.S. food culture, and a more public eating culture will emerge, shaped by the ideology, literature, and architecture of domesticity in the early republic but rooted, as the material in this chapter argues, in early modern feast and banquet literature and transatlantic pantomime theater. Out of this *olla podrida* of environmental, cultural, and political forces will emerge a charged eating culture, in which racially marked and working-class bodies are as closely bound to food imagery as they are infused with a suppressed political affect barely contained by eating spaces and the literary forms they produce.

By focusing on the hearth and then the kitchen not simply as ahistorical spaces but as work sites whose symbolic function changed radically across the eighteenth and nineteenth centuries, even when actual architectural changes may have lagged quite far behind, I join in a long line of feminist critics who have investigated the central role of cooking spaces in organizing and defining the value of female labor and the valence of women's political and cultural citizenship across the nineteenth century.[1] My interest in the hearth and kitchen as the literary and architectural sites from which the United States' eating culture emerges is an attempt to invest feminist, literary, and cultural criticism with a more nuanced idea of the links between food and literature across the nineteenth century, in part by connecting images of the hearth to the early modern and transatlantic cultural flows that consistently linked food and eating imagery to class and bodily inversion.[2] In this chapter, then, I build on these feminist critics' work to argue that the hearth and kitchen have a specific literary history of their own, which produced effects on nineteenth-century literature and its bodies through a persistent connection to orality, construed broadly as vernacular language, as eating and ingestion, and finally as a series of sensual and erotic intensifications centered on the mouth. Finding their literary heritage in the European and colonial hearth, the hearth and kitchen discourses I will examine adhere—"stick" in Sara Ahmed's useful term—to those subjects who labored with or close to food.[3] As the United States' hyperembodied notions of class, race, and gender were expressed in terms of food—the central matter of the kitchen—so the bodies that labored in kitchens came to be represented, in the unconscious of popular culture, as food. Materialization, and the material conditions that make possible the exemplary act of consumption, are thus central concerns of this chapter.

If the seeds of the images that became the late nineteenth century's obsessive kitchen and food comedies about race lie in the hearth and kitchen literature of the late eighteenth and early nineteenth centuries, those images, as I will show, germinate in earlier representations of class difference and inversion. Class must be at the center of this chapter if we are to understand, first, the series of transformations by which the fireplace- and hearth-centered kitchen became the modern kitchen and, second, the articulation of the kitchen as a separate room from the rest of the house, a change that paralleled the articulation of class difference in the antebellum United States. It is in literature of the hearth—sometimes represented as the fireplace or chimney—that I trace the legacy of a discourse that came from Europe to the New World and linked the hearth to storytelling, ingestion, and moments of theatrical and carnivalesque class, gender, and (at times) species inversion.

The hearth lingers in the memory of antebellum U.S. writers, suturing food and eating to literary culture. As it disappears as a practical space, the hearth reemerges as a specter that haunts later overdetermined representations of the kitchen and the racially burdened bodies that labored there. In other words, what began as early modern and colonial-era class discourse was exploited to provide the protocols for later mid- and late nineteenth-century narratives of racial difference and consolidation. The hearth, with its link to dirt, the pleasurable possibilities of transformation, inversion, and bodily fluidity, repeatedly returns to haunt the complex public food cultures that descended from it and in particular the hegemonic project of white middle-class embodiment.

As we understand the political economy of domestic space through discourse, so should we understand the cook. The kitchen is not only where the cook performs her designated labor; it is the space from which the cook, that servant-figure so broadly stereotyped over the past two centuries, threatens to speak. In so doing she threatens to infuse the food she produces—that her employers will eat—with the stifled political affect that the walls of the kitchen are supposed to contain. Thus, not only does the kitchen come to be associated with the mouth, more specifically, with the mouth that will not close (and thus the mouth that laughs, eats, speaks, and screams); it becomes the central space where the threatening porosity between bodies—most specifically between ruling-class and subaltern bodies—is most apparent. As a practice, the intimacy of everyday nineteenth-century middle-class life necessarily took place across categories and spaces of social difference within the home. The cook who knew the tastes of the master, the mistress, and the children knew an intimate detail about them, a secret, something beyond her subordinate function. The cook inhabited the mouths of her "superiors" at the same time as she functioned as a proxy for their mouths in the cooking spaces of the home. Like the hearth, the cook's mouth lay at the center of domestic well-being; the food that passed from the hands and body of the kitchen servant to the dining room figuratively passed through her mouth to the mouths of the master's or mistress's family; it was therefore fraught with the possibility of poison, pollution, and race and class contamination.

Beyond the lines of class and race, other boundaries are upset in relation to eating and cooking in the kitchen's unconscious, boundaries that also parallel the evolution of the United States' scientific and juridical racisms. The line between human and animal seems to disappear in stories that revolve around the hearth, but so does the line between person and *thing*, an image that becomes more important in pre–Civil War literature such as Harriet Beecher Stowe's *Uncle Tom's Cabin*. Food thus becomes a metalanguage for multiple forms of difference in these passages, as animals exhibit human consciousness and human bodies are presented as food objects, often as meat. The kitchen, in turn, is increasingly the space into which disorder, garbage, contagion, dirt, noise, and other abject sensory experiences are projected. Those projections, all associated with the ideological work of disgust and therefore constituted by disgust's other, desire, stick to the kitchen's residents, the hyperembodied subjects—disruptive, forbidden, marginally social, and therefore deliciously attractive—who come to be associated with its labor and products.

Hearth, Fireplace, and Chimney

Cooking was one of the central activities of colonial and early U.S. homes in the Northeast; it was generally performed around fireplace-hearths. Indeed, through the mid-nineteenth century, for most people in the mostly rural United States, the fireplace continued to be the central space around which members of the household met and socialized. The size of the traditional hearth is an indicator of this centrally unifying function. In the seventeenth century many New England houses were built around massive stone chimneys, as were most houses in Plymouth Colony and Rhode Island. In order to keep new rooms warm houses often expanded through add-ons to the main house, usually on the side of the house where the chimney was located. This house arrangement was slightly different in the Chesapeake area, where houses, particularly those of the genteel class, tended to be framed by chimneys on opposite ends of the house.[4]

Not surprisingly, most of the original homes in British North America followed on the vernacular architectural designs of their early modern counterparts in England. As historian John Crowley has written, "The plans, amenities, and finish of the houses in which most Americans still lived at the end of the eighteenth century—room-and-loft house plans, wood and clay chimneys, few and small windows, and construction from local raw materials—would have earned them the derogatory designation 'cottages' in England."[5] In early New England homes often resembled the two-room buildings of southeastern England, with one room designated for sleeping and storage, another for cooking, sleeping, and eating. The division between these spaces was marked by the central fireplace.

For most colonists what constituted home improvement was not expanding the size of the house structure but rather adding then-expensive windows and window panes, which allowed more natural light into the home and moved reading, writing, and household duties away from the light afforded by the central fireplace. Artificial lighting using candles, whale oil lanterns, and tallow was expensive. As Jane Nylander points out, making candles was part of the regular regimen of domestic duties, and the household manufacture of candles for home use persisted in rural areas until the advent of cheap kerosene in the late 1860s.[6] The expense of glass windows was due partly to the cost of transport. Francis Higginson, writing to advise his friends in England about coming to America and New England's plantation, reminds them that "here are yet neither markets nor fayres to buy what you want." Thus, one must bring a number of goods not only to furnish but to build the household, among which are "glasse for windowes and many other things which were better for you to think of them than to want them here."[7] Oiled paper was commonly resorted to instead of glass. Still, the best and cheapest source of illumination was, by process of elimination, the central fireplace, which could be used for indoor entertainment and domestic activity on cold days and evenings, as well as for cooking.

Because the colonial house had not yet developed the kind of specialized spaces and furnishings that are allowed in a society that has developed "fayres" and markets and manufacturing, the technological issues relating to cooking and domestic labors pertaining to food were inseparable from those related to heating and light. Faced with cold temperatures they could never have imagined before colonizing the northern Americas, heat was a central concern for colonists and their descendants. This was partly because fireplace technology was so poor: in fact, such was the inefficiency of fireplace construction that by 1637 colonists had cleared most of the old-growth forest from Massachusetts Bay to warm themselves. Within these homes, fireplace chimneys sent a great deal of heat up and outside, and lack of insulation—cracks in the house's wooden frame, for instance—made retaining heat in the room difficult. To produce a minimal level of comfort, then, a prodigious amount of wood had to be used, which exacerbated another problem, because if heat leaked out, smoke often stayed in.[8]

In fact the colonists transplanted fireplace models from England and continental Europe that were outsized, considering the "cottage" size of their houses. They were often so big that one might consider the fireplace a room of its own: at times dominating an entire wall, the hearth was often topped with an enormous low-hanging hood that cooks and others had to stoop under to stir up the fire. On cold days the prized seat of the house was in fact *inside* the fireplace and next to the fire. More than a few feet away it might still be cold enough for water to freeze; too close and one got burned. Cotton Mather complained in his diary entry for January 23, 1697, that "in a warm Room, on a great Fire, the Juices forced out at the End of short Billets of Wood by the Heat of the Flame on which they were laid yett froze into Ice at their coming out."[9]

Such was the importance of developing fireplace and domestic heating technology that Benjamin Franklin himself turned his considerable talent to this issue, writing a pamphlet in 1744 that proposed a new technology for stoves based on Dutch and German stoves.[10] Franklin criticized then-current heating technologies, arguing that "the large open Fire-places used in the Days of our Fathers, and still generally in the Country, and in Kitchens" kept very little warm and, further, polluted the room with smoke unless a door to the outside was kept open:[11]

> [It has] generally the conveniency of two warm seats, one in each corner, but they are sometimes too hot to abide in, and at other times incommoded with the Smoke; there is likewise good Room for the Cook to move, to hang pots, &c— . . . [But] the cold Air so nips the Backs and Heels of those that sit before the Fire, that they have no comfort 'till either Screens or Settles are provided.[12]

Although Franklin proposed his "Pennsylvania Stove" in 1744, due to the poor but still-costly state of iron-forging technology, stoves were generally slow to catch on for domestic use. The unsightliness of iron stove vents and longstanding ideas about the unhealthiness of closed rooms and warm air also contributed to the general resistance to stoves. Additionally, not all stoves, even those built into fireplaces, necessarily improved cooking technology.

I will return to the stove later on in this chapter, but what I want to make clear here is that the fireplace remained not only at the literal center of the colonial northeastern house but at the symbolic center of domestic life for the strongest of material reasons. And since it was the central source of evening light across all regions of the colonies and early republic, it was the central source by which to read and write as well as to cook, converse, or simply sit. It is no surprise then that the connection between literature and the hearth has a solid lineage in the United States: as I will show in the next section, in early nineteenth-century literature the hearth recurs as a space within and around which discourses of social inversion might take place. Drawing on early modern discourses of food and eating, as well as images lifted from transatlantic theater, hearth-place literature collapsed boundaries between classes of humans and species, drawing on the imagery of food for its focus on transformation and metamorphosis.

Hearth and Literature

An early children's book titled *Dame Trot and Her Comical Cat* nicely demonstrates that cooking and the hearth fire were intertwined with literature and social intercourse.[13] Published in 1809 in Philadelphia, this small lyrical pamphlet with its sing-song meter was clearly designed to be read aloud.[14] The poem itself had been well-known as a nursery rhyme in oral repertory of England for over a century; the Dame Trot character, usually played by a man, was a regular character in gender-bending pantomime performance.[15]

Accompanied, as the title page says, by "sixteen elegant engravings," the chapbook narrates (and images, in woodcuts) the anthropomorphic antics of Dame Trot's cat (fig. 1). In this story, the hearth and the fireside are represented—both in narrative and in the engravings that accompany the text—as the household's normal and central literary space and as a site of comic inversion and transformation, with cooking functioning as a comic device. The story opens,

> Here you behold Dame Trot, and here
> Her comic Cat you see;
> Each seated in an elbow chair
> As snug as they can be.
> Dame Trot came home one wintry night,
> A shiv'ring, starving soul
> But Puss had made a blazing Fire
> And nicely truss'd a Fowl.[16]

While the humor of the scene into which Dame Trot enters rests on the idea that her cat has made a fire and a meal, the normalcy of the background against which is set the cat's defiance of the norms of catlike behavior is almost always the hearth—out of sixteen in total, there are eleven woodcuts set in front of the hearth—thus giving the hearth a central role in the narrative. Beyond the delightful insights into eighteenth- and early nineteenth-century cooking—in one illustration the poultry hangs on a string in front of the fire, a traditional method for roasting meat wherein the spinning string hypothetically allowed the meat to cook all around and through—the poem and the accompanying images designate the fireplace-hearth as a space of playful boundary confusion (fig. 2).

The poem proceeds as a series of domestic vignettes largely without narrative, as the cat prepares breakfast for Dame Trot, rides on the dog's back, and then shaves the dog and dresses up as a "lass":

> The Dame was pleas'd, the Fowl was dress'd,
> The table set in place,

Figure 1. "Dame Trot and Her Comical Cat," from *Dame Trot and Her Comical Cat* (Courtesy American Antiquarian Society)

Figure 2. "Dame Trot came home one wintry night," from *Dame Trot and Her Comical Cat* (Courtesy American Antiquarian Society)

> The wond'rous Cat began to carve,
> And Goody said her grace.
> The cloth withdrawn old Goody cries
> "I wish we'd liquor too";
> Up jump'd Frimalkin for some wine,
> And soon a cork she drew.[17]

In the accompanying woodcuts the hearth literally frames the space within which the absurdity of the idea that a cat might cook, drink, or dance can make sense, thus shaping the comedy of the book:

> Next morning Puss got up betimes,
> The breakfast cloth she laid;
> And ere the village clock struck eight,
> The tea and toast she made.
> Goody awoke and rubb'd her eyes,
> And drank her cup of tea,
> Amaz'd to see her Cat behave
> With such propriety.[18]

Figure 3. "The Dame was pleas'd, the Fowl was dress'd," from *Dame Trot and Her Comical Cat* (Courtesy American Antiquarian Society)

The reference to propriety proposes the idea of animal sociality, even in a story in which other animals are consumed. Above all, the cat is continually working—making a fire, trussing a fowl, finding and uncorking wine, acting out, in all ways, the labor of a maid—or wife—to the end of pleasing a single, aged woman, always a liminally social figure (fig. 3). Dame Trot is thus transposed, to her own amazement, into an upside-down world within which animals can perform human functions in setting up one of the most regimented of social activities, the meal.

Aristotle, in the *Poetics*, considers that the socially low and the ugly define the comic, as the socially high and the beautiful define the more serious genres.[19] It is perhaps because of the many social rules attached to bodily functions such as eating, which can be so easily located in the social space of the low and the ugly, that food culture has long been connected to comedy. Discussing the history of banquet literature, Michel Jeanneret writes,

> Food and drink belong to the generic and stylistic registers that are traditionally vulgar: to associate them with serious and noble themes is to upset the accepted hierarchy, to join orders which are conventionally separate

> and to confuse the normal relations between form and content. This incongruity produces a crack in the system and generates comedy; furthermore it gives received vocabulary and discourse a shock which gets rid of the cobwebs and revitalizes them.[20]

Jeanneret's important work traces the connection between food, eating, and literature from the classical through to the early modern period. As he shows, the history of vernacular European literature, of local languages, and in particular of nonsense poetry and language is tied to food and eating. Attacking humanism and classical thought, the food literature of the sixteenth and seventeenth centuries reveled in polyphony, lower-body humor, and vulgar pig Latin jokes, many of them found in stories of outrageous meals and grotesque banquets.[21]

This pre-Enlightenment history would perhaps be irrelevant to this project if European culture stopped at the shore; but as scholars of transatlantic culture have also documented, early modern European influence is ever present in colonial and early U.S. literature and, via eighteenth- and nineteenth-century pantomime, in theater as well. In that literature we can still discern clear traces of the European discourse of vulgarity and grotesquerie best captured by Bakhtin:

> The grotesque mode of representing the body and bodily life prevailed in art and creative forms of speech over thousands of years. From the point of view of extensive use, this mode of representation still exists today: grotesque forms of the body not only predominate in the art of European peoples but also in their folklore, especially in the comic genre. . . . It is the body that fecundates and is fecundated, that gives birth and is born, devours and is devoured, drinks, defecates, is sick and dying. Whenever men laugh and curse, particularly in a familiar environment, their speech is filled with bodily images. This boundless ocean of grotesque bodily imagery within time and space extends to all languages, all literatures, and the entire system of gesticulation.[22]

In this system of humor, food imagery is exploited for its references to the otherwise suppressed or masked physiological functioning of the body and in so doing gestures to the temporary inversion of social hierarchies that accompanied the classic feast and festival: "The grotesque . . . does not have to respect hierarchical distinctions: it freely

Figure 4. "The cloth withdrawn, Old Goody cries," from *Dame Trot and Her Comical Cat* (Courtesy American Antiquarian Society)

blends the profane and the sacred, the lower and the higher, the spiritual and the material. There are no *mesalliances* in its case."[23] While the Dame Trot story does not quite explore the life of the lower body to Rabelaisian extremes, perhaps because the hearth keeps the narrative at the site of ingestion and not excretion, the poem does make a quiet revolution out of upending the relationship between human and animal in a space and time defined by eating, cooking, and drinking. The comic meal provides the stage for this interspecies meeting, as both participants open their mouths together—toward each other—to eat, drink, dance, and laugh (see fig. 4).

Dame Trot herself was, as I mentioned, a pantomime figure, one performed *en travesti.* We should expect that a chapbook about her would be intertextually associated with the transatlantic culture of pantomime theater, in which nursery stories and fairy tales were performed. Daphne Brooks writes that "the [antebellum] culture of performance responded to the uncertainty of corporeal autonomy [in modernity] by producing a range of liminal and embattled types and icons. These figures prowled the colorful world of nineteenth-century transatlantic theatre and performance, a universe that trafficked in panoply of phantasmagoric bodies."[24] In fact, the cat as a servant, or maid, is taking on a role that, in Dame

Trot's world, was performed often, if not most often, by African Americans. Racial categories and norms seem to lie just outside this particular chapbook, although an audience familiar with transatlantic pantomime culture might well have made the association between animal bodies and minoritarian bodies. Still, in one way the household of our stereotypically cross-dressed figure has indeed elevated the animal to the human place—although the carnivalesque logic is incomplete, inasmuch as Dame Trot is not downgraded. Instead, her wishes are fulfilled—she is served by a drinking cat and a dancing dog, who both then join her at her table, providing her with service and company. The fine line between genders and species as it appears here presages the later depictions of encounters between classes of people as they will continue to take place in the spaces devoted to eating.[25]

These inversion themes also appear in another children's tale, titled *Think Before You Speak; or, The Three Wishes.*[26] Published in England in 1809 and in Philadelphia in 1810, *Three Wishes* has an explicitly class-based cautionary message derived from magical happenings that take place around the hearth. The story tells of a poor man, "Homespun," and his wife, Susan, who are "honest folks in humble life / Who liv'd contented with their lot / And lov'd the comforts of their cot."[27] One night they are sitting at the hearth talking ("And o'er the fire the parents sat / Engaged in sober, social chat") when a fairy—whom Homespun had previously saved from being hunted when she was disguised as a hare—appears to grant them three wishes.

After debating whether they wish to be rich farmers, merchants, or lords and ladies, they retire to sleep. Before doing so, however, Susan accidentally spends the first wish:

> Our choice requires the coolest head;
> So rake the fire, and we'll to bed.
> Susan, the happiest wife on earth,
> Set all to rights, and brush'd her hearth;
> And said, These embers burn so clear,
> *I wish we had a pudding here!*
> Methinks 'twould broil so clean and nice;
> I'd make it ready in a trice:
> She spoke—and in the chimney rumbled
> A noise—and down a pudding tumbled![28]

As shown in the third engraving, Homespun rants over the pudding as his wife shrinks away:[29]

> Her tongue itself forgot its use,—
> Tongue once so ready at excuse!
> Mean time the husband storm'd and rated,
> Swearing no man was e'er so mated;
> And call'd his spouse—like savage shameless
> By ugly words that must be nameless,
> To throw our fortune thus away!
> Are'nt you a stupid idiot—hey?
> Such want of thought your folly shows,
> *I wish the pudding on your nose!*
> The words escap'd, he gain'd his wish.
> The pudding, rising from its dish,
> On Goody Homespun's nose was stuck
> So fast, no power on earth could pluck.[30]

Again, the hearth becomes a space of inversion and change: it is there that the fairy—who appears earlier as a hare but is saved by Homespun's empathy for her across species lines—transmogrifies and reappears to offer the three wishes that will transform the Homespuns' class status; it is also there that Goody Homespun's body transforms into food. The whole is framed, as in *Dame Trot and Her Comical Cat*, by a backgrounding hearth, both in the lyrics themselves and in the illustrations—and, no doubt, in the way that the lyrics were read, out loud, in the home, near a hearth.

More radically, speech in *Three Wishes* has embodied consequences, for, empowered by the fairy's gift of three wishes, the Homespuns' idle talk becomes speech act: what they enunciate becomes reality. The narrative ultimately curbs the potential of that (albeit magical) power, and the book wraps up when Homespun spends the third wish to get the pudding off his wife's nose:

> And to relieve thee from this evil
> I wish the pudding at the devil!
> Obedient to this prudent wish,
> The pudding fell, and in its dish
> Flew up the chimney as it came,
> And thus restored the suffering dame.[31]

By the end of the poem the Homespuns have learned their place, to "Temper our hopes with moderations / And suit our wishes to our station."[32] But for a brief moment, around the hearth and in fact through the hearth, their power of imaginative speech is unlimited, even if it escapes their control.

More specifically, the performative potential of the peasant body—specifically the woman's body—is anchored and limited by its bodily proximity to food when the pudding, which Susan first imagines and then wishes for, finally becomes stuck to Susan's face ("Sad Susan wav'd her head in woe / The pudding too wav'd to and fro").[33] In *The Poetics and Politics of Transgression*, Stallybrass and White argue that the fluid hyperphysicality of the working-class body was a central projection of the emerging bourgeoisie of the Industrial Revolution.[34] While Goody Homespun's body becomes stuck to the pudding, the pudding can also be read as a metonym for the nonbourgeois body: a package made up of pretty much anything and sewn up and cooked in a soft bag of skin.[35] In this poem the hearth, as a space that deals with food, is an important site of liminality: for in the image of the housewife's body joined to the food object we see that the body (and in particular the working-class body) threatens to escape the limits of sociality and become fleshy foodstuff, to become at least partially indistinguishable from those other animals we choose to turn into food. The boundary between the genders is in question here as well, when we consider that *pudding* is also a slang term for the penis: the image that accompanies this passage shows a long penislike protrusion dangling from Goody Homespun's face into her lap, as her husband comforts her in front of the fire.[36] And finally, the line that demarcates the inner body from the outer world is also reversed, when the association of pudding with guts and viscera turns the body inside out, putting intestinal membranes on the outside of Goody Homespun's body, just as a pudding is encased in its skin.

This is the comic logic of a world in which animals take on the role of humans and speech acts bring about physical events: it is a world of transformations linked to the world of food, itself a metamorphic referent, standing in for the steps through which dead flesh and organic matter are processed, changed, and then ingested to become living matter. The theme of inversion also promises the opposite: any person has the possibility—as an organism—of being metamorphosed into food and devoured. In raising the question of who gets to eat and who gets eaten or, alternatively, who is a "who" and who is a "what," the literature of the hearth-space both fixes and destabilizes social hierarchy—the Great Chain of Being—through the transformative metaphor offered by cooking, itself captured in literature which then might be read, out loud, at a cooking site.

Thus, the hearth, which is the "center" of the house, can also be the space at which numerous decenterings play off each other, around and within which hierarchically related entities are reconfigured. In these texts the lines between human and animal, like those between the human body and food, are defined in terms of a naturalized social hierarchy, in which the human is not an animal and the human body is not food. This theme repeats in *The World Turned Upside Down; or, The Comical Metamorphoses*, a chapbook published first in London by the prominent printing house Dicey and Marshall and then republished during the 1780s and 1790s in the United States.[37] The chapbook contains a series of poems of seven stanzas, each with a concluding poetic moral of four lines. Each poem is accompanied by an engraved illustration. In each of these poems some relationship in the social hierarchy is inverted in order to punish an individual who abuses or fails to properly administer his power: thus, a butcher who tortures animals is butchered by them, a deer shoots a gamekeeper, and a hare roasts a cook over an open flame. The last poem is accompanied by a striking depiction of the cook being basted on the hearth by a rooster, or cock. Basting here signifies both to its strictly culinary meaning and also to its slang meaning as a beating or whipping: food comes to signify the body at its extremes of sensation, at its barest animal form:[38]

> If fortune smile, her favours prize
> Nor let your wealth be wasted;
> Or like the cook, before your eyes,
> You'll by the world be basted.[39]

One can well imagine how these texts, which also gleefully depict anti-aristocratic violence and other forms of insurrection, would have been received in the first quarter century after the revolution.[40] In fact, the American edition of this chapbook was reprinted with far more elaborate illustrations than the original English version contained, indicating that "I. Norman," the publisher, thought the book was worthy of some financial investment.[41] Of the thirty poems in this chapbook, fourteen involve animals rising against humans, and six in particular involve animals hunting, fishing, or butchering men. Another poem tells of an abused maid who switches places with her mistress. In this poem the illustration depicts her ordering her mistress about in a kitchen in which the hearth takes up the entire right-hand wall of the picture:

> The woman drudging in that place;
> (Observe the print beside)
> Was one of those that catch disgrace,
> And bait the hook with pride.
> The maid who us'd to watch her call
> And at her back was ready,
> By her impudence, and downfall,
> Is now become her lady.
> MORAL:
> Ye fair-ones ne'er be arrogant;
> Be of this tale observant;
> Misfortune may your bliss transplant,
> And each become a servant.[42]

In these chapbooks, marvels and revolutions may be recounted, but the function of the hearth does not change. In the illustrations and the poems, the hearth is, as always, the normal site that links cooking spaces and eating. It is in relation to the hearth that the literature could tie its themes of class fluidity and bodily transformation, in which the differences defining social hierarchies were overturned. The hearth space represents a site where classes—of people and of things—met and where the normal order of transformations took place; it is also the space in which the order of transformations might be inverted, even if only temporarily. Further, as performed in *The World Turned Upside Down*, it was also a space where social bodies could be reduced—debased—into animal fleshliness.

What I also want to point to in these poems is the importance of food as a metalanguage for the strangeness of the body and, thus, I wish to argue, for the thingness, the quiddity even, of the body. The food that tends to be represented in these stories is meat, which, while derived from the animal, is recognizably in the same category as human flesh. It is, as animal studies scholars and animal rights activists have noted, permissible to eat meat because animals represent a lower social order than humans, and even then this is not true for all animals: Pets such as Dame Trot's cat and dog are in a separate category.[43] Those that are eaten are not persons but things, and their thingness is the result of a system of social degradation. For a human to take the place of an animal means becoming the object of a similar social degradation. To be socially degraded, then, to be completely other with relation to the human, is one of the conditions of being edible. At the many points in these stories in which the human body becomes food we see that what defines the social boundaries that govern the edible and the tabooed is the degree to which particular bodies are made marginal within the social world, or how they become other to some image of the human in the domestic space where food is cooked.

And yet these stories of transformation and inversion are also obsessively occupied with similarity: between cook and hare, between nose and pudding, between body and flesh. Human flesh, over which the social exerts its control, naturally resembles the flesh of other animals. Visibly, humans are isomorphic to other animals, sharing eyes, limbs, internal organs, and the like. In order to cook and eat animals in good conscience, humans must negate that likeness. And, on the human side, this community of negation grounds the transcendentally human in a process by which is produced both the modern subject and its human and animal others. In these chapbooks human bodies are both defined and haunted by the uncanny resemblance between their own bodies and those devalued beings we kill to make meat. Food, which is the result of the convergence of a physical and a symbolic process, recurs as a trope through which this resemblance can be explored; in these texts the fireplace-hearth is clearly the literary site most often associated with the possibilities, and threat, of that resemblance.

Orality and Abjection in the Kitchen

Although it is one of the arguments of this chapter that the early modern and early U.S. discourses of inversion as they appeared in relation to the food and hearth continued to lie beneath images of food and eating across the rest of the century, it is important to remember that the processes by which food and the human are coded are local and historically specific. The kind of proximity to cooking and eating that colonists and early nineteenth-century Americans experienced would shift in tandem with regional changes in kitchen technology and domestic architecture across the nineteenth century. In the first thirty years of the nineteenth century, more homes were built with kitchens; at the same time, stoves began to replace fireplaces both in the kitchen and in other rooms. As stoves replaced fireplaces, American writers of this generation, who had grown up with hearths and most probably learned to read and write by firelight (as well as by daylight, of course) became nostalgic for the open fire. Priscilla Brewer's work on the development of cooking technology in the United States demonstrates that from the 1820s through the 1850s, when the days of the hearth started to recede from living memory, a number of authors lamented its loss, the fireside poets being perhaps the best known of them.[44] Nathaniel Hawthorne joined his voice to the general dislike for stoves when he wrote his plaintive 1843 short essay "Fire Worship."[45] He writes, "It is a great revolution in social and domestic life, and no less so in the life of a secluded student, this almost universal exchange of the open fireplace for the cheerless and ungenial stove. On such a morning as now lowers around our old gray parsonage, I miss the bright face of my ancient friend, who was wont to dance upon the hearth and play the part of more familiar sunshine."[46] More than a simple aesthetic loss, for the narrator the end of the fireplace signals the beginning of modernity, a beginning that blots the "picturesque, the poetic and the beautiful out of human life."[47] By taking classical "Promethean" fire and forcing it to labor on "a half dozen sticks of wood," the stove has upset the fundamental economy of the house. Hawthorne balances this loss of an interior picturesqueness against a former age in which "sixty cords of wood" were consumed by the hearth—"almost an annual forest." For the narrator, the passing of the fireplace marks the end of an era of social communion, marked in particular as the end of communal storytelling and talking:

> It is my belief that social intercourse cannot long continue what it has been, now that we have subtracted from it so important and vivifying an element as firelight. . . . There will be nothing to attract these poor children to one centre. They will never behold one another through that peculiar medium of vision the ruddy gleam of blazing wood or bituminous coal—which gives the human spirit so deep an insight into its fellows and melts all humanity into one cordial heart of hearts.[48]

Fire here is in the first place a source of the visual, shaping the ways that children see each other—and thus perhaps shaping the first experiences of vision as a social sense. For Hawthorne it also lays the foundation of sociality in the connection between fireplaces and speech: "[Without fire] domestic life, if it may still be termed domestic, will seek its separate corners, and never gather itself into groups. The easy gossip; the merry yet unambitious Jest; the life-like, practical discussion of real matters in a casual way; the soul of truth which is so often incarnated in a simple fireside word,—will disappear from earth."[49] For the narrator, to get rid of the fireplace is to undermine the very definition of the domesticity. This descent into modernity is a fall away from orality and simplicity—from the "simple fireside word"—and into specialization and noncommunication, as families seek the four corners of the home, facing away from each other and aborting all traditional forms of speech. If the hearth and fireplace were the center of domestic orality, it is unsurprising that the chimney flue was often referred to as the "throat"; the fireplace, it might be said, was the mouth of the house.[50]

Melville reworked Hawthorne's lament in his quirky short story "I and My Chimney," which some critics have seen as a direct response to "Fire Worship":[51]

> It need hardly be said, that the walls of my house are entirely free from fireplaces. These all congregate in the middle—in the one grand central chimney, upon all four sides of which are hearths—two tiers of hearths—so that when, in the various chambers, my family and guests are warming themselves of a cold winter's night, just before retiring, then, though the time they may not be thinking so, all their faces mutually look towards each other, yea, all their feet point to one centre; and when they go to sleep in their beds, they all sleep round one warm chimney, like so many Iroquois Indians, in the woods, round their one heap of embers.[52]

As feminist cultural studies has turned to the study of the interior space of the household, "I and My Chimney" has come under new critical scrutiny. Millette Shamir, for instance, sees "I and My Chimney" as Melville's defense of an older model of patriarchal domesticity, antedating that of the post-Revolutionary era, in which the gendered division of labor in the household was reflected in the house plan.[53] Shamir argues that the chimney, closely tied to the narrator's sense of self, represents a masculine, phallic selfhood that resists being accessed by public discourses of domestic (read: feminine) respectability or even by women at all. Other critics, notably Bertolini and Wilson, have seen in "I and My Chimney" a crucial literary expression of the production of different masculinities within the order of antebellum domesticity, expressed through Melville's use of architectural form.[54]

While these critics have persuasively illuminated both the phallic ("'Your chimney, sir, you regard as too small, I suppose, needing further development, especially at the top?' 'Sir!' said, I . . . 'do not be personal.'")[55] and anal ("Yes I dare say there is a secret ash-hole in the chimney; for where do all the ashes go to that we drop down the queer hole yonder?")[56] symbolism of the chimney, it is important to acknowledge the moments when Melville's chimney symbolism gestures to the mouth. For instance, the narrator insistently draws attention to his own mouth, specifically the bodily parallels between his own pipe smoking and the smoke that emerges from the "huge, corpulent old Harry VII. of a chimney."[57] But the mouth is not only the site of drawing in and breathing out smoke—a product on the border line between the edible and the nonedible, the clean and the dirty (or "sooty") thing. It is also the site of the verbal. Significantly, the written word, in the story, is aligned with the architect Mr. Scribe—a name denoting the architect's connection with textuality—and the narrator's wife, against whose machinations the narrator protects the chimney—while supplementing the oral word by letter, the form in which he communicates with the architect.

> The truth is, my wife, like all the rest of the world, cares not a fig for my philosophical jabber. In dearth of other philosophical companionship, I and my chimney *have to smoke and philosophize together.* And sitting up so late as we do at it, a mighty smoke it is that we two smoky old philosophers make.
>
> But my spouse, who likes the smoke of my tobacco as little as she does that of the soot, carries on her war against both. I live in continual dread lest, like the golden bowl, the pipes of me and my chimney shall yet be broken.[58]

While the hearth place is a place of masculine reverie, as Vincent Bertolini has argued, it is also, Melville reminds us, a site associated with comic orality: "philosophical jabber" even. If we reconsider the story through the lens of the spoken word, we see that the narrator's hostility to his wife's temporality is about a hostility to a futurity that he sees as tied to print culture: "While spicily impatient of present and past, like a glass of ginger-beer [my wife] overflows with her schemes; and with like energy as she puts down her foot, puts down her preserves and pickles, and lives with them in a continual future; or ever full of expectations both from time and space, is ever restless for newspapers, and ravenous for letters."[59] In

"I and My Chimney" the chimney is definitively not connected with eating and food as it is in the other stories I discuss here, perhaps because the masculinist terms of the story demand that cooking and food be connected to femininity, as in the passage just quoted. Instead, the chimney is the site of a kind of physical and social abjection as the narrator (whose words are "jabbering" to his wife), "philosophizes" to his chimney, which comes to stand in variously for his mouth, his anus, and his penis, sitting alongside it happily covered in soot and resisting the attempts at domesticating and modernizing the house made by his wife.

In his stubborn commitment to this hyperembodied existence, the delightfully perverse, if misogynist, narrator of "I and My Chimney" attempts to resist what Michel de Certeau called "intextuation," the shaping of the flesh by textual, or disciplinary, pressures. De Certeau writes, "The intextuation of the body corresponds to the incarnation of the law; it supports it, it even seems to establish it, and in any case it serves it. For the law plays on it: 'Give me your body and I will give you meaning, I will make you a name and a word in my discourse.' . . . The only force opposing this passion to be a sign is the cry, a deviation or an ecstasy, a revolt or flight of that which, within the body, escapes the law of the named."[60] Even as the narrator is, paradoxically, entirely a creature of Melville's text as well as a response to Hawthorne's text, his hyperembodiment as object—his thingness—resists legibility within the wife's domestic scheme. As de Certeau indicates, the narrator's resistance to intextuation takes place through recourse to his body but also to the oral—the "cry." Thus, when the narrator comes to writing a letter to Scribe the architect, the only instance of his writing inside the text, he has no implements to write with and must leave the house to find and fashion a quill. He closes the letter,

> "We shall remain,
> "Very faithfully,
> "The same,
> "I and my Chimney."[61]

This desire to remain the same, to resist a modernity that is leaving the revolutionary epoch behind and advancing into a different regime of domesticity, characterized, as Shamir argues, by the power of the feminine over interior household arrangements, can be seen as more than simply a desire to cling to the past; it is also a desire to cling to an embodied, orally authentic present. The story is narrated in the past tense, as a memory, it is true, but the narrator takes pains to point out the presentness of the narration:

> From this habitual precedence of my chimney over me, some even think that I have got into a sad rearward way altogether; in short, from standing behind my old-fashioned chimney so much, I have got to be quite behind the age too. . . . I never was a very forward old fellow, nor what my farming neighbors call a forehanded one. . . . As for my belonging to the rear-guard in general, certain it is, I bring up the rear of my chimney—*which, by the way, is this moment before me*—and that too, both in fancy and fact.[62]

The narrator is caught in an impossible temporality that he takes pains to elaborate: he is at the back of the crowd (rearward), and thus he is behind the times; he is not future-oriented (forward, also meaning pushy), and thus he cannot prepare for the future (he is not forehanded). And while he clearly defines himself as old-fashioned, he also makes clear that contra the "continual future" of his wife's preserves and plans, he is rooted in the present. Specifically, he tells his story in the *now*—the "this moment"—of the spoken word.

The final passage of "I and My Chimney" brings up its central (and, indeed, entitling) project, namely, the blurring of the line between human and object and the constitutive relationship between domestic architecture and the subject that inhabits it: "Some say that I have become a sort of mossy old misanthrope, while all the time the fact is, I am simply standing guard over my mossy old chimney; for it is resolved between me and my chimney, that I and my chimney will never surrender."[63] The back-and-forth between the nominative-case "I" and the objective-case "me" points not only to the identification between the mossy old narrator and the mossy old chimney but, as well, to the identification between the narrator and objects, generally. At times the narrator and the chimney are subjects of the sentence ("I and my chimney will never surrender"); at other times they are objects ("it is resolved between me and my chimney"). In the former the narrator and the chimney are mutually objects of the verb action "resolve": the tense is passive. In the latter clause they are both subjects ("I and my chimney will never surrender"). In that echo of "me and my" and "I and my" the doubling between chimney and narrator is itself redoubled. Melville's attachment to the "double-house" model—that is, the house that centers on a single hearth—reworks Hawthorne's nostalgia (with the reference to "mossiness" surely alluding to Hawthorne's association of "moss" and "manse") without entirely abandoning it; more than simply carrying on Hawthorne's defense of the spoken word, he takes on the hearth as a space of masculine embodiment, an embodiment that ultimately renders the narrator *other* to himself by blurring the line between his body and his chimney, between subject and object.

The hearth is thus a space that ties textuality and orality together, a space that Hawthorne and Melville, as writers, melancholically see as tied to the authenticity of the spoken *now*. In writing against the technological future, however, they cling to a space that the chapbooks—books no doubt similar to those they had encountered in their own childhoods—had portrayed as a fixity against which the fluidity between social categories might be performed. Read aloud, the chapbooks suture together the oral and the written in scenes framed by—and staged at—the hearth. Ironically, the nostalgia for the hearth is itself a resistance to a different kind of inversion, in which the home fires, situated on the ground, are themselves turned upside down, lifted above the floor and contained in an iron case. The loss of the hearth as a writerly and literary space displaces the author from the chapbook's powers of bodily and social transformation—most particularly associated with childhood and therefore the writer's past—and banishes his work to the isolation of modern liberal individualism, as typified by the autonomous reader, consuming text in isolation, forbidden, in the regime of middle-class mores, even to move his lips. Orality is indeed in recess here.

Across the five decades spanned by the stories I have discussed here, the hearth and fireplace recur as important literary spaces. While the children's chapbook stories of the period just after the Revolution make the hearth the framing background against which the story is both told—read out loud—and dramatized as the space of cooking, eating, and drinking, both Melville's and Hawthorne's short stories yearn for the hearth/chimney as the sign of a lost sociality. This literary nostalgia for the hearth arose alongside a widespread unease with the "cheerless" stove that had replaced the open cooking fire. By the 1860s, one could choose between a small stove and a "range," which was fitted in where the hearth used to be.[64] The stove itself was often, as Ruth Schwartz Cowan puts it, a "monster" with "four to eight cooking holes on its top surface (or surfaces, since some of the early stoves were "stepped"), two or three ovens for warming and baking (the heat being controlled by proximity to the firebox and by dampers), and attached reservoirs dispensing hot water."[65] This arrangement didn't last very long, however: by the time Melville came to write "I and My Chimney" the cookstove and heating stove had been separated, with the heating stove becoming the "very efficient 'base burner' (which had the fire at its base and a magazine for maintaining a continuous supply of fresh coal above)."[66] It was in the face of this mechanism, the product of new American industry and a new use of American natural resources—especially iron and coal—that those writers most invested in developing a domestic ideology that linked female virtue and labor to the private space of the home sounded an alarm.

It was not only the fireside poets but also the authors of domestic manuals who ostensibly sought to establish middle-class white women as sovereigns of their own empires, who saw as suspect and dangerous the new technology associated with food labor. In 1841 Catharine Beecher wrote,

> Stoves are used on account of the great economy of fuel thus secured. A common large box-stove, set in a hall, with a long pipe, and a drum in a distant room, will warm the hall and three or four other rooms. The chief objections to stoves, are, the dryness of air which they induce; the disagreeable smell of the iron; and the coldness of the lower stratum of air, producing cold feet in those who are subject to this difficulty.[67]

Although Beecher was clear that the stove was a far more efficient means of heating a house, as well as cooking for a family, her introduction of the stove emphasizes the objections over the efficiency. Not only does she devote relatively little space in her *Treatise on Domestic Economy* to working with or maintaining the stove; what text she does devote is full of warning: "If a person is apparently lifeless, from the effects of coal smoke, fresh air, friction, poultices on the feet, stimulants to the nostrils, and hot drinks, such as pepper and ginger, should be administered with much perseverance."[68] Each of the house plans printed in the *Treatise* assumes that homeowners will heat their homes with fireplaces and not stoves. The nostalgia for the hearth was, it appears, not limited to male writers.

However, as middle-class domestic spaces were articulated in tandem with the rise of non-manual labor as a defining class characteristic,[69] kitchen labor and working with the raw materials of food was pushed away from the front-of-house activities to become an increasingly hidden labor activity—at least from the perspective of the owners of the house.[70] This shift is most tellingly revealed in antebellum domestic manuals that generally designed homes to have kitchens that were separate from the living and dining rooms.[71] The early impulse to rationalize the domestic sphere and thus to contain the aspirational energies of middle-class women within the home was often focused toward ordering that which was already seen to be inherently disordered. At the same time, as numerous feminist historians have pointed out, the emergence of the industrial economy meant that the domestic labors that women had traditionally carried out—those described by domestic manuals—became socially devalued as they were divorced from productive importance. Jeanne Boydston writes,

> In addition to its specific implications for women, the ideology of spheres, and the pastoralization of housework that lay at the heart of that ideology, both represented and supported larger cultural changes attending the evolution of early industrial capitalism. The transition to industrialization was not only material: it was ideological as well, involving and requiring new ways of viewing the relationship of labor to its products and of the worker to his or her work.[72]

The ideology of domesticity as defined and disseminated by authors such as Catharine Beecher encoded these changes by both elevating the importance of the sphere of domestic labor and inserting it into the modern discourses of rationalization and professionalization. In this way the housewife, while safely inserted in the domestic sphere, is held at arm's length from the labor that she commands from the Irish or African American maid, who actually performs the chores of cooking and cleaning.

Nowhere did these discourses more clearly emerge than in antebellum domestic manuals, in which domestic labor was depicted as an endless struggle against disorder and chaos. For instance in 1824 Mary Randolph wrote in *The Virginia Housewife*,

> A regular system must be introduced into each department which may be modified until matured, and should then pass into an inviolable law. The grand Arcanum of management lies in three simple rules,—"Let every thing be done at a proper time, keep everything in its proper place, and put everything to its proper use." If the mistress of the family will every morning examine minutely, the different departments of her household, she must detect errors in their infant state, when they can be corrected with ease; but a few days' growth gives them gigantic strength; *and Disorder, with all her attendant evils, is introduced*.[73]

Sixteen years later Catharine Beecher concurred when she famously wrote,

> There is no one thing, more necessary to a housekeeper, in performing her varied duties, than *a habit of system and order*; and yet the peculiarly desultory nature of women's pursuits, and the embarrassments resulting from the state of domestic service in this Country, render it very difficult to form such a habit. But it is sometimes the case, that women, who could and would carry forward a systematic plan of domestic economy, do not attempt it, simply from a want of knowledge of the various modes of introducing it. It is with reference to such, that various modes of securing system and order, which the Writer has seen adopted, will be pointed out.[74]

The first edition of Lydia Maria Child's *The American Frugal Housewife* is an excellent example of this disorder rendered into text.[75] Primarily a conglomeration of recipes, and therefore more cookbook than domestic manual, the first edition of *The American Frugal Housewife* is far more impressive as a textual struggle against disorder than as a systematic guide to household order, frugal or otherwise. Lacking a table of contents, the book presents the reader with a mash-up of home remedies, cleaning tips, and recipes in no particular order, recalling the receipt books that early modern European women brought over to the Americas. The last few sections consist of a series of household hints, ranging from things to do with ear wax to restoring elasticity to feathers.[76] Child seemed to recognize that the state of her own book might bode ill for the frugal housewife who picked it up, looking for a system of home economy, when she wrote in her somewhat poetic opening paragraphs,

> The true economy of housekeeping is simply the art of gathering up all the fragments, so that nothing be lost. I mean fragments of time, as well as materials. Nothing should be thrown away so long as it is possible to make any use of it, however trifling that use may be; and whatever be the size of the family, every member should be employed either in earning or saving money.[77]

The image of gathering up fragments nicely captures the sense of chaos held at bay, but it did not hold at bay Child's early reviewers, who harshly criticized the organization of the book. In later editions, Child radically reorganized the text.

Middle- and upper-class women writers responded to the devaluation of domestic work and their own changed relationship to the management of physical chores not only with reformist writings meant to restore social value to women's work but also through the explicit discourse of cleanliness. Beneath their rhetoric, however, it is not difficult to discern the reality that domestic work was an ongoing struggle against dirt, disease, and decay. In the chapter of *The Treatise on Domestic Economy* titled "On the Care of the Kitchen, Cellar, and Storeroom," Catharine Beecher writes,

> It is very important, for every man who wishes to have his daughters brought up with good domestic habits, to secure a light, neat, and agreeable kitchen. Such an arrangement will make this part of the house more attractive to his daughters, more comfortable for his wife, and better secure the contentment of domestics. For this reason, cellar-kitchens are undesirable, besides being often unhealthful.[78]

What is clear from these passages is that the kitchen was associated with infection, and the new designs that sought to push the kitchen out of the household's foregrounding activities ran into the old notion of the disease-causing "miasma," a combination of stale air and the mephitic exhalations of the earth.[79] Cleanliness, advised Beecher, meant not only keeping dirt at bay but also making sure that refuse and bad odors were funneled out of the house and that cleaning materials did not further dirty that which they were meant to clean:

> A kitchen should always have a sink, with a drain to carry away all slops; and this drain should never empty on the surface of the ground near the house as it is both unhealthful and uncleanly. It is best to whitewash the walls of a kitchen, as it makes it lighter, and tends to remove all bad smells. . . . The sink should be thoroughly washed every day, and often scalded with ley or hot suds.[80]

In addition, three pages of Beecher's kitchen chapter helpfully detail how to get rid of vermin, which, in an era of spotty waste disposal and lack of sewage systems, was no doubt a vital concern for her readers.

Some writers, such as Sarah Josepha Hale, whose *Good Housekeeper* was published three years before Catharine Beecher's *Treatise*, explicitly addressed the devaluing of kitchen labor. In the last chapter of Hale's book she printed a short story in which a husband attempts to hire a cook for his household but cannot afford to do so:

> There must be something radically wrong in the present fashions of society. An educated man thinks it no shame to do the business of his profession, whatever it may be. I work hard in my store every day. But women, who have been educated, think it degrading to put their hands to any household employment, though that is all the task we assign to our females. A lady would be ashamed to be seen in her kitchen at work. O, how many are now sitting at ease in their pleasant parlors.[81]

This piece of fiction is startling given that historians of housework tell us that even with the presence of a core of African American and Irish servants, most white, middle-class women in the mid-nineteenth-century United States ended up doing much more manual labor than sitting in parlors.[82] What this story tells us, as I noted earlier, is that the marking of manual labor as the great distinguishing characteristic of the working class had consequences for the middle-class domestic scene, as the meaning and value of manual work had begun to change.

Two further issues emerge from Hale's story: the first is that of the increased importance of domestic help in middle-class home life; the second is that of the parlor as an important space opposed to the kitchen. As Faye Dudden has shown, domestic workers increasingly became an important part of the middle-class home during the 1820s and 1830s.[83] The flood of Irish immigrants in particular created an army of hands that lowered the cost of domestic labor. The effect of this was to exert a status pressure on the middle-class household to hire such labor, so that the middle-class family could increasingly occupy itself in the household with entertainment and other forms of dining room and parlor life.[84] In pushing the kitchen away from the household's stage-front activities, household architecture reflected the specialization that divided the owner's public and social spaces from the kitchen, which was becoming the exclusive province of the domestic worker. Indeed, the architectural plans in Catharine Beecher's *Treatise* favor putting the domestic's bedroom next to the kitchen. As Dudden points out, this expectation accompanied the shift in attitudes toward the role of those who were performing physical chores in the house, from the daughterly role that relatives and other forms of female help played in colonial homes to the more servile and servantlike role that professional domestics were expected to play in the mid-nineteenth-century period.

Catharine Beecher firmly addressed issues of power in the household when she wrote that

> in all classes, different grades of subordination must exist; and that it is no more degrading for a domestic to regard the heads of a family as superiors in station . . . than it is for children to do the same. . . . They should be taught that domestics use a different entrance to the house, and sit at a distinct table. . . .
>
> The Writer has known cases, where the lady of the family, for the sake of convincing her domestic of the truth of these views, allowed her to follow her own notions, for a short time, and join the family at meals. . . . The experiment was tried, two or three times; and, although the domestic was treated with studious politeness and kindness, she soon felt that she should be far more comfortable in the kitchen, where she could talk, eat, and dress, as she pleased.[85]

It is clear, then, that the emergence of the kitchen as a newly separate and abject space coeval with the increasingly class-stratified American culture meant that the kitchen became that space in the middle-class home most closely associated with class difference.

The Kitchen and the Vernacular

That class difference significantly overlapped with ethnic difference became apparent as increasing numbers of Irish women immigrated and went into domestic service; the "Biddy" and the "Bridget" soon became stock characters in the midcentury discourse on servants, on a par with the stereotypically black "Dinah." Writing on domestic life thus increasingly discussed interactions with foreign and black women, and the nascent fashion for dialect writing found a new literary setting in the kitchen. Publishing under the pseudonym "Christopher Crowfield" in the *Atlantic Monthly*'s serialized version of the *House and Home Papers*, Harriet Beecher Stowe wrote, "The complaints made of Irish girls are numerous and loud; the failings of green Erin, alas! are but too open and manifest."[86] In another Stowe story, "Our Second Girl," published in *Atlantic Monthly* in January 1868, a mysterious Anglo-American girl is an exemplary servant in a house full of Irish servants. Upon her leaving, "the servants in the kitchen, with the warm-heartedness of their race, broke out into a perfect Irish howl of sorrow; and at the last moment, Biddy, our fat cook, fell on her neck and lifted up her voice and wept, almost smothering her with her tumultuous embraces."[87] These nonverbal howls could only come from the kitchen. Irish women, tellingly, were often referred to in terms of food language—they were "raw," as is shown in this passage from Catharine Beecher and Harriet Beecher Stowe's *American Woman's Home*:

> A lady living in one of our obscure New-England towns, where there were no servants to be hired, at last, by sending to a distant city succeeded in procuring a *raw Irish maid-of-all-work, a creature of immense bone and muscle, but of heavy, unawakened brain.* In one fortnight she established such a reign of Chaos and old Night in the kitchen and through the house that her mistress, a delicate woman, encumbered with the care of young children, began seriously to think that she made more work each day than she performed, and dismissed her.[88]

Just as the incipient industrialization of the United States exploited the muscle power of the immigrant, so, too, did the aspiring domestic household; but management in the one sphere as in the other had to concern itself with inculcating skills, which were, in turn, identified with the national project. As these servants with their linguistic and religious differences—their non-WASPness—increasingly populated the servant-labor pool, middle-class writing on domesticity became more concerned with the governance of the house, and the rhetoric of domestic work came to overlap with that of missionary and other forms of benevolent work. Wrote Beecher and Stowe, "The mistresses of American families, whether they like it or not, have the duties of missionaries imposed upon them by that class from which our supply of domestic servants is drawn."[89] In this metaphoric economy the kitchen became an uncivilized space, the women who worked within it unfinished or uncooked; the project of running a home was metonymic of the civilizing work of empire.[90]

The kitchen also came to represent domestic insurrection, as the hot-tempered and insolent cook became a staple trope of domestic literature. Sarah Josepha Hale wrote,

> One of the faults which a cook should most seriously guard against, is bad temper. . . . Her employment, in the summer season, is not a pleasant or healthy one—obliged as she is, to be over the hot fire, and confined, often,

> in a dark, close kitchen. It is in the power of the cook to do much for the comfort and prosperity of the family; if she is economical and conducts with propriety, the whole establishment goes on pleasantly; but if she is cross, *intemperate*, and wasteful, the mischief and discomfort she causes are very great. Never let the family have reason to say—"The cook is always cross!"[91]

The cook became an important figure at this time as domestic roles were increasingly defined: unlike other domestics, the cook, as Hale said, had "privileges—mistress of the kitchen, the highest wages, and, the favorite always of her employers."[92] The cook, as I pointed out earlier, retained a privileged and intimate knowledge, that of the tastes of the household family; that intimacy in turn shaped the privileged status accorded her by her employers, who provided her the best possible food and their backing in the organization of the "downstairs" hierarchy; for it was in the power of the cook to make her employers lives miserable, and costly, by ruining food.

Finally, the kitchen became, in much of the language around domestic economy, the space that served to represent all space that "belonged" to domestics. In Mrs. John Farrar's 1837 *The Young Lady's Friend* ladies were advised to keep their families out of the kitchen while the servants had their meals: "I have been in some families, where the comfort of those who eat in the kitchen is as scrupulously guarded as those who eat in the parlour, and no one is permitted to ring the bell till the domestics have had a quiet half hour for their meal, and children are forbidden to open the kitchen door during that time."[93] This practice was exacerbated in the South, where there were often separate cooking facilities from the main house. Caroline Gilman wrote in her novel *Recollections of a Southern Matron*, published in 1838, "The distance of the kitchen from the house at the South often repulses housekeepers, both in cold and warm weather, from visiting it frequently; indeed, a young woman often feels herself an intruder, and as if she had but half a right to pry into the affairs of the negroes in the yard."[94] Most domestic manuals advised young women to learn how to cook so as to supervise their cooks and take over their work when they left, as servants seemed to do so often. But increasingly the kitchen came to seem like a foreign territory—literally inhabited by foreigners—within the middle-class home.

Barbara Ryan has argued in her essay "Kitchen Testimony" that middle-class fears about what servants might observe and speak about had a very real source: the publication of memoirs by servants and ex-slaves (many of whom had themselves served in houses) became a literary trend in the nineteenth century when indenture laws and traditional servant-employer relationships went into decline.[95] In fact, the phrase that Ryan uses in the essay's title, was itself coined by a man reputed to have been the lover of Catharine Forrest, the Shakespearian actress whose adultery against her husband was established in a sensational trial by the testimony of a servant. As Ryan shows, *Home Journal* editor Nathaniel Parker Willis campaigned against the legal validity of servants' testimony when he complained in his magazine about "testimony exclusively from the kitchen, and below it."[96]

As I have pointed out, the hearth was closely connected with orality, reading, and writing. In the new furnace-oven system of domestic architecture, as Ryan's illuminating article shows, other kinds of close ties were forged between the kitchen and speech. The term *testimony* as Ryan adopts it from Willis points to the spoken word, to a specifically juridical form of oral narrative (oriented toward "telling the truth") that is also nonetheless not a written contract—although, in the police procedure of the period, testimonies were signed by the testifier, who often could not read them. While Ryan uses the term to describe all forms of servant and ex-slave narrative, I want to push her analysis further by considering that, as I have argued, the kitchen was already linked to the oral. Such a linkage emerged in the household subconscious as the domestic space was reorganized to "hide" the kitchen. The threat of the servant-witnesses—who, as "secret" observers, could penetrate the mysteries of the private sphere—was deflected by devaluing their position in giving testimony, inasmuch as they were the inhabitants of the house's abject below-stairs space, the space, as Catharine Beecher reminds us, of damp and illness—and even lower, below the kitchen, as Willis would have it. Orality clearly was associated with the linguistic form that represents the kitchen's threateningly back-of-house, vernacular literary production; that orality threatened to upset the orderly performances taking place at the front of the house.

Perhaps the clearest connection between the mouth and the kitchen was set down by Robert Roberts, the African American author of *The House Servant's Directory*.[97] Although Roberts's book is consistently cited in studies of housework and domesticity, it has been shockingly undertreated by historians and critics, despite its status as the first book by an African American published by a commercial press, as well as the first American domestic manual to be written by and for house servants. This oversight is no doubt because of the avowedly apolitical and nonsubversive tone of the book, which seems to counsel servants' submission and acceptance of the "various stations in life [that] are appointed by that Supreme Being, who is the giver of all goodness."[98] While I will not go into the politics of this detailed and knowledgeable book here, it seems worthwhile to note that Roberts not only used the success of his book to invest widely in Philadelphia real estate and become a well-off professional caterer but that he then went on to become an active Garrisonian and an outspoken opponent of African colonization schemes. And in fact, even read as a text complicit with the established antebellum order, the sheer amount of text that Roberts dedicates to containing the subversive energy of servants seems a noteworthy recognition of the resentment that must no doubt have brewed below stairs.

Nowhere is the threat of servant insurrection more apparent than in Roberts's discussion of the role of the cook. Roberts's method in the book is to present a bottom-up point of view of the upper-middle-class house: to this end he provides detailed instructions for formal dining service as well as household cleaning. In the section containing advice to cooks close metaphoric ties are drawn between speech, food, and the space of the kitchen. In this section of his book Roberts draws directly, as he acknowledges, from the text of William Kitchiner's late eighteenth-century British book *The Cook's Oracle*; Robert finds Kitchiner's book to be of enough relevance to his American audience that he edits it and reprints it in his own book.[99]

The majority of Roberts's advice to the cook regards her mode of speaking, both to fellow servants and to the "master or mistress." The following long sentence offers a typical example of Roberts's advice:

> We hope the culinary student who peruses these pages will be above adopting the common, mean and base, and ever unsuccessful way of "holding with the hare, and running with hounds."—of currying favour with fellow servants by flattering them and ridiculing the mistress when in the kitchen, and then prancing into the parlour and purring about her, and making opportunities to display all the little faults you can find (or invent) that will tell against those in the kitchen, assuring them, on your return, that they were praised, for whatever you heard them blamed; and so, excite them to run more extremely into any little error, which you think will be most displeasing to their employers, watching an opportunity to pour your poisonous lies into their unsuspecting ears, when there is no third person

> to bear witness of your inquiry—making your victims believe it is all out of your sincere regard for them—assuring them . . . "That indeed you are no busybody that loves fending nor proving, but hate all tittling and tattling—and gossiping and back-biting," &c. &c.[100]

The trope of food as poison—the most feared power of the cook—governs the moralism of the passage. Still, in Roberts's reproach to the positional jockeying of downstairs servants, he is unable to conceal the spirit of play that seems to emanate from the cook's space. The cook's range of expressive possibilities, like her semiautonomous power, is wide. She may flatter and ridicule, purr and invent, pour poisonous lies, assure, tittle-tattle, or backbite. It is not simple gossipy subversion but in fact fiction—tittle-tattle, a form of the oral that reverts almost to the pure, babylike production of sound and is all the more dangerous for what it conceals under the surface of innocence—that threatens middle-class domestic social order, as Roberts's repetition of the word "invention" indicates.

The sheer amount of advice to the cook regarding her mouth and voice is astonishing in this passage: further advice includes "A still tongue makes a wise head" and "Saucy answers are highly aggravating and serve no good purpose" and "Muttering on leaving the room, or slamming the door is as bad as an impertinent reply."[101] This may in fact be because as the most important female domestic, cooks were no doubt in a better position to speak their minds than were other servants; nonetheless, the volume, as it were, of advice on speech demonstrates the link between orality and the kitchen. And in fact Roberts draws a direct line between speech and the cook's mouth and from there to the mouths of the master and mistress of the house:

> A faithful servant will not only never speak disrespectfully to her employers, but will not hear disrespectful words said of them.
>
> Apply directly to your employers, and beg of them to explain to you, as fully as possible, how they like their victuals dressed, whether much, or little done. . . .
>
> Do they like soups and sauces, thick or thin, or white or brown, clean or full in the mouth?[102]

The cook must not only "watch her mouth," but, in a different way, she must learn to inhabit the mouths of her employers such that she can anticipate their tastes. The line from speech to taste is direct.

In these passages the cook's mouth is represented as a tool of her trade; she is enjoined to take care of it as though it were her best knife:

> It is impossible that the most accomplished cook can please [her employers'] palates, till she has learned their particular taste. . . .
>
> To taste anything in perfection, the tongue must be moistened, or the substance applied to it contain moisture, the nervous papillae which constitute this sense are roused to still more lively sensibility by salt, sugar, aromatics, &c.
>
> If the palate become dull by excessive tasting, one of the best ways of refreshing it, is to masticate an apple, or to wash your mouth well with milk.[103]

The viscerality of these passages reveals the cook's physical vulnerability to the workings of power—it is quite within the employer's purview to enter the cook's mouth in order to discipline her tongue. In a more abstract sense orality gives the cook her access to power as well; while her mouth may be subject to middle-class discipline, she has access to her employers' mouths as well. In fact the cook's entire worth hinges on her mouth: it metonymizes her essential value as a cook.

The passages Roberts appropriates from Kitchiner professionalize taste, disciplining it and putting it to the service of the middle-class household. The cook must remain ever conscious of what goes into not only her mouth but her employers':

> The incessant exercise of tasting, which a cook is obliged to submit to during the education of her tongue, frequently impairs the very faculty she is trying to improve. "'Tis true, 'tis pity, and pity 'tis," (says a grand gourmand,) "'tis true her too anxious perseverance to penetrate the mysteries of palatics may diminish the *tact*, exhaust the power and destroy the *index*, without which all her labour is in vain."
>
> Therefore, a sagacious cook, instead of idly and wantonly wasting the excitability of her palate, on the sensibility of which, her reputation and fortune depend, when she has ascertained her relative strength of the flavour of the various ingredients she employs, will call in the balance and the measure, to do the ordinary business, and to preserve her organ of taste with the utmost care, that it may be a faithful oracle to refer to, on grand occasions, and new compositions; of these an ingenious cook may form as endless a variety, as a musician with his seven notes, or a painter with his colours.[104]

In other words: don't eat too much. Here we see the republican fear of too much sensation that I will explore in my later discussion of spice in Sylvester Graham's writings. In depicting proper and improper speech as bound to proper and improper eating Roberts's book provides insight not only into the spatial semiotic of the kitchen but also into the connections between language, food, and power. The cook's power lies, here, in exercising orality: in eating and in speaking. Both, by presenting the possibility of poisoning, project a sense of the unconscious power dynamics at work in the antebellum household, as the old "mossy" manners of the republican era pass into history.

Of all the domestic manuals printed in the nineteenth century, Roberts's may contain the most graphic representation of the orality of the kitchen. And while Roberts's book is concerned with professionalizing servant labor, he is nonetheless aware, as his account of kitchen behaviors reveals, of the possibility of radical inversion that kitchen space and kitchen labor just barely seem to contain. In taking the reader directly inside the cook's mouth Roberts's text demonstrates the hypervisscerality both of the servant's body in the symbolic economy of the middle-class house and, by analogy, of the kitchen space, which, it is important to note, he attaches to no other space in the house.

Although the kitchen only emerged as a new space in the homes of most middle-class citizens during the nineteenth century, it was already, discursively, a significant political and cultural battleground. What should be clear by now is that it did not emerge from a void: rather, the space of the kitchen carried forward significant meanings inherited from its previous life as a hearth. The shifting meanings attached to the U.S. kitchen cannot be divorced from other widespread social changes, including the new economic structure of the republic and the accompanying shift in gender ideologies as well as the consolidation of discourses of racial difference and the emergence of an immigrant servant class. The complex of changes that were occurring in the sphere of the national economy, such as the technological changes in heating and cooking technology that dispensed with earlier wood-based heating, cooking, and illuminating in favor of coal, oil, and iron, also contributed to the changing shape of the kitchen; at the same time, these changes were perceived and encoded within a literature that was suffused with a widespread nostalgia for the "old-fashioned" kitchen hearth with its democratic tradition of orality and storytelling.

As middle-class culture increasingly identified itself with disciplined and regulated front-of-house performance, the kitchen receded from polite discourse and took on associations with labor that seemed to have less and less productive value. This lack of value in turn attached itself to the servants, who were increasingly seen as foreign, vernacular, and hyper-embodied. At the same time, the longstanding association of the fireplace and hearth with storytelling and orality seems to have both lingered and mutated in the concerns that the middle-class had with "kitchen talk." These new concerns grew among an old vocabulary, but that vocabulary, as we saw from Melville and Hawthorne, was increasingly heard as "jabber," as extralinguistic, subsocial nonsense that came from minoritarian spaces and subjects, even as it constituted—perhaps because it constituted—a threat to the social order. If the cooking/storytelling tradition of transformation and inversion could plausibly be encoded in the children's chapbooks of the republican era as, essentially, comic and emancipating, by the midcentury the dynamics of the kitchen genre were changing, seeming barely to contain the threat of class and race alchemy.

Perhaps Robert Roberts said it best in his introduction to *The House Servant's Directory* when he wrote, defending "domestic" servants against immigrants, "To borrow a phrase from the kitchen, our Aboriginal servants need *grilling*."[105] In the heated economy of the kitchen raw servants, immigrant and otherwise, were, by the cheapness of their labor, both drivers of the new framework of middle-class gentility and the introjected subversives of it. In fact for "raw" servants domestic labor might be—as it was for Robert Roberts, a free man in the North—just one rung on a class ladder they were indeed trying to ascend. If the transformational possibilities of the kitchen offered significance to anyone, it was to them most of all.

In this chapter I examined the formal and thematic issues that arise when we consider literature in which the hearth plays a central role. I argued that the hearth and therefore cooking labor are associated with vernacular speech, with the fluidity of the subaltern body, and, finally, with the boundaries that lie between seemingly dichotomous social groups: men and women, upper and lower classes, humans and animals. As we will see in the following chapters, the kitchen in particular and eating and food culture broadly retain these connections across the century. Attached to subaltern and minoritarian bodies, these images morph alongside the changing middle-class house, shifting class and race relations, and an increasingly nationalist concern with the bodies that make up the United States.

The next chapter looks at reformist attempts to manage and contain the alchemical threat of eating and food culture in the writings of Sylvester Graham and William Alcott. By the 1830s, the dietary reform movement emerged out of temperance discourses to make what came to be an indelible mark on the politics of food in the United States. At the center of this dietetic project was an anxiety about asserting and maintaining the stability and superiority of what was rapidly becoming the racial identity at the heart of the national project: whiteness. Although the food reform movement was an attempt to rationalize the United States' diet, it nonetheless counted on the threat of bodily dissolution as a result of incorrect diet in order to assert its regimes of self-care. But while food and eating culture had in the past formed a metalanguage for the comedy of class difference, by the 1830s the national project of expansion, in concert with the concretization of domestic ideologies, shifted the question of difference away from class and toward the consolidation and protection of whiteness as the nation's de facto racial identity.

2

"She Made the Table a Snare to Them"

Sylvester Graham's Imperial Dietetics

As one of the century's best-known antimasturbation campaigners, Sylvester Graham has long been thought of, particularly in popular histories of food and medicine in the nineteenth century, as the apotheosis of nineteenth-century quackery.[1] This chapter argues against the ongoing tendency to treat Sylvester Graham's work as a punch line for the rhetorical excesses and perversities of his period. Excessive he is indeed, but as scholars have shown, the perversities with which Graham was associated—masturbation and vicious consumption among them—have a significant place in literary history.[2] Indeed, when it comes to conversations about Graham—whom I take to be among the most breathtakingly literary of the antimasturbation campaigners—we might echo Eve Kosofsky Sedgwick's words, when she writes of the furor surrounding her "Jane Austen and the Masturbating Girl" paper presented at the 1990 conference of the Modern Language Association, "An exploration of the literary aspects of autoeroticism seemed to leave many people gasping. That could hardly be because literary pleasure, critical self-security, and autoeroticism have nothing in common."[3] The perverse intensity of Graham's interest in the signs, symptoms, and practices of what Bruce Burgett has called "heterosensualities"—the sensations, languages, and metalanguages of both alloerotic and autoerotic desire—seems to have had the effect of turning critics away from a detailed consideration of his work.[4] Instead, it seems, discussion of Graham's writing is pervaded (and cut short) by an unending giggle factor. As we will see, the deeply catachrestic—that is, the slippery, sensual, and savory—nature of his writing can make Grahamite logic difficult to parse. Inhabiting that difficulty, however, produces a singular portrait of early nineteenth-century "sexual" economies, whose signs and practices have evaded the subject-centered (and genitally oriented) methodologies of post-Foucauldian sexuality studies, but whose unveiling can point us toward new readings of the canonical and noncanonical writers that were impacted by Grahamite thought, Herman Melville and Louisa May Alcott among them.

Graham's writings illuminate the relationship between eating and sexuality by linking the cultural history of wheat and bread to vice, morality, and national formation; in turn, his implicitly racialized and civilizationist construction of an ideal American diet—what I see as the political unconscious of eating culture in the United States—allows for a reconfiguration of Foucault's theory of biopower in the antebellum context. My inquiry here works in conversation with historians and theorists of sexuality who have taken up Graham's writing to make useful insights into male sexuality in the period, as well as with scholars in the separate field of food studies, where Graham has been situated as one character in a pantheon of eccentric nineteenth-century food reformers.[5] Few scholars, however, have put these two seemingly separate concerns—food and sex—into productive conversation; some have even dismissed the idea that eating can be a dissident form of pleasure.[6] Gayle Rubin writes in her groundbreaking article "Rethinking Sex," for instance, that "the exercise of erotic capacity, intelligence, curiosity, or creativity all require pretexts that are unnecessary for other pleasures, such as the enjoyment of food, fiction, or astronomy."[7] That Rubin pairs food with fiction in much the same way that Sedgwick paired masturbation with fiction is important: all of these activities point to interiorized and imaginative pleasures that seem to defy capture in language. As this chapter will show, in the 1830s eating is in fact quite closely linked to what Rubin calls "the exercise of erotic capacity."[8]

My argument unfolds in four sections. In the first section I will explore bread as a commodity and symbol in early American media culture—mainly newspapers and domestic manuals—in order to enlarge our understanding of the social meanings that accrued to wheat and bread during a period that spans, in kitchen terms, the transition between the hearth and the stove, with all that that suggests in the reorganization of the domestic space. In the second section I look at Graham's *Treatise on Bread and Breadmaking* (1837) to unpack his formulation of the relationship between diet and racial supremacy. The third section elaborates on Graham's ideas about the body in civilization with a short look at William Alcott's *The House I Live In* (1839), a popular anatomy primer of the period. The final section examines Graham's *The Lecture to Young Men on Chastity* (1839) to examine the erotics of Grahamite antimasturbation discourse as it constructs white female sexuality—the masturbating girl and her luxury-loving mother—in a comparative and fantastic framework with the alternately chaste and incestuously polygamous practices of South Pacific islanders.[9]

What is at stake across all these texts is the constitution, protection, and reproduction of the chaste, white body; at the center of that project is the erotic and political life of the mouth. The interconnected ideologies of domesticity and U.S. empire were, across the nineteenth century, diffused across multiple branches of the print media, from novels and domestic manuals to medical how-to books and temperance tracts, creating a series of symbolic links between nation, home, and body deployed in the service of keeping each term tightly bound to the other. Across all these genres, images of breached borders, of orifices and openings in the body and weak joints in the home, were meant to symbolize threats to national-cum-familial well-being. The mouth, a socially visible opening in the body, was one site where the threat of racial inversion and bodily dissolution lingered.

In an epoch that saw the first emergence of commodity culture, exposing the bourgeois household to new ways of managing the household economy, coupled with an intense discussion of U.S. expansion that had everything to do with divisions over slavery, the mouth was an overdetermined site for both the domestic politics of pleasure and the enforcement of norms. In this period, in other words, we can begin to trace an ideological line from the borders of the nation—which were in almost-constant flux—to the kitchen—an opening in the home through which commodities flowed—and finally to the political life of the mouth—a dense and eroticized point for the transfer of power. These complex mechanisms are, as we will see, early expressions of biopower as it came to be unevenly configured in the United States. Through them we can trace the outlines of nonnormative desires that have thus far escaped our postsexological understanding of sexuality as genitally centered, desires that emerge in and around the mouth, that space that William Alcott called a "door" into the interior life of the body.[10]

The American reform movement was synchronic with the Second Great Awakening, both movements reaching their apogee during the 1830s and 1840s, when the twin issues of slavery and imperialism, converging in the Mexican war and the conflict over the admission of new slave states, polarized political stances in the new nation.[11] While the Great Awakening was certainly a nationwide event, the reform movement was generally a northern event that evolved in tandem with the rise of Unitarianism and the dissolution of Congregationalism's place as the establishment church in New England. While the various reform movements were infused with a deeply Christian orientation, they "coalesced as discrete movements partly to address tensions within the society that were not being effectively addressed by churches or the state."[12] Movements such as abolitionism and women's rights tended to be associated with the more liberal Unitarians; evangelists, including the fiery Lyman Beecher, rode the hobbyhorse of absolute temperance.[13]

In spite of the fact that Ralph Waldo Emerson, in 1844, counted temperance and diet in the front line of the reform movements of his time, contemporary historians have tended to treat temperance as the least important of all the reform movements and dietetic reform—the stepchild of that movement—hardly at all.[14] Discussing dietetic reform as part of a number of movements for corporal discipline, which transposed a waning theology of otherworldly perfectionism into a this-worldly ideal of the perfect physique, one historian writes that the movement was "little help with the deeper, less tractable problems of nineteenth-century America: poverty, economic uncertainty, and crime among them."[15] Another historian, writing on the culture of reform, leaves temperance out of the discussion because it did not "[redefine] the structure of public discourse in the way that women's rights or antislavery did."[16] Graham and his followers, including the more moderate William Alcott and his cousin Bronson Alcott, would have disagreed, arguing—along with the temperance groups from which their movement emerged—that the whole point was the union of physiological and moral well-being with civic virtue.

By contrast with historians, scholars of literature and print culture, have argued for the central importance of the temperance movement in the formation of both the public sphere and the literary culture of the early republic.[17] Michael Warner in particular has argued that the temperance movement was central to the emergence of an "early national pattern of association": "Even before the arrival of the new steam presses . . . tract writers and newspapermen were developing the basis of a mass public. Not only were temperance societies and newspapers expanding; they incorporated an awareness of non-state society in the culture of their membership and readership."[18] Starting in the 1990s, an enormous amount of cultural studies scholarship has looked at the rise of civic culture and the place of sociability in forming modernity's disparate and overlapping public spheres. In a classic chapter in *Democracy in America* (1840) on public associations, Tocqueville wrote,

> The political associations that exist in the United States are only a single feature in the midst of the immense assemblage of associations in that country. Americans of all ages, all conditions, and all dispositions constantly form associations. They have not only commercial and manufacturing companies in which all take part but associations of a thousand other kinds religious, moral, serious, futile, extensive or restricted, enormous or diminutive.[19]

For Tocqueville, what the salon does in aristocratic societies, providing a venue for an education in sociability and the sentiments, was accomplished in America by associations in which "feelings and opinions are recruited [and] the heart is enlarged."[20] What Tocqueville did not remark on was how many of these associations were dedicated to the linked issues of health, diet, and morality, creating the prototype of a nationally identified therapeutic personality. Inseparable from the constitution of the public sphere, then, was the intimate constitution of the private citizen. Dietetic reform may not have explicitly joined the argument over slavery, women's rights, or imperialism, social issues that threatened to fracture the nation, but it did draw force from those more obviously political issues as it asserted itself in the cacophony of the public sphere, where it helped shape the national conversation around eating, that seemingly most quotidian and universal of bodily acts. It did so by telling new stories about the country's daily bread.

Bread in the United States during the Revolutionary and Antebellum Periods

In the early republic bread recipes did not appear in cookbooks. Amelia Simmons's 1796 guide *American Cookery*, for instance—long described as the first American cookbook—lists no bread recipes, although there are several recipes for sweet cakes and puddings, including one "flour pudding."[21] Susannah Carter's 1765 *Frugal Housewife*, a book that was originally published in London but that saw at least five reprints in the colonies and the early republic, likewise does not have a section for bread; rather, both books focus on recipes for meat and sweets.[22]

We might surmise that this was because baking bread was too widely known about and done in the eighteenth century for the recipe books to pay it any heed. In the newspapers of the early republic bread seems to be an ongoing topic of conversation: a search for the word *bread* in the "Early American Newspapers" database results in 1,138 hits.[23] In the *Columbian Magazine*, one author, writing pseudonymously as "Philanthropos," exemplified the rhetoric surrounding bread in the newspapers when he wrote,

> Bread has generally been considered as *the staff of life* to man, being the most important and universal article of his sustenance. For this reason, it is the practice of all wise states to subject the price and quality of this grand staple of our food, to the regulation of the civil magistrate. . . . Of such importance is the article of bread, that the government of every country ought to hold a controlling hand of those circumstances, within its reach, which may have a tendency to augment the price of this commodity.[24]

These articles not only make it clear that wheat was at a financial premium during this period but that it was widely viewed as a staple food item on which the state needed to impose some controls.

The volume and diversity of the newspaper and magazine articles dealing with the topic of bread and wheat in this period is remarkable, and the fact that those discussions took place in the print medium that was so central to the creation of the "imagined community" of the nation, seems noteworthy.[25] Bread clearly formed a topic of ongoing interest for the newformed republic, where the cost of flour had a direct impact on the staples of the average citizen's everyday diet.[26] Wheat was so important to the European colonizers that it was among the first seeds Columbus brought with him to the "New World"; one economic historian of the wheat industry has written that "it was traditional for the early colonists to take wheat seed with them to the new country."[27] The colonies were easily able to supply their domestic population with foodstuffs, while the initial farming system in the South was oriented toward the export of a nonfoodstuff, tobacco, which was later joined and surpassed by cotton. In the North, where wheat, rye, and oats were better adopted to the soil type, wheat culture did begin to flourish by the beginning of the eighteenth century, especially as the forests were cleared. Wheat soon overcame the difficulties of the New World and became a staple crop for home consumption and export.

Initially, wheat did not flourish as successfully as corn, an indigenous plant, a difference which underlined the growing divide between the southern and northern colonies; by the beginning of the eighteenth century the middle colonies, in particular New York and Pennsylvania, became known as the "bread colonies," as they produced most of the wheat and flour that was exported to the southern states and the English Caribbean colonies, which in return exported sugar—some of which was distilled into rum in New England—and tobacco. By the middle of the eighteenth century soil depletion as a result of monoculture (single-crop farming, particularly of tobacco) led more southern colonies, including Maryland and Virginia, to begin farming wheat as well.[28] Yet southern cooking, as John Egerton notes, adopted corn and its various products—for instance, hominy—from the very beginning. And Egerton points out that during the antebellum period the economy of the region, dependent on nonfood cash crops, was barely self-sufficient when it came to food: "Even in its antebellum heyday, it was a spare and repetitive sufficiency. The majority of its people, black and white, sustained themselves primarily on the same basic foods the colonists at Jamestown ate: corn and pork."[29]

In the early republic, however, the South was not the only area to suffer from anxieties concerning its basic grains. Many authors were eager to find ways for people to use less wheat to make bread, with the general proviso that these alternative breads would come in as a distant second best to bread made entirely of wheat.[30] In one article, titled "On Carrots as an Ingredient for Bread," the author remarks that "carrot meal, mixed with twice as much wheat-flour, or with one-part wheat-flour and one part flour of Indian corn, makes a very cheap, savoury, and nourishing bread. . . . We must not, in times of scarcity, object to it, because it may not be altogether pleasing to the sight."[31] Other articles in northern newspapers report on experiments to find other substitutes for wheat, including potatoes, rice, pumpkin, oats, and, as a joke, sawdust.[32] Anxiety about bread became especially pronounced in the decades after the American Revolution, for a variety of reasons. There was a range of panics that the needs of the new nation would outstrip its hard-won supply. Wheat was also grown for export at an accelerating rate, which in turn was dependent on transport in regions where rail and water connections had not been fully developed. In addition, the American South became a net importer of grain as its agriculture, despite the depletions of monoculture farming, was increasingly devoted to cotton and tobacco. Thus, wheat and other grains entered into the complicated and unstable nature of capitalist interactions at the local and national levels. The question most concerning the newspaper writers, who were largely writing for an audience of small landholders and artisans, seemed to be, How should the government stabilize the price of basic commodities so that families could survive? How, in other words, were Americans to keep bread on the table? The issue of guaranteeing the cost of flour and finding ways to make bread cheaply occupied a lot of print space from the 1780s forward.

The magnitude of popular interest in bread may also have been due to the changing dietary habits of Americans. Early in the nineteenth century many reformers were concerned with the increase in meat consumption and the decline in the amount and quality of bread production. Thus, in 1839, Sarah Josepha Hale wrote in the preface to her *Good Housekeeper*,

> Foreigners say that our climate is unhealthy; that the Americans have, generally, thin forms, sallow complexions and bad teeth.
>
> Is it not most likely that these defects are incurred, in part if not wholly, because the diet and modes of living are unsuitable to the climate, and consequently to the health of the people?
>
> Could public attention be drawn to this important subject sufficiently to have a reform in a few points—such as using *animal food* to excess, eating *hot bread*, and swallowing our meals with steam engine rapidity the question of climate might more easily be settled.[33]

In Hale's *Good Housekeeper* bread has its own chapter, right after a general treatise on healthful eating and drinking, in which she argues for "a mixed diet, bread, meat, vegetables and fruits, as the best, the only right regimen for the healthy."[34] Bread is, indeed, singled out for praise in the preface: "The art of making *good bread* I consider the most important one in cookery, and shall therefore give it the first place in the 'Good Housekeeper.'"[35] Hale, however, presents herself as a moderate who does not want to go all the way with the advocates of vegetarianism, one of whom had, by this time, made a name for himself as a lecturer: Sylvester Graham. It is intriguing that vegetarianism, which was relatively new in the country, was already well-known enough that Hale feels she needs to refute it: only two years after the publication of Graham's *Treatise on Bread and Bread-making* domestic manuals have departed from cookbook tradition exemplified by Amelia Simmons and entered into a broader conversation with reform movements.

Beyond the debates about *what* to put on the table authors of domestic manuals and other food reformers were in uniform agreement about *why* the U.S. diet needed policing: each and every reason ties diet to the strength of the national political order. Reflecting the increasingly racialized science of the era, which relied on notions of climate and environment to make claims about civilizational supremacy, Hale writes that "in every country where a mixed diet is to be found, . . . it is that portion of the human family, who have the means of obtaining beef at least once a day, who now hold dominion over the earth. Seventy thousand of the beef-fed British govern and control ninety millions of the rice eating natives of India."[36] The beef-eating British had by this time become a stock stereotype to explain Britain's rise to power in the world. Hale, however, seeks to improve on the imperial lust of the mother country. She links the omnivorous diet—which embodies a republican virtue of balance not found among the British—to racial and imperial superiority. Hale's worry is that "the tendency in our country has been to excess in animal food. The advocates of the vegetable diet system had good cause for denouncing this excess, and the indiscriminate use of the flesh."[37] In this semiotic field, where food groups and choices are associated with body types and body types with political power, bread holds a special place—it is both a vegetable dish and a central religious and political motif. Hale, along with other food writers, reinscribes it into an equation with democratizing, republican bodies, bodies that counter the imperialist impulse that derives from an obsessively animal-product diet.

The comparative framework between the colonial British and the American body is critical: in Hale's comments British and Euro-American bodies are in peril because their diets are dislocated from their national climates. As Ann Stoler and others have noted, colonial powers were very interested in each other's strategies for racial and national formation, poring assiduously over each other's policies in an effort to render their own internal legislation more effective, aggressively policing "the intimate as a strategic site of colonial governance."[38] Colonial powers legislated diet, personal hygiene, and sexual behavior in the colonies in an effort to preserve racial continuity.[39] In comparing American, South Asian (Indian), and British bodies Hale associates the United States (a former colony) with other spaces colonized and ruled by Europeans and reveals diet as a crucial technology through which nations are formed as communities against racial, moral, and physiological contamination. As the old ideology of republican virtue of balance gave way to antebellum anxieties, one of those anxieties was precisely that the Americans who descended from the English and Scots would be drowned in the flood of new immigrants coming from Germany and Ireland. Not all domestic manuals made these transnational connections explicit, but all of them connect diet—and thus domesticity and female labor—to the republican project.

In Eliza Leslie's 1840 *Directions for Cookery*, for instance, breadmaking is connected to national well-being, which is in turn associated with the country's agrarian past.[40] Leslie calls for city women to relearn the bread-baking skills of "those who live in the country," recommending the activity as economical, healthful, and good exercise for the hands and arms.[41] Leslie also argues against excess in meat eating:

> There is much more danger of excess in using animal than vegetable food. The reason is, that meats can be cooked in a greater variety of ways, are more condensed by cooking and made so "savory" by seasoning, &c. that the taste is tempted when the appetite is satisfied. Not so with plain bread: let it be made in the best possible manner, still we seem to decide, as if by instinct, the exact point when we have had enough.[42]

The excellence of bread, for many of these writers, lay in the fact that it was an unstimulating food, one that would not tax the body's digestive energies or lend itself to aggravating the nerves. In this vein Catharine Beecher writes in a chapter of her *Treatise on Domestic Economy* called "Nourishing and Unstimulating Food," "The first and most important of these foods are called *farinaceous* substances. Of these, wheat stands at the head, as the most nutritive, safe, and acceptable diet to all classes and in all circumstances. This can be used in the form of bread, every day, through a whole life, without cloying the appetite, and to an extent which can be said of no other food."[43] There has yet to be any broad study of bread consumption in the colonies or early republic. However, a few general trends are clear. The near invisibility of bread in cookbooks before and just after the American Revolution stands in sharp contrast to the near obsession over bread in cookbooks of the antebellum period. Perhaps bread simply was not as appreciated before the colonies revolted. But soon after, it seems, bread leapt into the national consciousness. By the antebellum period the many cookbooks and domestic manuals, with their fervent apologies for bread and denunciations of excessive meat consumption—always linking bodily health to the well-being of the body politic—seem to indicate that for authors of domestic manuals and food reformers alike bread was a significant item in their agendas for a healthy citizenry.

By the 1830s wheat production had begun to spread west to the prairies following westward migration; aided by advances in technology and transportation, wheat production doubled between the late 1830s and the late 1850s.[44] The soil and climate of the plains states proved to be excellent for wheat cultivation, and the vast expanses of land enabled the large-scale farming that made the crop truly profitable. Thus, to advocate for bread as a republican food in this period was to advocate an economic model that supported U.S. expansion and economic autonomy. The home in which bread was at "the center of the plate" was a self-sufficient homestead, an image of the republic in miniature. The commonplaces that surrounded bread—"the staff of life," the very image of a daily food in the Bible—made it a kind of secular sacrament for a community of consumers who, by partaking of the substance, seemed to mingle their own physical constitution with that of the nation's, unpolluted by the richer foods of decadent monarchies or the exotic fare of the tropics.

Graham's Bread Treatise

Of all the many signs of moral and physical contamination, for which reformers were constantly on the lookout, the reputedly widespread practice of masturbation among the young was one of the most vexatious. An act easily hidden, masturbation was both the sign of a youth who had escaped the scope of parental surveillance and a reason for the further extension of that surveillance. The reform discourse that addressed the "sin of Onan" sought to flush the masturbator from his or her lair by cataloguing the supposed corporeal signs that betrayed the habit, imagining rigorous cures for it, and worrying about its contaminative effect. Though masturbation was so hidden that one had to slyly infiltrate the privacy of its supposed practitioners in order to spot it, it was also, in this discourse, a powerful attractor which could set in motion a train of copycat masturbators. Along the way the United States' anti-Onanism campaigns, like their European forebears, helped invent one of modernity's first subaltern sexual identities.[45] The particular conjoining of dietetic reform with anti-Onanist campaigns also expressed an idea of the mouth as a sensual and erotic space, one which must be disciplined lest counternormative desires burst forth.

Sylvester Graham's particular contribution to the anti-Onanist movement was to propose that a vegetarian and bread-centered diet would cure what he saw as the era's epidemic of masturbation. Between his 1837 *Treatise on Bread and Breadmaking* and *The Lecture to Young Men on Chastity* two years later, as well as in his other work, Graham produced one of the most influential articulations of the connection between diet and moral well-being in nineteenth-century America. Emerson, with his eye for American characters, called him the "poet of branbread and pumpkins," although he also noted—instinctively connecting the nutritive and the political—that "there is a limit to the revolution of the pumpkin, project it along the ground with what force soever. It is not a winged orb like the Egyptian symbol of dominion, but an unfeathered, ridgy yellow pumpkin, & will quickly come to a standstill."[46] Emerson was prescient in one sense, as Graham's celebrity lasted only a decade; his influence, however, continued across a century.

As we have seen, Graham was far from the first to focus on bread as a central dietary staple. But while contributors to early American newspapers and the authors of antebellum domestic manuals spilled a fair amount of ink talking about the importance of wheat and bread, or "farinaceous foods," Graham's writings on diet crystallize, in delightfully perverse passages, many of the meanings circulating around this everyday food. Bread, for Graham, signified domestic order, civic health, and moral well-being; ingesting more bread, he promised, would produce healthy bodies and homes and ensure America's place in the pantheon of civilized nations. A close reading of the dietetic program in these two Graham texts, including two appendices to the *Lecture* that have been hitherto ignored, uncovers a semiotic economy in which eating, domesticity, race, and national formation assume sometimes interchangeable places with relation to each other, to the point where diet seems synonymous with domesticity, and race with the correct diet, all caught up in a system of mutual dependency. Here is revealed the intimate workings of republican bodily technologies within the imperial ambitions and transnational spaces of the antebellum period. In this context bread becomes far more than a staple carbohydrate: it is a symbol of the close relationships between eating, technologies of the self, and burgeoning mythologies of race and nation in the antebellum United States.

Initially trained as an evangelical minister, Graham first entered into public view in 1830, when he accepted a post with the Pennsylvania Temperance Society. Over the next decade he produced eight books and became a fixture of the northeastern lecture circuit. The extent of his interests was wide, including the importance of Sunday school, the spread of cholera, and, of course, the importance of sobriety.[47] By 1833 he had started touring extensively and was known especially for his views concerning the relationship between vice and correct diet; in those few years he managed to articulate a dietetic program whose highly metaphorical qualities reflected the concerns of the reform period and ultimately spawned a number of influential nineteenth-century health reform movements, often referred to as "Grahamite."[48] In the 1839 edition of *Good Housekeeper*, Sarah Hale introduces the recipe for "brown or dyspepsia bread" with an acknowledgment: "This bread is now best known as 'Graham bread'—not that Doctor Graham invented or discovered the manner of its preparation, but that he has been unwearied and successful in recommending it to the public."[49]

Graham proposed several methods by which young men and their families could ensure a chaste lifestyle and thus preserve their virile energies and moral well-being. These included hard beds, cold-water bathing, and purity of thought.[50] By 1837, however, Graham came to promote wheat as a wonder-working food that would prevent masturbation in particular and digestive or sexual overexcitement generally. The collective effect of bread eating would be to reinvigorate tired American energies.

Graham's clearest explanation of the importance of bread to the American diet is found in his 1837 *Treatise*. As in many popular writings, the *Treatise*'s biblically derived rhetoric around bread is heavily laden with the ideology of early nationalist racism, what might more precisely be thought of as "civilizationist," that is, relying heavily on a language of civilizational hierarchy.[51] Graham's anxious detailing of bread preparation hinges on establishing the causal link between "farinaceous foods" and civic health, from which he derived a number of insights about American consumer habits. Graham opens the *Treatise* with a history of bread, beginning with "primitive inhabitants of the earth, [who] ate their food with very little, if any, artificial preparation."[52] He narrates the beginning of grinding nuts, seeds, and grains on stones and continues through to the discovery of fire, constructing the story of bread as the story of the rise of civilization from the primitives through Mosaic times. "Even after the establishment of the Hebrew nation in Palestine, . . . at the period of the highest refinement of the Jews, in the arts of civil and domestic life, their fine flour, from which their choicest bread and cakes were made, was, in comparison with modern superfine flour, extremely coarse, ground mostly by females, in hand-mills constructed and kept for that purpose."[53] What is interesting in this history is the importance that Hawaii—here called the Sandwich Islands—holds for Graham. Not only does he footnote his story about primitive techniques for baking with fire with the comment, "In this same manner the Sandwich Islanders cooked all their food, when they were first discovered," but he concludes the section in which he describes farinaceous foods around the globe—Asia, Africa, Scotland, and Ireland—with a discussion of the Pacific Island diet: "The bread of the inhabitants consists of the plantain, bananas, yams, bread-fruit, and other like vegetables, simply roasted, baked, or boiled."[54] As we will see in the discussion of Graham's *Lecture*, the South Pacific has a key role to play in the United States' self-imagining in the period.

In the *Treatise*, however, the Sandwich Islands are but a footnote to his larger comparative project. For Graham all "civilizations" consume some kind of farinaceous food, or "bread-stuff":

> From Rome the art of bread-making very slowly found its way over considerable portions of Europe. A thousand years after Julius Caesar first entered Britain, the rude people of that country were little acquainted with raised bread. . . . In Eastern and Southern Asia, rice constitutes the principal bread-stuff; and this is generally prepared with great simplicity. In Middle and Western Asia, and in Africa, bread, though made of different kinds of grain, is prepared with almost equal simplicity. In Scotland, Ireland, and indeed throughout Europe generally, barley, oats, rye, potatoes, peas, beans, chesnuts [*sic*], and other farinaceous vegetables constitute the bread-stuff of most of the laboring people, or peasantry.[55]

In this anthropological mapping of the farinaceous world, perfect yeast-leavened bread (such as the type that Graham will teach his readers how to bake in the *Treatise*) is a mark of progress to which other nations must aspire. While Graham would have his readers baking and eating "the most beautiful and delicious bread—perfectly light and sweet," by contrast Asia, Africa, and the crude people of historical Britain and present-day peasantry all live on "simple" bread-stuffs.[56]

The language of "civilization" bleeds almost seamlessly into the language of "civic life," as "our" local diet—that of Graham and his American audience—is tied to a set of "virtuous" practices that justifies a hierarchical ranking of civilizations: "In all civilized nations, and particularly in civic life, bread, as I have already stated, is far the most important article of food which is artificially prepared; and in our country and climate, it is the most important article that enters into the diet of man."[57] This rhetorical leap in turn allows Graham to extrapolate from a particularity—"our country and climate"—to a universality—"the diet of man."

The text does at times vacillate between celebrating primitivism—associated with "cooling" and raw foods—and distancing the "civilized life" it attributes to its readership in the United States from those primitives, except insomuch as Graham sees these examples of primitivism as living relics of the civilized world's prehistory. This bifurcation prefigures Lévi-Strauss's separation of the raw and the cooked and his attribution of cooking to civilization, with the key substitution of leavening as the sign of advancement.[58] What is interesting, however, is that the semiotic economy here is attuned to a language of excitement and sensual disorder that Graham will further develop in the *Lecture*:

> If man were to subsist wholly on uncooked food, he would never suffer from the improper temperature of his aliment. Hot substances taken into the mouth . . . serve more directly and powerfully to destroy the teeth, . . . and hot food and drink received into the stomach, always in some degree debilitate that organ and through it, every other organ and portion of the whole system, . . . increasing the susceptibility of the whole body to the action of disturbing causes.[59]

Leaving the question of these "disturbing causes" vague for the moment, Graham continues, "While man obeys the law of constitution and relation which should govern him in regard to his food, he preserves the health and integrity of his alimentary organs, and through them of his whole nature. . . . If he disregards these laws, and by artificial means greatly departs from the natural adaptation of things, he inevitably brings evil on himself and his posterity."[60] The issue, then, is at least in part one of sensory overexcitement, which starts with heat in the mouth and builds until it overcomes the rest of the body, expanding outward until it wreaks havoc on man's future generations, "his posterity." The language attached to individual well-being easily slips into the language of body politic:

> And therefore it is of the first consideration, that its character should, in every respect, be as nearly as possible, consistent with the laws of

> constitution and relation established in our nature; or with the anatomical construction and vital properties and interest of our systems.
>
> If we contemplate the human constitution in its highest and best condition, in the possession of its most vigorous and unimpaired powers—and ask, what must be the character of our bread in order to preserve that constitution in that condition? The answer most indubitably is . . . the coarse unleavened bread of early times.[61]

In this passage the discourse on eating and embodiment is informed by the republican language of governmentality in that the "improper temperature of the aliment" can debilitate the "human constitution." The body is here a precise analogy for the state.

Like a great deal of antebellum writing on vice and virtue, Graham's writing is frenetic, obsessive, and frankly prurient, a perfect specimen of the genre that David Reynolds has called "(im)moral reform," a genre that enacts and performs exactly what it seeks to abolish.[62] Graham's catechrestic language can make it difficult, as I have noted, to parse his logic. However, it is in exactly these rhetorical strategies that I find traces of what I term *queer alimentarity*, a form of nonnormative sensuality that centers on orality and the mouth. That is to say, even before the publication of his specifically anti-Onanist writing, Graham's work imports language generally associated with venery and sensuality and ties it to the language of eating. For instance, what tears down "the laws of constitution and relation" and the "vital properties and interest of our systems" for Graham is "gross and promiscuous feeding":

> The people, generally, are contented to gratify their depraved appetites on whatever comes before them, without pausing to inquire whether their indulgences are adapted to preserve or to destroy their life and health. . . . There will soon reach us, as a nation, a voice of calamity which we shall not be able to shut our ears against, albeit we may in the perverseness of our sensualism, incorrigibly persist in disregarding its admonitions, till the deep chastisements of outraged nature shall reach the very "bone and marrow" of the human constitution.[63]

This sense of eating as (possibly) depraved and promiscuous would seem, to the modern reader schooled in understanding sexuality, to borrow from the realm of sexuality. Such a reading, however, flattens out Graham's anatomizing of a perverse and nonnormative geography of desire, in which eating—and therefore the mouth—is in fact supercharged with an erotic intensity that easily spreads through the entire body, "outraging" nature to its "very bone and marrow." My point here is that in talking about eating as a form of depravity we are not dealing in displacement. Rather, what I am naming *queer alimentarity* is a form of sensuality, *in and of itself*, one with, according to Graham's fevered prose, the power to disrupt both the individual body and the social order. Indeed, each of Graham's terms here—*depravity*, *grossness*, *perversity*, *incorrigibility*, *outrage*—implies that social disorder is the inevitable result of indulging in the senses at the expense of virtuous behaviors oriented toward upholding orderly systems of feeling, being, and acting. Improper eating is, in this symbolic economy, a mode of "sensualism" that is described with the same language as forms of "venereal" indulgence and is linked as a practice, through a highly racialized language, to the question of the nation's "posterity."

This idea of eating as a form of sensual pleasure that works against the nation's interests is not disconnected from the forms of social inversion linked to cooking and eating in the early literature of the United States. In Graham's work we can detect an unfinished shift in eating culture away from the boundary confusions of early modern hearth-centered literature toward a biopolitical moment in which technologies of self-care such as sexual hygiene and diet—the two particularly linked in Graham's work—were tied to civic and state well-being. What I am characterizing here as a biopolitical turn in nationalist narratives of food and eating was linked to the culture of reform, which encompassed a disparate group of movements including temperance, abolition, and early feminism. These groups characteristically construed politics to be a matter of collective action, but as a political model, reform politics based that collectivity on the individual body, which they interpreted as a site of personal transformation.[64]

In this narrow crevice between the desires of the individual body and the fate of the national body Foucault's notion of "biopower" takes particularly interesting root. According to Foucault, biopower is constituted by "numerous and diverse techniques for achieving the subjugation of bodies and the control of populations," including the disciplining and regulating of bodies, or "anatomo-politics," and "biopolitics," or the regulating of the species body, "imbued with the mechanics of life and serving as the basis of the biological processes."[65] The term *biopower* in this chapter, however, accounts for very specific and local discursive moves concerning food in the American antebellum culture, what we might think of, if we were to follow Foucault's narrative of the consolidation of biopower as the joint workings of anatomo-politics and biopolitics, as an early or transitional moment in the uneven consolidation of bodily and regulatory disciplines in the service of capital and state power. It may be useful to recall here the link that Foucault posits between the imposition of medical and psychiatric discourses of wellness and the emergence of the nation-state, with its need to track its "'population' as an economic and political problem: population as wealth, population as manpower or labor capacity, population balanced between its own growth and the resources it commanded, . . . with its specific phenomena and its peculiar variables: birth and death rates, life expectancy, fertility, state of health, frequency of illnesses, patterns of diet and habitation."[66] Foucault, of course, is thinking of post-Revolutionary French and British societies, with their fairly centralized governments. In the context of the nineteenth-century United States, with its weaker and dispersed governmental power, its regional differences, its "peculiar institution" slavery, and its less homogeneous secularization, Foucault's formulation cannot be applied in quite the same way. Michael Warner has linked the temperance movement to a "statistical consciousness, combined with a vast network of non-state associations and an equally vast body of print," but he is quick to note that temperance "brought a mass public into awareness of itself and its *distinctness* from the national state."[67] Indeed, in the early nineteenth century there was not much of a state infrastructure dedicated to the "right of the social body to ensure, maintain or develop its life": that came later, when, in the early twentieth century, Progressive-era reformers built on the work of their reformist antecedents and implemented change at the federal and state level.[68]

Grahamite biopower is located in the interspace between the state, from which it was excluded as a radical movement, the public sphere, where it competed with other reform movements to gain the people's ears, and the nation, which it figured as an ideal futurity against which the present might be compared and regulated. As the child of both the temperance movement and anti-Onanism campaigns, the dietetic movement also styled itself as an attempt to press politically on the most intimate sphere of domestic life. Just as drink and masturbation decayed the body and the mind, so too did a diet embracing the foreign commodities made available by the expanded sphere of consumerism have a subversive and perverting effect on the antebellum American body. The movement sought to promote its message by tapping into the political energy of republicanism as a discourse of self-improvement and civic belonging.[69]

In doing so in a period of rapid national expansion—a period marked by an explosion in wheat production as the western borders and reach of the nation expanded, decimating Native cultures, while whaling and merchant ships made trading inroads into the South Pacific—dietetic reform inevitably encountered the epistemological challenges generated by increasingly fraught definitions of race and empire, which it sought to manage by anchoring the nation to ecological and increasingly essentialized ideas of racial embodiment. In Graham's work—and indeed in many domestic manuals—wheat became symbolically overdetermined in this way because of its connection to what Amy Kaplan identifies as the "paradox of . . . imperial domesticity," in which the home "becomes the engine of national expansion."[70] What Kaplan calls "manifest domesticity" operates through antitheses which absorb and define the foreign: the foreign exists both within and beyond the boundaries of the domestic, as the domestic—here, the nation—expands as part of an imperial project. In the context of this close relationship between the home and the nation middle-class women's domestic work becomes a process of civilizing and colonizing which is invaluable to the building of empire.[71]

Certainly, bread is linked to Graham's hostility against female entry into the public sphere and an argument for the central place of women in the home. Graham writes, "Who that can look back thirty or forty years to those blessed days of New England's prosperity and happiness, when our good mothers used to make the family bread, but can well remember how long and how patiently those excellent matrons stood over their bread troughs, kneading and molding their dough?"[72] Concentrated within this single food item is a host of complex and meaningful cultural values that derive as much from its preparation as from its consumption. Bread in this scenario is work intensive, with the laborer being the matron herself, rather than a servant. The matron's time is evidently taken up by the labor and thus devoted to the home, rather than to shopping or displaying herself. These properties of breadmaking sustain the domestic order; it signifies an affective regime in which the "bodily and intellectual and moral" well-being of the husbands and children of the nation lie in the no-doubt roughened hands of the middle-class wife and mother.[73] Domestic well-being is signified by "perfect" bread and by the containment of middle-class female labor within the domestic space.

Dietetic expressions of the biopolitical were thus linked to what Ann Stoler has called "the education of desire": the intimate schooling of the body and of sentiment at the heart of European colonial projects, a schooling that had and that saw its own particularly nationalist articulations in the United States in the early republic and the antebellum period.[74] The period between the Louisiana Purchase and the Civil War saw the acceleration of an expansionist project that, in the end, created the continental United States. These projects of national embodiment linked national formation to the consolidation of whiteness as the dominant racial position in the United States, and they took place in a broad comparative landscape, one in which reformers looked to three sites to shape a micropolitics of daily life: laterally to other colonial spaces, backward to their own European genealogies, and forward toward their often imperial futures. Within these three temporal landscapes the United States succeeded in performing what John Carlos Rowe has called the "rhetorical legerdemain" of both identifying imperial injustices with the former colonizer, Great Britain, and justifying its own imperial efforts, particularly the expansion of U.S. territory into western North America, as part of national "consolidation" in the name of democracy.[75]

That the commodity to solve the problem of gross sensuality—oral and otherwise—had to be wheat was no coincidence.[76] Graham's work, in its commitment to wheat, directs the United States' imperial and civilizing agenda toward the intimate and quotidian functioning of its citizens' bodies, re-creating internally what the country was in the process of manifesting at its borders. When Graham writes, "They who have never eaten bread made of wheat, recently produced by a pure virgin soil, have but a very imperfect notion of the deliciousness of good bread; such as is often to be met with in the comfortable log houses in our western country," he is attempting to direct dissident alimentary desires toward the American West, using the imperial imagery of virgin soil waiting to be fertilized as a sign on which pleasure (deliciousness) is displaced.[77] In a further fantasy (playing on an enduring American myth) the scene of the eating of this delicious wheat bread is placed in a "comfortable log cabin" such as is found in the West. What sanctifies this pleasure is its civic meaning, for the bread will enter into the very mouths of an audience he invokes as "us, as a nation."[78] In this way the bodies of the citizenry—from the inner space of their mouths through the coils of their digestive tracts—are implicated in the rapid expansion of American territories into the apparently empty, untouched—virginal—spaces of the West. Eating becomes what Ann

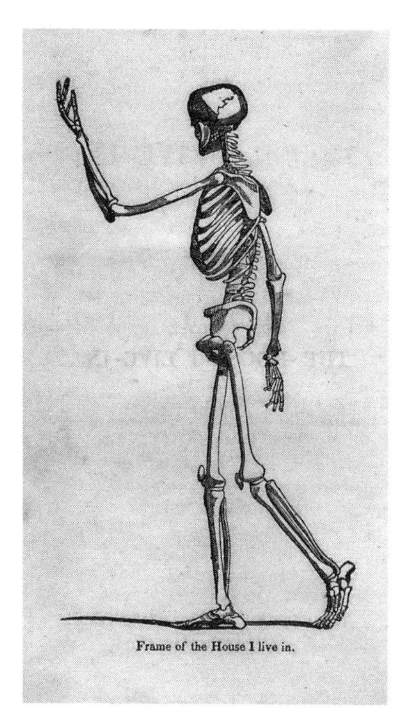
Frame of the House I live in.

Figure 5. "Frame of the House I Live In," from William Alcott, *The House I Live In* (Courtesy Department of Special Collections, Stanford University Libraries)

Stoler, borrowing from Albert Hurtado's social history of California, has referred to as an "intimate frontier": "a social and cultural space where racial classifications were defined and defied."[79]

Graham's *Treatise on Bread and Breadmaking* tells us that we might think of eating as a racializing practice that exists on a rhetorical continuum with dissident and nonnormative forms of sensuality, a continuum that was constructed through the comparative anthropological fictions of primitive and savage life that underwrote the United States' self-fashioning as the nonpareil of white civilization.

Figure 6. "Another Sort of Huts," from William Alcott, *The House I Live In* (Courtesy Department of Special Collections, Stanford University Libraries)

Figure 7. "Tents," from William Alcott, *The House I Live In* (Courtesy Department of Special Collections, Stanford University Libraries)

William Alcott: Body, Home, and Nation

If Graham's *Treatise* sets up a symbolic association between the body, the house, and the nation, in which each of these sites fully represents the other, the regulation of one came to seem impossible without regulating the others. These concerns, and the comparative racisms on which they were based, were not limited to Graham's writing: consider, for instance, a text of William Alcott's, Graham's reformist associate. *The House I Live In* was one of the most important and widely reprinted children's anatomy textbooks of the nineteenth century, first published in 1834 and with at least thirteen editions in as many years.[80] Throughout William Alcott's book, he draws parallels between human physiology—represented by the human skeleton, an image of which is captioned "Frame of the House I Live In"—the accoutrements and construction of the middle-class house, and ethnic and national identity (see fig. 5). In the 1837 edition he describes a genealogy of houses, starting with the wigwam: "Among what we call savage nations, buildings are very simple in their construction, and rude in their appearance. They are often nothing more than *huts* formed of the trunks of trees driven into the ground. . . . They are covered with bark and some of the holes are perhaps covered with mud or clay."[81] Alcott narrates the progress and development of human dwelling from the wigwam to clay domes (see fig. 6) to the kraals of South Africa and the tents of the Tartars and Bedouin Arabs (see fig. 7). He finishes this progress narrative with a detailed diagram of a two-story wooden house that charts and

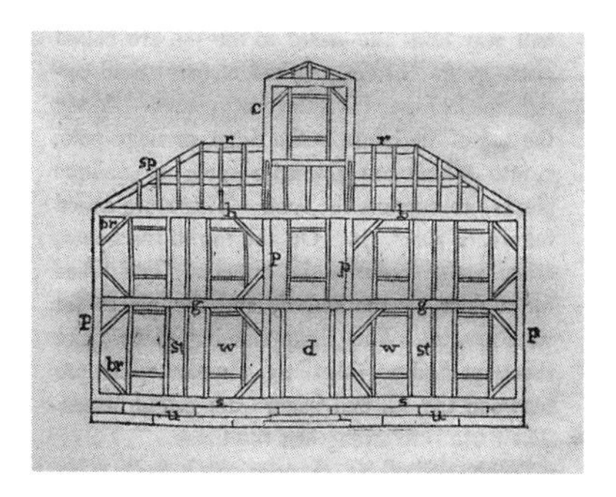

Figure 8. Diagram of the "house," from William Alcott, *The House I Live In* (Courtesy Department of Special Collections, Stanford University Libraries)

labels each element of the supportive structure of the house (see fig. 8). The tent and the kraal are represented as exterior and completed constructs; the house, on the other hand, is a plan using letters as variables to label the parts. Here, in short, is the Enlightenment notion of the progress of civilization, from the primitive—which requires little intellectual labor—to the civilized—in which objects are first designed by the intellect. If the teleology of progress—constructed through a comparative relationship between disparate European colonial projects—governs the flow of these pictures, it is also clear that a normative logic governs the middle-class house and its inhabitant, the middle-class body.

According to this metonymic logic, every theme Alcott introduces about the body has an impact on the house and nation, and vice versa. Thus, Alcott's detailed worrying over the supportive and protective elements of the house reveals an anxiety about the nourishment and preservation of the civilized body and its vulnerability to unwanted penetration. The skeleton becomes the "frame-work" of the house, while the shoulder and elbow joints become "hinges," the mouth, ears, and nose become "doors," and the esophagus becomes a "trap-door" to the basement. Just as the house without a good septic system is liable to miasma, the body's digestive system from mouth to anus requires elaborate attention, from chewing all food items to a proper liquid pulp to disposing of them in an orderly fashion. The ills that result from lack of order in the body—choking, for instance—are also ills that effect lack of order in the household—which, in the closed system of body and house, can operate to induce illnesses such as stomach pains, dysentery, and other illnesses caused by mephitic exhalations. As we saw in the previous chapter, in the antebellum culture cellars and dampness were associated with disease—perhaps for good reason, given the lack of resources for waste disposal in country and urban homes. In Alcott's vision the body/house is thus ever susceptible to collapse and/or pollution and ever in need of shoring up against the threat from without.

Significantly, in William Alcott's anatomy primer it is "primitive" and "savage" homes that are most vulnerable to penetration by the elements. Progress, then, is a process by which the body, through its dwelling, isolates itself from the environment. Nations, which are on a higher stage than savage tribes, are also represented through their houses, while the houses themselves are extensions of the body. But just as the savage is threatened by the environment that can so easily penetrate his or her domicile, the civilized person is threatened by exterior intruders too, most notably in the form of food. However much the civilized body, domicile, and nation seek to seal themselves off from the exteriority of nature, they can never wholly succeed without some impossible act of sewing up the mouth and orifices, without becoming entirely isolate. This would, of course, mean death—and so the body, the house, the nation has to possess outlets in order to eat and breathe and excrete. These, in turn, form permanent danger zones, threatening illness, savagery, and instability, providing a perpetual platform for reformist zeal.

But it is not simply imperfect or savage construction that threatens the being that Alcott calls "the inhabitant of the house": in perhaps one of the purest exercises in periphrasis in nineteenth-century U.S. writing until *Moby Dick*, the "doors" of the house are situated in the "cupola," or skull.[82] Alcott writes, "I have called the mouth and ears and nostrils doors. . . . All sound, smell, taste, &c. come to us through these passages, and the machinery or organs near and within them. Why then may they not properly be called doors?"[83] Of these, he asserts, "the mouth is the most important door in the human frame. . . . If the mouth were to fail—if this door were closed forever—there is no substitute. . . . Our frame would soon decay, and mingle with their kindred dust."[84] Life itself is thus made possible by the mouth; for this reason, having "entered" the body through what he calls the front door, Alcott spends a considerable number of pages describing the digestive tract, from the interior of the mouth (an "apartment" or "entrance chamber"), down the "food pipe," and through to the stomach and intestines.[85]

It is, of course, a comparison that must be continually repaired, since it is the inhabitants of the house, not the house itself, who eat the food.

What keeps the threat of moral and physical collapse at bay, for Alcott, is a Grahamite diet. The civilized body—which, like the house, becomes an intentional object—may produce and preserve an interior space, but it is ultimately dependent on an exterior providing it with food. Just as domestic labor depends on the labor that occurs out of doors—or at least out of the home's door—to keep the household going, so too does the body depend for its capabilities—its healthiness—on the fruits of alien labor.

In the works of Graham and Alcott the chain of associations between the body and the household, and the household and the nation, orients the doctrine of nutrition, anatomy, and housekeeping alike toward the nationalist project. Graham's and Alcott's work also enables us to locate these alimentary discourses within, as Bruce Burgett writes, "the contemporary project of grounding domestic institutions in intimate and bodily practices, which in turn could be exported as signs of (imperial) civility and (racial) freedom, . . . [as well as the] broader context of civilizationist discourses that underwrite a wide array of nationalist and imperializing projects."[86]

Antebellum reformist foodways serve as allegories through and against which imperialism and its attendant anxieties are managed and rendered inevitable. At the risk of oversimplification, there is a fundamental similarity between the worries of Graham and Alcott—what goes into the body and how it comes out—and the broader concerns of antebellum America. As the country functioned more and more like an empire, it fretted about what came into its borders—including the absorption of new populations into the nation—and simultaneously sought to spread its borders further and further out into the west and south. What we see in Graham's dietetic reform project is the antebellum imperial agenda distilled down to the intimate and quotidian functioning of the body: in this way the continuing materialization of the body, through the performative and physiological functions of eating, is metonymic of the continually expanding physical borders of the United States.

The Table as Snare: The Lecture to Young Men on Chastity

The Lecture to Young Men on Chastity, published in 1839, two years after the *Treatise*, elaborates Graham's theory of the body, describes the problem of "self-pollution" in youth, and suggests corrective dietary and hygienic measures. In the *Lecture*, as in the *Treatise*, food and reproduction constitute "two grand FUNCTIONS of [man's] system [that] are necessary for his existence as an individual and as a species."[87] Graham echoes the anatomical-cum-architectural schema of the body laid out by William Alcott across the dozens of pages in which he enumerates the effects of excessive masturbation (excessive here defined as anything from once to constantly) and sensual indulgence. The descriptive detail is extraordinary: Graham runs his prose across the skin of the body, through the nervous system, between and inside the sexual and digestive organs, and offers a range of affective and behavioral indications—from blushing in the company of women to languor to a morbid sensibility. The end result of venereal indulgence is either an explosive rupturing or the gradual degradation of the body's borders: "It is by abusing his organs and depraving his instinctive appetites, through the devices of his rational powers, that the body of man has become a living volcano of unclean propensities and passions."[88] The volcanic activity here is not simply a matter of emissions: the masturbator drools and dribbles, he is covered with pussy sores and pimples, he has tooth decay and diarrhea, his eyes become glassy and fall back into their sockets. The erotic object of Graham's palpating narrative ultimately decays and falls apart, becoming less an object of desire than of disgust.

In the *Lecture* Graham continues to show the same concern with "farinaceous foods" that had taken him down the path of reformed dietary practice in the *Treatise*. There, as discussed earlier, Graham starts the discourse on bread as an exegesis of the Bible, in which the term *bread* "comprehends all farinaceous vegetable substances that enter into the diet of man."[89] In the *Lecture* farinaceous food is again praised for providing healthful fare for those suffering from "irritation and oppression" in the intestines, for it counters the effects of gluttony, highly spiced foods, and spirits with its wholesomeness and coolness.[90] He recommends farinaceous foods as counterpoisons, which will return the body to a primitive but morally refined state of virility and virtue. In this sense *farinaceous* expands to include not only wheat but also any indigenous foods that provide the digestive system with enough roughage to keep it both cool and fit, preventing overheating and enervation.

While Graham's writings have been rediscovered by cultural studies scholars in search of antebellum texts on male sexuality, there are two stories contained in an appendix to the *Lecture* which have not received the attention they surely deserve. There are fifteen notes at the end of the *Lecture*, listed alphabetically from A to O, which either serve as elaborations and commentary on the text or offer case studies that support Graham's theories. In particular, the first appendix—Note A—which Graham offers as anthropological evidence for his project, seals the latent connections between diet, sexuality, domesticity, and empire by constructing an analogous relationship between the masturbating daughter of a wealthy family and the story of the survivors of the mutiny on the *Bounty*. Note A contains two anecdotes. The first describes a highly respectable family "of considerable distinction for their wealth, refinement and piety." Graham makes particular note of the eldest daughter: "Long before this child could speak with sufficient distinctness to be understood by any but the mother, she was taught to repeat, morning and evening, and on various occasions, little prayers and hymns, adapted to her age. . . . All that a pious and devoted mother could do, by way of religious instruction, was done, to train her up in the nurture and admonition of the lord."[91] Sixteen years later, Graham visits the family again and finds the children unruly and ill-behaved. Once again he turns his attention to the eldest daughter:

> What surprised me most was her excessive lasciviousness. Wantonness manifested itself in all her conduct, when in the company of males; and I ascertained that when she was alone with a gentleman, she would not only freely allow him to take improper liberties with her, without the least restraint, but would even court his dalliance by her lascivious conduct. Being consulted in regard to her health, I found that she was addicted to the practice of self-pollution and had greatly injured herself by it.[92]

The central question that Graham poses is how such a child, raised under the piety and purview of her religious mother and teachers, could come to this licentious state. The young woman's injuries are temperamental and moral ones: excessive masturbation has eroded her self-control, making it impossible for her to distinguish socially appropriate and inappropriate behavior. The sexual sin—self-pollution, or masturbation—most closely associated with isolation here resolves its diagnostic challenge, that is, its essentially antisocial dedication to solitary pleasure, by exhibiting signs of itself in public.[93] Graham diagnoses the daughter's fault as a domestic fault, originating with the mother, who had

> wholly disregarded the relations between the bodies and souls of her children—between their dietetic habits and their moral character. She truly "made the table a snare to them"; and they literally "fared sumptuously every day." Indeed, she prided herself on setting the best table in town. Highly seasoned flesh-meat, rich pastry, and every other kind of rich

> and savory food, and condiments in abundance, together with strong coffee and tea, and perhaps occasionally a glass of wine, were set before these children for their ordinary fare. The result was just what was reasonably to be expected; and sorrow and tears were the reward of the afflicted mother.[94]

In this anecdote Graham spots the root viciousness of the female-dominated domestic sphere in the mother's departure from the bland diet that republican reformers took such pride in to the conspicuous consumption of excitants and rich and savory food. The tongue, which is accustomed to such sensual pleasures at the table, leads to the search for other debilitating bodily pleasures, such as the daughter finds in rubbing her genitals. Hence, a habit of indulging in sumptuary foods leads to "self-polluting" practices and to moral blindness. Graham lingers, in the sensuous details just quoted, on the spectacular carnality of the table, making clear the relationship between female domestic pride and skill, the eroticized diet, the young woman's licentiousness, and the decadence of an era that has overturned the primitive and healthy diet for the modern saturnalia of foods.

While this story organizes itself around the masturbating daughter, in fact it is the mother's unchaste consumption that occupies the causal center of this story and that must ultimately be reined in. Eating is thus invoked as a sensual and erotic experience connected to the mother's taste for exotic fare and played out in the daughter's masturbatory activities. In a vaginal term suggestive of both lesbian and incestual desire the mother's seductive table, that sign of her spending and shopping pleasure, is described as a "snare"; through that delicious "snare," eating and masturbation become inextricably linked.[95]

As historian Jeanne Boydston, among others, has pointed out, at the same time that new forms of gendered domesticity were being produced in the early republic and antebellum period, women were taking on domestic shopping duties formerly allotted to men.[96] Graham's domestic parable is located in the cusp of this shift. What the mother has not resisted outside the house, in the public market, is spending the household wealth on sensual foods that are a sort of prologue to her daughter's inability to restrain herself when she is "alone with a gentleman." The social and moral threat posed by female spending in the public sphere finds its expression in the domestic unconscious; the spending female is an invitation to physical and moral degeneracy because she perversely, if unconsciously, elaborates on the metaphor between unwise spending and the illicit "spending" of sperm.

Most of the foods that constitute a threat to the body in this story are marked as "foreign" and "exotic" to the United States (spices, coffee, sugar, tea, and wine), whereas most, if not all, of the cures for the problem of excessive masturbation and the degeneracy of the body lie in local and domestic produce (milk and bread, for instance). The problem is that of misbehaving bodies—of, literally, "spiced" bodies. Graham writes, "I found that this lasciviousness was not confined to the oldest child: all the children were more or less spiced with it, according to their age."[97]

Here, then, is the threat that middle-class women's financial power and foreign luxury pose to the integrity of the middle-class home, a threat of bodily dissolution and infection through the inappropriate eating of foreign imports. For antebellum middle-class white women, leaving the home—going out the front door—to buy supplies for the "most important door" in the house—the mouth, in Alcott's terms—required navigating the contradictory symbolic boundaries of the home, which, of course, followed them. It opened the home up to the possibility of infection, just as the immigrants coming through the kitchen opened the interior space up to the alien and the free borders opened up the national body to the possibility of debility and disease. The intervention of the Other at the household table, embodied in luxury items such as wine, tea, and coffee, drained the coffers of the house and the nation and presented the threat of sexually coded changes that might overthrow piety, reverence, and modesty in future generations.

However, congress with foreign bodies is not always a matter of uncomplicated relations of inequality. Rather, it involves ambivalent forms of identification and rejection, desire and disgust, intimacy and alienation. In this first story the foreign excitants threaten to become the totality of the consumer, concretizing diet as a central term in the imperial metonymy between body, home, and nation.[98] In this first story all three bodies, actual and political, can be returned to the regime of worldly asceticism through the total rejection of the foreign and a rededication to the unprocessed and primitive, which are, fortunately, offered by domestic growers. The second of Graham's stories in Note A of the appendix, however, presents an antithetical dynamic.

Set in the South Pacific, the second story recounts the mutiny on the British ship *Bounty*. Contrary to the first story's representation of a sealed domestic sphere, Graham's second narrative reveals another reality of the political economy—the subordination of the American economy to British hegemony, which created a series of lateral identifications between the antebellum United States and other British colonies. It is important to read the seeming contradictions of antebellum food culture through the history of U.S. imperial expansion and the complex relationship of the United States to Britain, its former ruler and greatest customer, as well as its industrial rival; similarly, it is important to recall the United States' ambiguous position as a postcolonial power in a world in which Europe's colonial powers were expanding.

In Graham's story from the 1830s food and sex emerge as central themes in a premonitory fantasy of imperial expansion. Here commodity consumption and the desire for land serve as catalytic desires for interactions across national, regional, and ethnic differences, despite the fact that racial unity would have to be sacrificed in any expansion of American territory. Absorbing these alien others and "Americanizing them" is a constant preoccupation in a nation that is both militarily aggressive and open to successive waves of immigration. In this story, more than any other, the metaphoric qualities of "farinaceous" foods are stretched to include foods not indigenous to North America but that nonetheless evoke the cooling qualities of Grahamite bread.

The story begins with the mutiny on the *Bounty*. Escaping the ship, the mutineers first go to Tahiti, where they take native wives, and then to Pitcairn's Island, along with some native males and their wives. The natives mutiny against the mutineers, and all adult males "of both colors" are killed, except for one: an Englishman, who rather Edenically renames himself "John Adams," perhaps not coincidentally the name of the second president of the United States. Adams oversees the upbringing of the surviving nineteen children, and there, living either in chaste equanimity or polygamous harmony with all the remaining wives, he raises a race of children "in uniform good health": "Infants were generally bathed three times a day in cold water, and were sometimes not weaned for three or four years; and when that did take place, they were fed upon food made of ripe plantains and boiled taro root, rubbed into a paste. . . . They have no bowel complaints, and are exempt from those contagious diseases which affect children in large communities."[99] The narrative follows the children into adulthood:

> Their beds were mattresses composed of palm leaves, and covered with native cloth, made of the paper mulberry tree. Yams constitute their principal food, boiled, baked, or mixed with cocoa-nut, made into cakes, and eaten with molasses extracted from the tee root. Taro root is no bad

> substitute for bread; and bananas, plantains and appoi are wholesome and nutritious fruits. They but seldom kill a pig, living mostly on fruit and vegetables.... They are subject to few diseases.... They are certainly a finer and more athletic race than is usually found among the families of mankind.[100]

A number of representations merge into one another here. First, we see that the model of the noble savage so prevalent in Enlightenment discourses emerges in the ideal of the Pacific Islander raised without the taint or temptation of modern life. Second, we see the parallel that Graham has set up between the idea of the noble savage and the white child. There is an implicit comparison between the young men to whom Graham is lecturing and the allegory of the growing nation into which he inscribes the story of Pitcairn Island. Because Graham is using the example of mixed-race Tahitian children to make a point about American bodies, we cannot assume that the racial politics at play here is simply the familiar one, with its hierarchy of dwellings, body types, and races and that in the southern United States had the force of law to enslave a large minority of the population. On the one hand, as in the previous story, white American bodies have to remain untainted by contact with the foreign—they need to remain "unspiced"—an image that gestures to the need to shore up the boundaries of the white body. On the other hand, we see that white American bodies can profit by comparison with the foreign, though only when foreigners are appropriately located in their own bioregional spaces.

Once again, these politics of comparison reveal what Ann Stoler has called "[colonial] circuits of knowledge production and racialized forms of governance [that] spanned a global field."[101] In this story U.S. bodies are *like* Tahitian bodies, a likeness that is underlined by the mixed British-Tahitian heritage of the subjects. These bodies are not, however, of equal standing: Graham ends the story by informing the reader that the Tahitians will one day become an important race—but are not one yet. However, the importance of the comparison lies in the cultural value assigned to these two sets of subjects, both of whose lineages are simultaneously expatriate and, as the argument seems to go, indigenous. Mixed-race Pitcairn subjects can lay claim both to British origins and to the land they live on. What is at stake in Graham's dietetic program is reforming the epicurean American consumer's body so it, too, can make a similar claim. As though Graham's narrative is haunted by the American Revolution, we see the same crucial elements: the sailors revolt against British tyranny and establish their own state, literally becoming the founding fathers of a new race; and the narrative comes to a close when all adult males except John Adams are killed off, eliminating the threat of native insurgency and the cultural or political—or culinary—legacy of the British sailors.

The narrative of the mutiny on the *Bounty* compulsively reenacts the colonization of the New World and thus, by analogy, restages the problem of naturalizing the former British colonists' claim to what had formerly been British North America, through the metaphor of indigeneity. In so doing the metaphor erases the historical presence and agency of the actual indigenous inhabitants of the land, by both murdering the men and sexually conquering the women. Within this miscegenative framework Graham co-opts indigeneity for the project of colonization. The story becomes a case study for the elaboration of his own domestic dietetic argument, even though, again, the analogies at work here need constant repair and overlook discontinuities in the story (for instance, John Adams is, on one level, a founder of a race and, on another level, a traitor to his race, inasmuch as his companions were slaughtered by the Pitcairn Islanders). Similarly, the project of producing normative sexual models that we saw in the previous tale of the masturbating daughter here rests nicely next to Adams's possibly polygamous practices. The inhabitants of Pitcairn's Island are both shining examples of the ideal of human health and, as primitive peoples, sign and symbol of the physical possibilities that Americans have abandoned in their commitment to consumer lifestyles that depend on foreign commodities.

Here, as always in Graham's writing, bread or bread substitutes take on an organizing role. Correct eating—yams and "cocoa-nut" made into cakes, and taro root as a substitute for bread—take on this central role because within the schema of nineteenth-century science, bodies were best maintained and cured by local produce—a longstanding nationalist formulation that we can trace back through, for instance, the cultural geography of British medical botanists and other scientists of early nation-states.[102] This logic, however, posed a particular problem for settler nations that had visibly imported their fauna and flora with them—a problem that Graham solved with his formulation of a paradoxical Euro-American indigeneity organized around wheat, that symbolically important European grain that the Jamestown settlers had worked so hard, and so vainly, to cultivate. Within this logic indigenous South Pacific islanders maintain their "natural" morality, because they consume only that which grows where they live.

The term "paradoxical Euro-American indigeneity" here refers to the ways in which the United States, as a settler nation, both co-opted and erased the bodies of native peoples in order to naturalize the European claim to the land. Yet the immigrant paradox is that these settlers change the very land that, according to the strictures of nineteenth-century science, produces the foods that are healthiest for their bodies. Between the nation's health and the nation's produce there lies a shadow. For Sylvester Graham the farinaceous rule, which elevated bread to the fulcrum of bodily health and moral character, governed the semantics of food production. Whether from wheat or from taro root, bread—the biblically appointed heart of the European diet—became the cure-all for bodily woes. Fortunately, the virgin soil of the American West, by its very virginity, allowed the immigrant to import this idealized "local" plant culture; it is in this act, of the rapidly Americanized immigrant spreading westward, planting the grains which can be milled into the staff of life, that the American stakes his or her claim on the ground.

However, if Graham is, on the one hand, claiming that we are what we eat, he is also demonstrating that what we are, like much of what we eat in the era following the Columbian exchange, is always dislocated and relational, reiterated and reconstructed by our quotidian acts. John Adams, the Edenic first and last man of Pitcairn Island, passes on his generational wisdom to his heirs, having no luxuries to tempt him off the path of virtue. The pious, elegant, and wealthy lady of Graham's first story, on the other hand, forgets the frugality that instilled moral character into her generation and debauches her children, corrupting their libidos with the rich and savory foods that she brings to the table. In both constructions correct eating, like correct sexual behavior, is understood as a performative act of national identification and formation. In eating as national subjects flesh is called into social being through a model that understands race as anchored to some of the most intimate of biological functions.

I take my cue here again from Ann Stoler's work, in which she reinserts race as a central issue in Foucault's *History of Sexuality*, arguing that the policing of the body and the body politic in Europe and its colonies was enacted through a "hierarchy of moralities, prescriptions for conduct and bourgeois civilities [that kept] a racial politics of exclusion at its core."[103] Stoler argues that in neglecting the comparative possibilities of empire and imperial outposts Foucault's *History of Sexuality* "misses key sites in the production of that discourse, discount[ing] the practices that racialized bodies, and thus elid[ing] a field of knowledge that provided the contrasts for what a healthy vigorous body was all about."[104] Graham, in juxtaposing his two narratives, produces the shock resulting from the contact of the colony with the metropole, in a discourse based on—as we also saw in William Alcott's anatomy book—exactly the sort of comparative, transnational framework that became more prominent in the antebellum years. As America's contact with other peoples grew—from increased immigration into the country, from the continual expansion of the country's borders, and from the tales that trickled back from whalers and missionaries—so too did depictions that paired the wild and the raw, the cultured and the uncivilized. We see this juxtaposition in the appendix to Graham's book, between Pitcairn and daily life in the metropole, and also between that book, physically present on the *Lucy Ann* when Melville was part of its crew, and the Tahiti that was one of the whaler's destinations.

Graham's fetishization of farinaceous foods allows us to see the importance of the idea of indigeneity in a settler nation that was, from its inception, built on imperial (indeed, genocidal) principles. In Graham's domestic-cum-dietetic proposal North American indigenous peoples are entirely absent from nationalist discourse; at the same time, only a few years before the consolidation of the official policy of manifest destiny, in Graham's work we find the national gaze already turning westward toward the Pacific. Graham's discussion of the South Pacific is built on far more than a simple contrast of bourgeois white cosmopolitanism against an exotic colonial other; in his idealization of the Pitcairn Islanders, and their murderous creation/violent genesis, he both negates their existence and identifies with their dietary resolve. Through his contradictory depiction we also find nascent hints of an argument for annexation.

Graham's vivid dietetic imagination visibly projects social hierarchies and social identities onto food and the scene of eating in the domestic unconscious. Food and spices from the tropics are coded as dangerous or luxurious—which, politically, is already inscribed in the national founding myth in the story of the rebellion against the tax on tea, one of the foreign substances that Graham found to be morally debauching. The projection of concepts of "healthiness" onto "indigenous" American foods[105]—whether or not those items were in fact native to the Americas and, as we have seen, often *because* they were not—reveals reformers' anxious need to solidify borders that seemed to be getting more and more blurry. The blurring of these borders, between the public and private, between the savage or "raw" Irish cook in the kitchen and the civilized cuisine of the dinner table, between the enjoyment of food and the wanton abandonment to sexual urges, gnawed at the boundaries of the body and the body politic. At the same time, this managing of racial, sexual, and dietetic anxieties, a project overseen by the ever-diligent woman of the house, demonstrates an effort to shore up the imaginary contiguities among nation, home, and body and between majoritarian political groups and the spaces to which they laid claim. The sheer corporeality of the heavy meals and the heavy bouts of self-abuse—the seemingly irrational demands of the body and of embodied existence—threaten to dissolve social, familial, and often national boundaries. To consume wheat bread, with its power to cool the skin and diminish aggressive sexual energies, was, in Graham's formulation, to hold all these threats at bay.

In one bourgeois American household in the 1840s, at least, the meals were frugal and meatless—in that of William Alcott's cousin Bronson Alcott. By 1873, and with the publication of his daughter Louisa May Alcott's novel *Work*, which I discuss in chapter 4, bread was firmly constituted as a metonym for women's domestic labor, and wheat signified the vast inner spaces—the belly, perhaps—of the United States. The virgin soil had been conquered by the plow and the threshing machine and was becoming the bread basket. Only twenty years later, in the lyrics to "America the Beautiful," Katharine Lee Bates wrote,

> O beautiful for spacious skies,
> For amber waves of grain,
> For purple mountain majesties
> Above the fruited plain!
> America! America!
> God shed his grace on thee
> And crown thy good with brotherhood
> From sea to shining sea!

By the 1870s those amber waves were entirely contained within the domestic borders of a still-hungry empire: the lands "from sea to shining sea" had been fully consumed.

Sylvester Graham and his followers articulated one of the founding dietetic reform discourses of nineteenth-century America, with the result that American meals, at least, were blander—even if no evidence has come to light that Americans masturbated less after consuming less exciting foods. Harvey Levenstein has noted that even at the end of the nineteenth century "a relatively light hand with spices continued to characterize cooking. . . . Many people shared the notion of antebellum food reformer Sylvester Graham that they stimulated inordinate appetites for sex."[106] The Grahamite movement spawned a journal, the *Graham Journal of Health and Longevity*, which ran for three years and five volumes and was edited by Garrisonian abolitionist David Campbell and then, later, William Alcott.[107] William Alcott was also the first president of the American Physiological Society, a group dedicated to lecturing on the physical sciences. Across cities and towns there were even Graham boarding houses, where followers might resist temptation and adhere to the Spartan diet.[108] Alcott later went on to design physical education regimens for American public schools.

There is no doubt but that Graham's dietary advice offered a nutritional improvement on the general diet of the time. Nonetheless, its nutritional properties were almost accidental, traced not by some diagnosis of the real processes of digestion, in which Graham had no training—indeed, for which there existed no training we would recognize as medical by today's standards—but against the alchemy of the always-threatening body. Emerson's poet of the pumpkin may have taken on the garb of the scientist of the pumpkin, but his categories and theories immediately read biological processes into social terms.

The project of constituting America was not, of course, a project of dietetics alone: it was shared across a number of reform movements. Graham and Alcott found their voices in the temperance movement but used the vocabulary of "temperance" broadly to include a total style of life, in which abstaining from all enervating substances would be at the center of a new, moral form of domestic consumption. In fact, they were marginal figures as far as the tendency of the United States' economy was concerned. Industrialization and foreign trade in the United States, as well as the Civil War, soon radically changed the economy from the one that Sylvester Graham knew in 1838; the industrialization of all parts of food production made a mockery of his apparently staid republican ethos. But if the political effect of the reform movement was only partly successful, another legacy—shaping the terms in which Americans understood themselves—lived on, testifying to the fact that we can no more separate eating and ingestion from the understanding of the bourgeois self than we can separate it from the prevailing codes of sexual desire. Dietetic reformers anxiously charted the inner spaces of the American body and in so doing made apparent the reform movement's desire to bind those spaces into the political future of the nation.

3

"Everything 'Cept Eat Us"

The Mouth as Political Organ in the Antebellum Novel

The Venus [speaks]:
Petits Coeurs
Rhum Caramel
Pharaon
Bouchon Fraise
Escargot Lait
Enfant de Bruxelles
(Rest)
Do you think that I look like
one of these little chocolate brussels infants?

—Suzan-Lori Parks, *Venus: A Play*[1]

Toward the end of Suzan-Lori Parks's play *Venus*, the embattled Saartjie Bartman, also known as the Venus Hottentot, is offered a box of chocolates by her lover and captor, the Baron Docteur. Parks's 1997 play dramatizes the life of Bartman, a nineteenth-century woman who was brought to England from Africa as a freak-show performer because of her allegedly large buttocks and hips. When the real Saartjie Bartman died in 1815, Georges Cuvier—botanist, zoologist, and the model for the Baron Docteur character—dissected her body and preserved her genitals—pickled them, actually—in a jar at the Musée d'Homme in Paris. There, along with a plaster cast of her buttocks, they remained until the 1980s, when public pressure caused the museum to remove them from view. The body parts were finally returned to South Africa and buried in the town of Hankey in 2002, to much fanfare in the South African press. Over the past two decades historians, theorists, and artists have rediscovered Bartman's life; she has become a central example of the confluence of scientific racism and commercial entertainment in the nineteenth century.[2]

Parks's play, then, deals with a woman who had, in the 1980s, become a symbol of the Western desire both to know, in the most intimate detail possible, and to conquer, with any amount of violence, the black body—especially the black female body. While the events Parks is dramatizing are European, she, as an American, does not have to explain the cultural connections between Bartman's body and the chocolates, molded into little figurines, given by her lover. The theme of the black body as food is massively present in American culture, encoding all the ambivalence and terrible violence of American racial politics.[3]

I argue in this chapter that the libidinal logic of American racism leads to the extreme image of the black body itself as food. This bizarre image emerges from the complex web of racial relationships, as though to find a compromise between white America's twinned emotions—desire and fear—nothing will do but to actually internalize and obliterate blackness. This desire is represented with a blatant urgency in the scene quoted in the epigraph, in which the Venus eats chocolate bonbons, holding and directing her lover's gaze as he watches her and masturbates. An "exotic" food item introduced to Europeans through the colonial conquest of Mexico, chocolate is today associated with sexuality, female desire, and romantic love. In these passages, however, chocolate's color, history, and cultural valences bear the much more complex weight of a metaphoric association with the black female body.

The image of the black body as food finds its roots in the violent intimacies of the slave economy and continues to be expressed today in a variety of visual and literary representations of black bodies, including Little Black Sambo, Aunt Jemima, and Uncle Ben.[4] The image has also found a trenchant response in the work of black artists such as Parks—whose Venus works within the slim margins of her political agency to attract, manipulate, and hold the Baron Docteur's gaze while she eats chocolate reproductions of her body—and Kara Walker, whose installations *Vanishing Act* and *The End of Uncle Tom* reverse the trope of black edibility to depict blacks consuming whites.[5] Doris Witt has made the rich point that the numerous images linking black subjects to food are "products of the dialectic between commodity capitalism and popular culture"; the results of this merger—everything from the ubiquitous bottles of pancake syrup, made in the shape of a woman's body, to the still-available licorice baby candy, from *The Gator and the Pickaninny* film discussed in the introduction to the gator-bait advertisements discussed in the chapter 5—are, Witt argues, "created to suture contradictions of racial, ethnic, gender, and class difference."[6] Black abjection and black beauty, forced slave labor and the fantasy of the black female caretaker, nostalgia for the "innocence" of plantation life and the endless history of racist violence: Parks plays with these contradictions—unties the bandage and opens the wound—that lie beneath these representations seen throughout the nineteenth and twentieth centuries.

In this chapter I look at some early iterations of black edibility in three antebellum novels: Nathaniel Hawthorne's *The House of the Seven Gables*, Harriet Beecher Stowe's *Uncle Tom's Cabin*, and Harriet Wilson's *Our Nig*. The latter two, of course, more explicitly grapple with issues of race and power. However, within the escalating antebellum debate about the place of black subjects in the future of the nation all of these novels use the image of the black body, metaphorized as food, in conjunction with the project of construing—and at times critiquing—the idea of whiteness.

I earlier explored the nutritional ideologies of the antebellum era and their connections to the formation of whiteness. Here I continue to examine images of the mouth and ideas of orality as they relate to the architecture of the house, as well as the intertwining of white identity with images, figures, and representations of eating and consumption. There is a key difference, however, in how food is considered and used. Grahamite dietetics relied on prohibitionist or distancing strategies—the *rejection* of certain foods—to defend a nationalist formation of whiteness threatened by the expansion of both America's borders and consumer culture. In this chapter, by contrast, we will encounter the trope that bell hooks once called "eating the other," that is, the constitution of whiteness through the *internalization* of racial difference.[7]

These three texts are, of course, very different: on a purely aesthetic level and even at the level of genre Hawthorne's romance, Stowe's sentimental maternalism, and Wilson's autobiography-cum-novel are far apart. And yet these texts do speak to each other, if I may anthropomorphize, in their desires to repel each other's most sacred beliefs: Hawthorne is intent on refuting literature's apparent feminization in the sentimental novel; Stowe rejects masculine legal and economic discourse; and Wilson works to unravel sentimentalist myths of white female abolitionist benevolence. Although I will only discuss the latter point at length in this chapter, my point here is to note that their separate goals do to some extent position these novels in a tacit polemic about the thorny questions of race and gender. What is more pertinent to my project, however, is that these texts converge in their shared images and objects—the black body as food—and in their shared spaces—nineteenth-century houses and kitchens, built, as argued earlier, on and around the semiotic bones of the colonial home. While all three novels figure these tropes in the contexts of their different political projects, in all these texts the edible black body is linked to white, and primarily female, embodiment. My goal is to build on earlier discussions of the white-black racial dialectic by pushing the bodily politics of these novels past the skin and heart—past color and past feeling—and into the mouth and stomach.[8]

These texts also inaugurate a new theme which will continue through the rest of the book; we will follow the moments when the ingestion and figuration of blackness, if the reader will forgive my belaboring of the metaphor, *chokes*—in other words when blackness pushes back at its devouring racial other and thus not only rejects white desire but also complicates the mythology of whiteness itself. To reprise an earlier comparison/metaphor, the black body is always "sticky" in the white domestic unconscious, just like the syrup in the Aunt Jemima bottle. But there is a limit to how much the white body can absorb the black subject; and typically that limit is reached when the black body inhabits its own stickiness, pushing back in order to get stuck in the craw of whiteness. Once situated, blackness is not easily obliterated by the aggressive and devouring white body, nor, by analogy, will black subjectivity be so easily erased by the nation itself. In these texts blackness enters into and *upsets* the white body and therefore the white body politic in all senses of the word. It is no coincidence that the white body faces the crisis of its disunion in the antebellum period; the United States' republican project comes undone in these years precisely over the issue of the violent exploitation of the black subject.

Inseparable from Graham's fascination with the bodies of distant natives at the edge of the nation's fantasy empire, domestic whiteness in these pre–Civil War texts is cannibalistically dependent on its racial other, through what Toni Morrison has tactfully called, on the one hand, "the process of organizing American coherence through a distancing Africanism" and, on the other, less gentle, hand, "the parasitical nature of white freedom."[9] In "eating the other" the white self affirms liberal interiority through the metaphor of assimilation and digestion; blackness is the precondition, in these texts, on which whiteness is made material, both as body and as political actor. But as we will see across these three texts, even when compressed into objecthood, black subjectivity does not, and will not, give itself up so easily.

Modernity's Cannibals: Hawthorne's House of the Seven Gables

> The way us niggers was treated was awful. Marster would beat, knock, kick, kill. He done ever' thing he could 'cept eat us.
>
> —Charlie Moses, ex-slave, testimony from the Works Progress Administration[10]

Perhaps the most famous representation of the black body as an edible object in U.S. literature takes place in Hawthorne's 1851 *House of the Seven Gables*, in which a young boy enters Hepzibah Pyncheon's store to buy a "Jim Crow" cookie.[11] The boy enters the house "sideways," through a door cut into the side of the house to make an entrance for the shop; the boy's purchase is Hepzibah's first sale and thus her initiation into the market economy. In this chapter eating is quickly associated with class identity:

> A lady—who had fed herself from childhood with the shadowy food of aristocratic reminiscences, and whose religion it was that a lady's hand soils itself irremediably by doing aught for bread—this born lady, after sixty years of narrowing means, is fain to step down from her pedestal of imaginary rank. Poverty, treading closely at her heels for a lifetime, has come up with her at last. She must earn her own food, or starve![12]

Hepzibah's real hunger, in the present, is contrasted with her replenishment, in the past, on food's double—its "shadow." Feasting on "aristocratic reminiscences," however, has led her to this moment in which her "narrowing means" has so thinned her out that she can no longer resist the pressure to eat real food. Hepzibah's entry into marketplace modernity implies that her aristocratic history has rendered her barely physically present, a ghost in the vibrant commodity culture that the boy so easily inhabits. Her hunger, in other words, drives her entry into the marketplace, in which she must earn—one of capitalism's barest puns—her own bread.

Hepzibah's repugnance for her role as shopkeeper thus vies with the necessity of earning a living. When the young boy comes in and asks for the Jim Crow cookie in the window—"The one that has not a broken foot!"—Hepzibah refuses the penny payment he offers for the gingerbread.[13] The boy leaves the store with the cookie and soon returns:

> No sooner had he reached the sidewalk (little cannibal that he was!) than Jim Crow's head was in his mouth. . . . She had just placed another representative of the renowned Jim Crow at the window, when again the shop-bell tinkered clamorously; and again the door . . . disclosed the same sturdy little urchin who, precisely two minutes ago, had made his exit. The crumbs and discoloration of the cannibal-feast, as yet hardly consummated, were exceedingly visible about his mouth.[14]

In the mock heroic inventory of Hepzibah's goods that had preceded this scene the Jim Crow cookie is presented as though it were "executing his world-renowned dance, in gingerbread," referring to the bawdy humor of antebellum blackface and thus to the impulse for racial impersonation that underlies that medium's structuring joke.[15] But if this gingerbread is conceived as the white impersonation of black performance, its destiny is to be ingested, in all its mock black physicality, by the young Ned Higgins, a mock white "cannibal."

Higgins's "cannibal" eating of the cookie gestures to the sublimated recognition of species-likeness that is always registered by the term. As Peter Hulme has written, across modernity cannibalism has signified the total primitive otherness against which Western rationality—and its installation of the putatively ungendered and deracinated "human" as its subject—measured itself. This dialectic—between what Stuart Hall has called "The West and the Rest"—points to the ways that the imperial project underpins European Western modernity as a whole.[16] And yet, while a moral repugnance toward the ingestion of one human by another radically undermines the human privilege of the eater, it also underlines the humanness of the observer. But from another perspective, by designating the eating of one body by another to be cannibalism (and thereby worthy of repugnance), we acknowledge the likeness between the subject and object, establishing both positions to be, in the very least, circus-mirror images of each other's humanity. Indeed, from an ontological perspective, as Maggie Kilgour has shown, the act annihilates the difference between self and the eaten other, making one body of the two.[17] In this way cannibalism acknowledges and performs sameness; on the level of epistemology, however, cannibalism constructs difference.

Staging that encounter, the Jim Crow gingerbread is eaten, and the upshot of Higgins's cannibal feast is that he remains and indeed returns, wanting another bite of the other. However, the "crumbs and discoloration of the cannibal-feast" return us to the scene of the minstrel theater with which we began. Like a photonegative of blackface makeup, Ned Higgins's white face is marred by the crumbs around his mouth—in contrast to the typical blackface makeup in which a black face is caricatured by white (or red) lips surrounded by a thick white outline. Hepzibah's entry into capitalism is thus marked not only by her opening a store inside her home but by selling a food item that invokes the theatrical slave body both in its presentation and in its consumption.[18] The idea of a Jim Crow cookie seemingly reduces the black body to total dehumanization, as it allows the consumer to digest and symbolically destroy that body. But the opposite, as discussed earlier, is also true. The "impish" Jim Crow who "execute[s] his world-renowned dance," and whose remains ring the mouth of the white child, is anything but passive, especially in a world such as that of the novel, in which objects are so relentlessly animated for their symbolic value. The cookie carries enough auratic power that it attracts Higgins's notice above any of the other items in the window; its power also infects Higgins's body with its own "primitive" likeness—he becomes a cannibal.

If Hepzibah aborts her first commercial transaction when Higgins asks for the Jim Crow gingerbread, she cannot afford to give her merchandise away again when the "little cannibal" comes in for a second exchange. This time she gathers her courage together and demands payment:

> "Well, here it is for you," said Hepzibah, reaching it down; but, recognizing that this pertinacious customer would not quit her on any other terms, so long as she had a gingerbread figure in her shop, she partly drew back her extended hand, "Where is the cent?"
>
> Looking somewhat chagrined, he put the coin into Hepzibah's hand, and departed, sending the second Jim Crow in quest of the former one. . . . It was done! The sordid stain of that copper coin could never be washed away from her palm. The little boy, aided by the impish figure of the negro dancer, had wrought an irreparable ruin . . . as if his childish gripe had torn down the seven-gabled mansion.[19]

Sánchez-Eppler has argued that children consistently figure in Hawthorne's fiction as the sign of commodity capitalism, "suggesting how closely Hawthorne associates the market with children."[20] She argues, further, that the popular understanding of children as little primitives during that period represents the "felt similitudes between the project of raising good, white, middle-class, Christian, American children and raising an economic and cultural American empire."[21] This is why, as she demonstrates, Hawthorne can call Higgins a cannibal: here, as in the larger cultural discourse, both while children and the objects of empire figure as primitive beings.

The child's "gripe," as Hawthorne puts it, nearly tears down the mansion, that space that had enclosed Hepzibah Pyncheon, for her first six decades, outside the flow of history and within the strictest of domestic confines. "Gripe" here denotes the clutch of this "true-born Yankee's" hand, but it also motions to the medical meaning of "spasmodic contractions, often in the bowels, as in colic pains."[22] That Hepzibah has been a paid party to the mock cannibalism of Higgins's consumption not only threatens the total dissolution of the assumptions that have governed her private life but also signals toward profound—literally deep—(in)digestive effects as she is forced to enter the market unwillingly. Indigestion is thus not only of the body here: Hepzibah stands for her house. Higgins's cannibal feast has violated the rules of exchange that govern the aristocratic household, in order that Hepzibah herself may eat. Her ability to earn her own bread, as it were, depends on the gluttonous child who puts the second Jim Crow, "in quest of the first one," into his gut.[23] Such a profusion of sweetness—such stickiness—unsettles house and body.

While the admittedly stale cookie seems to disagree with the child, another effect of the interaction is that the coin "stains" Hepzibah's palm. The racial implications of the child's consumption, as blackness penetrates the white body, are also enacted on Hepzibah's body, newly implicated in the market economy. Her hand is stained not black but copper, an amalgamated color signaling both to many shades of brown and to a highly conductive metal. The stain marks her participation in, and facilitation of, the murderous "cannibal feast." However, later in the chapter the coin becomes a talisman, "fragrant with good" and "endowed with the same kind of efficacy, as a galvanic ring":[24] "Hepzibah, at all events, was indebted to its subtile operation, both in body and spirit; so much the more, as it inspired her with energy to get some breakfast, at which . . . she allowed herself an extra spoonful in her infusion of black tea."[25] At many points, then, the text connects the constitution of the white body with the consumption of blackness. And yet, as noted, that racial algorithm is paradoxical: because the white child's consumption is referred to as cannibalism, the cookie's otherness is annihilated at the same time as it is consumed; on the other hand, that difference remains behind, marking the child's face as it makes its way through his digestive system. But it is also implied that Hepzibah changes color, the child's appetite serving as proxy for her own; indeed, although the chapter begins with Hepzibah's morning, she does not have breakfast until after she has a few sales. No coincidence, then, that Hepzibah, hungry because she has waited to eat, gives herself an extra infusion of black tea: both she and Higgins are reenergized and reembodied, fed even, by their encounter with Jim Crow.

It is worth taking a moment here to think through the implications of the energizing ingredients at play here: tea, ginger, sugar, and—as in the epigraph that began this chapter—chocolate, particularly as they come into contact with an overarching interest of this study, sweetness. We saw in chapter 2 that in antebellum temperance and food reformer texts these ingredients—all products of Asia or the tropics—were generally understood as vicious, overstimulating, and therefore dangerous to a white, nationally identified body and body politic; tea, as I will discuss in the next chapter, was one commodity in a global commodity exchange founded on the sale of opium to China. Likewise, sugar, a commodity repeatedly linked to blackness in this chapter, circulated as part of a colonial trade circuit in which, as Mimi Sheller writes, "sugar and molasses were exported [from the Caribbean] to North America 'in return for . . . beef, pork, cheese, corn, pease, staves, plank, pitch and tar.'"[26]

Sugar and molasses were thus inextricably linked to the slave trade, both in colonial British North America and in the early republic. Sidney Mintz argues in his classic work on sugar, a foundational work in food studies, that the Caribbean sugar plantation, with its murderous consumption of slave life and labor, was the "laboratory" in which modern industrialism was forged. As the Industrial Revolution boomed, Europeans—including their colonist and then American cousins—developed the taste for both bitter drinks such as coffee and tea that needed the addition of sugar and sweetened goods such as candy and jam, all of them cheap and easy sources of carbohydrate energy. This shift in the Western palate and the resultant demand for sugar was enormous, and, in the minds of abolitionists, that desire for sugar was inextricable from slavery's moral "stain."[27]

Sugar, then, seems to have been linked to the slave body securely enough that Hawthorne could casually turn a popular image of blackness in popular culture into a sweet. Thus, even before Hepzibah breaks with her "shadowy past" and finds her palm stained the text implicates her both in the national sin and in transnational modernity, through the products she manufactures and sells: brown sugar, bits of "delectable candy" known as Gibraltar Rock, gingerbread and Jim Crow cookies (made, as Esther Howland's 1845 New England cookbook tells us, with molasses), and, curiously, "sugar figures with no strong resemblance to the humanity of any epoch."[28]

Hawthorne surely knew that the image of the "stain" produced by slavery was as common in abolitionist literature as it was in the proslavery South, though in each region it signified differently. In the abolitionist North slavery was a stain on the nation's conscience; in the proslavery South the stain referred to the stain of race—the one drop of black blood—that tainted any mixed-race body. In citing both the popular trope of the stain, then, and the sweetness of the black body linked to colonial and tropical slave production, the coin that lands on Hepzibah's palm in exchange for her spicy and sweet cookie links her store and her body to a modernity founded on the radical asymmetries of colonialism and ties Ned Higgins's cannibalism to the standard tropes of the abolitionist movement.

In Hepzibah's shop modernity is sweet and deeply transformative, down into the gut of the subject and back again. Sheller writes that "Caribbean and Asian commodities fed into—and literally fed—a new capitalist world that tied together far-flung markets and created a new international division of labour, affecting the meaning of work, the definition of self and the very nature of material things."[29] Sheller's tying together of the global and the intimate in the transformations of the modern world is key: the Pyncheon family's "galvanization" into modernity is a central concern of the text, and this passage places race at the center of this shift, symbolized later in the novel by the daguerrotypist's new modes of photographic representation, the train and its almost psychedelic effects on Clifford, and, finally, the union of the Maule and Pyncheon families and their move into a heterosexual futurity, through the romance between Holgrave and Phoebe.[30] In the novel's bizarre and violent "consummation," as Hawthorne calls it, between whiteness and blackness, blackness is defined by an irresolvable doubleness: it is both inanimate and "dancing," both "renowned" and replaceable, the white man under the blackface made of gingerbread. However, blackness is *always* desirable and *always* animating of whiteness.

The potency of blackness holds true even when Hawthorne exhibits his problematic ambivalence toward slavery,[31] by connecting white consumption with both debilitating and energizing results: the gripe and the stained palm, Hepzibah's exhaustion and her newly energized physicality.

Importantly, while it is the male child who consumes the cookie that Hepzibah sells, nonetheless it is her body that is most radically remade when the coin for Jim Crow crosses her palm in a part of the house that, by that act, is made into a public, commercial place. If we take up Hawthorne's galvanic metaphor, the racial energy of the Jim Crow cookie passes from Higgins's mouth to his gut through to the penny and into Hepzibah, connecting all of them to a marketplace in which race is a symbolic and defining marker.

In *The House of the Seven Gables* the black body is portrayed as food in terms far more explicit than in either of the two novels that I explore in the next two sections. But that frankness ultimately offers the critic a new site through which to track the anxious formation of white racial dominance in the period, as well as the connections between those formations, the nation's entry into modernity, and the intimate life of the body. The figure of the Jim Crow cookie reveals that while modernity forces the encounter between domestic (here, seemingly aristocratic and female) space and capital,[32] for Hawthorne that meeting forces a racialized incursion into the white body—here, as in Graham's stories and William Alcott's anatomies, that body is metaphorized as a house. Given these violations, the scene clearly portrays the fantasy of white liberal selfhood as atomistic, complete and whole, to be just that: fantastic. When the incursion of market concerns into the Pyncheon house is rendered as the violation of its intimate inner spaces, the intimate inner and outer spaces of the white body—the mouths and digestive systems of both Hepzibah and the child and the skin of the former—are similarly revealed as both public and vulnerable.[33]

Written during the heat of national debates about slavery, *The House of the Seven Gables* seems to ignore the issue that threatened to sunder the nation. In this very small but significant scene, however, we see that despite Hawthorne's terror of miscegenation and his discomfort with reformist causes, through the use of the cannibal metaphor the text here not only recognizes a basic species-sameness between the races; it also indicates that as a condition of the modern era, blackness must and will enter into and change the white body and thus the white body politic. Hepzibah's shop is a liminal site—both temporally and spatially—between private and public, between Puritan past and capitalist modernity. The cookie's path from production to consumption—from kitchen to shop to street and body—offers insight into the mutual constitution of the white female body and the slave body. In that formulation, black bodies might well circulate as objects, but blackness also held in its "gripe" whiteness and the nation seemingly predicated on it.

In citing amalgamation here it is of course impossible to ignore the issue of the coerced and illicit sexual relationships that helped stimulate white anxieties over racial purity and pollution in the nineteenth century. Sex, as an act that threatens the myth of racial purity, always haunts eating; it tugs, for example, at the word Hawthorne uses to describe Ned Higgins's ingestion of the Jim Crow cookie: "consummation." In the libidinal economy in which the body stands for the house and the house stands for the body, the mouth—which, as we saw in the last chapter, was analogized in William Alcott's text for children as a "door"—is the space within which the porous and eroticized boundaries between the races are both traced and erased.

In the domestic unconscious in which white racial desire is forged as an alimentary desire for interracial contact one possible investment for that desire is profoundly, even promiscuously, queer: we can even see the Jim Crow cookie scene in *The House of the Seven Gables* as an example of what I have previously termed *queer alimentarity*. The cannibal union between the chocolate-coated cookie and the white child inaugurates same-sex intimacy, which is "consummated" in Ned Higgins's mouth, throat, and gut. These doors and passageways also frame a drama of intraracial desire, when Higgins sends "the second Jim Crow cookie in quest of the former one." The mouth can perhaps function as a passage for these desires because of its oblique relationship to normative, genitally focused heterosexuality: not sexually reproductive but rather central to the reproduction of the owner's body, the mouth is an erotic space, one into which may be put articles that represent both the same sex and/or different races.

This polymorphous eroticism, focused on the mouth but digestively disturbed, points us to another doorway into and out of the body: the anus. For if digestive upset is provoked by the internalization of the foreign object through the mouth, indigestion, the childish "gripe" caused by Jim Crow, is a sign of what happens when the metabolic process is reversed, when the bowels speak back to the stomach. Refusing the easy excretion of matter from the body, the digestive tract registers its unhappiness to the larger body. Rather than immediately processing and then ejecting the other—both the digested and undigestible portions—the indigestion that shakes the Pyncheon house is here also sign of the homoerotic union between two Jim Crows and the young boy. This union, flavored with the products of the domestic and international slave economy, shakes the foundation of the Puritan past on which the narrative of U.S. modernity—here represented by the eponymous House of the Seven Gables—has been built. In this way both ingestion and indigestion come into view as political processes of specific importance to those bodies inevitably associated with excretion, abjection, and expulsion from the social body.

As with the self-abusing daughter in Graham's *A Lecture to Young Men on Chastity*, children are adept at unlocking the sexual secret of rich, savory, and sweet foods. In these delicious encounters the consuming body is allowed to publicly enjoy otherwise forbidden pleasures—to make cannibal feasts of cookies. Meanwhile, though Hepzibah is initially stained by the coin exchanged for her Jim Crow gingerbreads—the symbolic consummation of the moment that began when she "took down the bar from the shop door, making the entrance free"—she finds that the destruction of her "ladyhood" is actually animating, so that "the healthiest glow that Hepzibah had known for years" appears on her face, and she allows herself an extra infusion of "black tea." Hepzibah's market exchange has its own erotic valence.[34]

Here I wish to step back for a moment to take in the larger role that orality plays in *The House of the Seven Gables*. The novel begins, just a few pages before Hepzibah's cannibal feast, with the regurgitated blood on Colonel Pyncheon's ruff (the seeming fulfillment of the wizard Maule's dying curse—"God will give him blood to drink!") and ends with regurgitated blood on Judge Pyncheon's shirt bosom. The first death occurs as the colonel is celebrating a "ceremony of consecration" for the newly built house; the second death keeps Judge Pyncheon from a mockingly inventoried political dinner. The medical cause of these deaths is left unexplained, though Hawthorne notes that Judge Pyncheon was to see the doctor about, among other possible symptoms, "a disagreeable choking, or stifling, or gurgling, or bubbling, in the region of the thorax, as the anatomists say."[35] However, physical cause aside, it is indisputable that the text describes the deaths of the Pyncheon patriarchs as the return of the historically repressed in the material form of unsavory and undigestible blood, stuck in the Pyncheon maw. It is a striking image, given that Maule cursed the Pyncheons to *drink*, not vomit, blood. We are told that the judge is an aggressive eater: greedy for the property that would have otherwise gone to Clifford, the judge has an "ogre-like appetite . . . [and is] a great animal, . . . a great beast."[36] In the deaths of both the governor and the judge the Pyncheon propensity for devouring land—for unethical consumption—returns to haunt its patriarchs.

Maule's curse—"God will give you blood to drink"—is, in a sense, one of cannibalism, but, strangely, while the curse is realized as an aborted form of autocannibalism, because of the Pyncheon patriarchs' failure to ingest the blood—they can only regurgitate it—the curse fails. Their deaths, then, refuse both interiority and otherness. The contrast is clear here with Hepzibah and Ned Higgins, who are implicated in cannibalizing the black body, as a precondition of their entry into the modern, capitalist world. The end result for the Pyncheon men is one of systemic breakdown. The bodies of the Pyncheon patriarchs are stopped violently; they sit in death and stare, unseeing, at nothing, haunted by the past they cannot absorb or reconcile with and, therefore, without a place in the modern landscape that Hepzibah and Clifford manage (albeit barely) to enter.[37]

In a novel in which Hawthorne so often uses ekphrasis to drive the narrative forward the continued attention to the mouth and throat is striking. While Maule's prophecy hangs over the house, it is not fulfilled in the death of the oppressively patriarchal Pyncheons: they do not die from drinking blood but pass from the intermediate state of gurgling blood or "awkwardly" ingurgitating it to *re*gurgitating it, spitting it up onto and staining ruffs, beards, and shirts. As happens throughout the novel, Hawthorne coyly leaves the question of representational accuracy open; the narrative voice chimes in that he "never did hear, and therefore cannot describe [the gurgling sound]." Indeed, the legend of the gurgling blood is passed down via oral tradition, and, in line with Hawthorne's *Fire Worship*, discussed earlier, orality is associated with the kitchen hearth: "ancient superstitions, after being steeped in human hearts, and embodied in human breath, and passing from lip to ear in manifold repetition, through a series of generations, become imbued with an effect of homely truth. The smoke of the domestic hearth has scented them through and through."[38] Here Hawthorne intertwines the dual social function of the mouth: it is both for speech and, like other products of the hearth, for eating, if not always for ingestion. Superstitions, he seems to say, like all open-hearth cooked foods, have a smoky scent; after steeping in the human heart(h) we might conclude that homely truths have both a smoky and a bloody flavor.

In *The House of the Seven Gables* the mouth is a gateway, a stage even, that links the social world to the interior—the gut—of the social and political self. In leaving the "crumbs" of each of these feasts visible—be they cookie or blood—the text asks whether that gateway is untroubled, its processes free of conscience, and its desired objects easily assimilated. The answer is rarely as simple as the anxious white body would like it to be. Part of the inevitable ambiguity here is because the mouth, as I have argued already, must be seen not simply as a passageway but as a stage; far from being a mere physiological site for the ingestion of nutrients, the white mouth is public space whereupon the racialized erotics of the modern encounter are played out. Hawthorne's novel allows us to see that mouth as a physical space on and through which history—as discourse or as justice—flows, fixing and unfixing racial and sexual desire, and being.

Reader as Eater in Uncle Tom's Cabin

A domestic space—a house—names both the text and the narrative in Hawthorne's novel. Another classic American domestic space—a cabin—names Harriet Beecher Stowe's 1852 novel. In *Uncle Tom's Cabin*—as we would expect, under the sign of the domestic dwelling—images of eating, ingestion, and the mouth proliferate. But Stowe's is clearly a different domestic space, in which her abolitionist and feminist goals complicate Hawthorne's representation, even as they share a thematic interest in both white embodiment and female participation in the public sphere. As many critics have noted, the kitchen is a crucial space in Stowe's best-selling novel of the mid-nineteenth century.[39] Stowe's kitchens, at their most idyllic, lure the reader in with passages that linger on the intertwined pleasures of food and language; at their most problematic, the class and race inflections that construct the cultural life of the antebellum kitchen allow Stowe to speak in a broadly racialized (and, it need not be said, no doubt inaccurate) vernacular that would otherwise be forbidden to her.

In *Uncle Tom's Cabin*, five interconnected representational strands create the complex of food, orality, and African American bodies. The first is the particular literary function of the kitchen. The second is the representation of African Americans as food themselves, an image that was literally materialized in Hawthorne's Jim Crow cookies and that, in the discourse on slavery, circulates as a common trope for the objectification and commodification of slave bodies. That system and its metaphors are a precondition for both white women's embodiment and their emergence into the public sphere. The third is the figure of the cook, who appears in the literary kitchen as both the threat of domestic disruption—a threat that may or may not enter the dominant subject's body through his or her open mouth—and the subject on which is exercised the performance of white middle-class female power. The fourth strand lies in the links between slavery, the South, and death and plays out, according to the digestive logic of the novel, in an excremental symbolism that supports Stowe's commitments to recolonization, what we might read as a form of expulsion from the body politic. The fifth and minor strand is the ongoing connection between kitchens, food, and vernacular speech.[40]

Throughout the novel Stowe sets up parallels between slaves and food that underline her desire both to unveil and to trouble the status of slaves as "living property."[41] In the first chapter, for instance, Eliza's child Harry is made to scamper and dance after a handful of raisins that Shelby has thrown to the floor, while the slave trader Haley suggests that the child can be sold into another position as a waiter: "Why, I've got a friend that's going into this yer branch of business—wants to buy up handsome boys to raise for the market. Fancy articles entirely—sell for waiters, and so on, to rich 'uns, that can pay for handsome 'uns. It sets off one of yer great places—a real handsome boy to open door, wait and tend. They fetch a good sum."[42] The phonetic echo here between "raisin" and "raise" is set off by the visual parallel that is implied between Harry and the raisins—each small and black, each on the floor.[43] It is also the first instance in the book of a theme that, outside the book, is represented in cultural artifacts throughout the nineteenth and twentieth centuries: a fascination, in the white imaginary, with the dermatological differences between white and black skin. Both Harry and the raisins are, in the racist mythos of the nineteenth century, sun-darkened. This apparently material difference in turn offers a host of possibilities, a flood of metaphors that are themselves enabled by the ways in which black bodies have historically been impregnated with marketplace significance.

The implicit analogy between slaves and food develops further when Shelby attempts to distract Haley from his discussion of Eliza's market worth. Food here begins to play a more complicated role than it does in *The House of the Seven Gables*, as the cabin is set in the South, where slavery is the rule, rather than in the free North. Thus, the black bodies in question are not metaphorized in terms of gingerbread but are real human selves, manipulated in the unsavory language of the trader:

> "By Jupiter . . . ther's an article, now! You might make your fortune on that ar gal in Orleans, any day. . . ."

> "I don't want to make my fortune on her," said Mr. Shelby, dryly; and seeking to turn the conversation, he uncorked a bottle of fresh wine, and asked his companion's opinion of it.
>
> "Capital, sir,—first chop!" said the trader. . . . "Come, how will you trade about the gal? What shall I say for her—what'll you take?"[44]

Again the rich metaphorical possibilities offered to the language of slavery by the language of food are picked up in this passage when Shelby's clumsy attempt to distract Haley from Eliza replaces her figure with a glass of wine. The language here is decidedly that of the mouth: Shelby's "dry" language is countered and refuted by the "wet" language of the bottle of wine he is offered as distraction.

Haley refuses to be distracted by the food and wine and refers to both the wine and Eliza with the phrase "first chop": as the first cut of meat off a carcass. Eliza thus is a first-rate article, her monetary value and lack of human value reduced, by analogy, to that of a bottle of first-rate wine or a cut of meat. Here, the line from human object to food object becomes clear; further, Eliza's commodification allows Stowe to play on the connections between sexual and alimentary desire. We return again, as well, to the ways that the language of food allows for the exploration of the fine line between animal and human: here, however, the line has a particularly racist connotation, as Haley attaches Eliza's body to the category of animal—and, of course, not just any animal but a dead animal slaughtered for human consumption.

As black bodies (and their fates) are bandied about in the mouths of Haley and Shelby, we see the first of many instances of the tongue's importance. But the novel—and Stowe's interest, it seems—moves quickly beyond the polite conversation of these two men. In the many moments of orality to come, as we will see, the sensual pleasure allowed to the tongue becomes a template for the representation of transgressive desires.[45] The erotic pleasures here metaphorically associated with the mouth are allowed to do because, as we have seen earlier, the era's reproductive-oriented norms associated the erogenous with the genitals. Carrying forward Graham's association of illicit eating with the broader categories of vice and appetite, the mouth in *Uncle Tom's Cabin* is a space where other possibilities, here clearly understood by Stowe to be amoral and sexually abusive, were allowed to appear.

What the issue of orality also speaks to is Stowe's dexterity with minstrel dialect. Ann Douglas captures Stowe's transgressive relationship to vernacular (theatrical) speech and its social implications when she writes that "Stowe knew the vernacular and the wit it inspired were officially off limits to American women."[46] As Douglas explains, Stowe, like many of her contemporaries, was clearly intrigued with the literary possibilities of American vernacular. In fact, Stowe opens the first chapter by marking the linguistic—and therefore class—differences between the slave-master Shelby and the trader Haley. She comments that Haley's "conversation was in free and easy defiance of Murray's grammar, and was garnished at convenient intervals with various profane expressions, which not even the desire to be graphic in our account shall induce us to transcribe."[47] We can see from the first that Stowe is interested in the cultural politics of speech. In the scene between Shelby and Haley the pattern of speech is clearly inspired by the wine and brandy that are on the table. Theirs is a messy exchange indeed to be "graphically" reproduced by an upper-class white female writer, marked as it is by the mutual interpenetration of food, wine, vernacular speech, and economic need, all of which function to enable discussion, by antebellum cultural norms, of the unutterable. If Stowe cannot transcribe the "various profane expressions" used by Haley, that space which remains exterior to the language that is allowed to be used in parlor conversation returns as that which can be eaten: food here marks both the limits of what is sayable—speech patterns at the edges of social decorum—and the realm of what is unsayable, namely, Haley's desire to possess Eliza's body sexually.

Vernacularity gestures to regional identity in the same way that vernacular food—intimately connected to local and everyday ways of being—describes the boundaries of, and differences between, identities. In *Uncle Tom's Cabin* the use of the vernacular marks the intersection between the body and language, as the discursively constructed hyperembodiedness of the "lower orders"—those peoples who are represented as food—by definition influences and shapes the language of middle- and upper-class whites. As a woman writer and thus a writer bound to a propriety built on norms of race, gender, and class, Stowe dares popular convention by trying to reproduce the sound of "actual" talk. Her use of food language gives her a resource to explore the limits of another domain exterior to what "can be said," that in which the ineffability of bodily sensation brings us close to those desires that hover at the edge of permitted social discourse—the domain of temptation, seduction, and violence. To taste food, and to taste certain forms of desire, is to experience that which cannot yet be put into words.

Stowe's fascination with the vernacular is nowhere as well displayed as in the first kitchen scene in the book, in chapter 4. We have already seen how the nineteenth-century kitchen, particularly in its literary incarnations, gains much of its aesthetic and political import from the ways that it carries its much more democratic and carnivalesque history forward. In particular, we have seen how the modern kitchen, which begins with the replacement of the fireplace as the main tool of cooking, can never quite be separated from its earlier literary associations with the hearth, as a site of bodily inversion, hypermateriality, and vernacularity. I want to revisit the kitchens in *Uncle Tom's Cabin* as spaces where the racism encoded in the systematic comparison of blacks to food finds its center. In this symbolic structure the kitchen, then, assumes a special value not only because it represents a meeting place between separately coded—if not separately functioning—spheres but because it is a site associated with the material life of the body as it is represented in food culture, where, as Gillian Brown has argued, the affective life (the "woman's domestic sphere") is most closely integrated with economic life (where the slave labor of producing and processing food occurs).[48]

As I stated in the introduction, my move to consider domesticity in *Uncle Tom's Cabin* from the "back of the house" is an attempt to think about the ways that food and kitchen imagery begins to account for the perceived viscerality of difference but also the ways that food metaphorizes fleshly experience at the, and as a, limit of linguistic expression, in particular through vernacular language. The mutual constitution of the vernacular and the culinary makes itself visible most obviously in the character Chloe, who is the first of a series of cook figures to appear in the novel. Across the nineteenth century the mammy figure—who is inevitably a cook—is often characterized by a sort of succoring benevolence as well as a minstrel-show stereotyping that provides the text with its racist levity. The comedy of the mammy lies in what seems to be her empowered place in the household. From the kitchen she seems to speak from power, but a power that is undercut by the broad vernacular of her speech and her "natural" embrace of manual labor:

> "What does get into ladies sometimes, I don't know; but sometimes, when a body has the heaviest kind o' 'sponsibility on 'em, as ye may say, and is kinder '*seris*' and taken up, dey takes dat ar time to be hangin' round and kinder interferin'! Now, missis, she wanted me to do dis way, and she wanted me to do dat way; and, finally, I got kinder sarcy, and, says I, 'Now,

> Missis, do jist look at dem beautiful white hands o' yourn with long fingers, and all a sparkling with rings, like my white lilies when de dew 's on 'em; and look at my great black stumpin hands. Now, don't you think dat de Lord must have meant *me* to make de pie-crust, and you to stay in de parlor?' Dar! I was jist so sarcy, Mas'r George."
>
> "And what did mother say?" said George.
>
> . . . "Says she, 'Well, Aunt Chloe, I think you are about in the right on 't,' says she; and she went off in de parlor. She oughter racked me over the head for bein' so sarcy; but dars what 't is—I can't do nothin' with ladies in de kitchen!"[49]

Chloe's physicality is central to this scene: large and comforting, she has "stumpin" hands made for making "pie-crusts." Chloe's monologue, in which she seems to assert a power that rests in the kitchen, obscures the material suffering—and punishing labor—that in actuality played out in the kitchens of slaveholding plantations. Any incipient power—crucially, the power to talk back, or to be "sarcy"—suggested by Chloe's berating of Mrs. Shelby is negated in two ways. First, Chloe's speech is never really articulated to Mrs. Shelby but only repeated and acted out secondhand, to a minor power of the household—the young Master George. Indeed, the spectacle of a black woman publicly berating or confronting a white woman in a northern kitchen would have been almost unimaginable in the terms of the time; in slaveholding states it might have been mortally dangerous.

The second strategy that Stowe uses to contain and manage the political force of Chloe's speech lies in the passage's elaboration of the black-body-as-food theme, which is packed into the notion of "sarcy-ness." Sauce, as we saw in Sylvester Graham's work, was the kind of savory item that bore an ambiguous moral reading. Here, in the idea of Chloe's sauciness, lie the volatile politics that Stowe barely covers with the veneer of comedy. Although Chloe's kitchen insurrection is contained and repressed not only in its method of recounting but also in her avowed commitment to what is, in a sense, her own servitude, nonetheless it is also true that Chloe's "sarcy-ness" also contains the threat of her intimate association with the Shelbys. That is, in representing Chloe's berating of Mrs. Shelby as sauciness Stowe hints that her sauciness is a dish that the Shelbys must swallow. Chloe's speech—her sauciness—threatens to reach into the mouths, throats, and bodies of those who listen to her, even as they might desire to consume her.

Significantly, *sauciness*, a word with its roots in the Latin *salsus*, in fact means "salty," or "savory." Traditional femininity, in sharp contrast, depends on sweetness—a subject whose power is palatable, whose desires go down easily or who has no desires at all. Given the contrast, the intimate transactions between mistress and slave—within the kitchen's contrasting simultaneity of intimacy and inequality—can turn these alimentary metaphors into a threat against the domestic hegemony of white womanhood. This is something different, something more, than the previous associations of blackness with sweetness.

Consider, for instance, Stowe's use of the term "stumpin" to describe Chloe's hands in the passage quoted earlier. While the term works to contrast Mrs. Shelby's parlor femininity with Chloe's laboring physicality, implying even a disabled body, the term also alludes to the idea of political speech.[50] These hands, the undeniable evidence of her physicality, give her a platform from which to speak—like the politician arguing his political platform, they enable her, literally, to make her own "stump speech." Like her saucy words, Chloe's hands speak with a certain political import; thus, the products of those hands, "meant" to make piecrusts, also carry the heavy weight of an unsayable political critique, one that tempers the sugary and entertaining sweetness otherwise associated with the black body.

Chloe's edibility is not simply a self-applied trope but, in a sense, a metaphor for the way her work (of making food for whites to eat) has eaten her:

> A round, black, shining face is hers, so glossy as to suggest the idea that she might have been washed over with white of eggs, like one of her own tea rusks. . . . A cook she certainly was, in the very bone and centre of her soul. . . . She was always meditating on trussing, stuffing and roasting. . . . Her corn-cake, in all its varieties of hoe-cake, dodgers, muffins, and other species too numerous to mention, was a sublime mystery to all less practiced compounders; and she would shake her fat sides with honest pride and merriment, as she would narrate the fruitless efforts that one and another of her compeers had made to attain her elevation.[51]

What haunts the figure of Chloe is not simply the problematic representation of her happy and willing servitude but rather that her physicality comes to embody her labor. She offers the fruits of her labor first to Master George—who eats even before Chloe's children, as Stowe not uncritically notes—and then, descending hierarchically, to her husband and children.

She is not allowed to own the value attached to her craft, and thus the object of her craft engulfs her, transforming her flesh into the very product of her labor. Stowe's Mammy is an object of pleasant consumption—for the reader as for the slave-owning characters—at the same time as she is one barb in Stowe's antislavery critique.

This portrayal of Chloe as an object of consumption also embeds itself in the narrative as a discussion of Chloe's essence, in the culinary sense.[52] This food trope is carried further as her face itself becomes a sort of cake, as shiny as though she were glossed with "white of eggs." The parallels here between Chloe and the chicken clearly draw on folkish images of the busy mother hen; however, their comic status is undermined by what awaits those animals—trussing and roasting. It is a parallel that makes us see through the benevolence of the barnyard imagery to the very real specter of terror that haunts the slave body, a terror that is ultimately enacted in Tom's death during the climactic scene of the novel.

The centrality of the kitchen within the cabin makes the young George's appetite for Chloe's food—her pan-cake—an important thematic concern, as their dialogue and the early action of chapter 4 is dominated by his eating. When she describes George stuffing himself with Chloe's baked goods—which are, we have established, analogous to Chloe herself—while her children wait to one side, hungry, she is leveling her critical gaze at George, at his imperiousness and sense of entitlement, just as surely as she levels her criticism at Haley. Indeed, both George and Haley perform the same gesture, throwing food to the floor for black children to eat; George, despite his ambivalent construction as a benevolent slaveholder, is nonetheless a slaveholder. Until the religious meeting that closes the chapter George is "always ready for anything that makes him of importance":[53]

> "Ah, Mas'r George, you don't know half your privileges in yer family and bringin' up!" Here Aunt Chloe sighed, and rolled up her eyes with emotion.
>
> "I'm sure, Aunt Chloe, I understand all my pie and pudding privileges," said George. "Ask Tom Lincon if I don't crow over him, every time I meet him."
>
> Aunt Chloe sat back in her chair, and indulged in a hearty guffaw of laughter, at this witticism of young Mas'r's, laughing till the tears rolled down her black shining cheeks, and varying the exercise with playfully

> slapping and poking Mas'r Georgey, and telling him to go way, and that he was a case—that he was fit to kill her, and that he sartin would kill her one of these days; and, between each of these sanguinary predictions, going off into a laugh, each longer and stronger than the other, till George really began to think that he was a very dangerously witty fellow, and that it became him to be careful how he talked "as funny as he could."[54]

The mounting aggression and deep sadness that underlies this passage is astonishing once it is read closely.[55] While clear that Master George's sense of privilege—his "pie and pudding privileges"—is here exercised in his right to eat first and best, as well as in his congruent ability to read and write, it is simultaneously clear that Chloe is pushing and prodding him to a revelatory extreme of self-importance. While the minstrel mugging of the scene would on first glance make her to be its comic object, in fact she has stuffed him full of himself, making *him* the object of the joke. Chloe's laughter operates, here, as a "hidden transcript" in James Scott's sense of the word, diverging from the public transcript of the dominant class by engulfing it, quoting it, and, through exaggeration and parody, hiding its offstage feelings in plain sight.[56] The sublimated aggression of Chloe's playful "slaps" and "pokes," twinned with her tears, masks what she is actually saying: "sanguinary predictions" that George should "go way," that he is "fit to kill her" and "sartin would kill her." Each laugh sounds "louder and stronger" than the last as Chloe slaps and pokes him; the joke, as Stowe makes clear, is on George, even if the power is with him. In Chloe's bloody speech "sanguinary" violence emerges as a bitter aftertaste, the visceral and vicious underbelly of antebellum comedy.

Here, then, is Chloe's "sarcy-ness," sneaking in such that it only lingers on the edge of George's, and the reader's, awareness: George begins to think that he "was a dangerously witty fellow, and that it became him to be careful how he talked 'as funny as he could.'"[57] Stowe's text subtly asserts Chloe's humanity both through stifled political affect *and*—by recognizing her human consanguinity—as sentient being. What is most consumable in the kitchen is the bodies of the slaves themselves, but Stowe is also able, in this chapter, to inhabit that analogy to take fierce critical aim at both the white appetite for those bodies and the white appetite for racist comic discourse.

How then are we to understand the desire on the part of the white subject to devour blackness in *Uncle Tom's Cabin*? And what does this desire tell us about eating, and the body, in this novel? The representation of black bodies as food furthers Stowe's engagement with the problem of black commodification, even as the text turns on the white desire to consume and internalize blackness. This schema of representations points us toward a latent understanding in the text concerning racial difference as an American problem: race will not be banished. But the dream of maternalist humanitarianism that runs through the relationship of the mistress and her female slave—on which the white woman's understanding of her own moral superiority is based—is stripped in these passages to its bloody consequences, where it stands revealed as an appetite that degrades the eater and the eaten alike.

In engaging with the symbolic possibilities of literary cannibalism Stowe signals that the lines that divide blackness from whiteness are fine and fragile; the humanity of the one echoes the other. At the same time, the white desire to devour black subjectivity also indicates the desire to annihilate it, to recognize the black subject only in terms of her capacity to regenerate whiteness. The language of the novel allows Chloe to inhabit the cannibal metaphor, to use it to reach into the mouth and gullet of the white body. Here again the white child's body is used to reach white women—Stowe's white maternal readership—where it nudges them toward self-knowledge about their implication in the reproduction of racial inequity.

In dividing up Chloe's body and feeding it to George, Stowe offers up the black body as the materially dense object that the racist ideologies of the nineteenth-century United States saw it to be. But even if Stowe allows, and perhaps even encourages, Chloe's critique of slavery, as many critics have noted, she is ultimately unable to separate white enjoyment of and desire for black bodies from her critique of slavery's dehumanization. Stowe's representation of this desire complicates her feminist agenda, for in positing white women as avatars of social change, in interpellating them directly in her text, she positions them as mediators and consumers of black subjectivity. The text thus ultimately upholds white female bodily hegemony even as it indicates Stowe's awareness of its bloody visceral consequences. In encoding eating as a readerly act, particularly in this highly politicized novel, the representation of the enslaved body as tied to the materiality of often-appetizing food products reveals, as Saidiya Hartman has discussed, that "rather than bespeaking the mutuality of social relations or the expressive and affective capabilities of the subject, sentiment, enjoyment, affinity, will, and desire facilitated subjugation, domination, and terror *by preying upon the flesh*, the heart and the soul."[58] If

Stowe's representation of blackness as food serves to develop the metaphor of objectification, like Hawthorne's it also renders the black body appetizing to her readers. And while the invitation to consume blackness is not explicit, the extensive food metaphors would seem to indicate that the desire to commune with and consume blackness is latent in the text.

Beyond the ingestion of the racial other, the hegemony of the white body is ultimately only possible if the internalization of the black body is followed to its logical and digestive endpoint. Indeed, as the text of *Uncle Tom's Cabin* relies on the idea of black deliciousness, it is clear that Stowe's manifest resolution is excretory: the final step—one that is as convenient as it is essential—is for the black body to be expelled toward the darker regions of the world. Ultimately, Eliza, George, and their family move on, as processed and exported American products, to Africa, a theme to which I will soon return.

In the novels of oppositional writers such as Harriet Beecher Stowe and, as I show later, Harriet Wilson, white appetite signifies unthinking privilege and aggression, but it also represents the desire on which both white female citizenship *and* the future of the postemancipation republic rests. The text thus aligns the white reader with sentimentality's political paradox: to empathize with the slave is to internalize her, but to do so is also to annihilate her subjectivity. Therein lies the problem on which so many early and contemporary relationships between feminist white women and people, especially women, of color has foundered: if black citizenship is to be tested out in white women's bodies via a set of figurative relationships that includes metaphor and analogy, black citizenship, on its own terms, will always be obscured.

While the novel's problematic interracial politics were meant to propel white women into the sphere of public abolitionist action, the novel also invited white women into a relation with the idea of blackness that was not dissimilar to the theatrical tropes of minstrel blackness with which white men were already engaged in the public spaces of popular culture: when the first interracial scene in the novel is the dance performed by a four- or five-year-old "octoroon" who is briefly called "Jim Crow," it is evident that the classic tropes of minstrelsy will be wound through this text. Stowe's innovation is to translate the burlesquerie of the Jim Crow troop into scenes of regular life in the planter's domestic sphere; this infusion of the minstrel world into the domestic novel places the so-called private culture of the white woman into an embodied relationship to blackness, by appropriating the inherently male realm of public theatrical performance.

As Sanchez Eppler writes, Stowe also advances her nascent feminism by positing her readers' bodies as analogous to the body politic, both absorbing and appropriating racial difference.[59] White women's politicization thus mediates the perilous state of the "divided house" of the nation. In this relationship Stowe assumes white women to be as aggressively desiring of an intimate communion with blackness as are the white men performing on the minstrel stage. However, rather than positing blackness as the theatrical projection of whiteness's absented affective states, blackness is at least in part here a subsumed element of white interiority and feeling.

Food metaphors seem to continue this merger of public and private desires, of political feeling rendered personal.[60] As domestic space—in particular the kitchen—is the space in which vital interracial exchanges take place, it is there that the text engages in forms of racial play—including, as we have seen, vernacular speech—otherwise reserved for men in public spaces. But there are other contestations, expressed through the trope of eating, which reveal not only Stowe's mastery of her craft but also a committed critique of entitled white embodiment that complicates her borrowing from the minstrel stage. Again in chapter 4 Stowe's depiction of the broad humor of Chloe's kitchen reveals a subtle game of power, inextricable from the politics of who-gets-to-eat-first and who-gets-to-eat-best. A close look at Stowe's language in this scene reveals that it is a game that hinges on but also unerringly skewers white appetite.

Of course, most of *Uncle Tom's Cabin* happens outside of Uncle Tom's cabin. In tracing the domestic psychopathology of food in the opening chapters of the novel we came to the final moment in the digestion of the sweet black body: its excretion. As I pointed out and as many critics have noted, Stowe's solution to the question of black citizenship in 1852 was expulsion: to Canada, to Africa, and, as a final solution, to the next world, in death. The theme of excrement—or, in Bakhtin's words, of the "bodily lower stratum"—necessarily holds a vital place throughout this discussion but emerges nowhere more clearly than with Stowe, who engages so deeply with cloacal imagery of rot, decay, and death in her depiction of life on Simon Legree's plantation, where Tom is sent to work after St. Clare dies and the St. Clare slaves are sold off.[61] Of the entrance to the plantation she writes, "The place had that ragged, forlorn appearance, which is always produced by the evidence that the care of the former owner has been left to go to utter decay. . . . The ground was littered with broken pails, cobs of corn, and other slovenly remains. . . . A noble avenue of China trees . . . [grew] amid discouragement and decay."[62] When Tom looks into the slave huts, he finds "rude shells, destitute of any species of furniture, except a heap of straw, foul with dirt."[63] Arriving at the Legree plantation, then, the slaves find themselves in the bowels of the nation: Stowe gives the chapter in which the slaves arrive at their new home the title "Dark Places."

The taboo connection between eating, defecation, and the dark interior spaces of the body always hovers over the racial politics of food. The Grahamite dietetic project arose in the same culture that continued to exclude African American subjects from the vestiges of full juridical subjecthood, thrusting them outside the legal parameters of contract, citizenship, and enfranchisement even as some states instituted gradual emancipation. Particularly within the context of chattel slavery and plantation labor, however, these subjects were figuratively—and literally, in terms of their labor—connected to refuse, garbage, and, most pertinent to the question of African recolonization, to a literal and symbolic ejection from the U.S. body politic. As Achille Mbembe has written, "In the context of the plantation, the slave condition results from a triple loss: loss of a 'home,' loss of rights over his or her body, and loss of political status. This triple loss is identical with absolute domination, natal alienation, and social death (*expulsion from humanity altogether*)."[64]

If the white relationship to the black body has been portrayed, as we have seen, through the metaphor of consumption, and if the assimilation of the black body through the white mouth is also accompanied by images of sticky resistance or even digestive upset, we must follow the metaphor eschatologically, to the point at which it becomes a fecal absolute. Achille Mbembe's remarks help us to see the salient stages in the solution to the problem of the black body in the antebellum United States. While the southern white house lives on the profit from slave labor, the laborer, under the burden of social death, lives as a dead thing. In the political unconscious the slave is ultimately fated to "material destruction." The body of the dead slave, devoid of its exchange and labor value, is a form of refuse and *the* form of refuse. It is refuse itself. Stowe tells us early on that the Legree plantation is a site of mass death, when Legree says, "I don' go for savin' niggers. Use up, and buy more, 's my way. . . . When one nigger's dead, I buy another."[65] When a slave dies, then, he is completely without value; even Legree refuses to take money for Tom's body from George Shelby. The movement through the intestinal canal of the national body and into death, or the state of being refuse, is clear: as the slaves are shipped down the Mississippi—"up the red, muddy, turbid current, through the abrupt tortuous windings of the Red river"[66]—they come to reside in a space of total nonhumanity. It is Stowe's humanizing gesture—a refusal of the black body as mere refuse—to have George Shelby embrace Tom's dying body and then bury it within sight of the Legree plantation.[67]

Digestion and defecation were far from comic issues in the period. Given the concern with digestion as a sign of overall health, even the most prim of antebellum anatomical primers obsessed over excrement, though of course in relatively sanitary terms: *The Laws of Health*, Alcott's sequel to *The House I Live In*, has an entire section on defecation, and his autobiography—*Forty Years in the Wilderness of Pills and Powders*—narrates in detail the relationship between his diet and the evacuation of his "alimentary canal." Such a concern, Alcott is quick to point out, reaches back to Locke, who wrote a section of his *Essays Concerning Education* on training the bowels to pass a stool once a day.[68]

Additionally, and more to the point in a novel obsessed with death and the life beyond, Stowe was clearly using tropes out of Dante's *Inferno*, a text that, as some scholars have argued, is structured as a voyage into the mouth, through the stomach and intestines, and, in its final stages, as excremental expulsion.[69] The language of hell is everywhere in the last third of *Uncle Tom's Cabin*. That Stowe was familiar with Dante is testified to by the many references to Beatrice and the *Inferno* in her novel *Agnes of Sorrento*, and the Dantean metaphor of excretion as the ultimate end to travel through the seven uncomfortable levels of hell certainly fits Tom's journey south through the various slave states.[70] Indeed, as Karen Halttunen has written, Stowe's appropriation of the gothic tradition interprets Legree's haunted house as the ultimate form of mental hell.[71] The eschatology of the novel—even when it comes to Topsy and the Harris family, who are displaced northward into Canada and then into renewed life in Africa, in the opposite direction from Tom—destines the black body to ultimate ejection from the body politic.

The rectum, Leo Bersani tells us, is orality's absolute other: unspeakable, abject, and symbolic of the sexual drives of those subjects—sodomites—most closely aligned with social and actual death.[72] Indeed, P. Gabrielle Foreman argues that Tom's final beating at the hands of Legree, Sambo, and Quimbo contains all the symbolic force of male-to-male rape, further positioning the South as the site of anality.[73] But if we push our analysis of the anal beyond the most obvious theme of sodomy, we return to this study's overarching metaphor, which is that of indigestion. As we have seen, the novel's solution to the problem of black citizenship is undoubtedly one of ejection. But if we consider the gothic themes of the Legree plantation, in particular Cassy's haunting of Simon Legree, there is another, parallel reading: that slavery as a fundamental injustice gets stuck inside the body politic, rendering it ill with symptoms that were all too familiar in antebellum America, afflicted as it so often was with typhus, diphtheria, and epidemic outbreaks of cholera. These symptoms were diarrhetic to a horrifying degree—many a family experienced the expiration of a loved one in a nightmarish burst of excretion. Stowe might have had intimate experience of this kind of death in the cholera epidemic that struck Ohio in the late 1840s, as she was writing her novel.[74]

Teresa Goddu's idea of the gothic as the haunting of history is particularly pertinent here.[75] If history can haunt a home, as Cassy—hidden in the attic with Emmeline, whom she seeks to protect from Legree's sexual abuse—haunts the Legree plantation in the gothic-tinged last third of the novel, and if the body forms a metonymy for the house, we might think of intestinal distress as an introjected gothic; in particular, indigestion becomes the return of the repressed as the indigestible black subject pushes back against her consumer, upsetting the white body politic even as she is sold into death. Just as with the underhanded force of Chloe's monologue, the intestinal trouble caused by the black body seems to subtly hint at the text's deeper ideas. The revolutionary potential of that metaphor, however, is not just contained within the novel—and American life—but rejected: reading *Uncle Tom's Cabin* through the conjoined images of consumption and indigestion reveals the ejection of blackness's upsetting element from the white body politic, a necessity both to the body politic's health—laid as it is on a foundation of white supremacy—and to its narrative logic.

The Open Black Mouth: Our Nig's Kitchen Scenes

> Every Black woman in America has survived several lifetimes of hatred, where in even in the candy store cases of our childhood, little brown niggerbaby candies testified against us.
>
> —Audre Lorde, "Eye to Eye: Black Women, Hatred, and Anger"[76]

While in one sense fieldwork has come to represent the space of the most abject enslaved black labor, *Uncle Tom's Cabin* and other texts tell us that the kitchen and food culture, considered broadly, are sites of primary importance in representing the visceral politics of the nineteenth century: certainly the dehumanizing images that were imposed on black subjects in the kitchen mirror the sort of brutality only unleashed on the animals that humans consume. While white desire for the black body appears in *The House of the Seven Gables* and surfaces even more strongly in *Uncle Tom's Cabin*, with Stowe's greater consciousness of the slave's hidden transcript, in our discussion it is Harriet Wilson's 1859 semiautobiographical novel *Our Nig* that gives us the fullest account of the black subject in this alimentary dialectic.

Wilson expresses, with gut-wrenching specificity, the critique and rebuff of white violence. In particular, Harriet Wilson's antisentimental text takes the domestic tropes of *Uncle Tom's Cabin* and uses them against that domesticity, bringing forward, as Julia Stern suggests, Wilson's own brutalized body to testify against the reality of domesticity in what contemporary readers have come to know as a house owned by a prominent abolitionist family. The work thus becomes an act of demystification. It is here that the autobiographical in *Our Nig* encodes the conventions of the gothic novel. Stern argues,

> In pitting gothic antinurture against sentimental maternity, Wilson reaches out to the same audience that embraced *Uncle Tom's Cabin*, a novel that, more than any other fictional work of the 1850s, is structured by a Manichean poetics of familial love. But Wilson's phantasmagoric representation of motherhood is far more critical than that of Stowe, whose vision is nothing less than redemptive.[77]

In her article Stern begins to develop the idea of what she calls the "food chain" as part of an economy of bestial metaphors at play throughout the novel. In particular, she persuasively argues that the more Frado is tortured, the less human and more animal she becomes to the eyes of the domestic figure, Mrs. Bellmont, and, in a continued perversion of maternal sentimentality, to her daughter.

Much of the violence perpetrated against Frado does echo that perpetrated against those animals consumed for domestic use. For instance, when Mrs. Bellmont threatens to "take the skin from her body," it is as though Frado's skin will be put to use as leather. When Frado becomes, as Stern says, "potential food"[78]—particularly when Mary throws a carving knife at her in the kitchen, charging her with being a "saucy, impudent nigger"—the metaphor that I have been exploring here, down to the always-ambiguous place of sauce, makes Frado into another piece of meat in the kitchen, in the eyes of the Bellmont girls.

However, there is no cushioning comedy in the sauciness, no sweetness to ameliorate the direct force of Wilson's prose. Food as metaphor for the black body has a radically different valence in *Our Nig* because it is not a pleasurable auxiliary to white female subjectivity and white embodiment; rather, the story calls on the reader to witness the trials undergone by a black self—by a black girl—in the process of becoming a full subject. The point of view has shifted here from white subjectivity and embodiment to Frado's autoethnographic project of fully inhabiting her own history and thereby envisioning a new future, one supported by her interpellation of a black intellectual public sphere.[79] In the service of that vision, much of the work of the novel is to make bodily pain visible and legible to the readership. Even more radically, the text for the most part refuses its audience—which Wilson imagines, as she tells us, as both white and black—the kinds of pleasure in consuming on which both Hawthorne and Stowe count. While Wilson does not entirely avoid borrowing from minstrel comedy in scenes that, like much minstrel comedy, rely on black proximity to pain, we are far from comedy here in this early instance of naturalist fiction.[80] And we understand, more deeply than perhaps Stowe did, Chloe's motives for keeping the "ladies" out of her kitchen when we see how Frado suffers from not being able to do the same: "It is impossible to give an impression of the manifest enjoyment of Mrs. B. in these kitchen scenes. It was her favorite exercise to enter the apartment noisily, vociferate orders, give a few sudden blows to quicken Nig's pace, then return to the sitting room with *such* a satisfied expression, congratulating herself upon her thorough house-keeping qualities."[81] To survive as a black servant in the free North, Wilson argues, is to risk being consumed alive. It is also to speak from the spaces that have otherwise been colonized by white desires. Thus, the kitchen functions as the primary site of Frado's domestic labor and her suffering; Mrs. Bellmont's repeated torture of Frado, not surprisingly, is referred to as taking place within "kitchen scenes." Here, as in *Uncle Tom's Cabin*, the opposition between the kitchen and the sitting room is defined by the difference between black female labor and white female leisure. Wilson allows us to see that which both Hawthorne and, to a lesser extent, Stowe do not allow us to see: the sadism of white female domesticity, which can exist as diversions, as little theatrical "scenes," even within an abolitionist household. The Bellmonts' kitchen is resoundingly not the site of happy production, vernacular comedy, and pleasant consumption.

In *Our Nig* Frado's body offers no nourishment to the white reader; rather, the narrative demands that the reader stand witness to starvation. Further, in *Our Nig* Wilson reverses the trope of the white mouth eager to eat the consumable black body; instead, the white appetite is confronted with its consequences. In a scene of stunning brutality, Mrs. Bellmont and her daughter beat Frado "inhumanely; then propping her mouth open with a piece of wood, shut her up in a dark room without any supper."[82] The image of Frado locked up, "her mouth wedged apart, her face swollen and full of pain," trumps any possibility of white desire. Instead, Wilson turns the reader's attention away from his or her own mouth and toward Frado's, which remains forced open, hungry, and wordless, stuck in the shape of a perpetual but silent scream.[83] This representation seems to render Frado's open mouth and face monstrous, but in doing so the image testifies to white inhumanity: the image of the black mouth opened is not simply a sign of physical torture; it confronts the figurative open mouth of the sentimental reader with its mirror image.

The monstrosity—and the tragedy—of the open mouth is central to rendering Frado's suffering visible, even as it locates Frado's pain beyond what is linguistically transcribable. Mrs. Bellmont's policy is to shut up all of Frado's expressive organs—she whips her for her tears, she beats her for reading, and she tries to "beat the money out of her." Mrs. Bellmont takes a sadistic joy—derives satisfaction—from consistently stopping up Frado's mouth to keep her from moaning. When beating Frado, she either props her mouth open with wood or stuffs her mouth with a towel—an effigy of a scream without the sound.[84]

Meanwhile, the men in the house suffer an almost dreamlike powerlessness even as they seemingly desire to spare Frado. In one incident Frado is so ill from caring for the sick James, and from "drudgery in the kitchen," that she can barely stand. Mrs. Bellmont comes into the kitchen and commands her to go to work:

> "I am sick," replied Frado, rising and walking to her unfinished task, "and cannot stand long, I feel so bad." . . . [Mrs. Bellmont] seemed left to unrestrained malice; and snatching a towel, stuffed the mouth of the sufferer, and beat her cruelly. . . . [Frado] bore it with the hope of a martyr, that her misery would soon close. Though her mouth was muffled, and the sounds much stifled, there was a sensible commotion, which James' quick ear detected. . . . "Call Frado to come here. . . ." Susan retired with

> the request to the kitchen, where it was evident that some brutal scene had been enacted.[85]

This "sensible commotion," the reader infers, is the sound of the beating and, despite her being gagged, ultimately speaks her pain to other parts of the house. And yet the powerful figure who "hears" this pain does nothing to stop the torture. Like God, about whom Frado learns, the male Bellmonts are both all powerful in theory and curiously powerless in practice. Thus, experiences that happen at the outer limits of human suffering are expressed in sounds that are outside of spoken language; while such utterances reach a bedridden figure of power in the "private" part of the house, they seem to arouse no meaningful action.[86]

In a seminal moment in the novel, Mrs. Bellmont's son invites Frado out of the kitchen and into the dining room to eat a proper meal. A crucial—perhaps *the* crucial—conflict takes place between Mrs. Bellmont and Frado in this scene, when Mrs. Bellmont refuses to let the child eat from a clean plate and instead forces her to eat from Mrs. Bellmont's dirty one. Frado hesitates for a moment, then gives the plate to her dog to lick clean before eating from it herself. In this excessive gesture, this surplus of servility, Frado turns the code of the master/mistress against Mrs. Bellmont: it is, in fact, a masterful gesture, one that upends humanism itself by signaling Frado's alignment with the animal, that figure that has historically served as the constitutive outside term to the construction of the human.

With regard to the links we have been following in this chapter, Frado's gesture—her inhabitation of what Marjorie Spiegel has called "the dreaded comparison" between animals and slaves[87]—can be seen as a radical alternative to the post-Enlightenment liberatory claims of those groups historically excluded from the humanist project. Although Frado is not a slave, of course, she does exist, as the title tells us, in "slavery's shadow." Beyond positing a rights claim, although she engages that strategy as well, Frado's subtle gesture reveals the Bellmonts' hypocrisy in its baldest form. By turning her back on an alliance with the human, deftly skewered as the remains left behind on Mrs. Bellmont's dessert plate, that is, a plate that has held sweets, Frado argues for a liberatory project that allies itself with the abject, refusing the logic of humanism itself. However fleetingly, Frado's willingness to share a plate that has been licked clean by—that is covered with—a dog's saliva offers a glimpse into a revolutionary possibility that we have already encountered in the hearth literature of half a century earlier: that of a world turned upside down.

In *Our Nig* we are far from the apparent idylls of Harriet Beecher Stowe's kitchens—Chloe's pancakes, Dinah's gourmet disorder, the Hallidays' Edenic breakfast. In Wilson's account the visceral subtext inherent to nineteenth-century kitchen scenes emerges as full and manifest, rather than partial and metaphorized, brutality. Though Wilson too uses the metaphor of body as food, she refuses to extend the invitation to consume to the normative reader, on whom *Uncle Tom's Cabin* relies. Readers thus face a stark choice: identify ourselves with Mrs. Bellmont, as sadists, or *against* the cruelty of white female domestic mastery and *with* the subject of the kitchen scenes. Reappropriating food's many tropes, Wilson brings black subjectivity into being as an open resistance to the sadism that lurks just below the surface of the "two-story white house"; in doing so *Our Nig* delivers a stinging rebuke to one of the backbones of nineteenth-century white female subjectivity and white embodiment. In that moment the kitchen becomes a reversed abattoir in which it is the white woman whose cruel appetite places her lower than a dog, who attempts to slaughter the human—the black servant—and who fails, dying rather miserably herself, while Frado ultimately survives beyond the limits imposed on her by the Bellmonts.

There is another mode in which the open black mouth is important, and it is an image that returns us to the material conditions that drive the book. For if Wilson refuses to be consumed, the need to eat is marked, from the beginning, as what primarily motivates the production of her story. As she writes in the preface, "Deserted by kindred, disabled by failing health, I am forced to some experiment which shall aid me in maintaining myself and child without extinguishing this feeble life."[88] Hunger—the need for embodiment at its barest physical level—lies at the very center of this text and helps explain its sense of urgency.

In repudiating the relationship between black objectification and white female empowerment—and the reliance of the former on the latter—Wilson works to claim public space for black subjectivity in the antebellum North by recathecting the body that Mrs. Bellmont insists on treating with impunity. Testifying to the hunger that drives the novel, blackness in *Our Nig* is not a function of anxious whites' efforts to embody themselves in a rapidly changing world; rather, Wilson makes a claim for black subjectivity beyond white cruelty and despite white benevolence. Frado not only feels; she bites back.

4

A Wholesome Girl

Addiction, Grahamite Dietetics, and Louisa May Alcott's Rose Campbell Novels

Aunt Betsey, there's going to be a new Declaration of Independence.
—Louisa May Alcott, *Work*[1]

The first line of *Work*, Louisa May Alcott's 1873 novel, opens on a revolutionary note. Revolution was in the air: the end of the Civil War had brought enormous change, beginning with the emancipation of the slaves and the passage of the Fifteenth Amendment. Three years after the publication of the novel Alcott's nation celebrated the centennial of the Declaration of Independence; the hundred-year mark was also in the air as a measure of the nation's success. Thus, when Christie Devon makes her announcement to Aunt Betsey, she is speaking into the zeitgeist. In fact, in *Little Women*, which was begun after *Work* but published before, Alcott introduces the same trope, comparing French girls to Americans, who "early sign a declaration of independence, and enjoy their freedom with Republican zest."[2]

In *Work*'s opening passage we find Christie, the novel's protagonist, engaged in the quintessential act of traditional domesticity: baking bread. She upsets the usual order of such a scene, however, with the momentous announcement that she will be leaving her aunt and uncle's home in order to make her own living. The search for such "work" furnishes the book with its main plot.[3] Though the novel was written over 130 years ago, its setting—an "old-fashioned" kitchen—and its initial act—kneading bread in a bread trough—still signal to readers today that this is very much a woman's novel. In baking bread Christie performs an act that continues to represent the quintessence of female domestic labor. The passage continues:

> "Bless and save us, what do you mean, child?" And the startled old lady precipitated a pie into the oven with destructive haste.
>
> "I mean that, being of age, I'm going to take care of myself, and not be a burden any longer. . . ."
>
> Christie emphasized her speech by energetic demonstrations in the bread-trough, kneading the dough as if it was her destiny, and she was shaping it to suit herself.[4]

In this cleverly subversive scene Christie—who translates her "republican zest" into energetic kneading—takes on the masculine prerogative of the founding document of the American republic ("all *men* are created equal"). Continuing the long line of nineteenth-century women writers who transposed political discourse into the daily language of middle-class women's lives, Alcott draws the reader's attention directly to the cultural links between bread, democratic citizenship, and female economic power.

Making bread—the kneading, the rising or fermentation, and the baking—thus becomes a metaphor for the formation of a live political self:

> "I don't see why you can't be contented. . . ." And Aunt Betsey looked perplexed by the new idea.
>
> "You and I are very different ma'am. There was more yeast put into my composition, I guess; and, after standing quiet in a warm corner so long, I begin to ferment, and ought to be kneaded up in time, so that I may turn out a wholesome loaf."[5]

In contrast to twentieth-century feminist configurations of the kitchen as a female prison, for this radical nineteenth-century woman writer domesticity and its elaborate skills are conditions that give rise to female independence.[6]

Like *Work*'s opening scene, Alcott's *Eight Cousins*, published two years later, also begins in the kitchen; both novels, as well, have significant scenes that involve women baking bread. But it would be a mistake to think of Alcott as simply assimilating the Grahamite ideas of her father or his group. Just as she makes her heroine, Rose, an orphan, Alcott suspends her own "inheritance" from her father, Bronson Alcott, and her childhood exposure to food reformers such as Sylvester Graham and her father's first cousin William Andrus Alcott. Instead, Alcott takes the freedom to explore, with no little ambivalence and irony, the moral economy of eating and other forms of consumption in a more advanced consumer society.

I return here to my concerns in chapter 2 by revisiting Graham's and William Alcott's reformist dietetics slightly outside the historical epoch in which they were framed. The racial and imperial hierarchies that traverse those antebellum texts are rearticulated in the postbellum period, as we will see, even as the symbolic circuits of body, nation, and home are somewhat expanded to allow for, if not accommodate, a limited embrace of racial difference, as well as new models of white female self-sufficiency. Alcott locates these reform projects within the context of the China trade, laying bare the international trade routes on which Graham's autarkic fantasies rested. More interestingly, she also puts the project of dietetic and biopolitical reform into conversation with its historical roots in the temperance movement by contrasting Rose's growth into moral womanhood with her cousin Charlie's decline into alcoholism. In doing so she reveals the biopolitical project of shaping white heterosexual futurity to be intimately imbricated in the production of addiction, both domestically and, in the context of the China opium trade, transnationally.

The post–Civil War texts I am examining here—the two Rose Campbell novels, *Eight Cousins* and *Rose in Bloom*—thus highlight the successes and limits of the Grahamite program in the late nineteenth century. His ideas provide Alcott—a privileged witness to radical reform movements in the antebellum period—with a perspective that both confirms and mocks the confluence of diet and ethnic and national identity. If Alcott's protagonist Rose is more ambivalent about embracing the ideology of "wholesomeness"—a key Grahamite word—that infuses her uncle's dietary programs, the series of novels ultimately accedes to the conflation of correct consumption with an ideal of white racial embodiment as founded on an identification with European foodways. And yet, as we will see, Alcott's ambiguous commitment to racial equality also open the novels to a limited and problematic tarrying with difference.

Eight Cousins and Rose in Bloom

The obsessive charting of Rose's physical, moral, and emotional growth in these two books is revelatory of Alcott's deeply biopolitical feminist project. That project, of course, advances as a disciplinary one, focused on shaping Rose's consent to a present and future that will be, in one of the books' favorite phrases, "useful." That pragmatic goal, founded as it is on the reform movement's moral dovetailing of health and self-improvement with liberal ideals of individualism, echoes Graham's own work when it centers narrative attention to the female body and generates an erotic interest that energizes the narrative. In particular, as Alcott's particular brand of early feminist biopolitics unfolds in the form of a domestic education for the orphaned Rose, rather than one outside the home in some institutional space—for instance, an orphanage or public school—its disciplinary and libidinal aspects overlap.

The sign of that tension is the orphaned teenager's relationship to her uncle, Dr. Alec; though consciously seeking to tame and intellectually dominate Rose, he never uses the raw patriarchal force that would surely be applied in a more traditional home. Alcott's fidelity to a republican strain of radicalism can be seen in the story of Rose's maturation, which is shaped to strike a careful balance between republican ideas of virtue and the claims of the body, the concept of the domestic space as women's rightful sphere, and Alcott's commitment to emergent liberal models of white female subjectivity. In Alcott's novels the woman who leaves home does not bring disaster to it, pace Graham; instead, she brings a domestic program of dietetic, moral, and physiological reform with her into the world, one that is ultimately recuperated by the household. Like those dietetic reformers whose programs she was well aware of, Alcott's project in *Eight Cousins* and *Rose in Bloom* melds the medical with the political, finding in the project of curing the female body a prescription for reimagining the female condition. Alcott is also in direct conversation with both Sylvester Graham and William Alcott, developing their interest in the production of a temperate, white body politic via her own nascent feminist politic and even indicating her allegiance with their work by folding their didactic projects into her own, at times borrowing directly from their own books.[7] What her frank engagement with their work also teases out is what Michael Warner has seen as the reform, or temperance, movement's invention of addiction; here, however, the racial undertones of that project are spelled out forcefully.[8]

Louisa May Alcott's favorite plot template is to trace the maturation of young men and women, a process judged relative to their place in a family group. Such a template girds *Little Women*, *Little Men*, and *Jo's Boys*, as well as the Rose series, *Eight Cousins* and its sequel, *Rose in Bloom*. The Rose novels trace Rose Campbell's coming of age from early adolescence to her love match and marriage to one of her cousins, and, as in *Little Women*, Rose's story is told as an allegory of choice. However, rather than four very different sisters who, in making their life choices, mark themselves as different models of female subjectivity, in the Rose novels the protagonist, under the guidance of her uncle, must first choose from among six aunts the best role models for her personality type and then choose from among her seven male cousins—she is the eponymous eighth—for her husband.

In the first novel in the pair, *Eight Cousins*, Rose, a rich young orphan, is adopted by her uncle Alec, following the death of her father; her mother, whom she closely resembles, has died from unexplained causes long before the story begins. There is an obvious erotic charge to the relationship between Rose and her uncle: we are told that Alec refused to speak to his brother, Rose's father, for years because they had both been in love with Rose's mother and that, as a result, Alec has remained a bachelor, leaving him to redirect all that affect toward Rose via his new paternal role. Over this level of erotic rivalries and substitutions Alcott layers another substitution, between the paternal and medical roles: from the beginning of the novel Alcott conflates physical and moral health by having Rose call her uncle-cum-father-figure "Dr. Alec," while he calls the lessons he administers to her "doses."[9] She learns, in the first novel, to turn to him for advice and guidance in everything. The end result of Rose's apprenticeship in Dr. Alec's house (which is at the same time performed by Dr. Alec as a kind of courtship, reprising the role he unsuccessfully played with Rose's mother) is that she learns to accept her uncle's point of view and models her choice of husband on her Uncle's example. These exchanges are openly understood in terms of the transference of romantic feeling: "the aunts understood how dear the child was to the solitary man who had loved her mother years ago, and who now found his happiness in cherishing the little Rose who was so like her."[10]

This overlapping of the libidinal with the edifying, and the moral with the medical, frames the project of raising Rose. In fact, Dr. Alec calls his parenting of Rose an "experiment" or "treatment":[11]

> "We will show [Aunt Myra] how to make constitutions and turn pale-faced little girls into rosy, hearty girls. That's my business you know . . . ," he added.
>
> "I had forgotten you were a doctor. [Said Rose,] I'm glad of it, for I do want to be well, only I hope you won't give me much medicine, for I've taken quarts already, and it does me no good."[12]

Dr. Alec's first act is to throw out Rose's tonics and medicines, many of them given to her by her aunts to cure her depression—an emancipating gesture that is at the same time an enclosing one, as it makes Rose more dependent on Dr. Alec. Their replacement introduces the first Grahamite element into the text. Interestingly, it enters not as an explicit program but as a deception. Alec replaces Rose's medicines—which are implied to be quack patent medicines—with new pills, which he has secretly made in his study from pellets of whole wheat bread:

> Just then Phebe came out of the dining-room with a plate of brown bread, for Rose had been allowed no hot biscuit for tea.
>
> "I'll relieve you of some of that," said Dr. Alec, and, helping himself to a generous slice, he retired to the study, leaving Phebe to wonder at his appetite.
>
> She would have wondered still more if she had seen him making that brown bread into neat little pills, which he packed into an attractive ivory box, out of which he emptied his own bits of lovage.[13]

Dr. Alec also forbids Rose any coffee: she is to have whole milk, which she is to milk from the cow herself:

> "Don't you think she ought to have something more strengthening than milk, Alec? I really shall feel anxious if she does not have a tonic of some sort," said Aunt Plenty, eying [*sic*] the new remedies suspiciously, for she had more faith in her old-fashioned doses than all the magic cups and poppy pillows of the East.
>
> "Well, ma'am, I'm willing to give her a pill, if you think best. It is a very simple one, and very large quantities can be taken without harm. You know hasheesh is the extract of hemp? Well, this is a preparation of corn and rye, much used in old times, and I hope it will be again."[14]

The contrast of the East and West, between the poppy pillow and the medicinal bread and milk, between hasheesh, extracted from hemp and used at the time for an anesthetic, and the bread, made of corn and rye, offers interesting insight into the transnational and domestic politics at play in the novel.

On one hand, the pills, secretly manufactured in the male part of the house, emphasize the vigorous and virile blandness of the food; on the other hand, the box in which they are laid emphasizes the transnational economics that bolster the affluence and middle-class morality of the Campbell clan, themselves purveyors of luxury Asian goods. In fact we are told early on that the Campbell family derives its wealth from the New England maritime trading economy, much of which comes from China, and most of Uncle Alec's cures come wrapped in packages—ivory boxes for the pills and a quassia cup for her milk—that are decidedly exotic.[15] These interconnections are introduced in the book's opening scene, when Rose is pictured moping around the "capital old mansion." The mansion, Alcott writes, is "hung all around with portraits of solemn old gentlemen in wigs, severe-nosed ladies in top-heavy caps, and staring children in bob-tailed coats or short-waisted frocks." But it is also "full of curiosities from all parts of the world; for the Campbells had been sea captains for generations."[16] Three paragraphs into the book, then, Alcott is at pains to point out not only Rose Campbell's wealth but also the historical conditions under which it was made. Significantly, the era of the sea captains is associated with a past that is itself becoming exotic, with its wigs and frocks. As is often the case in the historical romance, a series of portraits transforms historical time into family time, and vice versa—prefiguring the extended family reach from which Rose never exits.

In an attempt to keep the grieving Rose amused the chapter continues, "Aunt Plenty had even allowed Rose to rummage in her great china closet,—a spicy retreat, rich in all the 'goodies' that children love; but Rose seemed to care little for these toothsome temptations."[17] Rose grows "pale, heavy-eyed and listless" until, following the sound of birdlike singing, she finds her way through a "china-closet" and into the kitchen, where she meets Phebe Moore, who will play the working-class foil to Rose's progress into privileged adulthood:

> When she entered, not a bird appeared, except the everlastingly kissing swallows on the Canton china that lined the shelves. All of a sudden Rose's face brightened, and, softly opening the slide, she peered into the kitchen. . . . All she saw was a girl in a blue apron scrubbing the hearth. . . . Rose crept through the slide to the wide shelf on the other side, being too hurried and puzzled to go round by the door.[18]

Entering by way of the "slide," a chute attached to the china-closet through which household items are sent to the kitchen for cleaning, Rose finds her first moment of happiness in the novel. It is a happiness also marked by the novel's first flare of erotic desire: just before meeting the source of the chirping sounds Rose passes a set of china painted with swallows kissing each other. As the plates hint, the relationship between Rose and Phebe becomes one of the series's central love stories. Alcott's didactic project, though resolutely heterosexual and invested in traditional gender norms, thus reveals moments of same-sex desire, a product, perhaps, of what Kathryn Kent calls Alcott's "pedagogic erotics": queer pleasures produced through seemingly normative identifications.[19]

The now antiquated term "china-closet" referred to both "a private repository of valuables or curiosities"[20] and a small storage space or cupboard. Alcott's description of the space emphasizes the china-closet's architectural function and allows Alcott to build on the Orientalist theme by gesturing toward the nineteenth-century's craze for chinoiserie and japonaiserie, while at the same time keeping luxury apart from the kitchen—and therefore from Rose's future—by containing it within a closet. Rose's "slide"—from grief over her father's death, and a languorous depression, to interest in the world outside—is signified as an illicit exit, an illicit movement even, out of the mansion. She literally moves through the portrait hall, with its hint of the gothic aesthetic through the exotic display of the Victorian china closet, and into the prosaic space of the kitchen, where Phebe is on her knees sorting beans and washing the hearth. The slide, in its architectural sense, is a metaphoric birth canal: just as Rose is "reborn" as an orphan through the death of her father, so she is delivered from the pictures of the dead to a kitchen inhabited by a live girl, pushed forward by her "hurried" and "puzzled" desire to find the person and the space from which the bird sounds are coming.

The kitchen here assumes its symbolic role as the domestic sphere's a priori site of social interaction across class difference, a difference mitigated by gender sameness and represented, on the Canton china, as species sameness. Rose's first vision of Phebe as she peers from the other side of the slide is of a girl scrubbing a hearth—a space that, as we have seen, symbolizes an older domestic order, one that has been displaced by the stove and the rearrangement of the house's private and public spaces. Rose's slide from the china-closet to the hearth presages the plotline of class mobility that runs through the two novels and echoes the theme of class inversion that haunts earlier hearth-centered literature. Indeed, across the novels Phebe will attain middle-class status, marrying one of Rose's cousins, while Rose, who marries another cousin, acquires for herself the habits and ideas of a middle-class woman, albeit one with an inconveniently upper-class fortune. But if we are also to understand the Rose novels as a love story, of a sort, between Rose and Phebe, the encounter between the two of them at the end of the "slide" looks like something else as well, in which the hearth, which Phebe washes with dabs of soft soap, stands in for a space of intimacy and tenderness.

Here, as elsewhere in Alcott's writing, the exotic, the foreign, and the fashionable are rejected in *Eight Cousins* and *Rose in Bloom* in favor of Alcott's cherished working woman and her ethic of honest labor. In a purely republican rationale healthfulness is defined by Dr. Alec to be "domestic wellness" in the broadest sense of the term. Giving Rose bread pills returns us to the deep-seated belief that domestic produce—wheat, milk, oats, and beans—will produce healthful bodies, undisturbed by overenervation, listlessness, or depression. On another level, however, the presence of the quassia cup, the ivory box, and the other *objets* that lie around the Campbell home express the deeper structural change that has come about in the economy of the United States as it begins to represent itself in the world as a defender of trade. The Grahamite metonymy of nation, home, and body sounds quite the same in *Eight Cousins* as it did in *The Lecture to Young Men on Chastity* or *The Treatise on Bread and Breadmaking* almost forty years earlier, but Rose's engagement with these ideas reflects a distinct shift in the way difference is figured. The utopian possibility, in 1837, that a consumer society could be recuperated by an autarkic economy of domestic self-sufficiency—which finds different but related expression in Graham and in the nostalgia for the hearth discussed earlier—has become a casualty of history, of civil war and steam ships, of aggressive trade with Asia, and of a heightened rhetoric of trade and empire.

Rose's domestic cures, the legacy of Graham's identification of personal, moral, and national health, now come wrapped in Oriental splendor. Indeed, the chapter in which Dr. Alec unpacks her room begins with Rose milking a cow into her quassia[21] cup, and ends with her dressed in

> a purple fez on her blonde head, . . . several brilliant scarfs about her waist, . . . a truly gorgeous scarlet jacket with a golden sun embroidered on the back, a silver moon on the front, and stars of all sizes on the sleeves. A pair of Turkish slippers adorned her feet, and necklaces of camber, coral and filigree hung about her neck, while one hand held a smelling-bottle, and the other the spicy box of oriental sweetmeats.[22]

Orientalist exoticism—this almost literal shopping list of items—thus not only frames every corner of Rose's body, imprinting itself on all of her senses; it also frames the narrative and historical background of the novel.[23]

Though the conditions of the Campbell fortune are taken for granted by all the characters, it seems important to note that Dr. Alec's wholesome cures come packaged with a smack of the illicit. Oriental objects, and in particular Chinese objects, were central to the performance of upper-class status in Revolutionary and nineteenth-century America.[24] The first American ship to trade with Canton departed Boston in February 1784; by the beginning of the nineteenth century more than twenty vessels were visiting Canton every year.[25] Indeed, building the American trade with China was a central political goal of the first half of the nineteenth century, a pillar in the republic's ambitions for economic power.

If the Americans desired the caffeine in tea, then like the British before them they had to quickly became merchants in the opium trade to the Chinese. The trade triangle particular to the Chinese market began with U.S. merchants exporting sugar, coffee, furs, and wood from the Americas to India and Turkey, where they were traded for opium that was shipped to China.[26] In China opium was traded for silk, tea, and other commodities that were then sent back to the United States, where they were sold for profit.

Alcott's references to Canton china, poppy pillows, Turkish slippers, and, as I will discuss later, the presence of one of the Campbell uncles in India thus explicitly locate the Campbell family in the international circulation of goods in which opium—the same opium made from poppies that Dr. Alec rejects as an everyday medicinal in favor of Rose's bread pills—was a key commodity. Dr. Alec's diagnoses, as we have seen, are based on Grahamite beliefs, and his work with Rose is a familial manifestation of Graham's biopolitical urges; Graham, of course, owed his beginnings to the Philadelphia Temperance Society. For Alcott, then, American sobriety, and the luxurious objects that paradoxically frame it, are presupposed by the external production of opiate addiction. As we will see, however, addiction does not attach itself to Asian bodies but to American ones, albeit via an indirect association with Asian trade.

Closer to home, however, temperance, in its original meaning not as abstention but as temperateness or moderation, defines Alcott's idealized woman even as Rose mocks her own dietetic cure. Rose learns to avoid champagne, as it gives her headaches, and to shun fashion in favor of practical clothing and to practice frugality with regard to her own money. Rose's progression through the book—as a depressive "invalid" cured not by "tonics" and "old-fashioned doses" but by milk and bread pills—sends up the culture of female illness that has generated the assortment of patent remedies to which Rose has been a victim. Indeed, Dr. Alec also considers the false medicine a bit of fun: "There! If they insist on medicine, I'll order these, and no harm will be done. I *will* have my own way, but I'll keep peace, if possible, and confess the joke when my experiment has succeeded."[27] By the end of the book Dr. Alec's Grahamite optimism succeeds. The joke-experiment works, and Rose does not need to take medicine again: bread and milk cure Rose of her bodily ills. And, of course, she is no longer dependent on questionable medicines, many of which, as the temperance movement well knew, were in fact alcohol in disguise.

Alcott also retains and reworks Graham's fetishization of the woman who bakes bread at home. In the chapter titled "Bread and Button-Holes" Rose decides to learn the domestic arts. Says Dr. Alec,

> Housekeeping . . . is one of the most beautiful as well as useful of all the arts a woman can learn. . . . Cooking is one of the main things, you know. . . . I'd rather you learned how to make good bread than the best pies ever baked. When you bring me a handsome, wholesome loaf, entirely made by yourself, . . . I'll give you my heartiest kiss, and promise to eat every crumb of the loaf myself.[28]

As in the passages of *Work* that open this chapter, bread does not just signify surrender to the patriarchal diktat; it is an portentous product that signifies, as well, an emergent form of independent female subjectivity, although one still caught up in what readers of Alcott's other books will recognize as her particular nostalgia for the traditional—"old-fashioned" in her words—framework of self-sufficiency.[29] The two books are not dissimilar in their uses of bread symbolism: discussing *Work*, Glenn Hendler has argued that Alcott's model of sentimentality seeks to invoke a particularly gendered public sphere, paradoxically by describing her heroine's departure from the domestic—another gendered sphere—through the use of food imagery attached to her aunt's body, language, and labor.[30] As so often in nineteenth-century discourse, the product of food preparation and the qualities of the worker are merged. Thus, Alcott uses the language of breadmaking, as we have seen, to compare Christie Devon with her less adventurous aunt: "after standing quiet in a warm corner so long," Christie says, "I begin to ferment."[31]

Alcott's use of the language of yeast as alive, as indeed it chemically is, ties Christie and Rose alike to imagery of growth and maturation. Christie ferments—is catalyzed—beyond the limits of the traditional domestic sphere, only to return to a newly imagined domesticity at the end of *Work*, one formed by voluntary and loving associations with an interracial cast of women. Rose similarly associates herself with bread. For Rose, however, it is described as intellectual labor: "bread-making is not an art easily learned, . . . so Rose studied yeast first, and through various stages of cake and biscuit came at last to the crowning glory of the 'handsome, wholesome loaf.'"[32] Rose is taught not to leave the bread to burn: "I must *give my whole mind to it*. . . . [I] sat watching over it all the while it was in the oven till I was quite baked myself."[33] Across the Rose books as well as *Work*, then, bread is transformed within the Grahamite ideology, coming to symbolize white female subjectivity in formation, one that, despite the figuring of the girl's body as rising and baking like bread itself, does not take the passive position in a consumer culture—indeed, Rose's decision to learn bread baking comes as a result of her decision to "decide what trade" she would learn, "for rich people may grow poor, you know, and poor people have to work."[34] Christie's declaration of independence, and Rose's concern to be able to support herself, are materialized in the kitchen, where making bread requires intellectual labor and willpower as well as the correct ingredients.

Louisa May had a particularly intense exposure to dietetic reform: her father's disastrous utopian experiment Fruitlands, which she later parodied in the memoir-cum-novella *Transcendental Wild Oats*, was not only based on Grahamite principles but in fact exceeded them in severity by excluding all products produced through the death or labor of animals, including not only milk and butter but also silk and leather. All products produced through the labor of slaves were also banned, including cane sugar, cotton, and wool. No one was even to remove the worms from apples; history leaves unrecorded whether eating the apple worms was a trespass of the vegetarian rules or not.[35]

In *Transcendental Wild Oats* Louisa May Alcott describes the utopian diet designed by Charles Lane and Bronson Alcott as particularly hard on the mother, who has to prepare all of the meals:

> Cakes of maple sugar, dried peas and beans, barley and hominy, meal of all sorts, potatoes and dried fruit. No milk, butter, cheese, tea, or meat appeared. Even salt was considered a useless luxury and spice entirely forbidden by these lovers of Spartan simplicity. . . . Unleavened bread, porridge, and water for breakfast; bread, vegetables, and water for dinner; bread, fruit and water for supper was the bill of fare ordained by the elders.

> No teapot profaned that sacred stove, no gory steak cried aloud for vengeance from her chaste gridiron; and only a brave woman's taste, time, and temper were sacrificed on that domestic altar.[36]

The language Alcott uses to describe the mother's kitchen is in another register than that which she uses in describing Rose's or Christie's kitchen. Their kitchens are resolutely political and secular; the kitchen in *Transcendental Wild Oats* is religious and sacrificial. The sacrificed object is the female herself—her "taste, time, and temper" are juxtaposed to the negation of the "gory steak"—but clearly that negation establishes a brutal correlation between the mother's work and a helpless piece of meat.

It is symptomatic of the arbitrariness of the Fruitlands rule book that the first bread of the day, and only the first bread, should exclude leavening. Two explanations seem possible. The unleavened bread for the first meal of the day may have been something on the level of pancakes or another kind of breakfast bread. However, it also seems possible that founders Charles Lane and Bronson Alcott, in all of their impractical high-mindedness, might have declared yeast a living organism and therefore in need of Fruitlands' protection. Perhaps Bronson shared his cousin William's opinion that "neither leaven nor yeast ought ever to have been known. They are a filthy concern. Besides, fermented bread is a semi-putrid bread; that is, it has advanced one step in the highway to putrefaction."[37] Graham, who did not view yeast as a pollutant as William Alcott did, still recommended that yeasted bread not be allowed to ferment too long, thereby destroying the starch and gluten that made the bread healthy, sweet, and—a term used extensively by both Graham and Louisa May Alcott—wholesome. Overfermentation, of course, ran the risk of association with alcohol, in particular fermented drinks such as beer.

Our fermenting heroine Rose, herself a subject of dietary experimentation, never loses her dialogic autonomy, which emerges in her habit of parody and humor. At the beginning of the second Rose Campbell novel, *Rose in Bloom*, Alcott sends up food fads when she makes fun of Mac, her bookish cousin who has gone through a vegetarian phase. Rose tells Mac, "This is the latest hobby, then? Your letters have amused us immensely; for each one had a new theory of experiment, and the latest was always the best. I thought uncle would have died of laughing over the vegetarian mania: it was so funny to imagine you living on bread and milk, baked apples, and potatoes roasted in your own fire."[38] Yet while she mocks radical diets, Mac is the cousin who most approximates Rose's beloved Uncle

Alec, and it is he whom she will ultimately marry. Similarly, while Alcott has sufficient distance from her father's Grahamite experiments to make fun of them, in the 1870s she has not entirely departed from the reformist food ideas of the 1830s. Rose's ironizing gestures might, in fact, be read as a protest not against the Grahamite ideology as a whole but against its programmatic nature. A typical Rose response to the overt association of virtue and nutrition occurs early on in *Eight Cousins*, when Uncle Alec gives Rose porridge for breakfast:

> "Uncle, *are* you going to make me eat oatmeal?" asked Rose in a tragic tone.
> "Don't you like it?"
> "I de-test it!" answered Rose.[39]

Rose eventually does eat it, also abandoning her preferred but overstimulating breakfast drink, coffee. Yet her vehement dislike of oatmeal stems not from the taste of it; rather, "people are always saying how wholesome it is, and that makes me hate it."[40] Although Rose is never depicted as immoral, here one can trace an underground connection with Graham's vicious daughter. As we have seen, the vicious daughter, with her "spiced" body, arrives at a more clearly hedonistic and amoral conclusion in response to pleasures of the luxurious table: her uncontrolled masturbatory behavior. Rose, less extreme, must still be recuperated into a more temperate and "wholesome" program; rather than an addiction to vice, however, Rose objects to the notion that the mouth can be subject to an "ought."

Rose's willingness to protest—indeed her insistence on protest—while still remaining within the boundaries of Grahamite ideology, is a telling indicator of Alcott's relationship to the dietetic reform discourses she has inherited. While retaining her allegiance to reform dietetics, Alcott recuperates the masturbating girl's erotic energy, directing it toward another girl. She also retains the rebellious energies of Graham's vicious daughter, making the fanning of Rose's independence central to her Uncle Alec's project.

A "True Scotchwoman" and a "Highly Satisfactory Chinaman"

It should not be surprising that, given Louisa May's indebtedness to Grahamite discourse, the symbolic relationship between wheat bread and colonialism explored in chapter 2 on Graham firmly positions whiteness at the heart of her feminist project. But it is not simply bread that does this racializing work. In the oatmeal passage quoted in the preceding section Rose's uncle does not tout the nutritiousness of the food, nor does he even tout the taste. Instead, he comments, "You are not a true Scotchwoman, if you don't like the 'parritch.' It's a pity for I made it myself, and thought we'd have such a good time with all that cream to float it in."[41] The long-standing connection between oats and Scotland, once mocked by Samuel Johnson in his dictionary, is trotted out for Rose as racial bait—eat your ancestors' food and be well.[42] By contrast we see that in *Rose in Bloom* Charlie, the (in contemporary terms) alcoholic cousin whose indulgence in "vice" and "veniality," that is, whose failure to achieve the reform ideal of the temperate body, ultimately causes his death, is consistently connected with India and the East. In fact it is Charlie who is first introduced as the likeliest future spouse for Rose; it is his public drunkenness that causes her to reject his affections, with, as Alcott writes, "a spirit as proud and fiery as any of her race."[43] Charlie's father, Stephen, has spent years in India away from his family, weakening his masculine and paternal energy. As a result, Charlie is too headstrong for his own good, according to his uncles:

> "It is too late to 'order' [Charlie about]: Charlie is a man now, and Stephen will find he has been too easy with him all these years. Poor fellow, it has been hard lines for him, and is likely to be harder, I fancy, unless he comes home and straightens things out."
>
> "He won't do that if he can help it. He has lost all his energy living in that climate and hates worry more than ever, so you can imagine what an effort it would be to manage a foolish woman and a headstrong boy. We must lend a hand . . . and do our best for poor old Steve."[44]

After struggling to win Rose's affection by conquering his alcoholism, Charlie is about to travel to India to recover, when he is thrown from the horse that he has been riding, drunk. He dies soon after, leaving the way open for Mac, whose ascetic experiments with vegetarian dietetics had once seemed so comical to Rose.

The structural contradiction in which Charlie is entangled—he is on his way to the "Far East" to get better, even though it was the "East" that had claimed his father's patriarchal energies—rests at the heart of the United States' commercial and imperial ambitions. The foreign functions both as structuring difference and as material condition for the metropole: as I have noted, the danger of addiction is displaced onto the foreign, but at the same time, the affluence that arises from the sale of drugs, which is the economic subtext of the novel, makes possible the Orientalist affluence—and the affiliated vices—of Euro-American culture.[45] If scholars of temperance and the history of addiction are correct to say that the temperance movement created addiction, what Alcott's Rose Campbell novels make clear is that the inverse is also true. That is to say, the material production of opium addiction in China in fact funded the cultural logic of temperance, which I have argued in this book to be central to the uneven history of local biopolitical imperatives. These in turn were tied to the historical construction of whiteness in the antebellum and, as we see in these novels, the postbellum United States.

Alongside this unoriginal mapping of vice and virtue, then, it seems notable that Charlie's initial romantic interest—Annabel Bliss—ultimately replaces him with a Chinese character, Fun See. Alcott first introduces Fun See in the context of a chapter titled "A Trip to China" when Uncle Alec, by way of a "geography lesson," takes Rose to see the ship (named the *Rajah*) and the warehouse that hold her family's wealth. The stage has already been set, as noted, when we are introduced to Rose at the very beginning of *Eight Cousins*, surrounded by the family's Oriental *objets de luxe*. The pervasive presence of these items echoes almost perfectly what Edward Said characterized, in Jane Austen's novels, as "the geographical notation, the theoretical mapping and charting of territory that underlies Western fiction, historical writing, and philosophical discourse."[46] As Said remarked, in this wide field of Western literature that takes the West's imperial and neoimperial holdings as its constitutive edges, the superiority of the "observer—traveler, merchant, scholar, historian, novelist" is buttressed by a "cultural discourse relegating and confining the non-European to a secondary, racial, cultural, ontological status."[47] This secondary status is most obviously accorded to Fun See, about whom Alcott writes that he is "delightfully Chinese from his junk-like shoes to the button on his pagoda hat. . . . He was short and fat and waddled comically; his eyes were very "slanting," . . . his queue was long, and so were his nails."[48] Fun See is described, in other words, via all the clichés of neovaudevillian yellowface; without recourse to English he must even "pantomime" his words.[49]

This "highly satisfactory Chinaman," as Rose calls him, presents her with a gift:

> Out from the wrappings came a teapot, which caused her to clasp her hands with delight, for it was made in the likeness of a plump little Chinaman. His hat was the cover, his queue the handle, and his pipe the nose. It stood upon feet in shoes turned up at the toes, and the smile on the fat, sleepy face was so like that on Fun's when he displayed the teapot, that Rose couldn't help laughing.[50]

The doubling of the image of Fun See is startling. What was "highly satisfactory" about Fun See, to Rose, is that he is perfectly the "type" of Chinaman she recognizes—his personal traits, whatever they may be, are entirely absorbed in his ethnic and racial ones. Following this logic, the doubling of the Chinaman could be read as referencing the national fascination with twinned Asian bodies, as epitomized, for instance, by the well-known conjoined brothers Chang and Eng.[51] The teapot scene also continues the ongoing theme of the Orient as a site of commodity production: even a "satisfactory Chinaman," in other words, even Chinese citizens, become objects of consumption, linked to the rage for exotically decorated interiors. What I want to point to here, however, is the use of the Chinese body as container for tea. That is, returning to the notion that particular food objects can facilitate a national and racial belonging—wheat as Euro-American, "parritch" as Scottish—Alcott has Fun See himself embody and contain his country's most widely exported commodity.[52]

The doubling of Fun See's body displaces another "unsatisfactory" Chinese man in the room, Whang Lo, who is described as an "elderly gentleman in American costume, with his pig-tail wound round his head. He spoke English and was talking busily with Uncle Mac in the most commonplace way,—so Rose considered *him* a failure."[53] Whang Lo does not appear again in the Rose Campbell novels, further attesting to his failure to make an impression on Rose. Fun See, however, appears in both books. Alcott's body of work is not entirely subsumed by a stereotypical racial typology. In fact, in her short story "M.L."—an "amalgamationist" love story written after John Brown's failed raid on Harper's Ferry and pseudonymously published in Boston's *Commonwealth* newspaper—describes with surprising dignity the marriage between a white woman and a mixed-race man. Alcott's matter-of-fact presentation of the couple was well outside established codes of acceptability. Similarly, although the marriage of Annabel Bliss and Fun See is a matter of mockery, it elicits no condemnation from Rose. In fact, to compound the insult to white supremacy, Annabel has chosen Fun over Charlie, who is the first to tell Rose of the upcoming wedding:

> "Fun has cut me out and the fair Annabella will be Mrs. Tokio before the winter is over if I'm not much mistaken."
>
> "What little Fun See? How droll it seems to think of him grown up and married to Annabel of all people. She never said a word about him but this accounts for her admiring my pretty Chinese things and being so interested in Canton."[54]

The easy substitution of Annabel's desire for "pretty Chinese things" for her romantic interest in Fun See lies beside a third substitution: that of the addicted Charlie—denied patriarchal guidance as a result of his father's Oriental dissipation—in the place of the figure of the Chinese opium addict on whom the Campbell fortune rests.

It is perhaps to Alcott's credit that, six years before the passage of the Chinese Exclusion Act, the text strains against the racial hierarchies that seemed to grow stronger and stronger in the decades after the Civil War, by including an interracial marriage; perhaps Fun See's status as a foreign student, "who had come out to be educated," instead of a railroad worker or menial laborer, serves the same purpose.[55] Those critics who have engaged with the Rose Campbell novels, either from the perspective of Alcott scholars or from Asian American studies, have inevitably skewered Alcott's representation of Fun See, and there can be no doubt that Alcott's novel participates in a long tradition in the United States of stereotyping the Chinese immigrant and worker.[56] But this skewering should not simply merge Alcott with her era's general anti-Asian discourse, as that would make Fun See's marriage to Annabel incomprehensible. Visibly, Alcott does struggle to exceed, in an extremely limited fashion, the period's standard emptying out of Asian American subjectivity in favor of the ruling stereotypes of the day.[57] Although she does portray Fun See in classic yellowface terms, even going so far as to quote Brett Harte's "Plain Language from Truthful James," in which Harte made famous the term "The Heathen Chinee," this failure of imagination is only one side of Rose's perception of Fun See.[58]

While the marriage between Annabelle and Fun See is so accepted as to sink into the background of the narrative, the political possibilities of that union are certainly held in check—and not just by the distancing humor with which Fun See and the marriage are depicted. Rather, the real generator of racist assumptions is the language of geophysical belonging central to reformist physiology. The indelible Grahamite link between body, home, and nation eternally bars Fun See from ever quite transcending the marks of Asian difference, although those marks do seem to stretch to enfold the new "Mrs. Tokio."[59] And yet the one axis through which he gains visibility as, at least, a romantic subject is via the tropes of fatness and plumpness, descriptors linked both to Asian and white women's bodies. When, late in the first novel, an "improved" and "Americanized" Fun See comes to dinner, he attaches himself to Rose's overweight Aunt Plenty, "whom he greatly admired as the stoutest lady in the company; plumpness being considered a beauty in his country."[60] The desire for not-thin and therefore "unfashionable" women is clearly stereotypical, and both Fun See and Aunt Plenty, as well as Annabel, are sent up via the text's burlesque tone. Fun See's fatness—and his desire for fatness, for indeed Annabel Bliss is herself called "plump as a partridge"—is wielded against him as a mark of his lack of conventional Western manliness.

Plumpness in the nineteenth century, however, also represents health and well-being: Uncle Alec, for instance, rejoices to see his love object, Rose, plump after following his dietetic remedies and persuades her to abandon stiff belts and corsets. Furthermore, in a society in which the display of too much sexuality can lead to "viciousness," fat seems to contain sexuality. The "not elegant" Aunt Plenty represents a kind of ideal of womanhood in this respect, for, as Uncle Alec asserts when suggesting her as Rose's teacher in housekeeping, she is "genuinely good, . . . beloved and respected. . . . No one can fill [her place] for the solid, homely virtues of the dear soul have gone out of fashion."[61] Though it does not quite reach the ideal valence of Alcott's word "wholesome," Plenty's plenty-ness, as it were, is at the very least about being healthful. By her very name she is filling and not empty. Dr. Alec praises her, oddly, in just those terms: "there will be universal mourning for her when her place is empty."[62] Plenty's fatness, then, can be celebrated because she is filling her place; her body is occupying its correct space, fulfilling its proper role. That proper role, of course, is that of maiden aunt: chaste and celibate, even though her only kiss in the book comes from Fun See.[63] So too are the sexual possibilities between Fun See and Annabel contained behind the asexuality of their shared plumpness, although Annabel's "stoutness" is less a mark of her traditional womanliness and more a kind of a sign of her comic freakishness: at one point Alec refers to her as "that affected midget."[64]

No matter how forward thinking Alcott's ideas are, and no matter how much her writing strains against the standards of her era, these efforts make us aware of the limits that she, too, fails to transcend. Almost four decades after the publication of *The Lecture to Young Men on Chastity*, that is, by 1876 and the publication of *Rose in Bloom*, the earlier Grahamite connection of racial constitution with a diet linked to geographic and ecological origins continues as a racial—and racist—shorthand in which food objects stand in for ethnicity. Indeed, when Rose encounters Fun See for the first time, she echoes a decades-old conversation about Chinese food when she states her fears that Fun See will make her eat "a roasted rat, a stewed puppy, or any other foreign mess which civility would oblige her to eat."[65] By the second book Rose amuses herself by imagining Annabel "going to Canton some day, and having to order rats, puppies and birds'-nest soup for dinner."[66] Dietary differences, in other words, mark the boundaries between the races. To cross those boundaries means taking up new foodways; inversely, to take up those foodways means to cross those boundaries. In this way Annabel Bliss is referred to as "our fat friend, who will take to chopsticks whenever [Fun See] says the word"—"taking to chopsticks," or eating as the "heathen Chinee" do, thus forms a shorthand for becoming married to and, we assume, sexually intimate with an Asian man. It is Annabelle who will, in adopting the Asian diet, leave her whiteness behind; Annabel Tokio, née Bliss, will become Chinese. Though much changed between 1837 and 1876, Alcott remains rooted in the original Grahamite racial imaginary linking body to place, attesting to the fact that, brief as his appearance was in the public eye, his work laid the foundation for a food discourse that was foundational to the nation.

In *Rose in Bloom*, specifically, the comparison of Rose and Mac's determinedly chaste choices with Charlie's alcoholism sits atop the deep structural ironies that accrue from the trade in opium, tea, and sugar. The sea captains who provided the financial foundation of the Campbell family presumably were links in the trade that led to Chinese opium addiction and linked as well to the trade in the spices, tea, and coffee that Grahamites condemned. Not surprisingly, these links are not made by any of the characters in the Rose novels, and at moments the realities of the transatlantic trade are obscured. Rose, returning from her "geography lesson" aboard the *Rajah*, tells her aunt, "I have collected some useful information about China. . . . Principal productions are porcelain, tea, cinnamon, shawls, tin, tamarinds and opium."[67] Of course, the opium was produced *for* China, in India and Turkey, and carried to Chinese ports aboard European and American ships.

In addition to performing specific Grahamite principles of dietetic reform, both Mac and Rose, future Campbell spouses and inheritors of the Campbell fortune, choose to live frugally, shunning alcohol and framing their choices in the language of virtue. While the doomed Charlie is vain about his good looks and clothes, gambles, and struggles with alcoholism, Rose chooses modest attire, giving her dress money to a poor Irish woman so she can clothe her family and using her wealth to build a boarding house for impoverished and single "gentlewomen." Mac, who is variously described as "Spartan" and "sober," chooses a life of study and poetry. The last paragraph of *Rose in Bloom* unites Rose and Mac—whose very nickname asserts his Gaelic origins[68]—in common purpose:

> And, with a sort of desperation, she threw herself into his arms, clinging there in eloquent silence while he held her close. . . .
>
> "Now I'm satisfied!" he said presently, when she lifted up her face, full of maidenly shame at the sudden passion which had carried her out of herself for a moment. . . .
>
> [As Mac looked] at her as she stood there in the spring sunshine, glowing with the tender happiness, high hopes, and earnest purposes that make life beautiful and sacred, he felt now that the last leaf had folded back, the golden heart lay open to the light, and his Rose had bloomed.[69]

But if Rose and Mac's "earnest purposes" designate the chaste practices that bring them together, the eroticism of this passage also belies the reform movement's coeval production not only of the discourse of addiction but also of multiple forms of sexual identity. While the Rose novels close with the traditional marriage plot, conjoining the two most virtuous Campbells—in fact installing Rose as Mac's possession—they nonetheless brim with other erotic possibilities, beginning with the hint of upstairs-downstairs desire between Rose and Phebe and continuing with Dr. Alec, the bachelor who Rose briefly hints is a "dandy" but who remains, except for his love for Rose and her dead mother, emotionally and erotically indeterminable.[70]

As the final passage of *Rose in Bloom* manifestly states, the heroine's erotic potential lies at the heart, or perhaps as the telos, of the novels. Not only have the two novels laid Rose open (like the leaves of a book, as the passage implies) physically, morally, and emotionally, charting her development through adolescence and into womanhood, seducing the reader in the manner of the traditional bildungsroman (with the crucial difference that Rose is a woman), but she is the romantic object for two of her cousins. More subtly, Rose's marriage to her cousin Mac closes the unfinished affective circuit between Rose's mother and Uncle Alec that forms the incestuous subtext for the books, as Rose's love and desire for the man who most closely resembles her uncle restages and recuperates Alec's failed heterosexuality.

While Louisa May Alcott can certainly wax as poetic as Graham about baking wholesome bread, the self-sufficiency that seemed, in the antebellum area, to be a real solution to the problem of America as a republic and an imperial power does not, in post–Civil War society, seem to condition America's position in the world. It is not enough, in other words, to create a rigid boundary between what goes into the body and what stays out. America had become too immersed, both in its commercial appetites and its imperial desires, in the business of the rest of the world; similarly, the body and the home are also immersed in the outside world, with all its attendant delights and anxieties. The boundaries that were otherwise meant to contain the body, the home, and the nation are thus far more permeable in Alcott's work. The consumption of exotic items and profit from overseas trade and the emergent forms of female independence—including interracial marriage—that are predicated on more porous boundaries are only some of the new possibilities that she imagines for her protagonists.

5

"What's De Use Talking 'Bout Dem 'Mendments?"

Trade Cards and Consumer Citizenship at the End of the Nineteenth Century

The food reform movements that emerged during the antebellum period and that evolved to haunt the novels of post–Civil War writers such as Louisa May Alcott contained a remarkably prescient fear of the food culture that was to succeed them. By the Gilded Age, at the close of the nineteenth century, the bourgeois household seemed unable to resist the "rich, savory" foods to which Graham so objected. The tempted but generally abstemious approach to consumption of antebellum Anglo-America disappeared underneath an almost orgiastic flood of commodities.

I argued in the introduction that a truly materialist approach to the American culture of food would have to detach itself from the habit of fetishizing the consumer object that so often is found in cooking history, food studies, and "foodie literature" and, rather, understand the frameworks in which those objects are produced and eaten. In this chapter I take in the late nineteenth century and early twentieth century. In this period there was no transformation of the middle-class kitchen as radical as the change from hearth to stove, although the working-class tenement kitchen, with its lack of distinction between cooking and eating spaces, became of increased interest to bourgeois progressives. More broadly, however, during this era all aspects of food production in the United States experienced the most radical changes since the beginning of agriculture in the Middle East, some ten thousand years earlier.[1] By the turn of the twentieth century both demographics and technology were reshaping the way food was grown, consumed, and thought about. America's population was increasingly heterogeneous, and more and more people lived in cities, booming multicultural spaces that fostered the means to sell, buy, and eat products from around the world. Further, the invention of the McCormick threshing machine in 1831, which enabled the faster harvesting of wheat and an explosion in industrial production in general, meant that the growing of food was no longer the provenance of small farms and local markets but rather an industrialized agricultural system. These myriad evolutions created a public consumer discourse that shifted attention away from domestic production and toward public commodity consumption. Although popular images of the white woman in the kitchen continued to bear an important cultural valence, as did the black cook, the source of the food these women were cooking came from the grocery store, which increasingly supplanted the homegrown foodstuffs of the farm.

The technological sophistication of the logistical system by which food came from the farm to the market—the increase in the mileage of railroads and the new means of storage and temperature control, to name just two innovations—contributed to the massive change in food consumption. The first refrigerated railroad car, using block ice, appeared in the United States in 1851.[2] In the period from the 1870s to the 1910s the complex of railroads and preservation techniques made it possible to create a mass meat culture that expanded across the nation from slaughterhouse hubs such as Chicago, to ship seafood from the East Coast to interior cities and to diminish the dependence of the meal on the season.[3] Eating, in other words, became an industrial experience. Immigrant and working-class spaces such as the saloon, the restaurant, and the oyster house also flourished and were important spaces of public food consumption and social performance, as were the lunch counter and cafeteria, both of which were invented in the 1890s.[4]

For the upper classes the immense wealth made through speculation and industry created a whole new ethos of consumption. Harvey Levenstein recounts a banquet held at Delmonico's in 1880 to honor General Winfield Scott Hancock, the Democratic Party presidential nominee:

> The meal began, as most did, with raw oysters, whose abundance and popularity at that time made them perhaps the closest thing to a classless food. A choice of two soups was followed by an hor d'oeuvre and then a fish course. The preliminaries thus dispensed with, the *Relevés*, saddle of lamb and filet of beef, were then carved and served. These were followed by the *Entrées*, chicken wings with green peas and lamb chops garnished

Plate 1. Chase's Liquid Glue (author's collection)

Plate 2. Freud's Corset House (Courtesy American Antiquarian Society)

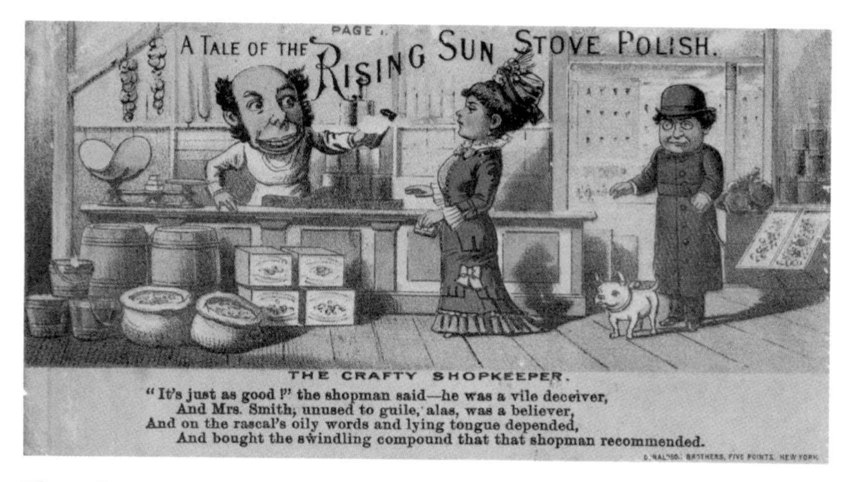

Plate 3. Rising Sun Stove Polish, "The Crafty Shopkeeper" (author's collection)

Plate 4. Rising Sun Stove Polish, "The Wretched Household" (author's collection)

Plate 5. Rising Sun Stove Polish, "The Beautiful Chromo" (author's collection)

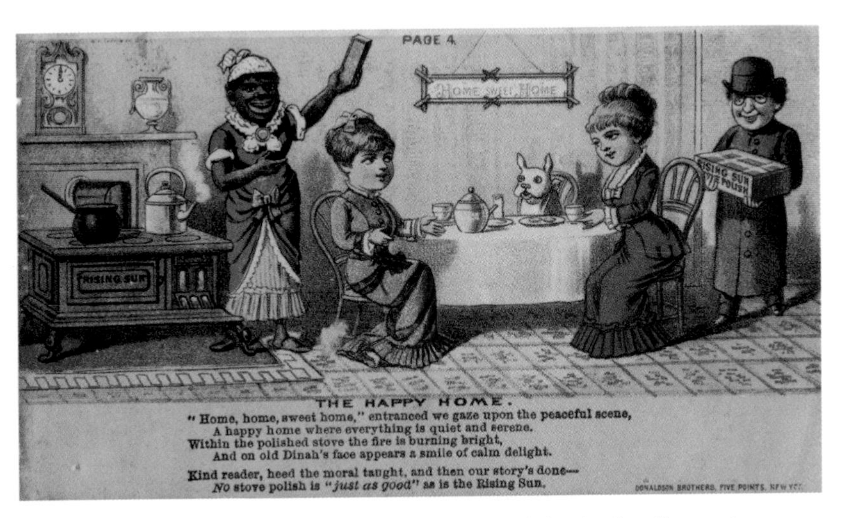

Plate 6. Rising Sun Stove Polish, "The Happy Home" (author's collection)

Plate 7. Rising Sun Stove Polish, "No Dinner?" (Courtesy American Antiquarian Society)

Plate 8. Clarence Brooks and Co., "The Scorner in the Corner Will Reply" (author's collection)

Plate 9. Clarence Brooks and Co., "I Hang Upon De Honey Ob Dem Lips" (author's collection)

Plate 10. S. H. Barrett & Co., Bandit King Co., "Fred Lyons and His Donkey" (author's collection)

Plate 11. Libby, McNeill & Libby's Cooked Canned Beef, "Othello, Act 2d, Sc. 3d." (author's collection)

Plate 12. Kerr and Co., "Kerr's Cotton Takes the Cake" (author's collection)

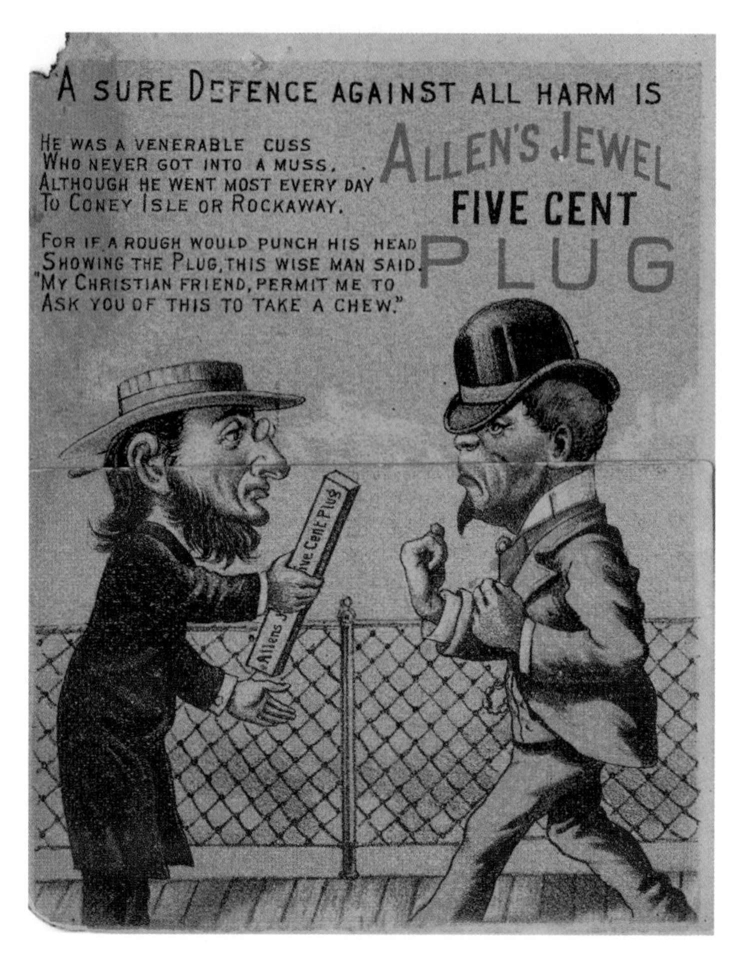

Plate 13. Allen's Jewel Five Cent Plug, folded metamorphic card (author's collection)

Plate 14. Allen's Jewel Five Cent Plug, unfolded metamorphic card (author's collection)

Plate 15. Merrick's Thread, "Dis Cotton Am Not Gwine To Break" (author's collection)

Plate 16. Libby, McNeill & Libby's Cooked Corned Beef, "John Ate the Delicious Meat . . ." (Courtesy American Antiquarian Society)

Plate 17. Paragon Dried Beef, "To Cure the Chinese Famine" (Courtesy American Antiquarian Society)

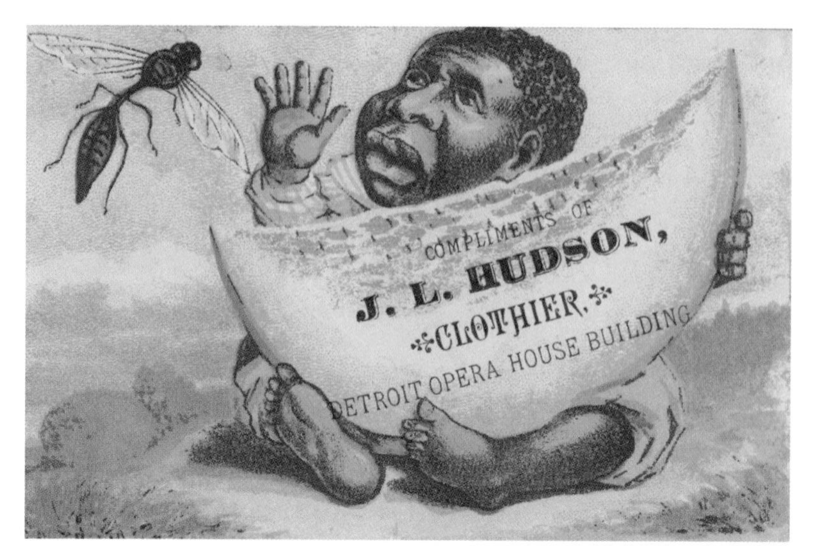

Plate 18. J. L. Hudson, Clothier, "Watermelon Baby and Wasp" (author's collection)

Plate 19. Merrick Thread, "Fooled Dis Tim Cully" (author's collection)

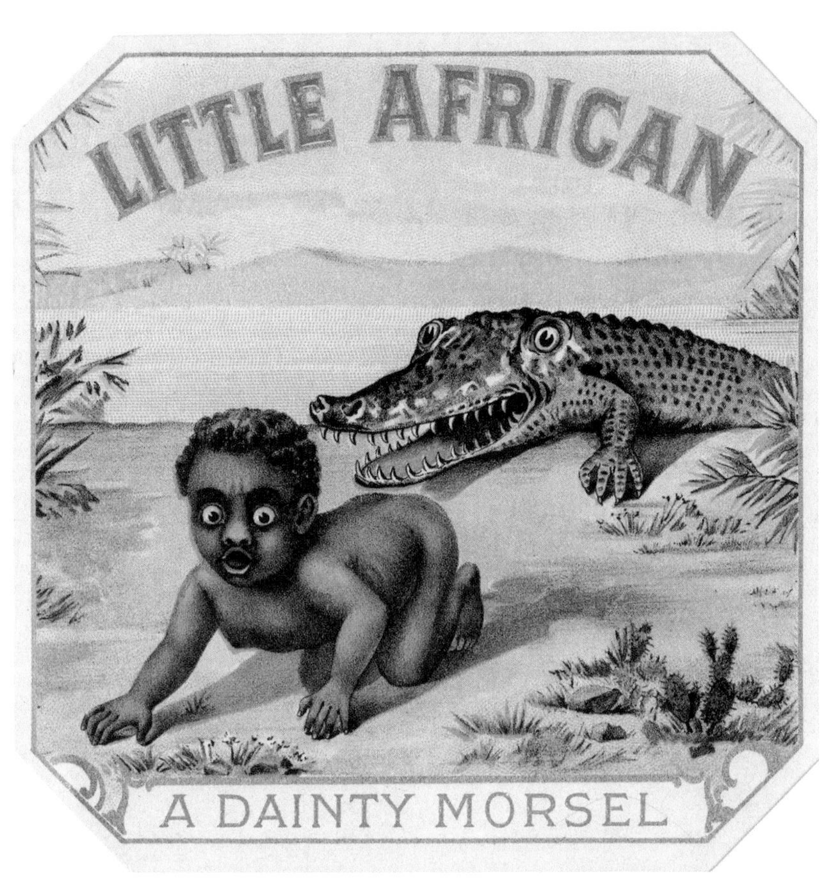

Plate 20. Little African, "A Dainty Morsel" (author's collection)

Plate 21. Sanford's Ginger (author's collection)

Plate 22. Lilliputian Bazaar (author's collection)

Plate 23. The Alden Fruit Vinegar (Courtesy American Antiquarian Society)

Plate 24. Fairbanks Rock Cordials

CLAY & RICHMOND. BUFFALO, N.Y.
" I Golly, I reckon dis OYSTER STEW is come from Race Brudders."

Plate 25. Race Brudder Oyster House (Advertising Ephemera Collection, Baker Library Historical Collections, Harvard Business School)

PAY HERE
CLAY & RICHMOND, BUFFALO N.Y.
"My pile is low, but I shall never be happy, I know, until I eat some OYSTERS at Race Bros."

Plate 26. Race Bros Oyster House (Advertising Ephemera Collection, Baker Library Historical Collections, Harvard Business School)

Plate 27. Dandy Jim (Courtesy Duke University Advertising Archives)

Plate 28. Atmure's Mince Pies (Courtesy American Antiquarian Society)

Plate 29. Ayer's Cathartic Pills (author's collection)

Plate 30. Candy Cane Seesaw, Ketterlinus Printers, Philadelphia

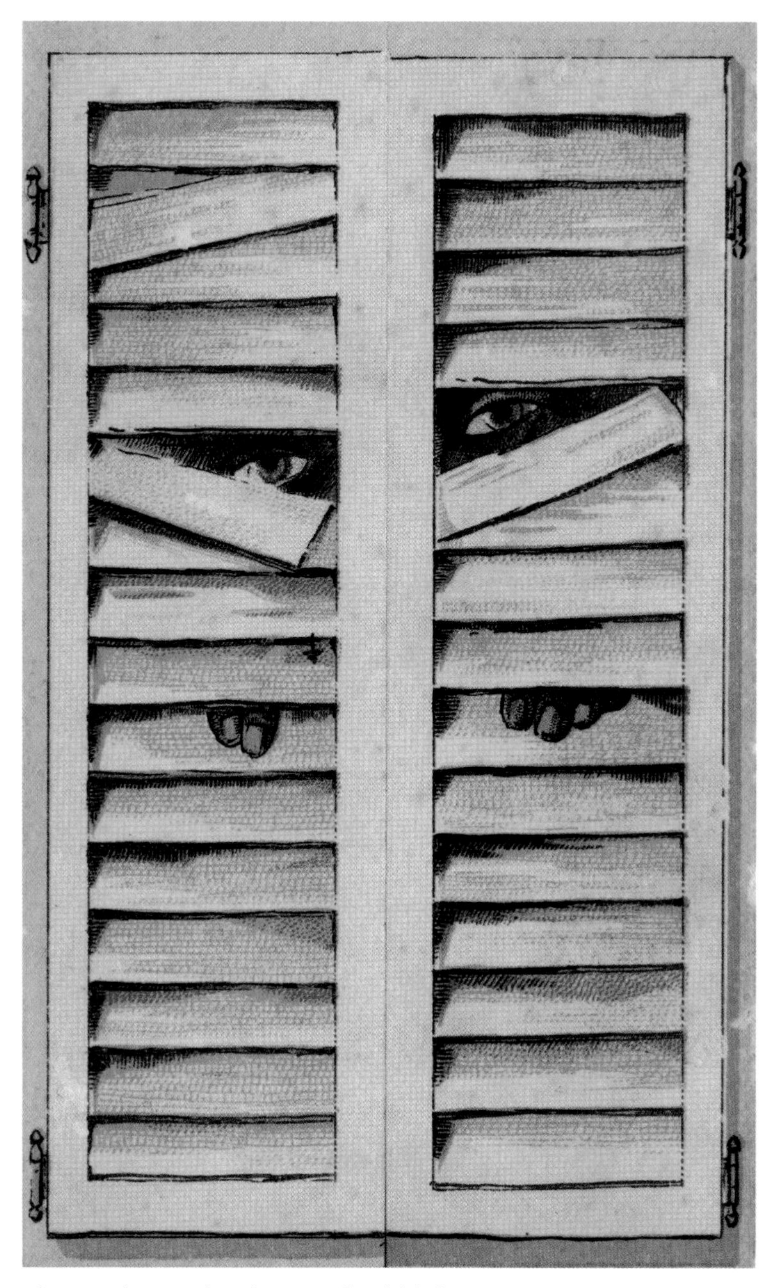

Plate 31. Chase and Sanborn Coffee, folded metamorphic card (Courtesy American Antiquarian Society)

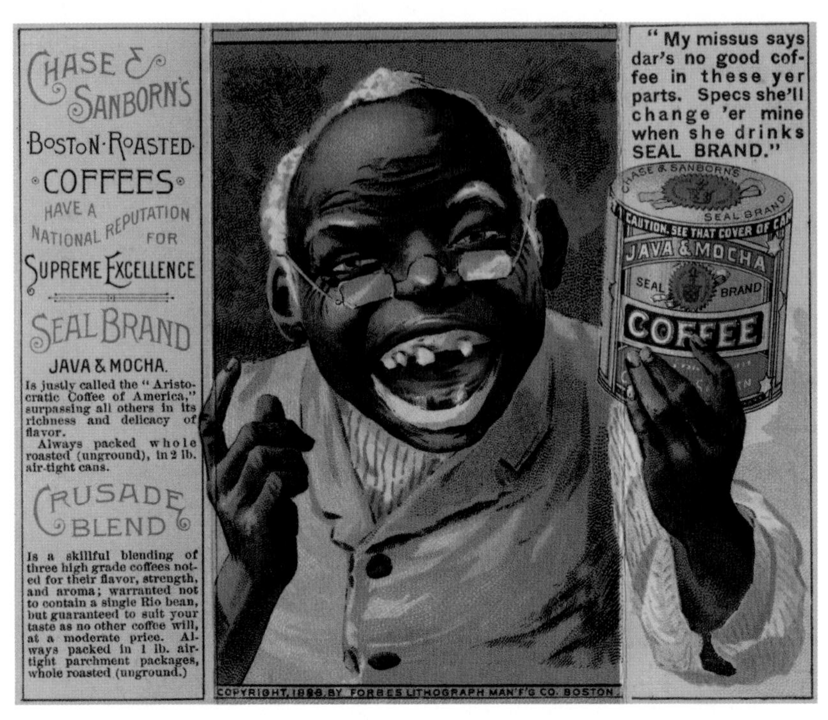

Plate 32. Chase and Sanborn Coffee, unfolded metamorphic card (Courtesy American Antiquarian Society)

Plate 33. Chase and Sanborn white man seersucker folded metamorphic card (Courtesy American Antiquarian Society)

Plate 34. Chase and Sanborn black man seersucker unfolded metamorphic card (Courtesy American Antiquarian Society)

Plate 35. St. Louis Beef Canning Co.: "My Friends! De Candidate dat eats dis yer beef . . ." (Courtesy Ben Crane, Trading Card Place)

Plate 36. Boston Codfish Balls (Courtesy Ben Crane, Trading Card Place)

Plate 37. Magnolia Hams, "What's De Use Talking 'Bout Dem 'Mendments," recto (Courtesy American Antiquarian Society)

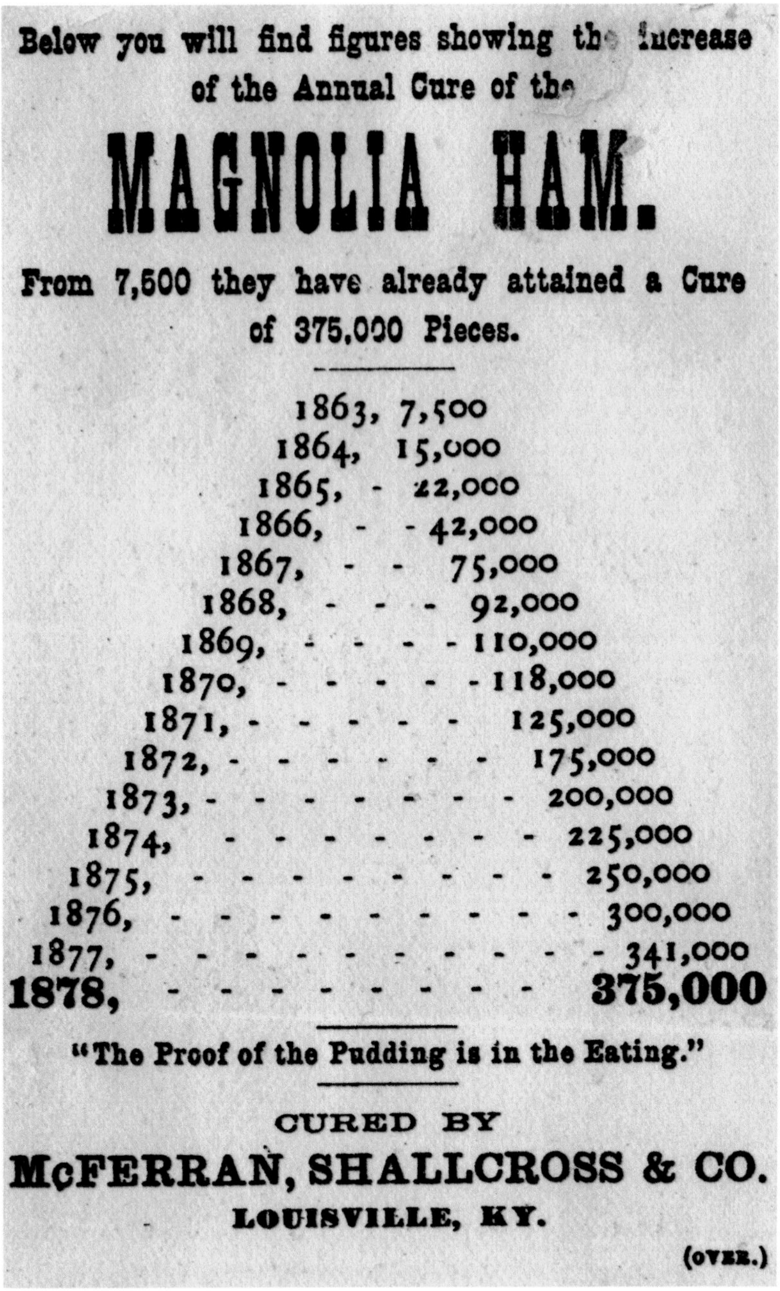

Below you will find figures showing the increase of the Annual Cure of the

MAGNOLIA HAM.

From 7,500 they have already attained a Cure of 375,000 Pieces.

1863, 7,500
1864, 15,000
1865, 22,000
1866, 42,000
1867, 75,000
1868, 92,000
1869, 110,000
1870, 118,000
1871, 125,000
1872, 175,000
1873, 200,000
1874, 225,000
1875, 250,000
1876, 300,000
1877, 341,000
1878, 375,000

"The Proof of the Pudding is in the Eating."

CURED BY

McFERRAN, SHALLCROSS & CO.

LOUISVILLE, KY.

(OVER.)

Plate 38. Magnolia Hams, "What's De Use Talking 'Bout Dem 'Mendments," verso (Courtesy American Antiquarian Society)

> with beans and mushroom stuffed artichokes. Then came *Terrapin en casserole à la Maryland*, some *sorbet* to clear the palate followed by the "Roast" course, canvas-back ducks and quail. For dessert, or rather desserts, there was *timbale Madison*, followed by an array of ice creams, whipped creams, jellied dishes, banana mousse, and the elaborate confectionary constructions so beloved by the French pastry chefs of the day, made to be a feast for the eye, rather than the palate. Fruit and *petits fours* were then placed on the table while coffee and liqueurs were served. With the exception of the canvas-backed duck, all the foods were prepared in a distinctly French fashion and labeled in French.[5]

Compare this with another political banquet, which Hawthorne imagines, in *The House of the Seven Gables*, in 1851, for Judge Pyncheon:

> Nothing in the way of French cookery, but an excellent dinner nevertheless. Real turtle, we understand, and salmon tautog, canvas backs, pig, English mutton, good roast beef or dainties of that serious kind fit for substantial country gentlemen as these honorable persons mostly are. The delicacies of the season in short and flavored by a brand of old Madeira which has been the pride of many seasons.[6]

The emphasis, in Hawthorne, is on a luxuriance of flesh, its manner of cooking subservient to its use—honest, seasonal food. On the other hand, the emphasis in the Delmonico banquet for Scott is on the taken-for-granted access to vast varieties of food and the decadence of its presentation, even down to the resplendent desserts that are hardly meant for eating at all.

To frame this shift another way: between roughly the 1840s and the 1870s the bourgeois descendants of the Puritans ate their food in an uneasy compromise between the scope afforded by their wealth and the morality expressed in Graham's temperance pamphlets. The denizens of the Gilded Age, by contrast, ate their food under the auspices of what one of their sharpest observers, Thorstein Veblen, called conspicuous consumption.[7] These shifts were paralleled by an equally dramatic increase in visual representations of consumption. By the end of the nineteenth century the nation was awash in various forms of advertising, including trade cards, magazine advertising, billboards, show cards, pamphlets, and traveling medicine shows. Just as transportation technology revolutionized what was eaten where, and what markets farmers, dairymen, or fishermen were producing for, the revolution in media was integral to the consumer phantasmagoria of the Gilded Age—the beginning of the unending barrage of visual stimuli that we now take for granted.

Although the argument here is a direct continuation of the previous discussions, my sources in this chapter are something of a departure from the rest of the book. On the surface at least, we will leave the textual testimony of fiction and nonfiction and turn to the new medium of chromolithographic advertising. Our earlier texts, as seen, abounded with visual references to a popular culture of image and performance. In turn, many of the images that we will turn to now are "texts" of their own and contain new forms of literature, such the advertising poem and the customer testimonial.[8] This chapter, however, is centered on a visual medium that I argue is relatively undertheorized.

Given this departure and given the general lack of discussion of reading methodologies for these cards in the critical and historical literature, in the first section of this chapter I defer my concern with food, eating, and race and explore the particular history of chromolithographic, or multicolor print, advertising—an admittedly long detour—in order to set the scene for what follows. In the second section I look at the trade card's connection to the black and white theater in the late nineteenth century, both with regard to its spectacular and narrative logics and in order to think through the identificatory frameworks through which these cards interpellate their viewer. In the third section I then return to my larger argument about orality, race, and embodiment, revisiting and developing our earlier inquiries into eating as a performative and social act. Building on the fundamentally theatrical modes of identification that I read in these cards, we will see how eating, and therefore the mouth, remains a site of importance in the consumer phantasmagoria of the late nineteenth century. Here consumer desire is cross-racial, borrowing from the tradition of racial impersonation, and intraracial, borrowing from the black theater and public sphere. The black mouth continues to serve as a proxy for the white mouth, for white *feeling*, but it also metonymizes the presence of the black consuming public, as it navigates the consumer phantasmagoria of the period, employing spectacular moments of visibility to become opaque—solid, in other words, present and real—in the intersubjective dialectic, the see-saw cathexis, between white power and black hunger.

The Archive and the Exuberance of Racist Affect

It is almost impossible to know how many trade cards were produced, though one scholar estimates that across the period of their production—roughly the 1870s through 1906, when the Food and Drug Act was passed partly in repressive response to the false claims perpetrated in patent remedy advertising—there were approximately "30,000 basic stock images in trade cards alone, each typically varied with each reprinting, resulting in many multiples of that number [in circulation]."[9] The term *chromolithographic* refers to the printing process whereby several stone slabs, each using a different color, are used to produce a multicolored effect; previous printing processes had limited lithographs—and advertisements—to single-color images. Trade cards, small rectangular cards meant to be handed out in grocery stores or included in product packaging, were designed by a wide variety of manufacturers, advertising everything from seeds to soap, and were produced by printers in every region of the nation and then carried by "drummers," or traveling salesmen. Indeed, trade cards were part of a general onslaught in advertising media in the period that also included posters, calendars, pamphlets, and show cards. Show cards, such as the one pictured in plate 5, were chromolithographic images mounted on boards and meant to be featured either on the sidewalk, on counters, or in store windows. Consumers often organized trade cards into albums, which were then passed down through families. Trade cards have survived in and out of albums, though albums were and are dismantled and sold individually. In the past 130 years of their existence trade cards, in other words, have been in constant motion across the country and between collectors.

As an early form of advertising, trade cards emerged in the late 1860s, when chromolithography became cheap and relatively easy to produce on both the small and large scale. Slipped into shopping bags at grocery stores across the country, included in product packaging, and, most importantly, featured at the 1876 and 1893 expositions,[10] the brightly colored imagery paired, as Jackson Lears has written, commercial products with "fables of abundance," including exotic and Orientalist imagery, scenes of idyllic domestic spaces, representations of mother goddesses, and other stereotypes of femininity, fecundity, and childhood.[11]

The social and emotional tensions that lie coiled in these images metonymize political agency in the conjoined tropes of commodity consumption, laughter, and ingestion. Their explosive energy, in part represented by the giddy use of color in the new printing technology and in part encapsulated in the action that these cards represent, demonstrates the aesthetic and political deployment of what Daphne Brooks, borrowing from Brecht, has called the "dissonantly enlightened performance" of "Afro-alienation." What Brooks also calls "too-muchness" produces moments of spectacular visibility that exceed the advertisers' intended and literal meanings.[12] In the era of conspicuous consumption the "too-muchness" of the black and Asian bodies as represented in these trade cards is of key importance. The affective excess and semiotic overload of these images encode the use of disgust to facilitate and accompany the white bourgeois consumer's disavowal *and* enjoyment of commodity pleasure.

Here I am understanding disgust as the form of pleasure-in-excess that often accompanies comedy.[13] Disgust here is married not only to the disavowal of big affect—joy, pain, desire, pleasure—away from the white, Protestant, middle-class body and onto black, Asian, and ethnic white bodies; it is also, seemingly inversely, married to envy and desire. Disgust thus is born of the everyday public encounter with bodies that seem to enjoy what whiteness is meant to disavow.

What we see in these cards is an explosive, outward-reaching physicality that registers the spectacular and sensory presence of nonwhites—in particular black subjects—in the spaces of the white urban public sphere, a presence no doubt kinesthetically shocking and politically threatening to the white and middle-class majorities, as attested to by the many violent and repressive responses to emancipation in the South and black migration to the North. The result is an affect that is unfamiliar to the contemporary consumer of advertising: it is one of shock as well as pleasure, disgust as well as desire. At the same time, these images often depict beauty, affection, and even tenderness, reflecting the erotic and intimate side of Eric Lott's foundational articulation of the simultaneity of love and theft.[14]

The theme of excess further relates to my research methodology in this chapter. With our liberal instinct to avert one's gaze from the intensely raced and exuberantly racist affect of these images, my guess is that at least some of those cards that our contemporary culture would deem as most offensive have been suppressed or destroyed; thus, we have no way of knowing the scale of the distribution of these images relative to what remains in archives and collections. Alongside our contemporary, potentially distorted view of the full extent of these cards, scholars have too often ignored these images. However, the lack of attention to these images seems worth pausing over. I was first drawn to think about this problem in the archives of Harvard University's Baker Business Library. One afternoon, while searching through the computer index of trade card images, the archivist whispered to me, sotto voce, that many of the images of nonwhites were probably missing because they had been destroyed for being overly negative and degrading.[15] The archivist's whisper remained in my ear as I wrote and researched this chapter, reminding me that the archive, and in particular the archive attached to minority presence in the Americas, is always either incomplete or inconsistent, always subject to the control and interests of its organizer and institutional location. As Roderigo Lazo writes, "control of the archive has epistemological and political ramifications."[16]

Not all trade cards are born equal, nor do they survive in the same ways. The archivist's whisper points us to the thorny question of what kinds of trade cards survived across the twentieth century, marked as it was by the shifting ideologies of race and rights, never mind market-related shifts in popular aesthetics, taste, and collecting practices. I raise this incident not only to demonstrate that we have no way of knowing how many of these images have been destroyed but to insist that against the liberal tendency to look away from racism we *must* look at these images—classic examples of racial kitsch—not only to render their historical weight visible and material but also to recognize both sides of their terrible ambivalence, their often loving and intimate as well as deeply hateful depictions of the copresence of whites and nonwhites in the urban spaces of the late nineteenth century.[17] It is, after all, only by looking and listening, by paying close attention to these cards through and in the strangeness of our historical distance from them, that we can begin to hear their ambiguities.

With this in mind I have roamed far to bring these images together, drawing my evidence in this chapter from a variety of sources, including collections at the Baker Library, the American Antiquarian Society, and the Duke University Advertising Archives. I am also drawing on ten years of attention to contemporary trade card collecting activities on two sites, eBay and the Trade Card Place, where thousands of trade cards circulate in much the same manner as they did in their original period: as objects of desire in and of themselves, circulating nationally and traded between collectors. These are artifacts that have outlived and surpassed their intended function as signifiers of particular commodities to become commodities in their own right, and as such, their value is subject to the consumer-driven logic of auction sites as well as to what Lazo has marked as the nation-building logic of archival institutions.[18]

From all these sources I have selected cards that bring together themes of racial difference with images of orality and eating; in other words I have created my own archive. Where possible I have made note of the copyright dates on each of these cards: however, the year of origin of a large majority of these cards can only be estimated from internal clues, as they are not dated. While I have selected images that address the themes that are relevant to this chapter, namely, images of (mostly) black and Asian consumers, it is also important to note that the majority of trade cards I have surveyed—I estimate about 90 percent—are made up of images of white children or white women. The general agreement among historians that most advertising was directed at white women and children seems to be borne out by the fact that most trade card scrapbooks in archives have been inherited from middle-class white women, the Bella Landauer collection at the New York Public Library being a prime example.[19]

Trade Card Histories: The Drama of Domesticity and the Spectacle of Black Theatricality

While cards were often marketed to white girls, as Ellen Gruber Garvey documents, advertisers counted on those girls becoming adult consumers and, further, hoped that their mothers would pick up the cards that children would leave lying around the house and thereby learn about their products.[20] Among young white girls collecting and trading these trade cards was a fashion parallel to the male craze for collecting stamps or baseball cards. Trade card manufacturers produced and marketed trade card albums and thematically organized trade card sets, and girls arranged them into individualized collections. Plate 1, for instance, shows a little girl pasting trade cards—here called "fancy cards"—into an album while her family looks on; a bottle of Chase's Glue floats in the foreground, equal in size to the girl and indicative of the extent to which these cards stuck in the country's booming consumer culture.

Although a product of a public commodity culture, trade cards were meant to be enjoyed in the home. As shown in plate 1, in which the girl is the central actor in the drama of commodity consumption, girls were a targeted demographic, but they were also clearly seen as a way to reach the entire family: in the picture the entire family is involved, from the mother who oversees the activity to the elder son who draws the advertising text on a curtain.[21] Only the father seems to be outside the collecting activity, though he nonetheless uses the product to fix a chair, an apparently acceptable use of patriarchal time. Chase's Glue does indeed cement everything, including the heteronormative family and its ordered gender roles.

Over the past two decades four separate strains of scholarship and critical commentary have dealt with these images: The first is African American and Asian American history, both of which tend to document the history of racist images as signs of the nation's fraught racial politics.[22] The second is feminist work; when images of nonwhites are explored here, it is almost solely with regard to what they meant in shaping white women as the ideal consumers of the late nineteenth century, what Ellen Gruber Garvey and Marilyn Mehaffy call "consumer citizens."[23] Another school of feminist work—namely, that of Anne McClintock and more recently Lori Merish—looks at the imperial intertexts for advertising, demonstrating that nineteenth-century commodity culture was underpinned by the semiotics and racial science of empire.[24] The final area of scholarship is business history, which focuses on printing and lithography houses and the growth of professional adverting in the period.[25]

Significantly, none of these strands of scholarship has examined these cards in relation to what I see as two major, overlapping, intertexts for this advertising: first, the nineteenth-century theater and its foundational configurations of gender, ethnicity, and race and, second, the increasingly interracial and the interethnic urban public spheres of the late nineteenth century. As such, except in those cases where explicitly raced images are noted and then dismissed as offensive, most of these studies spend little time considering images of nonwhites in trade card advertising as anything other than figments of an aggressive white racial imaginary.

There is, perhaps, another reading available to us. In reading these trade cards I am drawn to the repetition of themes across a wide variety of cards—and between collections—a repetition that testifies to the robust, and varied, identifications between eating and selfhood. The cards, created for countless companies, designed and produced by countless individuals, and distributed around the country, existed (and prospered) without any of the formal elements of marketing that we now take for granted—consumer surveys, coordination between advertisement and sales, specialists in the design of advertising, and so on. Success, therefore, required that the creators of trade cards trusted in the commonalities they shared with their targeted demographics. Their operating assumptions about what was and was not acceptable, alluring, or attention grabbing is revealed in the visual strategies and themes embedded in the cards and particularly in the remarkable repetition of themes. Over those strategies brooded a system of choreographed ethnic and racial character types largely borrowed from the late nineteenth-century theater, where, as historians have shown, white, nonwhite, and ethnic demographics constituted their own public spheres; within those dramatic spaces broad ethnic humor and various forms of dialect and cross-racial impersonation were the norm.[26] These cards, in other words, utilized a convenient and common shorthand for discussing the racial and ethnic other, which has particular consequences for our understanding of the interconnections between eating, race, and, now, performance.

To be clear, the traditional reading, which ties trade card advertising to the racist imaginary of the late nineteenth century, is not entirely out of sync with my thesis about the theater. For instance, with regard to popular white theater no production could have been more popular in the period than Gilbert and Sullivan operetta *The Mikado*, which played across the country and was immediately adapted and parodied in the black and Irish theater.[27] The play also appeared in advertising: plate 2, for instance, depicts three white women holding corsets in costumes alluding to the "geishas" that appear as characters in the operetta. The figures stand underneath Japanese writing in the left-hand corner, while under each figure we get their stage names: Pitti Sing, Yum Yum, and Peep Bo. Already here we see the link between theater, racial impersonation, and commodity consumption: to buy one of the wonderfully named Freud's corsets, the card implies, is to become a different person.[28]

As we saw earlier, the inchoate antebellum analogies between food and race had become, by the end of the Reconstruction period, a more organized shorthand for racial difference. Just as Louisa May Alcott compared the Asian character Fun See in *Eight Cousins* to a teapot, so here does the character of Yum-Yum in *The Mikado* take on a nickname associated with ingestion and the promise of deliciousness.[29] The three girls hold the corsets in various states of tightening, as though they were proffered to the customer who wants to try them on. Thus, the visual code of the image is "incomplete," waiting for the consumer's own body to fill it out. While Yum-Yum, the central figure, plays on the idea of racial difference as both sexual and edible, the figures support the construction of middle-class white womanhood through the association with the Orient as both a site of female repression, in the form of binding—whether foot or torso—and as the source, as we saw with Rose Campbell, of exotic self-adornment. This identificatory relationship with Japan was no doubt also enabled by the passage of the Chinese Exclusion Act, which allowed for increased Japanese immigration, until the 1907 "Gentlemen's Agreement" between the United States and Japan stopped Japanese immigration entirely, barring wives.[30]

Producers of trade cards, as mentioned earlier, assumed a shared text between themselves and the consumer. These cards were thus part of a public discourse, a cultural conversation that includes what we now understand as publicity; in fact, one of the many uses of trade cards was as publicity for the theater. The circulation of these cards was open and nondiscriminatory: the place in which advertising circulated was in the street or as something given by a shop or something displayed in a window. But the goal of these cards, like all advertising, was to create a desire for the advertised commodity. Unlike the theater, these products were primarily consumed at home; nevertheless, theatricality was a central modality through which advertisers and printers imagined a conversation with their prospective buyers. Thus, one of the great themes in the rapid advance of advertising's visual vocabulary was a dream image of the domestic drama—an image in which the product was essential and into which the viewer (and consumer) of that product could be assimilated.

A card series for Rising Sun Stove Polish nicely demonstrates this tying of theatrical convention to the internal space of the home. Plates 3–6, showing images that are printed on the back and front of two cards, detail the domestic trials of a Mrs. Smith, an ambiguously classed white woman who is tricked into buying the wrong stove polish by a crooked "shopman." The wrong stove polish results in a stove that will not work, an unhappy black maid, a stressed-out dog, and the imminent arrival of a husband who will find no dinner ready.

In plate 5, the third image, Mrs. Smith takes "a little ramble" with her friend Mrs. Jenkins "and at a splendid chromo in a window took a look." The "splendid chromo" is a large show card in the shop window depicting a happy woman in a ball gown enjoying the benefits of Rising Sun Stove Polish. After Mrs. Smith buys the polish domestic order is restored; the final card reads,

> "Home, home, sweet home," entranced we gaze upon the peaceful
> scene
> A happy home where everything is quiet and serene
> Within the polished stove the fire is burning bright
> And on old Dinah's face appears a smile of calm delight.

The reader will be unsurprised, at this point in the book, to see that the stove and the fireplace—the nostalgic image of the hearth and the reality of the stove—figure prominently in the dream of "home, sweet home." It is no surprise, too, that the ties that bind in this ideal domestic economy—in particular the requisite black domestic—are "sweet." But far from the reality of the early American/early nineteenth-century hearth, the card offers a dual conception of the new food culture: it continues to anchor the stove to the foundations of daily domestic order but at the same time locates the domestic sphere in a public commodity chain by tracing the consumer's steps between the place of purchase and the place of consumption.

Plate 5 is also interesting because it sets up the kind of modern visual schema on which advertising culture and ultimately film, in particular women's films, were to rest for the next century and beyond. Mrs. Smith is saved by becoming the *flâneuse*, the woman strolling on the boulevard, in the arcades, or in the department store.[31] The trade card series, just like the "splendid chromo" that Mrs. Smith sees within the trade card, attempts to induce identification with both the advertisement and the shop window, which reflect back to Mrs. Smith the idealized and imagined future emanating from the purchase of the pictured commodity.[32] This iconography is analogous to the nineteenth-century parlor game of *tableaux vivants*, in which guests and family members posed in famous literary or artistic scenes, forming the basis for what Roland Marchand calls "social tableaux," which provided "customers with a scene into which they could comfortably and pleasurably place themselves . . . as they aspired to be, rather than as they 'really were.'"[33] As the show card in the window of plate 4 demonstrates, the female consumer pictured in the window is far more elaborately (though scantily) dressed and relaxed than Mrs. Smith is: the successful use of Rising Sun Stove Polish makes her into a lady of leisure. The visual schema of the card series thus sets up a doubled or mirrored aspirational relation in which the card holder desires to be Mrs. Smith, who in turn desires to be the woman in the show card: Mrs. Smith, it might be said, models the trade card's ideal identificatory schema. On the other hand, the presence of the stove near the dining table renders the Smiths' outside the middle class, making the scene recognizable as an apartment or tenement.

While the foregoing is sufficient for a first level of analysis, close attention to this scene of commodity drama shows that there are more figures in this commodity drama than simply Mrs. Smith and her wise friend. Although the crucial interaction takes place between the two white women, Dinah the black cook appears in the second and fourth frame and in the happy ending reappears in far more elaborate clothing than her earlier work uniform. The bowler-hat-wearing man in the right of the picture, on the other hand, appears in every frame, though his presence is never explained: Is he Mr. Smith? Is he the sales representative for Rising Sun? Is he a proxy for the male spectator? Why in the final scene does he appear bearing a case of stove polish? In each of their appearances Dinah and the bowler-hatted man echo the emotional tone of each scene: distress or jubilation. So too does the dog, whose worried face in the crisis scene is rewarded in the final card with a seat at the dinner table and a bib tied around his neck.[34] The card is thus much more complicated than it seems at first look. Each of these figures partakes in the narrative as a spectator in, and mirror of, the central story, and each also seems to have his or her own minor, if not fully explicated, narrative. That is, Mrs. Smith has a supporting cast, all of whom play a part in making the domestic drama of commodity consumption into a public performance.

Most trade card images—the ones typically reproduced in contemporary greeting cards and calendars, depicting snowy Victorian Christmas tableaux or happy tobogganing scenes, for instance—represent idealized white women and children, which reflected back to the consumer her own idealized—and often, as in plate 5, eroticized—image. Idealized white femininity, as we have seen elsewhere, is an easy draw for readers and viewers alike; it is no surprise that the perfect woman (and her perfect children) are a staple of these cards. But what is surprising is how far these cards stray from the homogeneous white woman. Looking at a broader selection of these cards, it is clear that the newly available color printing technologies also provided a base for aesthetic experiments that allowed advertisers, printers, and artists to compete with each other in devising ever more distinct and identifiable images.[35] One new possibility was the detailed portrayal of ethnic and phenotypic difference—for instance, the ability to mark a character as Irish by making her hair bright orange. In an anxious post–Civil War world, portraying ethnic or racial difference thus became a central strategy in the mounting competition between manufacturers and service purveyors to attract and secure consumer desire.

The Gilded Age tellingly overlaps with the foundations of the Jim Crow regime, laid after the Republican Party officially abandoned the project of Reconstruction in 1877. Though the country grew gilded, the savagery of lynching became symbolic of the many forms of violence used to erase the constitutional gains of emancipation and to concretize the power of a white elite.[36] In 1882 Congress passed an act that sought to close off Chinese immigration to the United States. In the 1883 *Dred Scott* case the Supreme Court abrogated the 1875 Civil Rights Act that had mandated equal rights for all races in the public and civic sphere, opening the door to segregation throughout the country. Similar stories abound about other racial and ethnic groups during this period, which saw the sudden strengthening of a racist and race-based rhetoric among the exclusively white and mostly Anglo-Saxon governing class.

It is thus remarkable that, at the same time, the visual culture of Gilded Age consumption so often represents and envisions the nonwhite and the non-WASP body. If we rest on the classic story about white women, commodity consumption, and spectatorship in the nineteenth century, we run into cards that exceed or refuse a racially one-dimensional analysis. The card in plate 7, for example, also for Rising Sun Stove Polish, invokes a common theme in trade cards that advertise stove blacking, which, due to the fact that it was black, drew invariably reductive and objectifying connections between it and African American skin.[37]

In this card the theatricality of the scene is far more apparent: while the stage blocking and narrative form in this two-part card seems to invoke theatrical spectacle staged on what looks like baseboards, the drama, resolved with the happy meal, brings the high energy of a skit into the domestic space. The stove here makes a reappearance as a signifier, and indeed a character, in the skit; just as in other stove-blacking advertisements, the stove and the patriarch of the home seem to exist in a tension that the wife represents through her gestures and mood. However, in the two halves of plate 7, which are the recto and verso of the same pamphlet-like card, there is no white managerial presence. This poses the question of how, exactly, the spectator was "invited" into a scene that contains the fluid, transformative possibilities of kitchen and food humor that we found in earlier literature. That is, while transformation—here of the wife's mood and the tone of domestic life—is clearly promised by the commodity—and magic is, of course, the promise of the commodity fetish—neither class nor race nor even, despite the presence of the cat, the line between animal and human can be breached here. Nor does the broad humor invite easy identification on the part of the consumer; rather, the invocation of violence, as the wife threatens the husband with the defective stove blacking, would seem to invite the consumer's counteridentification.

The class orientation of the scene, signified as in the earlier Rising Stove series by the presence of the stove near the dining space, also confuses an easy reading of the narrative: for a population emigrating from rural cabin life a merged dining-cooking space would mean something very different, without, perhaps, erasing the reductive comedic representation. Sociologist Carl Kelsey, in a 1905 essay titled "The Causes of Negro Emigration," noted, "In many cabins of Virginia the one-roomed cabin has gradually disappeared, the stove has replaced the fireplace, and the table no longer sets forth corn-bread and pork. New wants have arisen."[38] Thus, while the dialect humor may be derogatory, the appearance of the stove here is an indicator both of geographic mobility and of rising social mobility; to a newly urban black spectator it might invite, perhaps on a very limited level, an aspirational relationship to the scene of the domestic drama and the commodities it depicts.

Once we look at these cards from the point of view of vaudeville and theater, it seems surprising that this aspect has been overlooked. Many of these trade card representations are manifestly borrowed from the skit and gag and minstrel formulas that, as Tom Gunning has suggested, ultimately governed early nonnarrative silent film, suggesting that we might treat the trade card as a bridging medium between the two forms.[39] Indeed, although there has been a great deal of literature linking the store window, advertising, and early film, scholars of nineteenth-century visuality have largely ignored trade cards, despite the fact that the early years of vaudeville and the latter years of minstrel theater coincided with the rise of film, the trade card, and the department store alike.[40] Advertisers and printers, by inscribing the consumer's gaze into their pictures in terms of the spectacle of nineteenth-century popular theater, created a form within which the images could be freed from more traditional or high-cultural iconographies; instead, their images could become desiring, imaginative, and geared toward broader forms of humor. Similar strategies were already at play in the larger market: printers and advertisers likely also had an eye on the theatrical advertising techniques of nostrum sellers, whose traveling shows borrowed from and included "banjo tunes and blackface capers stolen from the minstrel show" as well as "occasional performances of popular melodrama."[41]

If we consider the clear borrowing of theatrical tropes in trade card advertising, as well as the centrality of racial impersonation to the theater in nineteenth-century America, it seems clear that advertisers counted on a model of white racial embodiment that had grown simultaneously more mobile and more motile across the century. In order to attract the consumer desire of their (mostly) female audience, advertisers invited women to project themselves into the tableaux of their products. Advertisers, in other words, relied on the imaginations of these women and their ability (and desire) to see themselves, literally, in other skins. White middle-class girls and women, as an important consuming demographic and the target of these trade cards, thus seem to have been familiar with these projectile models of embodiment, just like the white men who enjoyed and participated in blackface spectacle starting in the antebellum period. We should not be surprised to know that by midcentury middle-class women were increasingly attending theater, usually under the guise of a morally improving matinee.[42] What these cards show us, then, is that late nineteenth-century trade card advertising is implicitly raced; one of the central functions of this racing, in turn, is to project white consumer desire into the body of the nonwhite other. In a culture not entirely at home with the excesses of the Gilded Age the rationale of that projection had a certain logic, as it might function to disavow consumer desire as a phenomenon experienced by white women. At the same time, that relationship was built on the obvious desire to appropriate those bodies and their affiliated excesses for themselves.

And yet, as I am arguing, this reading is not adequate to the historical fact of the presence of emancipated men and women in the urban arenas of the period. By the late nineteenth century black and immigrant consumers were increasingly visible, as was a severely delimited but nonetheless burgeoning black public sphere; most centrally, black children were also collectors of trade cards and trade card albums.[43] That public sphere asserted itself in black neighborhoods and through a wide and growing number of cultural manifestations, including black theater and its audiences, black newspapers, and journalism, as well as the coeval emergence of early film and urban black modernity in the 1890s, in which the cinema, as Jacqueline Najuma Stewart tells us, served as a "contested discursive and physical space in which migrating Black public spheres were constructed and interpreted, empowered and suppressed."[44]

What these trade cards tell us is that the theater in general and, for our purposes, black theater in particular operated as similar spaces of counterpublic formation. For instance, a series of cards printed under the name "Clarence Brooks & Co 'Fine Coach, Railway and Piano Forte Varnishes'" shows the black theater, depicting debates and performances that took place on stage and in front of black audiences. The card in plate 8 shows a public debate staged between black participants and for a black audience; the mediator exclaims, without a hint of the standard false black vernacular: "The Scorner in the Corner Will Reply." The audience is well dressed and includes members of both genders; glasses on some of the audience members lend the spectacle an intellectual air. The card in plate 9 is even more specifically theatrical, depicting a dramatic performance in which the protagonist has forgotten his lines. A prompter whispers the lines to him from stage left, while a lively audience only pays half a mind to the actors, talking and flirting among themselves and recalling what historians have consistently described as the rowdiness of nineteenth-century audiences. In this reinhabitation of the trope of the black body as food, an appropriation that was to continue across the twentieth century, from Jelly Roll Morton's "Jelly Roll Blues" to Destiny's Child's "Bootylicious," the actor's apparently forgotten line—"I hang upon de honey ob doze lips"—recalls the common troping of the black body as sweet. Here, however, that trope is appropriated in black performance for a black audience, describing the actor's desire for a black woman and, more specifically, honoring her sweet mouth and speech.

Black performers were of course present in the theaters and in the streets across the century, and that presence is registered in trade cards; the card in plate 10 advertises the 1885 appearance of black comedian and musician Fred Lyons, appearing in a production of a play called *The Bandit King*. A *New York Times* review called Lyons a "real colored comedian" who "plays the banjo and sings vociferously."[45] The card in plate 11 may reference blackface performance, but it may also reference the actor Ira Aldridge, whose Shakespearean performances purportedly often diverged into more colloquial and local interpretations, or, more topically, a production of *Othello* produced by Astor Place Company of Colored Tragedians, which was covered in a derogatory article by the *New York Times* in 1884.[46] The quotation on the card, from act 2, scene 1, inserts the can of cooked beef into a speech that Othello makes upon returning from war. The insertion of a vulgar commodity into Shakespeare's play mocks the actor, but it also sutures the culture of commodity consumption to the publicness of theatrical spectatorship. The heterogeneous mixing of kinds is, of course, also the subject of the play.

The lack of a white audience in these cards is key, particularly as a white audience appears in so many other cards that invoke black performance (see plate 12). Daphne Brooks's discussion of Afro-alienation opens up a way into reading these images against the topos of black transparency in the face of white identity. Reading across the transatlantic landscape of these "socially critical" performances, Brooks argues that we might think of these "acts as opaque, as dark points of possibility that create figurative sites for the reconfiguration of black and female bodies on display."[47] She writes,

> In what we may refer to as a "spectacular opacity," this cultural phenomenon emerges at varying times as a product of the performer's will, at other times as a visual obstacle erupting as a result of the hostile spectator's epistemological resistance to reading alternative racial and gender representations. From either standpoint, spectacular opacities contest the "dominative imposition of transparency" systemically willed on to black bodies.[48]

If the idea of opacity helps to enable emancipatory reading and performance strategies, then we must use the same frame for looking at what is generally regarded as racial kitsch. To look *at* these objects is to resist the liberal tendency to look away from or through racist images; instead, we might glimpse them as complex estimations of the presence of people of color in the public sphere, formed not only from the dominant white viewpoint but from a diversity of other counterhegemonic viewpoints as well. With this goal in mind I will resist the temptation to lapse into a conversation about the political valence of this advertising art as either a sign of black presence to be celebrated or a sign of racism to be condemned. As I hope to show, it is both.

The food narrative I followed in the first four chapters concentrated largely in the domestic space, where the production and consumption of food occurred. Yet, as far back as the 1830s, hints of a new regime of food consumption surface in the anxiety of Grahamite movements about "rich and savory" foods, spices and drinks that come into the body of the house from the outside, breaking down its autarky. In the Gilded Age the first forces of the consumer society were released; theater was a major intermediary in producing the images and narratives of this new consumer lifestyle. The theatrically produced spectator is present as a principle of construction in the modeling of consumer desire in the chromolithographic prints we have been looking at. They invite the consumer to imagine that he or she is the subject—the commodity user—of the advertisement, even as they use the stereotypes of comedy to make the commodities they advertise entertaining.

By citing various modes of ethnic and racial impersonation—white performers pretending to be black, black performers performing as black characters, white performers of various ethnicities performing other ethnicities—the world of commodity advertising invited the white consumer to try on—or to consume—new selves. Moreover, the racial ambiguity allowed for by the print genre—in which the viewer is never certain, in the way that a theatrical audience would be, what the original ethnicity of the performer is—allowed for a certain flexibility in imagining who the consumer might be. Despite the overwhelming preponderance of representations of white women in these advertisements, what other trade cards tell us is that we must not assume that consumer is always and only a white consumer. In addition, we must not assume that the white consumer is only identified with racial sameness.

The Other, Eating

Let us now return to the central theme of this book, by investigating a series of cards that represent people eating and consuming. In these cards the mouth becomes a space of interethnic and interracial encounter, part of a symbolic order in which ingestion is metonymic of an active relationship with commodity consumption, politics, and citizenship. To consume and to be consumed gain public political meanings. Additionally, in this unregulated and preprofessional advertising culture the fluid possibilities of eating in the early nineteenth century return in what Jackson Lears, in his landmark study of advertising, defined as carnivalesque imagery of commodity pleasure and physical transformation.[49] Produced at the end of the nineteenth century, these images illuminate the connections between spectatorship, desire, and racial embodiment as they were imagined in the period by printers and advertisers, whose desire to transcend the two-dimensionality of the image and to reach into the spectator's body is encoded in these images, with the purpose of awakening either the appetite or at least some surplus amount of attention. In this generative moment in advertising, a moment in which advertisers were training the consumer's attention span, sensual reactions produced a new kind of consumer—one modeled on the theater spectator rather than on the utilitarian buyer.

By depicting extremes of physical and affective experience—often pleasure but sometimes pain—these advertisements ultimately break down the rigidity within which racial embodiment is typecast, by refracting it through the metalanguage of oral consumption. That is, they stage encounters that show nineteenth-century commodity culture to have been an important sphere in which racialization takes place, mediated on the one hand through the senses and on the other hand through theater. As we will see, in the sphere of commodity consumption the production of race ultimately undoes its own logic: for just as the cards and pamphlets often attach extreme, even socially inappropriate, commodity pleasure to nonwhite bodies, the consistent trope of interracial and interethnic encounter as it happens through orality and consumption simultaneously points to a commodity culture that required this libidinously liberated racial moment as a mediating space between disparate and radically unequal demographics.

In the card pictured in plates 13 and 14 an Irishman and an observant Jew resolve their differences by sharing a plug of chewing tobacco. This advertisement plays out the theme of interethnic conflict, common not only to the urban scene but also to nineteenth-century theater:[50]

> He was a venerable cuss
> Who never got into a muss
> Although he went most every day
> To Coney Isle or Rockaway.
>
> For if a rough would punch his head
> Showing the Plug, this wise man said
> "My Christian friend, permit me to
> ask you of this to take a chew."

The conflict is then resolved with commodity consumption:

> The Savage breast is straightway soothed
> The upraised fist forthwith removed
> The rising storm becomes a calm
> The lion has become a lamb.
>
> MORAL:
> If you'd not fear an ugly mug
> Chew ALLEN'S JEWEL FIVE CENT PLUG.

The mouth here is the site in which a commodity of pure luxury—inasmuch as tobacco contributes no nourishment to the body—becomes the scene in which a discovered American taste can bridge differences of religion and ethnicity and create, in turn, a shared public space and culture.

As we saw earlier, across the nineteenth century the mouth consistently appears as a trope through which racial difference is both figured and resolved. I argue that the double function of the mouth—both in processing food into digestible matter and in producing sense—sutures that space to the domestic and civic production of language, to storytelling, and in particular to the performance and construction of vernacular idioms and identities. In entering into the mixtures of the social world, images of eating symbolize a solidarity that traverses social locations. While chewing tobacco is hardly food, in the Allen's Jewel ad open mouths bridge the conflict between two marginal citizens, the Irishman and the Jew, exclaiming the intimacy that arises when their proximity becomes that of the common enjoyment of a commodity. These are familiar stage figures of the period, as Irishmen and Jews were often represented, and represented each other, through caricatured dialect performance on the vaudeville stage. The stagelike wooden boardwalk on which the men in the ad stand underlines the theatricality of the images, while the metamorphic quality of the card—the fact that it flips open to shift the image from two subjects about to fight to two smiling subjects—points to its prefilmic qualities.[51]

The standard limits in our discussion of Gilded Age consumption, which focus solely on the creation of a normative white, middle-class, female consumer—indeed, one historian of consumption even argues that there are no images of blacks as consumers in the period[52]—eclipses moments in which the consumer could be a member of a multiethnic audience, drawn from the visible and longstanding phalanx/range of working-class people, European immigrants, free blacks, and other people of color—and, of course, men. That these images were often drawn from working-class life indicates that advertisers were concerned with reaching not only bourgeois Anglo-Americans but also these other populations, who, as many historians have noted, also made up vaudeville's early audiences and performers. Indeed, as in the chewing-tobacco ads in plates 13 and 14, produced by the prolific Donaldson Brothers printing house, many trade cards were in fact printed in the Five Points neighborhood, just below the Bowery, the creative center of New York's multiethnic working-class theater culture.

And yet, if consuming was figured in the postbellum era as central to American civic membership—a trope well explored by cultural and social historians—representations of non-Anglo-American consumers would seem to present complex and contradictory meanings, reflecting both the fear of free black and other non-Anglo subjects as well as an uneasy recognition of the changing ethnic, racial, and transnational landscapes of the period.[53] The card in plate 15 demonstrates this ambivalent relationship to black consumerism: the two figures enact the stereotype of the watermelon thief at the same time as they use the commodity for sale—Merrick's Thread—to contain the white figure. Thread is here used as a binding element (a descendant of the slave chain) to demonstrate the selling point of Merrick's Thread: it is strong and will not break. In the inverted world of the image it is the white owner figure who is bound and casts a horrified glance at the two young black men, who themselves look out calmly, smiling toward the spectator. Everything about the eating of these watermelons is inappropriate, and yet there is a jovial, pastoral mood about the scene. How was the spectator supposed to enter this scene?

When the trading cards portray immigrants and people of color using commodities in a manner that is outside the bounds of social conventions, it also questions the order under which the consumer lives. Here the normative grip of the white, middle-class consumer is loosened to acknowledge other consuming subjectivities. Unlike the domestic dramas, surveyed earlier, that end in peaceful eating scenes, the figures in these dramas—and indeed the background of the thread card implies a theatrical flat—cannot help but signal new forms of, if not black power, then black presence in the public eye. For one, the card reverses what is a common theme of thread advertising: the idea that black thread, like black skin, will not fade in the sun; instead, it hoists—lynches, even—the elderly white man on a white thread. But while the Merrick's Thread card follows the logic of post-Reconstruction racism by recasting black men as criminals, it also draws a clear parallel between eating, purchasing power, and racial power: the white figure has been immobilized by the (advertised) product in order to allow the two black men time to eat. The watermelon is, of course, a sweet fruit—but here the dialectic of sweetness through which the black body is consumed has literally been upended, as the white figure dangles upside down, lynched by the thread. And yet class mobility remains impossible, as attested to by the black men's bare feet and less elaborate clothing.

In drawing on theatrical tropes—and here again the thread card draws on the skit and gag formula, as well as the thieving formula that was soon to form the plot template for the earliest narrative films—commodity culture in these cards invites the potential consumer not only to try a product but to try on the appurtenances of the self that went with that product, to re-create and reembody his or her own skin. The tropes of embodiment in these cards display the fantasies of racial fluidity that lie at the heart of the period's theatrical and commodity culture. This connection seems particularly evident in an ad for Libby, McNeill and Libby's Cooked Corned Beef (plate 16). In this remarkable ad five men, apparently Chinese, dance about dressed in corned beef cans, their arms held in classical ballet's traditional designation of Oriental performance. The term *carnivalesque* seems particularly appropriate here: beyond the festive dancing of the Chinese figures the card certainly locates pleasure, and humor, in the belly, or the body's lower stratum: consuming Libby, McNeill and Libby's Corned Beef takes the eater directly to a joyful public performance in which social order—here, racial order—is temporarily inverted. As in most of these images the grotesquery—the sheer silliness of the body dressed in a corned beef can—contains the material political possibilities of the image. Laughter, in turn, signifies radical democratic potential as one dancing "John Chinaman" turns into a multitude, and the Asian man assumes—if only momentarily and if only problematically—a central and visible subjecthood in the card's visual schema. The landscape here implies foreign consumption: the name John, implying "John Chinaman," marks the consumer as Asian American, and the ever-seductive lure of China's population—a target market for American capitalism from the early decades of the nineteenth century—is signaled by the background. It is quite impossible to discern who it is the advertiser wishes to address, but the popularity of "yellowface" impersonation and of "John Chinaman" skits and songs once again implies that iconic models were taken from vaudeville's ability to stage multiethnic performance for multiethnic audiences.

The corned beef card brings eating and performance together as two interrelated modes of becoming. To eat corned beef here is to reembody oneself, both as food and as its container. The fluidity of possible embodiments in this card is remarkable: is John Chinaman an Asian man whose pleasure in consuming corned beef makes him dress in American goods? Is he becoming American? Is John a racial impersonator whose whiteness is both transmuted and reaffirmed through yellowface impersonation? Is he an Asian man playing Asianness on the stage? Can eating—as implied in Alcott's Rose Campbell books—change your race? There is no clear logic here, or rather it is the Freudian logic of condensation, into a single image, of conflicting desires. What emerges is a sense that that consuming, writ large, and eating, in particular, speaks to racial embodiment in such a way as to allow consumers to blur the borders of their racial selves, both consuming the other and becoming the other, if only temporarily.

The Chinese market is also represented in another ad, for Paragon Dried Beef, in which Uncle Sam sells dried beef to starving Chinese men against an Oriental backdrop (plate 17). The caption reads, "To cure the Chinese famine he acknowledges the 'fame in' Paragon Dried Beef." In this shameless advertisement the two figures stand on different kinds of ground, marking the economic exchange across national borders: the Uncle Sam figure stands tall and straight on green and grassy land, while the other side is dry and barren, scattered with dying Chinese men, one with his limbs twisted into impossible positions. American "aid" is nakedly figured as intertwined with commercial interests: in order to cure the famine, the Chinese figure must concede to the "fame in" Paragon Dried Beef. Food here becomes a tool of imperial conquest, as the conqueror can both exploit the foreign body and congratulate himself on his humanitarianism. The use value of this card is not, presumably, as an advertisement to the Chinese audience. Rather, it seems to exist to assert the symbolic presence of the Henry Mayo company. With the pun between "fame" and "famine" the reader is returned to the punning jokes of the minstrel interlocutor.

These advertisements not only display the relationship of the commodity culture to the theater; they demonstrate that advertisers—printers, designers, writers of captions—were immersed in the new racial and ethnic panoramas of the late nineteenth century. Trade cards, like the popular theater, asserted themselves as an important cultural space for the portrayal and working-through of social and political anxieties below the official discourse. What is also important to these advertisements is their own peculiar temporality: rather than unfolding in the event-space of the theater, these cards inject the theatrical into the realm of everyday commodity use. By theatricalizing the commodity these cards were a foray into what has become the standard practice of commodity culture, the blurring of the line between the self and the self as "actor" or star, a blurring which affects all social relations. Marx, in *Capital*, writes that the products of the labor process are imbued, in capitalism, with a certain anonymity: "As the taste of the porridge does not tell you who grew the oats, no more does this simple process tell you of itself what are the social conditions under which it is taking place, whether under the slave-owner's brutal lash, or the anxious eye of the capitalist, whether Cincinnatus carries it on in tilling his modest farm or a savage in killing wild animals with stones."[54] The trade cards fill in this anonymous blank—but they fill it in with fantasy. In creating these fantasies about both the situation in which the commodities are used and the process by which the commodities are produced, they constantly mitigate the harshness of capitalism while extending its reach into the domestic space.

The autarkic household for which even Louisa May Alcott is nostalgic is dissolved, just a few years later, by the theater of constant product flow. At the same time, the unconscious elements in this process—the harshness, poverty, and exploitation—which are repressed also constantly return, from the stringing up of the white man in the thread ad to the dying Chinese in the ad for corned beef. As such, the malleable embodiments on which these cards hinge offer insight into the quotidian nature of racial embodiment, its embeddedness not only in the fabric of everyday life but in the landscape of a national and transnational economy and political life.

Racial fluidity, as figured through what, to our vision, is the disturbing image of black children as edible objects—as for instance the Jim Crow gingerbread in *The House of the Seven Gables*—is a constant in the visual culture of the Gilded Age and accompanied the increasing harshness of the racist rhetoric and the tightening apartheid regime of segregation and second-class citizenship. Consider a trade card image of a black infant holding a huge piece of watermelon and raising a hand to ward off a gigantic wasp (plate 18). The longstanding racist association of African Americans with watermelon is legendary, but the hovering wasp begs the question of whether it threatens the watermelon or the child. Here again we see the simultaneous aggression toward and desire for the black body that we have witnessed in earlier pairings between African Americans and food objects. Which is the viewer supposed to want a bite of—the watermelon or the black child? And with whom and what is the consumer meant to identify?

Similarly, another ad for the Merrick Thread Company (plate 19) depicts a young black child suspended over water by a thread that he has used in his fishing rod. Beneath him an alligator awaits with open jaws: as in the previous ad for Merrick's Thread (plate 15) the durability of the thread is attested by the caption: "Fooled dis time, Cully. Dis cotton ain't gwine break." In another image that riffs on the popular image of the black child as "gator bait," this one taken from a cigar tin, a black baby is seen crawling up on the banks of a river in an advertisement for the Little African brand; an alligator just behind threatens to snap the child up (plate 20).

In these ads, blackness returns as appetizing and sweet; black babies are "dainty morsels" presented to the viewer in terms of their potential savor.

The sweetness that in *Uncle Tom's Cabin* exists between the normative white lady of the house and the black cook (where it operates as the substitute for civic equality) and that in *The House of the Seven Gables* links the Pyncheon house to transnational flows of capital is turned in these postbellum images to what is surely meant to read like good-natured mockery to the white spectator. Reembodiment in these images is not simply modeled through the projection or transformation of the consumer body into another body; it is about absorbing the other's body into one's own.

Blackness consistently appears being bitten, stung, or pinched, betraying a visual pleasure in black pain that is also a desire to taste it. At times the image is less overtly violent. Consider an advertisement for Sanford's Ginger, a "delicious summer medicine" (plate 21). In this card a black female child, sitting on a whole watermelon, holds a crying baby who is inside a watermelon that has been carved into the shape of a baby basket. In her left hand the girl holds a slice of watermelon that has a bite taken out of it. Her right arm is wrapped around a bottle of the ginger extract. As in an earlier advertisement (plate 18), bees and other insects gather over the children's heads, attracted by either the child or the fruit—one is not sure.

The verso side of the card claims that Sanford's, which consists largely of fine cognac, cures illness brought on by "Unripe Fruit, Unhealthy Water and Unhealthy Climates." Does this mean that the crying baby inside the watermelon is acting out this illness, displaying the consumer's "Cramps, Pains, Indigestions, Diarrhoea [*sic*], Colds, Chills, Simple Fevers, etc."? Does the baby then speak from inside the consumer's stomach or uterus, as though signifying the watermelon or the illness itself? This ambivalent representation offers multiple, fluid points of identification to the consumer. Here the black child is both consumer and consumed, healthy and unhealthy, the eater of the watermelon and part of the watermelon. Blackness here acts as the sign both of racial and physical degeneration and of health.

We cannot deny that many of the biting-themed cards—such as those in plates 22 and 23—demonstrate, without any ambivalence, the commingling of white pleasure and black terror that has, as Saidiya Hartman has documented, historically produced the spectacle of the black body in pain.[55] Our disgust at some of these images—our desire to look away—is for good reason. There can be no doubt that these comic images laugh at black pain. At the same time, these images nearly always use distancing techniques, disavowing white violence by making animals into human proxies, as in the card in plate 23, in which a dog bites an elderly man who is jumping over a fence with a basket of eggs.

That violence is deployed through biting or eating returns us forcefully to the role of the mouth in fixing and unfixing racial embodiment. The desire to bite both materializes and minimizes bodily violence; it inflicts pain, but it appears to do so only at the precise and relatively small point where human mouth meets human flesh; it is not shooting, cutting, or whipping. And yet biting is primarily a violence of childhood: it enacts the desire to destroy the other by consuming her, by obliterating the signs of her existence, or, at the very least, by reducing her physical presence in the world one mouthful at a time. In doing so, the biting image is complicit in "the sheer denial of black sentience" that is produced by the black body's history as object.[56]

If the denial of black sentience in these images is inextricable from the black pain they depict, the comedy of the desire to bite is telegraphed by the blackface mask, all exaggerated lips and eye rolls, with the white of the eye and the red of the lips always providing a strong contrast to the darkness of the skin. Such contrasts are another example of how these cards, and the era's visual culture in general, locate affective excess in the black body. These images project onto blackness the universal ungracefulness of the human body animated by the autonomic, that is, the liminally social, response to pain. In these extreme depictions the black body is posited as the negation of the normative—and controlled and sovereign—white body. At the same time, these cards deny the import of that pain by containing it within comic spectacle.[57]

However, despite the predominance of pain, as in the Sanford's Ginger cards, these are sometimes also images of black consumers and therefore of black pleasure in consumption. The child in the Merrick's Thread advertisement is indeed in danger of being eaten by an alligator but ultimately avoids being eaten—and even taunts his potential predator—because he has, as advertised, used Merrick's strong thread. By depicting black consumption through fishing and eating, many of these images characterize African American consumption as only liminally capitalist. However, African Americans are not always depicted consuming outside of capitalism. As waiters, caterers, and cooks, for instance, African Americans—both male and female—were central figures in the visual vocabulary of nineteenth-century food culture, particularly in the North. W. E. B. Du Bois explained in his study *The Philadelphia Negro* that between 1820 and 1870 catering was one way for northern blacks to attain a modicum of financial security. He wrote, "The whole catering business, arising from an evolution shrewdly, persistently and tastefully directed transformed the Negro cook and waiter into the public caterer and restaurateur, and raised a crown of underpaid menials to become a set of self-reliant, original business men who amassed fortunes for themselves and won general respect for their people."[58]

In the card in plate 24 a black cook makes bread while a young white girl looks on. Again, this scene is set in apparent incongruity against the company that it advertises. The scenes with which the company chooses to be associated are more idyllic—the social hierarchy between the black cook and the girl (dressed, no doubt, in tailored clothes) is a stable and cooperative one, in which servants—cooks and maids—were a significant factor in the lives of children. Importantly, in this period restaurants and cafeterias became working- and middle-class meeting spaces, as a public culture of eating emerged to rival the domestic table. In a pair of advertisements for a Chicago restaurant named Race Bros., a black man is seated on a stool eating from a bowl (plate 25). The caption reads, "I Golly, I reckon dis OYSTER STEW is come from Race Brudders." The uncannily named "New England Oyster and Coffee House" clearly hoped to benefit from the association with the depiction of blackness as jovial; but here the broad humor attached to blackness is linked to the "darky" appetite.[59] As a companion card shows, eating in restaurants was rapidly becoming part of urban culture across classes and races. For instance, in the second card in the series (plate 26) a white man in a top hat offers unhappy news: "My pile is low, but I shall never be happy, I know, until I eat some OYSTERS at Race Bros." Here the image parodies the middle-class obsession with digestion and excretion, while the representation of comic eating by both a white man and a black man hints that the bawdiness of eating and digestion may have been standard comic tropes of the period.

The common representation of African Americans as eaters as well as food to be eaten opens up the ambivalent possibilities inherent in a civic order sutured by Civil War and torn between segregation and limited political suffrage for blacks. Thus, if black appetite and black bodies evoke the comedy of the eater being eaten, they cannot fail also to represent the black subject taking, as it were, a bite out of the world. Metonymically, in the era's changing social order, such ambivalence implies the active presence of blacks in the culture of commodity consumption, their literal seat at the table—and, by implication, at the political table.

This fascination with African American bodies is often reflected in the fetishization of their mouths. In an advertisement for Dandy Jim chewing tobacco the viewer is invited directly into Dandy Jim's laughing mouth, whose teeth in turn are reflected in the advertisement's Art Nouveau gilded edges (plate 27). The advertisement for Dandy Jim chewing tobacco[60] picks up on another prominent minstrel-show figure: the northern black dandy, at other times also called Zip Coon. The dandy figure mocked the social aspirations of northern blacks at the same time as it played out, in performance, admiration for black urban bodily aesthetics.

What I want to get to here, however, is the connection between comedy and consumption that this advertisement so nicely encapsulates. Saidiya Hartman has suggested that in the antebellum period "the spectacular nature of black suffering and, conversely, the dissimulation of suffering through spectacle . . . all turn upon the simulation of agency and the excesses of black enjoyment."[61] Using blackness to represent and sell commodities reveals laughter, and by inference excess, to be an integral element of the new commodity culture. In commodity culture the use of the commodity almost invariably develops other uses, which are connected to creating lifestyles rather than merely satisfying basic needs. The scholarly interest in racial performance has, so far, concentrated on its explicit forums in the theater and in melodrama; as these cards show, however, theatricalized images, often with comic performance at their center, were an essential element both in commodifying the American lifestyle in the Gilded Age and in negotiating the new, postemancipation racial regime.

It seems essential to ask, what would it mean to read these often offensive representations on their own terms? That is to say, what if we bracket the whole project of reading blackness as a way of understanding whiteness? Instead, what do these advertisements have to say about black and other nonwhite consumers of the period? The demographic material on nonwhite consumers is limited but growing, as is the literature and scholarship on the black public sphere generally. Paul Mullins's archaeological work in Baltimore has shown that black households in the mid-nineteenth century engaged in consumer practices similar to their white counterparts.[62] However, as scholars have shown, each of the consumer demographics imagined by these advertisements formed their own public spheres in the contested urban spaces of the nineteenth century: thread, for instance, might be used by black seamstresses to make dresses for white women; tobacco might be chewed by black, Irish, and Jewish mouths. Further, each of these demographics produced their own hermeneutics in the same ways that they produced their own spectatorial practices.[63]

In this era of enormous immigration flows, both within and to the United States, and of enormous political and economic reorganization, the opportunity for a creative reimagining of the ideal consumer seemed more open than it had ever been. While the bourgeois white figure remained the ideal, deviation from this idea, in both the production process and the consumption process, was a clear possibility. We can assume that, like most people who work for a living, printers and designers of these advertisements were concerned as much, if not more, by profit as politics. And the creators of these images were, themselves, often immigrants and, in some cases, black.[64] Certainly by the beginning of the twentieth century producers were well aware of the benefits of targeting black consumers—as the history of tobacco marketing has shown, at times to deadly effect.[65] Perhaps, then, we might read these problematic images not simply as symptoms of a violent white imaginary but also as signs of the presence of nonwhites as, if not important or powerful, then at least visible consumer groups. We might even find moments of tenderness, affection, and loving intimacy.

In one advertisement for Atmure's Mince Pies, for instance, a shoeless boy eats pie on the sidewalk, his cheeks stuffed (plate 28). In another advertisement, for Ayer's Cathartic Pills (plate 29), an elderly country doctor holds a baby on his lap to feed her medication. Though neatly situated on the fine—and often nonexistent—line between romantic pastoral depiction and racial stereotype, this card also depicts a quite tender scene of familial, or at least medical, care. These are rare pictures indeed; more often the cards veer into the fantastic and comic. For instance, in another advertisement (plate 30) the interracial encounter is rendered playful and sweet, as a young white girl with an enormous hat that hides her face and a young black boy play seesaw on an enormous candy cane that seems to be mounted on a chocolate. The encounter is also eroticized, as the two figures straddle the same (presumably peppermint) pole, facing each other: we see here the return of the erotic life of the mouth in the ways that this advertisement promises its pleasures to any part of the body that touches the candy.

At other times, the too-muchness of blackness—what Sianne Ngai has called "the affective qualities of liveliness, effusiveness, spontaneity and zeal . . . [which] function as bodily (hence self-evident) signs of the raced subject's naturalness"—threatens to exceed the boundaries of the card.

The result, as Ngai writes in her discussion of the racial quality of animatedness, is "unanticipated social meanings and effects."[66] This is particularly true in the Chase and Sanborn Coffee metamorphic cards that fold out to reveal black men, apparently highly caffeinated. In the first card (plates 31 and 32) a pair of window shutters unfolds to show an elderly black man with missing teeth. Mouth wide open and finger raised, the man claims, "My missus says dar's no good coffee in these yer parts. Specs she'll change 'er mine when she drinks SEAL BRAND." Another remarkable metamorphic card shows a small white man standing on the closed side of the card in a seersucker suit and monocle and facing the cardholder with his hands on his hips (plate 33). When the card is opened, his body has been either transformed or replaced by that of a tall black man in a nearly identical suit, holding aloft a can of coffee and an advertising bulletin (plate 34).

The transformation in these cards, as in all metamorphic cards, is animated by the cardholder: the metamorphosis is subject to the owner/cardholder's will. But what I want to suggest here is that the animatedness of these cards exceeds their purpose—"generates unanticipated social meanings and effects"—in part because the cards directly address the viewer and in part because, as preserved across 110 years, the cards will not fold or entirely hide their inhabitants. Indeed, the closed cover of the first card shows the elderly man's eyes and fingers poking through closed window shutters; when the card fully opens, he addresses the viewer directly, the right finger raised while the imperfectly drawn left arm seems to be detached and gesturing at the reader, instructing us to sample from the can of coffee it holds. When the shutter opens, the man's mouth is of central importance. His imperfect teeth make him an object of humor, marking him as lower class, unable to afford whatever stood in for dental care in the period. What is interesting here is that not only do the shutters not contain the man but he also exceeds the frame of the advertisement. Further, the putative ugliness of his teeth would seem designed to evoke disgust on the spectator's part, pushing the consumer away from the man's body and denying the spectator any easy sense of impersonation and identification. Even the "missus" is displaced from the scene of consumption, as her accession to this new coffee is only speculated on; in fact, purchasing power seems to be in the hands of the pictured man, who will foist the new coffee on "the missus"—either an employer or his wife, perhaps—later. Here consumer affect is not pleasure but shock.

The second card, which shows the white man in the seersucker suit, also does not close. In this card, however, there is a gap between the man's upper and lower body that lines up with the waist of the taller black man inside the card. Imperfectly closed as it is, when the card opens, the white man disappears completely, as if exploded into thin air by a black self he can barely contain. When Huckleberry Finn says of Jim that he is "white inside," he is expressing the extreme edge of white liberal sentiment in the postbellum era. Here, however, in the carnivalesque images of the commodity culture the white man is "black inside." In failing to close—that is, in failing to contain racial difference—these cards stage moments of nonwhite visibility that exceed the total subjection of the contained black figure. More than that, however, in failing to close the cards undermine what Tara McPherson has called the "lenticular logic" of race. Such logic, which she argues finds expression in the postcards whose images shift when tilted in different directions, sometimes switching between white and black figures, "is a monocular logic, a schema by which histories or images that are actually copresent get presented (structurally, ideologically) so that only one of the images can be seen at the time. Such a logic represses connection, allowing whiteness to float free from blackness."[67]

What makes the Chase and Sanborn seersucker card so remarkable is that it complicates this lenticular logic by materially refusing to allow the white body to close itself off from its black alter ego and, further, by allowing the black body to overwhelm the white body in size. Ultimately, the card confuses the logic of blackface, rendering it impossible to tell which body occupies which. The animatedness of the racialized body here is clear: the black self cannot be contained but must press outward; he unrelentingly claims public space. The shuttered window card demonstrates this too-muchness as well; the elderly man's figure crosses the sill of the closed window to show us a can of coffee. In the face of the viewer the figure thus resists passivity, seeming to strain against the two-dimensionality of the card. His open mouth, uneven teeth, and direct gaze also push back at the viewer, refusing the traditionally consumed position of the black body and instead speaking to, back, and at the viewer. One should not fall back on any idea of unmediated black "resistance" to explain the excess registered in this card or others like it. But what is clear is that in its formal structure this card enacts the felt effect of black presence on the white public sphere: problematic, derogatory, and stereotyped but also irrepressible, insistent, and in the case of our Gilded Age Jim Dandy quite beautiful.[68]

The political register *is* at times made visible in other cards, when consumer culture is connected to black political enfranchisement. In an advertisement for St. Louis Beef Canning Company (plate 35) an elderly spectacled black man, in an Uncle Sam suit with an enormous yellow bow tie, stands on top of a can of canned beef to make a stump speech: "My friends!! De candidate dat eats dis yeah Beef is de man to be 'lected." Blatantly linking commodity consumption to citizenship, the man's patriotic outfit positions him within a narrative of national belonging, even as his strange spectacles, which seem to take up both of his eyes, and his stereotyped features accent his distance from normative physicality, even as the tagline urges a digestive political belonging.

Another advertisement, for Boston Codfish Balls[69] (plate 36), shows a black couple leaving the United States for Liberia. As they walk toward the left side of the card, a sign reads, "To Liberia, AFRICA," and the top-hatted man says, "We's Gwine Back to Our Old Ancestral Halls to Make Our Fortune Sure on Dees Codfish Balls." While the codfish card does not precisely draw an analogy between commodity consumption and political enfranchisement, aligning itself instead with recolonization schemes, it nonetheless indicates the ways that commodity capitalism is attached to forms of political power in the period: in leaving the United States the couple is nonetheless using their access to American commodities to establish a claim to another national space, ostensibly as Americo-Liberians.

An advertisement for Magnolia Hams (plates 37 and 38) is particularly interesting. The caption reads, "What's de use talking 'bout dem 'mendments when Magnolias is about?" The verso side of this card charts the growth of the Magnolia company from 1863 and establishes the advertisement's date as 1878, the year after the compromise that put Rutherford Hayes in the White House, signaling the collapse of Reconstruction and the advent of Jim Crow in the South. The possibility that African Americans might step into full civic membership in the American body politic is thus both figured and disavowed in this ad. Here, consumption, and specifically eating, is both symbolic of and a substitute for political enfranchisement and civil rights. The Magnolia ad both beckons to and rejects the interests of the black public: it gestures to the constitutional amendments that signaled the beginning of black enfranchisement and implies that African Americans can be distracted and pacified by a nicely cured piece of pig. At the same time, the advertisement for Magnolia Hams demonstrates the white fear that black citizens might begin to bite back.

And yet, as a southern card printed in the year after the failure of Reconstruction, the Magnolia Hams card reminds us that these artifacts, survivors of an era before a rationalized science of advertising, are limited in what they promise, not unlike commodity culture itself. For in essence, although the spectacular presence of blacks in advertising may be read with some more ambiguity than we have heretofore acknowledged—that is, as signs of an increasingly visible and empowered black public sphere—the extreme affect represented in these cards also testifies to another signification, one tied to the ages-old suspicion toward excess pleasure. For just as the advertisers of Magnolia Hams have sutured eating imagery to political power, in this card black power is also denied and contained, shunted toward consumer citizenship instead of democratic participation, mocked rather than celebrated. Further, the excesses of black enjoyment in these cards also point us backward to the vicious and masturbating daughter of the Graham parable, whose investment in pleasure enacts her mother's morally dubious spending power.

Borrowing Lloyd Pratt's term for the peculiar temporality of black vernacular in *The House of the Seven Gables*, it might be said that these cards "flicker": with political and purchasing power, with images of a public sphere whose archive is in many ways occluded to our view.[70] Their meanings also "flicker" back and forth between the before and after image, with the promise of commodity pleasure as experienced by the other and with the fantasy of a temporary excursion into that body. Eventually, of course, they all fail, as each card, which has somehow survived across the stretch of more than a century, outlives its purest, its inarguable purpose: to maintain customer interest in the product it advertises. For although these pieces of advertising ephemera have survived, almost without exception the products they depict have not.

Trade cards have had a surprisingly modest presence in literary and cultural studies, given the much-vaunted visual turn that has done so much to recast these fields in the past few decades. Their neglected role is perhaps due to the lack of "authors" among trade cards—many scholars are still more comfortable dealing with images or texts that can be traced back to a particular, nameable source, in contrast to the anonymity that veils both the origin and circulation histories of many of these cards. Nevertheless, the cards offer rich visual and textual insights into the late nineteenth-century mind-set.

I have tried in this chapter to present a thematic thread that winds through the visual culture of the Gilded Age, as that culture can be seen through the trading card. Because of their mass quantity, generally anonymous production, and often unstructured distribution, the trade card comes close to the kind of dream image Walter Benjamin theorizes: "To the form of the new means of production which in the beginning is still dominated by the old one (Marx), there correspond in the collective consciousness images in which the new is intermingled with the old. These images are wish images, and in them the collective attempts to transcend as well as to illumine the incompleteness of the social order of production."[71] Unlike the proletariat of Benjamin's Paris, however, who rose up to engage against capitalism, the American dream image tended to be one of full assimilation into the commodity process, making it a governing trope of personal and political identity in much the same way as the food object tropes the body. The transition from the antebellum order, with its anxiety about consumer culture, its division between free and slave labor, and its utopian dream of autarky, to the full embrace of conspicuous consumption in the Gilded Age was abundantly, even obscenely, registered in the world of trade cards. Inextricably linked, though often ignored, was the simultaneous decisive shift in American food culture, which both blurred the lines between domestic and public consumption and introduced, into the domestic sphere, the theatricalization of commodity use.

Theater, I argue, is the essential referent for the trade card. The advertisement of the commodity is mediated by the dramatization of commodity use and, by inference, the creation of new roles for the commodity user. Thus, in reading these cards we must necessarily consider the question of the spectator. If black bodies in these advertisements are without doubt put on display for white consumption as objects, these black bodies—insofar as they are consuming subjects—also invite viewers to replicate that consumption on their own by projecting their own bodies into the represented body. At the same time, these cards signal the presence of a black counterpublic sphere, sometimes represented by the black theater and at other times pointing to the growing black consumer demographic.

Consumption in these cards is thus partly figured in terms of racial impersonation, which at the very least points to the fact that the card encodes more elbow room in inviting the spectator into the drama of the commodity. This is a formal property of the production and distribution of the cards—the target audience is random enough that the advertisements for certain mass products (thread, canned meats, coffee) allow for the extension of the spectatorial-racial space. In this space white consumers are invited to imagine consumption by projecting themselves into nonwhite bodies, by imagining themselves to be nonwhite consumers, while nonmajoritarian or non-Anglo-American consumers are also given a certain leeway both to inhabit popular, white discourse and to invert hegemonic norms and sanctions. That is to say, we cannot assume a consumer who entered an entirely segregated public sphere, even as, politically, segregation became the official goal of much of the United States after the collapse of Reconstruction. Nor can we assume that the printers who produced the cards were always white, nor, most importantly, can we assume that the consumer population who looked at them was white.

And yet these cards do not only work by attraction; they also count on aesthetic repulsion. Consider the tone of so many of these cards and the apparently quotidian nature of the extreme and caricatured affect; it seems that discomfort was a very explicit strategy deployed by advertisers to capture consumer attention. In fact, it is not solely desire; it is a muddled and unstable mix of identification, desire, and disgust that constitute the viewing relationships in—that is, the affect invited by—these highly racialized trade cards. Many of these cards seem to be entirely foreign to our contemporary understanding of advertising as an instrument to construct desire. In sharp contrast, trade cards, particularly some of the metamorphic cards, seem to push back at the viewer, seeking to shock, surprise, and amuse, using racial violence to entertain but also seeking to engage the viewer's disgust. Nonwhite bodies here enact extremes of pleasure and pain; bodies exploding with affect encode the imagined hyperphysicality of nonwhiteness but also integrate the white consumer's felt experience of an increasingly interracial public sphere with the sensory experience of commodity consumption.

The presence of black consumers in these cards surely has many possible explanations. If for generations the black body was literally, in the minds of many Americans, a commodity to be sold, then it is no surprise that after slavery the black body seems made to sell other things. For late nineteenth-century whites, immersed in a Gilded Age but still uncomfortable with excess, the chromolithographic black body is the perfect target, a vessel bursting with physical, material abundance, which can surely absorb all that whiteness seeks to disavow.[72] As the image of the edible black body continues to show, the use of African Americans and other hyperraced subjects in chromolithographic advertising meant to incite white consumer desire is in itself a symptom of the profound but no less violent white desire for congress with the racial other. Images of black bodies in advertising that relate to food culture show that the messy politics of majoritarian racism was intrinsic to the economy of advertising imagery, even as they exist as signs of the presence of an active African American and ethnic buying public.

More essentially, however, black and other non-Anglo-American subjects push back in these advertisements: they are shocking, negative, motile, and *too much*—like conspicuous consumption itself. As the turbulent nineteenth century came to a close, trade cards attest to the presence of black and multiethnic consuming publics, who moved through urban and other consumer spaces claiming the right to both commodity pleasure and political citizenship.

Conclusion

Racial Indigestion

As I finish this book, I have been writing and thinking about food for almost two decades. From my beginning as a food writer and journalist and then on through my graduate education, food, eating, and the life of ideas have maintained an intricate relation to each other. Throughout my education I wrote about food; food and eating culture harassed me until finally I gave in and started the project that became this book.

This book had another prelife in a paper about Martha Stewart that I wrote as an undergraduate at York University. At the cookbook store where I worked while I was a student in Toronto I remember selling early copies of *Martha Stewart Living* magazine, fascinated with the alternatively vituperative or adoring relationship our (mostly female) customers had to Stewart and her work. When later I rewrote that paper, I came to realize that I would never really understand the Stewart ethos or aesthetic without delving deeper into her backstory, without understanding her in the context of the aesthetic, political, and alimentary history that produced her.

It was in that graduate paper that I began to think about the strange and perverse stories that we tell about food in our culture, stories that, as I came to understand, the United States has been telling about itself for quite a while. I argued that we might profitably read the commercial space of food culture, in particular the strange washed-out interiors, exquisitely lighted food items, and uneaten meals of Martha Stewart's high-WASP magazine, through related frames of race and the erotic. In particular, I came to believe that Stewart's work was defined by its coy relationship to ideas of vice and appetite, organized around the logic of masturbation, specifically around the spectacle of Martha Stewart's pleasure in her own product. In essence, I asked, is Martha Stewart a pornographer of (her own) white pleasure? And how did that come to be?

Martha Stewart's work is now only one example of what is truly an unprecedented explosion in food and eating cultures. And while my questions in that paper were specific to Martha Stewart, they have grown into larger questions: What is the historical relationship between food and race? When and why did eating become a way of asserting racial, not to mention class, identity? How does an act which is so policed and so overdetermined—eating—also come to be affiliated with transgressive pleasure, with sex, sexuality, and an eroticism that is all its own?

Today's foodie culture is only the latest expression of what I have been calling *eating culture* in this book. Although it finds its roots in the pleasures and visceral hierarchies of hearth and fireside life, across two centuries eating culture has managed to bifurcate political energies, as asceticism and vice, servant and mistress, hunger and pleasure, domesticity and empire, domination and democratic practice have battled each other from within the seemingly banal problem of what to put into our mouths.

I have traced that problem across five divergent cultural moments, via very different kinds of cultural, literary, prescriptive, visual, and dietetic texts. Beginning with domestic architecture in the colonial and early national period, chapter 1 looked at the technology of the stove that replaced the hearth. That technology, I noted, not only shifted the way in which food was cooked in the kitchen but was one part of a wholesale redistribution of spaces for labor, sociability, and privacy in the bourgeois household. In chapter 2 this redistribution of spaces was both acknowledged and resisted by a romantic conservative element in the antebellum culture, which advocated a nationalist and racialized food program centered on a metonymic relationship between nation, home, and body.

Chapter 3 saw the literature of domesticity and its deterrents think through models of white female empowerment that were predicated on desiring and violently consuming relationships to black bodies and subjects, who in turn refused their commodification as food objects in the racial logic of nationalist dietetics. Chapter 4 saw the reassertion of these dietetics in the adolescent novels of Louisa May Alcott, which once again linked proper consumption to the emergence of new forms of liberal womanhood, while linking the production of whiteness to the formation of other forms of vice domestically and abroad. Chapter 5 explored the explosion of commodities and new consuming publics in the last quarter of the nineteenth century via the invention of new visual technologies.

All these scenes of consumption reckoned with the increased commodification and modernization of food culture, with varying degrees of ambivalence, as indeed we do today. And at each of these moments eating culture was linked to the articulation of very different kinds of identities and political projects—as it is today.

At this moment of intense interest in the politics of food the need to think through the genealogy of U.S. eating culture and its twentieth- and twenty-first-century reincarnations seems pressing. Might these discourses find origin in earlier modes of biological racism and nationalism? In what ways does their need to rationalize the pleasures of eating continue to work as a technology for reproducing whiteness? How might the study of eating, of the mouth as a "dense transfer point of power" in the production of the biopolitical life of the nation, be put to work in denaturalizing racial formation and, equally relevant, class formation? What are the differences and overlaps between localism (eat within your own ecosystem) and Grahamite nativism (do not eat foreign foods)?

The colloquial nature of eating, its everydayness, and the biological imperative that makes eating a necessity often render it invisible as a highly discursive as well as material practice. To study and write about food, like eating it, is at times an unabashed pleasure. At these times pleasure itself perhaps functions as a kind of ethical alert. Examining the political and cultural meaning of eating culture, as those of us who work in the field well know, opens up a multitude of questions central to critical reflection about the production of asymmetrical social relations, both historical and contemporary.

In some ways I have tried to do for the cultural history of the mouth what Bersani did for the other end of the alimentary canal, in his seminal article "Is the Rectum a Grave?"[1] I have argued in *Racial Indigestion* that eating has a messy and promising history to tell about the dialectical struggles between pleasure and disgust, affect and aesthetics, dominance and resistance, and the interpenetrations of all of the above. Some of that history lies in the ways that the mouth is a stage for what I call *queer alimentarity*: a space where nonnormative desires can be played out. And indeed part of the work that I have done for the mouth in this book is to trace it as a site of radical *and* problematic pleasures.

Via the intertwined history of reform dietetics and U.S. biopolitics, however, we have also seen how in many ways the mouth is the rectum's pastoral other, a site of life-producing pleasure and a space of intervention into the well-being of an imagined nation. That biopolitical imperative is, as the link between white pleasure and black pain has indicated, matched in the nation's necropolitical energies, which are oriented toward consuming and destroying that which seems to threaten the internal order of the majoritarian class.

We might consider contemporary food tourism, in which cosmopolitanism at times subtends nativism as an elite practice, as the inheritance of that alliance between consumption and white bourgeois culture. Indeed, the experience of many food cultures as an indicator of a privileged urban and global mobility—or at least the performance thereof—can be as sure a sign of cultural capital today as is a cloth Whole Foods grocery bag. But perhaps we should not give in so easily, as reformers from Graham on have done, to the adoption or valorization of "primitive" foodways, without thinking through the colonial, even imperialist, pathways on which such commodity romances are and have been traced.[2]

If the related genealogy of the image of the black body as edible has anything to tell us, it is that while eating carries the metonymic power of encounters across difference it is often enough an asymmetrical encounter. And the trope of the edible black body has not gone away. In April 2010 a small news story broke about a publishing error found in a pasta cookbook published by Penguin Australia. In a recipe for tagliatelle with sardines and prosciutto the editors had somehow missed a typo, which called for cooks to add "salt and freshly ground black people"—instead of pepper—to the dish.[3] A small international furor led to the publisher pulling and pulping seven thousand copies of the book, in response to what the director of publishing claimed to be "quite forgivable" and a "silly mistake."[4]

Only a few weeks after the story broke it was reported that the book sold better after the scandal: "Advocating cannibalism, it turns out, can boost sales," reported the *Guardian*.[5] Although this incident took place in Australia, where blackness can have a quite different resonance than in the United States, the incident was widely reported in the United States, in the news and on food blogs. Typo or not, it is clear that the image of the black body as food continues to find resonance in our contemporary culture, linked to the forbidden pleasures of spice and to the production of elite foodways.[6]

The consuming body at the center of *Martha Stewart Living*, the viciously consuming Grahamite family, the assumed white audience of Edison's *Gator and the Pickaninny*, the consumer who rushes out to buy a recipe that calls for ground black people—these are diverse historical players, indeed. If this book argues anything, it is that they share a genealogy. But what I have also argued in this book is that the other will not go down easily but rather bites back. As Destiny's Child tells us, in the epigraph to the book, "I don't think you're ready for this jelly / My body's too bootylicious for you." If I were to continue the story of the black body's association with food into the twentieth century, as other scholars have done, we would see that the sweetness of the black body, food's valence as erotic pleasure, and the alliance between eating and sex have carried on and have been immensely productive in, for instance, blues culture and late twentieth-century black popular culture.[7]

This book has a different story to tell. I have long since stopped paying attention to food journalism, cooking shows, and magazines or food-centered cable channels, and I do not read *Martha Stewart Living* magazine anymore. Truth be told, I am a little tired of food and the cultural noise around it. But what I hope is that perhaps closer attention to the history of the mouth and eating culture might lead us through their various epistemologies to a more just ethics and practice of eating, not in order to shut down its pleasures but rather to share them more broadly and more critically, to dwell more insistently in sites and moments of discomfort and therefore to dream of a more ethical and life-affirming vulnerability to each other.

Notes

NOTES TO THE INTRODUCTION

1. A far-from-exhaustive list would include the recently published Parama Roy, *Alimentary Tracts: Appetites, Aversions, and the Postcolonial* (Durham: Duke University Press, 2010); Gang Yue, *The Mouth That Begs: Hunger, Cannibalism, and the Politics of Eating in Modern China* (Durham: Duke University Press, 1999); Cecelia Lawless, "Cooking, Community, Culture: A Reading of *Like Water for Chocolate*," in *Recipes for Reading: Community Cookbooks, Stories, Histories*, ed. Anne Bower (Amherst: University of Massachusetts Press, 1997); Emma Parker, "You Are What You Eat: The Politics of Eating in the Novels of Margaret Atwood," *Twentieth-Century Literature* 41:3 (1995): 349–369; Jennifer A. Ho, *Consumption and Identity in Asian American Coming-of-Age Novels* (New York: Routledge, 2005); Wenying Xu, *Eating Identities: Reading Food in Asian American Literature* (Honolulu: University of Hawai'i Press, 2008).

2. For earlier examples of body studies work with an interest in food and eating see Susan Bordo, *Unbearable Weight: Feminism, Western Culture, and the Body* (Berkeley: University of California Press, 1993); and Sander L. Gilman, *Fat Boys: A Slim Book* (Lincoln: University of Nebraska Press, 2004). See also Sander L. Gilman, *Fat: A Cultural History of Obesity* (Malden, MA: Polity, 2008). Two important predecessors to this book in dealing with race and food are Doris Witt, *Black Hunger: Food and the Politics of U.S. Identity* (New York: Oxford University Press, 1999); Psyche A. Williams-Forson, *Building Houses Out of Chicken Legs: Black Women, Food, and Power* (Chapel Hill: University of North Carolina Press, 2006); and also Melanie DuPuis, *Nature's Perfect Food: How Milk Became America's Drink* (New York: NYU Press, 2002). I am particularly indebted to Sander Gilman and my fellow students for their insights during Professor Gilman's summer seminar on fat and the body, "Body Matters," at the 2002 School for Criticism and Theory, Cornell University, Ithaca, New York.

3. Jennifer K. Ruark, "More Scholars Focus on Historical, Social, and Cultural Meanings of Food, but Some Critics Say It's Scholarship-Lite: Selected Books in Food Studies," *Chronicle of Higher Education*, July 9, 1999, http://chronicle.com/article/More-Scholars-Focus-on-Hist/15471/ (accessed May 23, 2011).

4. On the former see Laurier Turgeon and Madeleine Pastinelli, "'Eat the World': Postcolonial Encounters in Quebec City's Ethnic Restaurants," *Journal of American*

Folklore 115:456 (Spring 2002): 247–268.; Jordan Kleiman, “Local Food and the Problem of Public Authority,” *Technology and Culture* 50:2 (2009): 399–417. On the latter see, for instance, work in the field of human geography and rural sociology, such as E. Melanie DuPuis and David Goodman, “Should We Go ‘Home’ to Eat? Toward a Reflexive Politics of Localism,” *Journal of Rural Studies* 21:3 (July 2005): 359–371; C. Clare Hinrichs, “The Practice and Politics of Food System Localization,” *Journal of Rural Studies* 19:1 (January 2003): 33–45; David Goodman and E. Melanie DuPuis, “Knowing Food and Growing Food: Beyond the Production-Consumption Debate in the Sociology of Agriculture,” *Sociologia Ruralis* 42 (January 2002): 5–22.

5. The trend toward a certain kind of food history, which is concerned with tracing the history of a single commodity as it is introduced to a Western consumer demographic, marketed, and disseminated through various commercial venues, begs the question of how the subgenre arose and why it continues to flourish. Perhaps the answer is that publishers are banking on the basic bibliophagic analogy between reading and eating, both of these appetites driven by marketing, media attention, and the shifting class characteristics of food choices. See, for instance, the following, all on chocolate, surely the most overdetermined food commodity in circulation today: Deborah Cadbury, *Chocolate Wars: The 150-Year Rivalry Between the World’s Greatest Chocolate Makers* (New York: Public Affairs, 2010); William Gervase Clarence-Smith, *Cocoa and Chocolate, 1765–1914* (New York: Routledge, 2000); Sophie D. Coe and Michael D. Coe, *The True History of Chocolate*, 2nd ed. (London: Thames & Hudson, 2007); Meredith L. Dreiss and Sharon Edgar Greenhill, *Chocolate: Pathway to the Gods* (Tucson: University of Arizona Press, 2008); David Folster, *Ganong: A Sweet History of Chocolate* (Fredericton, NB: Goose Lane, 2006); Louis E. Grivetti and Howard-Yana Shapiro, *Chocolate: History, Culture, and Heritage* (London: Wiley, 2009); ICON Group International, *Chocolate: Webster’s Timeline History, 1585–2007* (New York: ICON, 2009); Arthur William Knapp, *Cocoa and Chocolate: Their History from Plantation to Consumer* (Charleston, SC: Nabu, 2010); Cameron L. McNeil, *Chocolate in Mesoamerica: A Cultural History of Cacao* (Gainesville: University Press of Florida, 2009); Marcy Norton, *Sacred Gifts, Profane Pleasures: A History of Tobacco and Chocolate in the Atlantic World* (Ithaca: Cornell University Press, 2010); Emma Robertson, *Chocolate, Women and Empire: A Social and Cultural History* (Manchester: Manchester University Press, 2010); Lowell J. Satre, *Chocolate on Trial: Slavery, Politics, and the Ethics of Business* (Athens: Ohio University Press, 2005); Susan J. Terrio, *Crafting the Culture and History of French Chocolate* (Berkeley: University of California Press, 2000); Allen M. Young, *The Chocolate Tree: A Natural History of Cacao*, 2nd ed. (Gainesville: University Press of Florida, 2007).

6. The most important of these is Jacques Derrida, “‘Eating Well,’ or the Calculation of the Subject: An Interview with Jacques Derrida,” in *Who Comes after the Subject?*, ed. Eduardo Cadava, Jean-Luc Nancy, and Peter Connor, 96–119 (New York: Routledge, 1991). Derrida’s work considers hunger, hospitality, and the ethics of knowing the other in this and other work; in general, of course, writing on the ethics of consuming animals is at the center of discussions of his ethics of eating. The question of the animal, particularly

in relation to race, is beyond the scope of this project, although I do touch on it briefly when considering the inversion of the animal-human distinction in hearth-centered literature. In general, however, it should be said that I am in accord with Derrida's reading of anthropophagy in *Eating Well*: in a very real sense, *Racial Indigestion* is a materialist, literary, and historicist expansion of Derrida's polemical proposal that "the so-called non-anthropophagic cultures practice symbolic anthropophagy and even construct their most elevated socius, indeed the sublimity of their morality, their politics, and their right, on this anthropophagy" (ibid., 114). *Racial Indigestion* attempts to answer Derrida's question—"What is eating?" (ibid.)—but, as I argue in my conclusion, agreeing with Derrida, understanding the social and cultural history of eating should not turn one away from it so much as propel one toward a more just inhabitation of the self-other dialectic that subtends the symbolic and metaphorical properties of eating. One feminist approach to the topic of eating would be Elspeth Probyn, *Carnal Appetites: Foodsexidentities* (London: Routledge, 2000).

7. Sara Ahmed's work on affect and the body is a good example of a productive focus on surface. For Ahmed, bodies (and bodies politic) ultimately take shape *between* surfaces or as the *effect* of surface, a term that appears and reappears in her argument: "It is through emotions that . . . surfaces or boundaries are made: the 'I' and 'we' are shaped by, and even take the shape of, contact with others. . . . The surfaces of bodies surface as an effect of the impressions left by others." Sara Ahmed, *The Cultural Politics of Emotion* (New York: Routledge, 2004), 83. Ahmed flirts with moments in which one body becomes vulnerable to another, arguing that the "feelings that are immediate, and which may involve 'damage' in the skin surface, are not simply feelings that one has, but feelings that open bodies to others" (15). However, she quickly retreats—in the next sentence in fact—from such assertions into the language of closure: "My analysis introduces the concept of 'intensification' to show how pain creates the very impression of bodily surface" (10). For Ahmed, concerned with the affective reproduction of social inequality, the boundedness of social groups and individual bodies serves an important, and persuasive, argumentative purpose.

My concern in *Racial Indigestion* is similar, but I am more interested in the horizontal intermixing of racial bodies and spaces and in the "roiling jumble of need, guilt, and disgust" that Eric Lott outlined as fundamental to the formation of whiteness in the United States. Eric Lott, *Love and Theft: Blackface Minstrelsy and the American Working Class* (New York: Oxford University Press, 1995). Minstrelsy, and the ambivalence of Lott's love-theft dynamic is central to this project; I echo both Ahmed and Lott in borrowing the language of cathexis from psychoanalysis to explore the conjoining of affect and aesthetics in the performance and dialogic constitution of race. The horizontal orientation of this project is probably why I largely ignore discourses of taste, which have been productively explored in the context of Enlightenment theories of aesthetics, as well as in sociological discussions of, in Bourdieu's term, *distinction*. I suppose it could be said that I am more interested in flavor: sweetness and later saltiness as well. On the discourse of taste see Denise Gigante, *Taste: A Literary History* (New Haven: Yale University Press, 2005);

Pierre Bourdieu, *Distinction: A Social Critique of the Judgement of Taste* (Cambridge: Harvard University Press, 1984); Timothy Morton, *The Poetics of Spice* (New York: Cambridge University Press, 2006); Timothy Morton, *Cultures of Taste/Theories of Appetite: Eating Romanticism* (New York: Palgrave Macmillan, 2004); Timothy Morton, *Shelley and the Revolution in Taste: The Body and the Natural World* (New York: Cambridge University Press, 1995).

8. Anthelme Brillat-Savarin, *The Physiology of Taste; or, Meditations on Transcendental Gastronomy*, trans. M. F. K. Fisher (New York: Everyman's Library, 2009), 15.

9. And of course, the literally dialogic nature of Brillat-Savarin's aphorism—"*tell me and I will tell you*"—only underlines this point.

10. In a much-quoted passage Judith Butler has argued that in considering the body, we understand "the notion of matter, not as site or surface, but as *a process of materialization that stabilizes over time to produce the effect of boundary, fixity, and surface we call matter.* That matter is always materialized . . . has to be thought in relation to the productive and, indeed, materializing effects of regulatory power in the Foucaultian sense." Judith Butler, *Bodies That Matter: On the Discursive Limits of Sex* (New York: Routledge, 1993), 69. Although Butler is interested in the *fiction* of site and surface, from the position of the eating body this account of the production of boundary, fixity, and surface, *even as effect*, seems insufficient. Rather, we are interested here in those spaces that remain open in the service of producing fictions of bodily materiality, thus unfixing their own work. More on this, of course, will follow.

11. Regarding this theoretical framework, the most important text continues to be Maggie Kilgour, *From Communion to Cannibalism: An Anatomy of Metaphors of Incorporation* (Princeton: Princeton University Press, 1990). For an important case study see Sharon Cameron, *The Corporeal Self: Allegories of the Body in Melville and Hawthorne* (New York: Columbia University Press, 1991).

12. The list of projects confirming the identity-making work of food and foodways is too extensive to do justice to here. For foundational work on this idea in Jewish dietary law, but also on the ways that food cultures produce a group's external boundaries and internal lines, see Mary Douglas, *Purity and Danger: An Analysis of the Concepts of Pollution and Taboo* (New York: Routledge, 2000). See also Bourdieu's discussion of working-class and bourgeois diet in Bourdieu, *Distinction*. Chapter 4, "The National Diet," is useful reading in Bob Ashley et al., *Food and Cultural Studies* (New York: Routledge, 2004). Carole Counihan's anthology *Food in the USA* offers several perspectives in the section "Food and the Nation," including Sidney Mintz's polemical article "Eating American," which asserts that there is no such thing as a U.S. cuisine while, it seems to me, paradoxically asserting that there is such a thing as U.S. food processes. Sidney Mintz, "Eating American," in *Food in the USA*, ed. Carole Counihan (New York: Routledge, 2002). In the now-classic *Revolution at the Table*, Harvey Levenstein disagrees with Mintz. Harvey Levenstein, *Revolution at the Table: The Transformation of the American Diet* (Berkeley: University of California Press, 1988). Recent popular work on U.S. foodways all hinges on the idea that there is such a thing as a national foodway. In particular see David Kamp, *The United States of*

Arugula: How We Became a Gourmet Nation (New York: Broadway Books, 2006); and Eric Schlosser, *Fast Food Nation: The Dark Side of the All-American Meal* (New York: Houghton Mifflin, 2001).

13. Sigmund Freud, *Three Essays on the History of Sexuality* (New York: Basic Books, 1975), 48.

14. It is worth noting that even Freud retains a rhetorical investment in the particular tactility of the mouth, referring to the mouth as a "mucous membrane," as though to emphasize the mouth's porosity, its difference from other, dryer sites on the body, on the one hand, and, on the other, to emphasize its similarity to the anus and vagina, both of which are described in the same terms. In fact, Freud seems to propose that all skin may *evolve* into mucous membrane in the case of the development of a sexual aberration. He writes, "In scopophilia and exhibitionism the eye corresponds to an erotogenic zone; while in the case of those components of the sexual instinct which involve pain and cruelty the same role is assumed by the skin—the skin, which in particular parts of the body has become differentiated into sense organs or modified into mucous membrane, and is thus the erotogenic zone *par excellence*." Freud, *Three Essays*, 35, italics in the original. See also ibid., 12, 16, 17, 18, 32, and so on. A full examination of the literary applications of Freud's theory of orality is unfortunately beyond the scope of this book.

15. See Michel Foucault, *The History of Sexuality, Volume 1: An Introduction* (New York: Vintage Books, 1990).

16. For more on the issue of the reform movement's production of a public and mass culture see Michael Warner, "Whitman Drunk," in *Publics and Counterpublics*, 269–290 (New York: Zone Books, 2005). On the production of individual interiority as the most important site of U.S. politics see Christopher Castiglia, *Interior States: Institutional Consciousness and the Inner Life of Democracy in the Antebellum United States* (Durham: Duke University Press, 2008).

17. Quoted in Catharine Esther Beecher and Harriet Beecher Stowe, *The American Woman's Home; or, Principles of Domestic Science* (New York: J. B. Ford, 1869), 120–121.

18. Butler, *Bodies That Matter*, 95.

19. William Ian Miller, *The Anatomy of Disgust* (Cambridge: Harvard University Press, 1998), 18. Sara Ahmed's work intersects with Miller's to argue that "the very project of survival requires that we take something other into our bodies. Survival makes us vulnerable in that it requires we let what is 'not us' in; to survive we open ourselves up and we *keep the orifices of the body open*." Ahmed, *The Cultural Politics of Emotion*, 83. Ahmed's brilliant work on affect generally in *The Cultural Politics of Emotion* is about understanding the ways that feelings "work as different kinds of orientations towards objects and others, which shape individual as well as collective bodies" (ibid., 15). My analysis of disgust in *Racial Indigestion* aligns itself with Miller's in that I see disgust to be a form of pleasure.

20. Bill Brown's work on materiality, on "thingness," opens up other useful questions, particularly in those moments when he engages with blackness as the a priori sign of the line between subject and object, or thing, in the American political unconscious. In "Reification, Reanimation, and the American Uncanny" Brown takes up the "ongoing record of

the ontological possibilities of slavery . . . which . . . persists within material, visual and literary culture." Bill Brown, "Reification, Reanimation, and the American Uncanny," *Critical Inquiry* 32:2 (2006): 207. Borrowing from anthropologists Arjun Appadurai and Igor Kopytoff, Brown seeks to emancipate materialist analysis from the limits of its concentration on the movement of commodities within capitalism's signifying chain to encompass the object's inherent ability to signify on and with the subject or, in other words, to develop meaning outside of commodity flow. This "uncanny" ability of things—in particular the objects of racial kitsch—to signify, to, in other words, come to life, is symbolic, for Brown, of the repressed history of those subjects who once circulated in the Americas as objects and commodities: "The American uncanny, as I've tried to describe it, might alert us to another dynamic as well: the possibility that our reluctance to think seriously about things may result from a repressed apprehension—the apprehension that within things we will discover the human precisely because our history is one in which humans were reduced to things (however incomplete that reduction)" (ibid., 207).

As much as I am indebted to Brown's opening up of the study of *thingness*, I am troubled by the absence of bodies in his work, particularly when his argument about studying things is meant to point us back toward the human. The absence of the body in Brown's work on race seems all the more surprising when one considers that the denial of human status to those humans designated as things through the combined interests of capital and juridical structures was historically based in perceptions of the lack of sentience and hyperembodiment of certain subjects vis-à-vis others.

Brown's primary object of study in this article, we should remember, is the Jolly Nigger Bank, a mechanical bank that takes coins that are slotted into its mouth; other objects include mammy cookie jars and a mammy mechanical bank, figures eating watermelons, or watermelons on their own, and finally a "Jolly Darkie Target Game," in which the player tosses balls into a mouth which can open and close. These are first and foremost objects that represent bodies; but all of these artifacts seek to take objects into, or in the case of the cookie jar to hold objects that will go into, a mouth. And this persistence of orality, of images of black ingestion or of the association of blackness with edibility and—as we shall see—sweetness, pushes us to think through the political life of the mouth, or as Davide Panagia has described it, "the mouth as a complex organ of political reflection." Davide Panagia, *The Political Life of Sensation* (Durham: Duke University Press, 2009), 19. Examining my archive via what I call *orificiality*—a trope that counters other, more "superficial" or epidermically oriented analyses—demands that we think about the return of history—what Teresa Goddu elsewhere has called the American Gothic—through the mouths of seemingly still images and representations of historically overdetermined bodies. But looking more closely to the mouth as a site—maybe *the* site—of political and affective "animation" in Brown's terms, what Sianne Ngai earlier called "animatedness," or what Ahmed calls "intensification" requires us to think about those apertures where the object and the subject open up to the world *and to each other*, sometimes as mirror images of each other, sometimes so that the one may devour the other. See Arjun Appadurai, ed., *The Social Life of Things: Commodities in Cultural Perspective* (New York: Cambridge

University Press, 1988); and Igor Kopytoff, "The Cultural Biography of Things: Commoditization as Process," in Appadurai, *The Social Life of Things*, 64–94. For a more detailed discussion of the "American uncanny" see Teresa A. Goddu, *Gothic America: Narrative, History, Nation* (New York: Columbia University Press, 1997). For a thorough discussion of the relationship of "animatedness" to race see Sianne Ngai, *Ugly Feelings* (Cambridge: Harvard University Press, 2005), in particular chapter 2, "Animatedness," 89–125. See also Bill Brown, *A Sense of Things: The Object Matter of American Literature* (Chicago: University of Chicago Press, 2004).

21. This connection between race and the metaphor of the food chain was first suggested to me in a footnote from Julia Stern's immensely helpful and brilliant article "Excavating Genre in *Our Nig*," *American Literature* 67:3 (September 1995): 460.

22. Daphne Brooks, *Bodies in Dissent: Spectacular Performances of Race and Freedom, 1850–1910* (Durham: Duke University Press, 2007), 8.

23. bell hooks, "Eating the Other: Desire and Resistance," in *Black Looks: Race and Representation*, 21–41 (Cambridge, MA: South End, 1999). Jacques Derrida also engages with the phrase "Eating the Other" in his discussion of hunger and the animal in "Eating Well."

24. Indeed I have at times considered subtitling this project "Rabelais in the United States" to underline my debt to these books. Bakhtin's important consideration of the grotesque as it relates to class, his valorization and recuperation of the life of the lower body, in particular the belly, and his discussion of the political work of laughter and the open mouth have importantly opened my sense for these things in American culture. I have also drawn on theories of early-modern banquet literature—in particular Michel Jeanneret's work—to think about the connection between food and language. I am interested in the long historical conjunction of food and eating culture with the counter-hegemony of the oral over the written and the vernacular over high culture discourses. In rereading Bakhtin I drew on Stallybrass and White's work, as well as Stuart Hall's important consideration and clarification of the importance of Stallybrass and White's development of Bakhtin's at times reductive high-low binarism. See Mikhail Mikhailovich Bakhtin, *Rabelais and His World* (Bloomington: Indiana University Press, 1984); François Rabelais, *Gargantua and Pantagruel* (New York: Penguin, 2006); Peter Stallybrass and Allon White, *The Politics and Poetics of Transgression* (Ithaca: Cornell University Press, 1986); Stuart Hall, "For Allon White: Metaphors of Transformation," in *Stuart Hall: Critical Dialogues in Cultural Studies*, ed. David Morley and Kuan-Hsing Chen, 287–306; (New York: Routledge, 1996); Michel Jeanneret, *A Feast of Words: Banquets and Table Talk in the Renaissance* (Chicago: University of Chicago Press, 1991). A related, though very different, term from the field of food studies is what Annie Hauck-Lawson, a contemporary food scholar, has termed *food voice*. While Hauck-Lawson defines *food voice* as the use of food as a channel of communication, particularly in ethnic communities, I am more interested in the conjoining of food with orality as a longstanding literary and cultural trope. See Annie Hauck-Lawson, "Introduction," *Food, Culture and Society: An International Journal of Multidisciplinary Research* 7 (Spring 2004): 24–25. See also Annie Hauck-Lawson, "When

Food Is the Voice: A Case Study of a Polish-American Woman," *Journal for the Study of Food and Society* 2:1 (1998): 21–28; and Michel de Certeau, *The Practice of Everyday Life*, trans. Steven Rendall (Berkeley: University of California Press, 1988).

NOTES TO CHAPTER 1

1. See for instance Gillian Brown, "Getting in the Kitchen with Dinah: Domestic Politics in *Uncle Tom's Cabin*," *American Quarterly* 36 (Fall 1984): 503–523; Jane Tompkins, "Sentimental Power: *Uncle Tom's Cabin* and the Politics of Literary History," in *Sensational Designs: The Cultural Work of American Fiction, 1790–1860*, 122–146 (New York: Oxford University Press, 1985). As I discuss in this chapter, there is a long line of feminist historians who have documented the changing architecture and technology of the kitchen.

2. Although domesticity remains at the center of much feminist literary criticism, some critics, such as Millette Shamir, have begun to examine the house in terms of the political and affective economy of its internally differentiated spaces. Shamir has noted that the plan of the bourgeois house began to change in the eighteenth century, with the upstairs coming to represent the sphere of privacy, and the main floor downstairs the more open (and hence public) space. In this shift in the interior space the fate of the kitchen was tied to a shifting sense of its function: from the hearth as a shared work and living space, the household plan came increasingly to mark the kitchen as wholly devoted to the production of food. Shamir cites a remark of Thoreau's, which casts a slightly paranoid view of these changes in interior design: "There is as much secrecy about the cooking as if [a host] had a design to poison you. . . . The parlor is so far from the kitchen and workshop," he laments, "how can the scholar, who dwells away in the Northwest Territory or the Isle of Man, tell what is parliamentary in the kitchen?" Quoted in Milette Shamir, *Inexpressible Privacy: The Interior Life of Antebellum American Literature* (Philadelphia: University of Pennsylvania Press, 2006), 204. In the shift to the architecture of the bourgeois home, the life of the hearth as gathering space, as cooking, reading, and working space, and crucially as social space is left behind, as each of these functions is banished, as Hawthorne and Melville will tell us, to its own separate corner. Nathaniel Hawthorne, "Fire Worship," in *Mosses from an Old Manse* (New York: Modern Library, 2003); Herman Melville, "I and My Chimney," in *Tales, Poems, and Other Writings*, 264–290 (New York: Modern Library, 2002).

Some of this scholarship has aimed at reconstructing the mechanisms through which domesticity helped to construct models of liberal selfhood. For instance Lori Merish argues in her study of middle-class interiority—both domestic and psychic—that "in sentimental novels, as well as in texts such as architectural pattern books and home decorating manuals, which codified domestic ideology, 'inside' was being established as the realm of fulfillment and emotional satisfaction: the Jeffersonian political ideal of the economic self-sufficiency of the individual homestead was being reconfigured as the domestic ideal of affectional self-sufficiency." Lori Merish, *Sentimental Materialism: Gender, Commodity*

Culture, and Nineteenth-Century American Literature (Durham: Duke University Press, 2000), 141. Resolving what Shamir sees as domesticity's ideological paradox—"how could domestic ideology reconcile the spirituality and ethereality of the domestic angel with her predilection for consumer objects" (ibid., 273)—Merish argues that the ownership of objects (and those humans see as objects) provides a template for the formation of the interiorized middle-class self. While for Shamir the house bifurcates into the feminized parlor and the masculinized study, the interior of the home is, for Merish, if not uniform and undifferentiated, then largely focused toward the front-of-house, or the parlor, as a privileged site of middle-class performance and commodity display. The interior of the house, then, models new forms of gendered and affective selfhood; in that model kitchen and food work became increasingly abject, part of the body work that is hidden from public performance. Given these critics' interest in the performative aspect of middle-class interiority, which was largely showcased in the house's more public areas, it is perhaps not surprising that in their work the kitchen is largely hidden from view.

Indeed, the literary thematic of the subordination of the kitchen in the regime of impression management that governed interior domestic space is not dissimilar from the pattern seen in other, more mainstream historical work. In historians' discussions of the middle-class house, and its corresponding narratives of refinement, either they emphasize the crass and premodern symbolism of the early modern and prerevolutionary hearth, or they leave it out almost completely. In Karen Halttunen's discussion of the rise of the parlor gentility in *Confidence Men and Painted Women*, for instance, she draws on Erving Goffman's work to define the social differences between the front and back of the middle-class house: in doing so, however, she names the kitchen only four times in her entire book. Karen Halttunen, *Confidence Men and Painted Women: A Study of Middle-Class Culture in America, 1830–1870* (New Haven: Yale University Press, 1982). Richard Bushman's discussion of the shrinking of the parlor fireplace as a correct backdrop for genteel conversation opposes that space to the "gaping maws of seventeenth-century cooking fireplaces" and mentions the kitchen not at all. He writes, "In the eighteenth century, fireplace openings in formal rooms were much smaller in every dimension than the gaping maws of seventeenth-century cooking fireplaces. Small fireplaces minimized the loss of heat up the chimney and by warming the entire room enabled people to fill the space rather than cluster at the fire opening." Richard Lyman Bushman, *The Refinement of America: Persons, Houses, Cities* (New York: Vintage, 1993), 5. If Merish's book does not directly address the kitchen, she doesn't ignore the mouth. In a gorgeous reading of masculine orality in her chapter on cigars, she writes, "the specifically *oral* desire associated with and engendered by the cigar manifests the cross-racial homoerotics of white male subject formation (cigar smoking as fellatio) as well as a historically resonant, cultural metaphorics of imperial cannibalism (cigar smoking as "eating the Other")" (Merish, *Sentimental Materialism*, 273).

3. Sara Ahmed, *The Cultural Politics of Emotion* (New York: Routledge, 2004), 89–92. I find Ahmed's formulation of stickiness useful in that it models history as a palimpsest in which meaning adheres to particular bodies, while at the same time registering the centrality of disgust in the production of everyday political discourse.

4. Amir H. Ameri, "Housing Ideologies in the New England and Chesapeake Bay Colonies, c. 1650–1700," *Journal of the Society of Architectural Historians* 56:1 (March 1997): 6–15. Ameri speculates that the Puritan dislike for ostentatious display put pressure on residents of New England not to emphasize their house's chimneys, as in England chimneys were generally associated with the gentry.

5. John E. Crowley, *The Invention of Comfort: Sensibilities and Design in Early Modern Britain and Early America* (Baltimore: Johns Hopkins University Press, 2001), 107.

6. Jane C. Nylander, *Our Own Snug Fireside: Images of the New England Home, 1760–1860* (New Haven: Yale University Press, 1994), 111.

7. Francis Higginson, *New England's Plantation: With Sea Journal and Other Writings* (Salem, MA: Essex Book and Print Club, 1908), 121.

8. Which raises the interesting question of whether colonial and nineteenth-century food *tasted* smoky.

9. Cotton Mather, *The Diary of Cotton Mather, 1621–1724* (Worcester: Massachusetts Historical Society, 1911), 216.

10. Benjamin Franklin, Lewis Evans, and James Turner, *An Account of the New Invented Pennsylvanian Fire-Places: Wherein Their Construction and Manner of Operation Is Particularly Explained; Their Advantages above Every Other Method of Warming Rooms Demonstrated; and All Objections That Have Been Raised against the Use of Them, Answered and Obviated; with Directions for Putting Them Up, and for Using Them to the Best Advantage; and a Copper-Plate, in Which the Several Parts of the Machine Are Exactly Laid Down, from a Scale of Equal Parts* (Philadelphia: B. Franklin, 1744).

11. Ibid, 5.

12. Ibid, 6.

13. *Dame Trot and Her Comical Cat: Illustrated with Sixteen Elegant Engravings* (Philadelphia: Wm. Charles, American Antiquarian Society, 1809).

14. The figure of Dame Trot has an interesting European history as the putative descendant of an eleventh-century female physician named Trotula, rumored, though probably not, a midwife and doctor at the Salerno medical school and reputedly the author of *De Passionibus Mulierum Curandorum*, or "Of the Diseases of Women." Trotula even merits mention in Chaucer's *Wife of Bath*.

15. See Iona Archibald Opie and Peter Opie, *The Oxford Dictionary of Nursery Rhymes* (New York: Oxford University Press, 1997), 320. For a discussion of cross-dressing in the pantomime see Shirley Ardener, "Male Dames and Female Boys: Cross-Dressing in the English Pantomime," in *Changing Sex and Bending Gender*, ed. Alison Shaw and Shirley Ardener, 119–137 (New York: Berghahn Books, 2005), 125.

There are mentions of Dame Trot and her Comical Cat in the New York Times up until at least 1879 when an anonymous reporter wrote that "Three hundred children from the Jewish Orphan Asylum will attend the last matinee of "Dame Trot" at the Fifth-Avenue Theatre to-morrow afternoon, on the invitation of Mr. Maurice Grau." "Amusements: General Mention," *New York Times*, November 28, 1879.

16. *Dame Trot and Her Comical Cat*, 3.

17. Ibid., 5–6.

18. Ibid., 10–11.

19. Aristotle, *Poetics*, trans. Malcolm Heath (New York: Penguin, 1996), especially sections 4 and 12, on tragedy and comedy, respectively.

20. Michel Jeanneret, *A Feast of Words: Banquets and Table Talk in the Renaissance* (Chicago: Chicago University Press, 1991), 102.

21. Rabelais's *Gargantua and Pantagruel* is only the best known of them. See François Rabelais, *Gargantua and Pantagruel* (New York: Penguin, 2006).

22. Mikhail Mikhailovich Bakhtin, *Rabelais and His World* (Bloomington: Indiana University Press, 1984), 318–319.

23. Ibid., 285–286.

24. Daphne Brooks, *Bodies in Dissent: Spectacular Performances of Race and Freedom* (Durham: Duke University Press, 2006), 23.

25. Indeed, Brooks notes that "whereas the pantomime employed the 'Benevolent Agent' or 'fairy godmother' character of the conventional nursery rhyme and fairy tale genre as a means of inserting play and possibility into the production of identity, the minstrel show relied on a repertoire of 'nonsense' songs, puns, and physical humor. . . . Blackface jokes and songs revolved around the transmutation of black bodies into animals, furniture, and—quite obsessively—food." Ibid., 27. More on this in chapters 3 and 5.

26. Catharine Ann Turner Dorset, *Think Before You Speak; or, The Three Wishes: A Tale* (Philadelphia: Johnson and Warner, 1809).

27. Ibid., 6.

28. Ibid., 8.

29. As a culinary footnote, Alan Davidson's *Penguin Companion to Food* (formerly the Oxford companion) explains that "pudding may be claimed as a British invention, and is certainly a characteristic dish of British cuisine." Alan Davidson, *The Penguin Companion to Food* (New York: Penguin, 2002), s.v. "Pudding." Amelia Simmons devotes eight pages of her *American Cookery* (1796) to pudding recipes. Amelia Simmons, *American Cookery; or, The Art of Dressing Viands, Fish, Poultry, and Vegetables, and the Best Modes of Making Pastes, Puffs, Pies, Tarts, Puddings, Custards, and Preserves, and All Kinds of Cakes, from the Imperial Plum to Plain Cake: Adapted to This Country, and All Grades of Life* (Albany, NY: C. R. Webster, 1796). Historically puddings could be sweet or savory, and early puddings (the earliest known recipe is 1617) were cooked in sausage skins, meaning intestine or stomach. Almost all of Simmons's puddings are sweet, however, and call for quite a bit of sugar: now, of course, "pudding" in America has come to represent what would then have been known as "milk pudding," made with flavoring, sugar, and loads of cornstarch. The pudding fits quite nicely into the *Three Wishes* story because it is a dish that is meant to cook slowly and steadily with low to medium heat. Thus, it is suited to be cooked in embers, as Susan wishes.

30. Turner Dorset, *Think Before You Speak*, 25–26 (emphasis in original).

31. Ibid., 30

32. Ibid., 32.

33. Ibid., 28.

34. Peter Stallybrass and Allon White, *The Politics and Poetics of Transgression* (Ithaca: Cornell University Press, 1986). To be fair, I am to a certain extent conflating the artisan and the proletarian body; the motif of the three wishes here is a transposition of Perrault's popular "conte de trois souhaits," in which the husband is a woodcutter and the food on the end of the nose is a sausage. Nonetheless my point here is that the one-fireplace room of the woodcuttings would have been read as not-genteel in the context of the early United States.

35. This is the way it is described in Amelia Simmons 1796 *American Cookery* anyway. Up until the seventeenth century, puddings were most often cooked inside an animal intestine or stomach, like haggis or sausage, unlike the gooey, sticky, cornstarch-laden sugar messes today thought of as "pudding." Simmons, *American Cookery.*

36. *Oxford English Dictionary*, 2nd ed. (online), s.v. "Pudding," http://www.oed.com (accessed March 14, 2011). The historical roots of the tale, which go back to Perrault's much-translated story of the "Three Foolish Wishes," make the penis allusion more explicit by making the food a sausage.

37. *The World Turned Upside Down; or, The Comical Metamorphoses: A Work Entirely Calculated to Excite Laughter in Grown Persons and Promote Morality in the Young Ones of Both Sexes: Decorated with 34 Copper Plates Curiously Drawn and Engraved* (Boston: I. Norman, 1794).

38. "Baste: To spoon or brush food as it cooks with melted butter or other fat, meat drippings or liquid such as stock." Sharon Tyler Herbst and Ron Herbst, *The New Food Lover's Companion*, 4th ed. (Hauppauge, NY: Barron's Educational Series, 2007), 48. According to the *OED*, basting also means "to beat soundly, thrash, cudgel." *Oxford English Dictionary*, 2nd ed. (online), s.v. "Baste, v. 2," definition 1a, http://www.oed.com (accessed June 12, 2011).

39. *The World Turned Upside Down*, 34.

40. Also, notably, *The World Turned Upside Down* shows many instances of children overthrowing parents. As Jay Fliegelman has shown, this was a widespread literary preoccupation in the period, pointing toward the rearrangement of family structures and certain modes of patriarchal authority, as well as to the rise of the Lockean model of education. Fliegelman writes, "English and American literature of the last half of the eighteenth century shared the same intense thematic preoccupation: familial relations. On both sides of the Atlantic, novelists, poets, playwrights, and anonymous authors of didactic periodical fiction joined together in an effort—an effort almost without historical precedent—to anatomize the family, to define 'the familial, the parental and the social duties,' and to prescribe the terms of a new ideal relationship between generations." Jay Fliegelman, *Prodigals and Pilgrims: The American Revolution against Patriarchal Authority, 1750–1800* (New York: Cambridge University Press, 1985), 9.

41. See the discussion of the 1764 Dicey-Marshall catalogue at the Birmingham Library website: "The Diceys and the Transmission of Cheap Print to North America," http://www.bham.ac.uk/DiceyandMarshall/intro3.htm.

42. *The World Turned Upside Down*, 30.

43. See for instance Cary Wolfe, *Animal Rites: American Culture, the Discourse of Species, and Posthumanist Culture* (Chicago: University of Chicago Press, 2003).

44. Priscilla J. Brewer, *From Fireplace to Cookstove: Technology and the Domestic Ideal in America* (Syracuse: Syracuse University Press, 2000).

45. Nathaniel Hawthorne, "Fire Worship," in *Mosses from an Old Manse* (New York: Modern Library, 2003), 107–114.

46. Ibid., 110.

47. Ibid., 106.

48. Ibid., 110.

49. Ibid.

50. "Throat, n.: . . . 6a. The part in a chimney, furnace, or furnace-arch immediately above the fire-place, which narrows down to the neck or 'gathering.'" *Oxford English Dictionary*, 2nd ed. (online), s.v. "Throat," http://www.oed.com (accessed June 12, 2011).

51. See for instance Lea Bertani Vozar Newman, *A Reader's Guide to the Short Stories of Herman Melville* (New York: G. K. Hall, 1986); Melville, "I and My Chimney."

52. Melville, "I and My Chimney," 271.

53. Shamir, *Inexpressible Privacy*, 81. I should clarify that I understand the separate spheres as an ideology and not a lived reality. Although much important work has been done to complicate ideas of separate spheres as quotidian functioning practice, it is important nonetheless to pay heed to the ideological force of the separate spheres doctrine. In that it could not be lived as such, we have much evidence; we have equally much evidence that it functioned as a felt standard against which many homes and lives were measured. See especially Cathy Davidson and Jessmyn Hatcher, eds., *No More Separate Spheres! A Next Wave American Studies Reader* (Durham: Duke University Press, 2002).

54. Sarah Wilson, "Melville and the Architecture of Antebellum Masculinity," *American Literature* 76:1 (2004): 59–87; and Vincent J. Bertolini, "Fireside Chastity: The Erotics of Sentimental Bachelorhood in the 1850s," *American Literature* 68:4 (December 1960: 707–737.

55. Melville, "I and My Chimney," 270.

56. Ibid., 285.

57. Ibid., 264.

58. Ibid., 289, italics added.

59. Ibid., 273–274.

60. De Certeau writes, "The intextuation of the body corresponds to the incarnation of the law; it supports it, it even seems to establish it, and in any case it serves it. . . . Perhaps the law would have no power if it were not able to support itself on the obscure desire to exchange one's flesh for a glorious body, to be written. . . . The only force opposing this passion to be a sign is the cry, a deviation or an ecstasy, a revolt or flight of that which, within the body, escapes the law of the named." Michel de Certeau, *The Practice of Everyday Life*, trans. Steven Rendall (Berkeley: University of California Press, 1988), 149.

61. Melville, "I and My Chimney," 284.

62. Ibid., 265, italics added.

63. Ibid., 290.

64. Ellen M. Plante, *The American Kitchen, 1700 to the Present: From Hearth to High-rise* (New York: Facts on File Press, 1995), 41.

65. Ruth Schwartz Cowan, *More Work for Mother: The Ironies of Household Technology from the Open Hearth to the Microwave* (New York: Basic Books, 1983), 54.

66. Ibid.

67. Catharine Esther Beecher, *A Treatise on Domestic Economy* (New York: Thomas H. Webb, 1841), 299.

68. Ibid., 303.

69. The question of when the middle class came to know itself as such is too large for this study to take on, but to clarify, my argument here is that the middle class is in formation in this period. I am working here with Stuart Blumin's idea of the middle class from his work in *The Emergence of the Middle Class* (New York: Cambridge University Press, 1989). In the eighteenth century, although the term *middle folk*, or *middling folk*, was in circulation, according to Blumin, the "middle" was a still-not-quite-defined social space. Although it referred loosely to artisans and "mechanics," or those who worked with their hands, in fact the urban social space, the "pedestrian city," was one in which people of different ranks met face to face. That said, the social hierarchy was far more rigidly defined in the preindustrial terms of *estate* and *rank*, and while Blumin argues that the Revolution offered mechanics and artisans a moment of political possibility for upward mobility, the rigidly hierarchical system of social deference based on rank still held during the early days of the republic. Thus, merchants held the most political power, while artisans and mechanics were at the lowest rungs, excepting slaves. Blumin argues that some ambiguity circulates around those artisans who were also proprietors, that is, who oversaw journeymen-apprentices or employees.

Blumin traces the change in conceptions of labor to the Jacksonian period that follows on the heels of the War of 1812. With trade routes opened up and the "transportation revolution" under way, the growing volume of produce and products that flowed through port cities led to increasingly specialized occupations surrounding trade, including sales, clerking, accounting, insurance, and managerial jobs. This in turn led to a boom in minor white-collar jobs and the segregation of manual work spaces from clerking, wholesale, and retail spaces. It is along this axis—manual versus nonmanual labor—that Blumin traces the line that divides the working class from the middle class. This spatial segregation had the effect of stigmatizing manual labor and the spaces it inhabits: the factory and the workshop. Additionally, there is an increasing specialization of retail spaces and a growth in the number of retail clerks, who are often apprenticing to be proprietors themselves. That said, it should be noted that Blumin ultimately argues that the middle class does not formally develop until after the Civil War.

70. Reaching back to the eighteenth century, in *The Refinement of America*, Richard L. Bushman writes that the "purpose of the eighteenth-century gentry house was to transform life within its walls. The house hid the everyday vulgar activities of cooking and work

in the back, in outbuildings, or in the cellar. In the front of the house were spacious rooms filled with light and warmth, where people stood or sat in conversation or at tea" (127). As Bushman shows, these changes did not reach the homes of "middling" folks until the nineteenth century.

71. It is important to read domestic manuals, with their valorization of the domestic labors of middle-class women, not as descriptive of a commonly existent space but, rather, as many historians have noted, as prescriptive and at times utopic. In disseminating early discourses of social hygiene, domestic manuals were both creating and being created by the new spaces inside middle-class homes.

72. Jeanne Boydston, *Home and Work: Housework, Wages, and the Ideology of Labor in the Early Republic* (New York: Oxford University Press, 1994), 159.

73. Mary Randolph, *The Virginia Housewife; or, Methodical Cook: A Facsimile of an Authentic Early American Cookbook* (Baltimore: Plaskitt, Fite, 1838), x, italics added.

74. Beecher, *A Treatise on Domestic Economy*, 144.

75. Lydia Maria Francis Child, *The American Frugal Housewife* (Boston: Carter and Hendee, 1830).

76. Child evidently expects the frugal housewife to transgress her scruples and her sense of disgust with her suggestion about the usefulness of "ear wax": "Nothing is better than ear-wax to prevent the painful effects resulting from a wound by a nail, skewer, &c. It should be put on as soon as possible. Those who are troubled with cracked lips have found this remedy successful when others have failed. It is one of those sort of cures, which are very likely to be laughed at; but I know of its having produced very beneficial results." Ibid., 116.

77. Ibid., 3.

78. Beecher, *A Treatise on Domestic Economy*, 366.

79. This idea has yet to disappear, as ongoing public panics about salmonella, raw chicken, and other food threats attest. One interesting story about the kitchen is Charlotte Perkins Gilman's "The Kitchen Fly," published at the turn of the twentieth century in her short-lived magazine, *The Forerunner*. In "The Kitchen Fly" Gilman proposes that kitchens be got rid of altogether. One of a long series of women who proposed utopian kitchen projects, as Dolores Hayden has documented, Gilman's commitment to the eugenics project makes her deployment of kitchen disgust very interesting, particularly in the context of the unfolding connection between race and food that I document over the next few chapters. Charlotte Perkins Gilman, "The Kitchen Fly" (1910), in *The Forerunner, Volume 1 (1909–1910): A Monthly Magazine*, 459–462 (Middlesex, UK: Echo Library, 2007); Dolores Hayden, *The Grand Domestic Revolution: A History of Feminist Designs for American Homes, Neighborhoods, and Cities* (Cambridge: MIT Press, 1982).

80. Beecher, *A Treatise on Domestic Economy*, 299.

81. Sarah Josepha Buell Hale, *The Good Housekeeper; or, The Way to Live Well and to Be Well While We Live: Containing Directions for Choosing and Preparing Food, in Regard to Health, Economy and Taste* (Boston: Weeks, Jordan, 1839), 152.

82. See Susan Strasser, *Never Done: A History of American Housework* (New York: Holt, 2000).

83. Faye Dudden, *Serving Women: Household Service in Nineteenth-Century America* (New York: Harper and Row, 1983).

84. This increasingly important parlor life is explored in Halttunen, *Confidence Men and Painted Women.*

85. Beecher, *A Treatise on Domestic Economy*, 201.

86. Harriet Beecher Stowe [Christopher Crowfield, pseud.], "Chapter IX: Service," from the *House and Home Papers*, *Atlantic Monthly*, January 1864, 442.

87. Harriet Beecher Stowe, "Our Second Girl," *Atlantic Monthly*, January 1868, 57.

88. Catharine Esther Beecher and Harriet Beecher Stowe, *The American Woman's Home; or, Principles of Domestic Science* (New York: J. B. Ford, 1869), 311, italics added.

89. Ibid., 326.

90. Amy Kaplan has explored close ties between domesticity and empire in her essay "Manifest Domesticity," in which she argues that the domestic served as a metaphor against which and through which the new outposts of U.S. empire were both contrasted and contained. She also briefly explores this metaphor in terms of the inner workings of the home when she writes that "the mother's ill health stems from the unruly subjects of her domestic empire—children and servants—who bring uncivilized wilderness and undomesticated foreignness into the home." Amy Kaplan, "Manifest Domesticity," in *No More Separate Spheres! A Next Wave American Studies Reader*, ed. Cathy N. Davidson and Jessamyn Hatcher, 183–208 (Durham: Duke University Press, 2002) 192.

91. Hale, *The Good Housekeeper*, 123–124.

92. Ibid., 124.

93. Mrs. John Farrar, *The Young Lady's Friend* (Boston: American Stationers' Company, 1837).

94. Caroline Gilman, *Recollections of a Southern Matron* (New York: Harper and Brothers, 1838), 126.

95. Barbara Ryan, "Kitchen Testimony: Ex-Slaves' Narratives in New Company," *Callaloo* 22:1 (1999): 141–156.

96. Quoted in ibid., 147.

97. Robert Roberts, *The House Servant's Directory; or, A Monitor for Private Families: Comprising Hints on the Arrangement and Performance of Servants' Work* (Boston: Munroe and Francis, 1827).

98. Ibid., lvii.

99. William Kitchiner, *The Cook's Oracle: Containing Receipts for Plain Cookery, on the Most Economical Plan for Private Families: Also, the Art of Composing the Most Simple, and Most Highly Finished Broths, Gravies, Soups, Sauces, Store Sauces, and Flavouring Essences: The Quantity of Each Article Is Accurately Stated by Weight and Measure; the Whole Being the Result of Actual Experiments Instituted in the Kitchen of a Physician* (Edinburgh: A. Constable; Cheapside: Hurst, Robinson, 1822).

100. Roberts, *The House Servant's Directory*, 140–141.

101. Ibid., 142, 143.

102. Ibid., 143.

103. Ibid., 144.
104. Ibid.
105. Ibid., xlvi.

NOTES TO CHAPTER 2

1. For an example of Graham as a contemporary symbol of nineteenth-century eccentricity and prurience see Chuck Klosterman, *Sex, Drugs, and Cocoa Puffs: A Low Culture Manifesto* (New York: Scribner, 2003), in which Klosterman writes, "Any breakfast historian can tell you that Sylvester Graham (1794–1851), so-called 'philosopher and nutrition crusader,' was the kind of forward-thinking wackmobile . . . ," etc. (119).

2. See Michael Warner, "Whitman Drunk," in *Publics and Counterpublics*, 269–289 (New York: Zone Books, 2005). See also Eve Kosofsky Sedgwick, "Jane Austen and the Masturbating Girl," in *Solitary Pleasures: The Historical, Literary, and Artistic Discourses of Autoeroticism*, ed. Paula Bennett and Vernon A. Rosario, 133–155 (New York: Routledge, 1995).

3. Sedgwick, "Jane Austen and the Masturbating Girl," 134.

4. Bruce Burgett. "Between Speculation and Population: The Problem of 'Sex' in Our Long Eighteenth Century," *Early American Literature* 37:1 (2002): 122.

5. See Ben Barker Benfield, "The Spermatic Economy: A Nineteenth-Century View of Sexuality," *Feminist Studies* 1 (Summer 1972): 45–74; Helen Lefkowitz Horowitz, *Rereading Sex: Battles over Sexual Knowledge and Suppression in Nineteenth-Century America* (New York: Knopf, 2002); and Stephen Nissenbaum, *Sex, Diet, and Debility in Jacksonian American: Sylvester Graham and Health Reform* (Westport, CT: Greenwood, 1980).

6. One important exception to this critical blind spot is Jordan Stein's wonderful essay "Mary Rowlandson's Hunger and the Historiography of Sexuality," in which he argues that Rowlandson's hunger—a major trope of her captivity narrative—can be read as the sign of a premodern sexuality that is significantly, deinstrumentalized from the matter of meeting the body's needs. My work on Graham here intersects with Stein's in that I see Graham as a transitional figure in what might become a nonlinear and nonprogressive history of systems of biopower in the United States. Graham seeks to discipline, and therefore render socially legible, deinstrumentalized drives within a binaristic logic of deviancy/normalcy, but in doing so he also recognizes them as socially significant forms of pleasure. Jordan Alexander Stein, "Mary Rowlandson's Hunger and the Historiography of Sexuality," *American Literature* 81 (2009): 469–495.

7. Gayle Rubin, "Thinking Sex: Notes for a Radical Theory of the Politics of Sexuality," in *Pleasure and Danger: Exploring Female Sexuality*, ed. Carole S. Vance, 267–293 (London: Pandora, 1992). The connection between sex and food also has deep roots in the history of population science, where, as Bruce Burgett tells us, Malthus understood food and reproduction as construing the two basic "postulata" controlling population growth. Burgett, "Between Speculation and Population," 125.

8. Thomas Laqueur links the rise of anti-Onanist discourse to the rise of both the novel and pornography as imaginative, and therefore individuating, media. Thomas W.

Laqueur, *Solitary Sex: A Cultural History of Masturbation* (New York: Zone Books, 2003). Sedgwick writes, "masturbation can seem to offer—not least as an analogy to writing—a reservoir of potentially utopian metaphors and energies for independence, self-possession, and a rapture that may owe relatively little to political or interpersonal abjection." Sedgwick, "Jane Austen and the Masturbating Girl," 135.

9. Sylvester Graham, *A Treatise on Bread and Breadmaking* (Boston: Light and Stearns, 1837); Sylvester Graham, *A Lecture to Young Men on Chastity* (Boston: Light and Stearns, 1838); William Andrus Alcott, *The House I Live In; or, The Human Body* (Boston: Light and Stearns, 1837).

10. Alcott, *The House I Live In*, 166. The phrase "political life of the mouth" was inspired by Davide Panagia's work in *The Political Life of Sensation* (Durham: Duke University Press, 2009). Panagia's fascinating project examines the "aesthetico-political dimensions of democratic life" (3) and, in one chapter on the Slow Food movement, "the mouth as a complex organ of political reflection" (19). I diverge from Panagia in that, in this project at least, I have not focused on flavor as a political thematic. However, as the following chapters will attest, my interest in the history and idea of sweetness as it attaches to blackness can certainly be thought of as an early instance of the politicization of the palate. Here, of course, Sidney Mintz's work is also critical. See Sidney Mintz, *Sweetness and Power: The Place of Sugar in Modern History* (New York: Penguin, 1986).

11. Ronald G. Walters, *American Reformers, 1815–1860*, rev. ed. (New York: Hill and Wang, 1997).

12. T. Gregory Garvey, *Creating the Culture of Reform in Antebellum America* (Athens: University of Georgia Press, 2006), 2.

13. Walters, *American Reformers*, 128–129.

14. See Ralph Waldo Emerson, "New England Reformers: A Lecture Read Before the Society in Amory Hall on Sunday, 3 March, 1844," in *Essays and Lectures*, 589–614 (New York: Library of America, 1983).

15. Walters, *American Reformers*, 173.

16. Garvey, *Creating the Culture of Reform*, 4.

17. See David S. Reynolds, *Beneath the American Renaissance: The Subversive Imagination in the Age of Emerson and Melville* (Cambridge: Harvard University Press, 1989).

18. Warner, "Whitman Drunk," 270.

19. Alexis de Tocqueville, *Democracy in America* (New York: D. Appleton, 1904), 593.

20. Ibid., 596.

21. Amelia Simmons, *American Cookery; or, The Art of Dressing Viands, Fish, Poultry, and Vegetables, and the Best Modes of Making Pastes, Puffs, Pies, Tarts, Puddings, Custards, and Preserves, and All Kinds of Cakes, from the Imperial Plum to Plain Cake: Adapted to This Country, and All Grades of Life* (Albany, NY: C. R. Webster, 1796), 27.

22. Susannah Carter, *The Frugal Housewife; or, Complete Woman Cook: Wherein the Art of Dressing All Sorts of Viands with Cleanliness, Decency and Elegance, Is Explained in Five Hundred Approved Receipts . . . to Which Are Added Twelve New Prints, Exhibiting a Proper Arrangement of Dinners, Two Courses for Every Month in the Year* (New York: G.

& R. Waite, 1765; reprinted 1803). For more information see "The Frugal Housewife, or, Complete Woman Cook" at the Michigan State Library's "Feeding America" website, last modified December 16, 2004, http://digital.lib.msu.edu/projects/cookbooks/html/books/book_02.cfm.

23. This is true when the results exclude articles containing the term *assize*, otherwise the count is significantly higher: announcements of state-regulated prices of commodities are common in newspapers of the period and do not usually discuss bread so much as announce the price of breadstuffs.

24. Philanthropos, "On the Regulation of the Price of Bread," *Columbian Magazine*, December 1789, in *American Periodicals Series Online, 1740–1900*, 714.

25. See Benedict Anderson, *Imagined Communities: Reflections on the Origin and Spread of Nationalism* (New York: Verso, 1991)

26. Some examples: "Remarks on Bread," *Christian's, Scholar's, and Farmer's Magazine*, April–May 1790, in *American Periodicals Series Online, 1740–1900*, 118; "Remarks on Carrots, as an Ingredient of Bread," *New York Magazine, or Literary Repository*, August 1796, in *American Periodicals Series Online, 1740–1900*, 424; "Review of an Account of Experiments Tried by the Board of Agriculture, in the Composition of Various Sorts of Bread," *Weekly Magazine of Original Essays, Fugitive Pieces, and Interesting Intelligence*, August 4, 1798, in *American Periodicals Series Online, 1740–1900*, 20; "On the Means of Making Bread from Rice," *South-Carolina Weekly Museum and Complete Magazine of Entertainment and Intelligence*, February 25, 1797, in *American Periodicals Series Online, 1740–1900*, 230; Christopher Cakeling, "Whimsical Distresses of an Attempt to Make Bread," *Literary Museum, or, Monthly Magazine*, March 1797, in *American Periodicals Series Online, 1740–1900*, 155; "Art of Making a Delicate Bread without Yeast," *Weekly Magazine of Original Essays, Fugitive Pieces, and Interesting Intelligence*, June 2, 1798, in *American Periodicals Series Online, 1740–1900*, 151.

27. Henry Adolf Knopf, *Changes in Wheat Production in the United States, 1607–1960* (Ithaca: Cornell University Press, 1967), 30.

28. Ibid., 33.

29. John Egerton, with Ann Bleidt Egerton, *Southern Food: At Home, on the Road, in History* (New York: Knopf, 1987), 21.

30. For some discussions of the fluctuation of wheat prices in the eighteenth and early nineteenth centuries see Richard Lyman Bushman, "Markets and Composite Farms in Early America," *William and Mary Quarterly* 55:3 (1998): 351–374.

31. "Remarks on Carrots, as an Ingredient of Bread," in *American Periodicals Series Online, 1740–1900*, 424.

32. "The Domestic Guide," *New York Weekly Museum*, December 7, 1816, in *American Periodicals Series Online, 1740–1900*, 96; John Draytonn, "To Make Rice Bread," *Archives of Useful Knowledge*, January 1813, in *American Periodicals Series Online, 1740–1900*, 272; T. Bridgeman, "Pumpkin Bread," *Workingman's Advocate*, January 2, 1836, in *American Periodicals Series Online, 1740–1900*, 151; John Pender, "Manufacturing Oats into Bread Stuffs," *Fessenden's Silk Manual and Practical Farmer*, December 1836, in *American Periodicals*

Series Online, 1740–1900, 118; "Wholesome and Nutritious Bread from Saw-Dust," *Journal of Health*, November 9, 1831, in *American Periodicals Series Online, 1740–1900*, 70.

33. Sarah Josepha Buell Hale, *The Good Housekeeper; or, The Way to Live Well and to Be Well While We Live: Containing Directions for Choosing and Preparing Food, in Regard to Health, Economy and Taste* (Boston: Weeks, Jordan, 1839), vii.

34. Ibid., 9.

35. Ibid.

36. Ibid., 11.

37. Ibid., 12.

38. Ann Laura Stoler, "Matters of Intimacy as Matters of State: A Response," *Journal of American History* 88:3 (December 2001): 893.

39. See Edward L. Ayers et al., *All Over the Map: Rethinking American Regions* (Baltimore: Johns Hopkins University Press, 1995); and Ann Laura Stoler, "Tense and Tender Ties: The Politics of Comparison in North American and (Post)Colonial Studies," *Journal of American History* 88:3 (December 2001): 829–865.

40. Eliza Leslie, *Directions for Cookery, in Its Various Branches* (Philadelphia: E. L. Carey & Hart, 1840).

41. Ibid., 22.

42. Ibid., 24.

43. Catharine Beecher, *A Treatise on Domestic Economy* (Boston: Thomas H. Webb, 1841), 5.

44. Knopf, *Changes in Wheat Production*, 49.

45. Or at least the mythology thereof. In fact both Foucault and Thomas Laqueur see the "incorporation of perversions and the specification of individuals," including the masturbator, as one of the hallmarks of the modern age. Michel Foucault, *The History of Sexuality, Volume 1: An Introduction* (New York: Vintage Books, 1990), 42, 45; Laqueur, *Solitary Sex*, 210.

46. Ralph Waldo Emerson, *Journals of Ralph Waldo Emerson with Annotations* (New York: Houghton Mifflin, 1911), 101.

47. See Sylvester Graham, *Thy Kingdom Come: A Discourse on the Importance of Infant and Sunday Schools, Delivered at the Crown St. Church, Philadelphia, December 13th, 1829* (Philadelphia: Wm. F. Geddes, 1831); and Sylvester Graham, *Lectures on the Science of Human Life* (Boston: Marsh, Capen, Lyon and Webb, 1839).

48. One example is the Battle Creek Sanatorium, founded and run on Grahamite principles by Harvey Kellogg. The modern analogy to the use of the Graham name would be the use of the word *Atkins* to describe any high-protein, low-carbohydrate meal or the nineteenth-century usage of the word *Banting* to describe dieting, after William Banting's *Letter on Corpulence Addressed to the Public* (London: Harrison, 1863). For a discussion of Banting see Sander Gilman, *Fat: A Cultural History* (Malden, MA: Polity, 2008), 81. The corpus of Atkins books is too enormous to account for here but seems to have been initiated in 1973 with Robert C. Atkins, *Dr. Atkins' Diet Revolution* (New York: Bantam, 1972).

49. Hale, *The Good Housekeeper*, 17. By way of evidence for Graham's status as the founder of his own farinaceous discourse, a search of the database of recipes in the "Feeding America" digital archive of cookbooks ranging from the eighteenth through the twentieth centuries reveals ninety-one Graham recipes, beginning in 1846 with Esther Howland's *The New England Economical Housekeeper* and continuing through the early twentieth century: these include Graham bread, Graham biscuits, and Graham Gems. Along the way Graham recipes can be found in the second edition of Catharine Beecher's classic domestic manual *Miss Beecher's Domestic Receipt Book* and the first edition of *Fannie Farmer's Boston Cooking-School Cookbook*, arguably the best-known American cookbook until *The Joy of Cooking*, as well as several Creole or southern cookbooks including Lafcadio Hearn's *La Cuisine Creole*. By the end of the First World War the term *Graham* was in wide enough use to be found in Florence Greenbaum's *International Jewish Cookbook*. The term, in most of these cases, seems to designate the use of what the early twenty-first-century consumer would call whole wheat flour. See Fannie Merritt Farmer, *The Boston Cooking-School Cook Book* (Boston: Little, Brown, 1896); Lafcadio Hearn, *La Cuisine Creole: A Collection of Culinary Recipes, from Leading Chefs and Noted Creole Housewives, Who Have Made New Orleans Famous for Its Cuisine* (New Orleans: F. F. Hansell, 1885); Esther Allen Howland, *The New England Economical Housekeeper, and Family Receipt Book* (Boston: S. A. Howland, 1845); Florence Kreisler Greenbaum, *The International Jewish Cookbook: 1600 Recipes According to the Jewish Dietary Laws with the Rules for Kashering; The Favorite Recipes of America, Austria, Germany, Russia, France, Poland, Roumania, Etc., Etc.* (New York: Bloch, 1919). For the complete database of cookbooks see http://digital.lib.msu.edu/projects/cookbooks/ (accessed May 2011).

50. Graham's writings are in dialogue with the continental European discourses on masturbation written in the seventeenth and eighteenth centuries. As Helen Lefkowitz Horowitz and Stephen Nissenbaum have written, Graham's first lectures, on the links among alcohol, sexual indulgence, and the cholera epidemic, drew on the writings of French physiologists Xavier Bichat and Francois J. V. Broussais, as well as those of the revolutionary-era American doctor Benjamin Rush, to develop "an understanding of alcohol and all stimulants as irritants of the natural system." Horowitz, *Rereading Sex*, 94. From Bichat, Graham borrowed the idea that all life was involved in a "continuous struggle for survival against the inorganic forces that surrounded them: life was a constant battle between the principles of vitality and those of physics and chemistry, and death was simply the victory of the latter over the former." Nissenbaum, *Sex, Diet, and Debility in Jacksonian America*, 20. From Broussais, however, Graham lifted the idea that the principal threat to human life was food and drink, "upon which living organisms depended for their survival but which literally invaded them from without" (ibid.).

51. See Hilton Obenzinger's *American Palestine* for a discussion of the representation of the United States as a modern Israel in the nineteenth century. Hilton Obenzinger, *American Palestine: Melville, Twain, and the Holy Land Mania* (Princeton: Princeton University Press, 1999).

52. Graham, *Treatise*, 10.

53. Ibid., 15.

54. Ibid., 12, 16.

55. Ibid., 15–16.

56. Ibid., 92.

57. Ibid., 26.

58. Claude Lévi-Strauss, *The Raw and the Cooked: Mythologiques, Volume 1* (Chicago: University of Chicago Press, 1983).

59. Graham, *Treatise*, 18.

60. Ibid., 19.

61. Ibid., 26.

62. Reynolds, *Beneath the American Renaissance*, 211–214.

63. Graham, *Treatise*, 35–36.

64. Christopher Castiglia's idea of the institutionalization of "interior states" is particularly relevant here, not only because it connects to the psychopathology of the temperance ideal's purified interior but also because it enters into conversation with earlier feminist work on domestic interiors. Castiglia defines interiority as the space of affect and intellect, of selfhood. He writes, "The increasingly discordant human interior (what I call the *nervous state*), with its battles between appetite and restraint, desire and deferral, consciousness and unconsciousness, became . . . a microcosm of the equally riven sociality of nineteenth-century America." Christopher Castiglia, *Interior States: Institutional Consciousness and the Inner Life of Democracy in the Antebellum United States* (Durham: Duke University Press, 2008), 2. This "discordant" interiority, which organizes itself around the pervasive image of "nerves" and the nervous state, is represented literally by both Graham and Alcott as they seek cures to suppress digestive upset and enervation and therapies that produce healthy, energetic, and productive domestic bodies through the regulation of diet. The isomorphism of nation and body is continued by the mapping of the physiological interior onto the interior of the house, itself undergoing massive changes. Both writers connect the inner passages of the body, from mouth through the digestive tract, to the civic life of the nation and the distribution of public or open and private or closed spaces of the household. Alcott in particular is painstakingly intent on tracking the passage of food from the mouth to the bowels and the rectum. In doing so, he opens up these interior spaces: he makes them *places* as complex and socialized as the middle-class home he uses as his extended metaphor for the body.

65. Foucault, *The History of Sexuality*, 139.

66. Ibid., 25.

67. Warner, "Whitman Drunk," 271.

68. Foucault, *The History of Sexuality*, 136. Ronald Walters writes, "The future of reform belonged to institution users—to men and women who regarded bureaus, agencies, and the government in general as instruments of social policy. I have in mind, of course, the stream of liberalism that flows from Progressivism through the New Deal to the 'Great Society' of the 1960s. . . . It tried to make the system run better." Walters, *American Reformers*, 222.

69. I use Ronald Takaki's definition of republicanism here: "In the republic, the people would no longer have an external authority over them, a father/king to restrain their passions and deny them luxury; they would instead have to control themselves. Whether or not they would be able to exercise self-control effectively depended on their virtue. . . . Republicanism and virtue would reinforce each other: moral character would enable republican man to govern himself." Ronald Takaki, *Iron Cages: Race and Culture in 19th-Century America*, 2nd ed. (New York: Oxford University Press, 2000), 8–9.

70. Amy Kaplan, "Manifest Domesticity," in *No More Separate Spheres: A Next Wave American Studies Reader*, ed. Cathy N. Davidson and Jessamyn Hatcher (Durham: Duke University Press, 2002), 188.

71. In Mrs. Hale's *The Good Housekeeper*, the matron of the household is advised to be kind but firm with the Irish cook, conjuring up a scene in which a friend instructed the new Irish maid: "The names of the articles of furniture in the kitchen, as well as their uses, were entirely unknown to her, and she had seen so many new things done which she was expected to remember that it must have made her heart sick to reflect how much she had to learn. But there was one thing she thought she understood which was to cook potatoes. These were done and she would show the lady she knew how to prepare them for the table." As it turns out, she even prepares the potatoes wrongly, which would have caused another "lady" of the house to throw the maid out, where she would have wandered "without knowing a place where to lay down her head in this strange country." But in Hale's scene all ends well: "My friend did not act in this manner; she expressed no surprise at the attitude of the girl and only quietly said, 'That is not the best way to peel your potatoes, Julia; just lay them on this plate, and I will show you how I like to have them done.'" In this way, in such kitchen scenes, the ladies in this "strange country" civilize its new inhabitants. Hale, *The Good Housekeeper*, 123.

72. Graham, *Treatise*, 92–93.

73. Ibid., 106.

74. See Ann Laura Stoler, *Race and the Education of Desire: Foucault's History of Sexuality and the Colonial Order of Things* (Durham: Duke University Press, 1995), 164.

75. John Carlos Rowe, *Literary Culture and U.S. Imperialism: From the Revolution to World War II* (New York: Oxford University Press, 2000), 5.

76. Wheat also took on meaning in relation to other commodities. As a vegetarian, Graham advocated for wheat as a full replacement for meat. As Sidney Mintz writes, advances in industrialization throughout the eighteenth and nineteenth centuries resulted in a shift in Western diets from a diet based in a "core" of carbohydrates, with "fringe" foods made of fats and proteins, to one in which meat increasingly became a central food. Sidney Mintz, "Eating American," in *Food in the USA*, ed. Carole Counihan (New York: Routledge, 2002), 146. By the 1840s domestic writers were already in disagreement with Graham about vegetarianism, even as they continued to advocate for bread as a central component of a healthy American diet. In 1844 Sarah Josepha Hale wrote, "There has been, of late years, much said and written respecting the benefits of adhering to a strict vegetable diet, and many excellent people are sadly perplexed about their duty in this matter, and

whether they ought to give up animal food entirely. As I profess to make my book a manual for those who wish to preserve their health, as well as prepare their food in the most judicious manner, I will here give a sketch of the reasons which induce me to recommend a mixed diet, *bread, meat, vegetables and fruits, as the best, the only right regimen for the healthy.*" Hale, *The Good Housekeeper*, 19.

Yet if Graham felt that he was losing his audience by preaching against "promiscuous feeding" on the dead carcasses of animals, he narrowed it even more by advocating for wheat against corn as the breadmaking grain of choice. This advocacy must be read, within the antebellum frame of reference, for its connotations of regional difference, the South being a region where corn-based breads continued to define the cuisine. That said, the replacement of corn by wheat was a strategy with a long and illustrious history in the Americas. Clara Olaya, discussing her work on foodways in the Latin American conquest, writes, "To convert the American Indians to the Catholic faith, the Spaniards had to talk to the Indians in food metaphors. For example, the Passion fruit and its flower were the metaphors used to explain the Passion of Christ to save the world. The American Indians had in high esteem their fruits: they marked the passage of time to celebrate the rites of passage from birth to death. In the meantime they were the sustenance and enjoyment of life. The chronicles of the Spanish conquest are full of descriptions on of how thousands of fruit trees were cut and cultivated plots burned to bring the Indians to their knees and join the European economy of wheat and grapes, the blood and body of the European man." Clara Olaya, email message to ASFS listserv (Association for the Study of Food and Society), October 15, 1999. Clara Olaya is the author of *Frutas de América: Tropical y subtropical: Historia y usos* (Barcelona: Grupo Editorial Norma, 1991).

As the single most important indigenous North American grain, corn had long played an important role in Native American cuisines and thus in the early European settler cuisine. Amelia Simmons's *American Cookery*, for instance, lists recipes such as "Indian Pudding" and "Indian Slapjack," and Joel Barlow's humorous nationalist poem "The Hasty Pudding" addressed corn as "The pudding of the bag, whose quiv'ring breast / With suet lin'd, leads on the Yankee feast." Simmons, *American Cookery*, 38, 49. For a discussion of the Barlow poem see Rafia Zafar, "The Proof of the Pudding: Of Haggis, Hasty Pudding, and Transatlantic Influence," *Early American Literature* 31:2 (1996): 133–149.

While it is not my intention to set up an overarching dichotomy between corn and wheat in this book, particularly given the differences between the United States' regional cuisines, in trying to understand Graham's project here it seems clear that, in relation to wheat, for Graham corn recedes into the background as a solution to the ills of the body politic. Corn is a healthful food for Graham, but it is not, as I show, the panacea that is wheat. One might, however, put Graham's 1837 document into conversation with recent conversations about corn and the contemporary American body in which, as Michael Pollan says, "If you are what you eat, and especially if you eat industrial food, as 99 percent of Americans do, what you are is corn." Michael Pollan, *The Omnivore's Dilemma* (New York: Penguin, 2006), 19. Viewed in this light, it is clear that Graham's project failed, and wheat—certainly, whole-grain wheat products—have receded from the American diet in favor of corn. From this failure one might indeed argue that corn and not wheat has come to define the American body; such seems to be the fate of all radical dietetic schemes. Still, it is interesting to note where Graham's and Pollan's work converges: Pollan's manifesto points the consumer toward "real" foods: whole grains, more vegetables, less processed meat and food, as in a sense does Graham. But whereas Pollan calls refined flour "the first fast food" (106), placing the production of white flour during the 1870s, Graham would disagree. Not only does Graham rail against processed flours in 1837; he is particularly harsh about chemical leavening, popularly used in the early part of the nineteenth century and reviled by Graham for making bread "sour" and nonnutritious. If one wanted to pick at Pollan, which I do not, one might call chemically leavened bread the first fast food.

77. Graham, *Treatise*, 34.

78. Ibid., 35. The classic discussion of this metaphor in U.S. literature is in Annette Kolodny, *The Lay of the Land: Metaphor as Experience and History in American Life and Letters* (Chapel Hill: University of North Carolina Press, 1984).

79. Stoler, "Tense and Tender Ties," 830.

80. Harvard Library lists thirteen editions, from 1834 to 1847.

81. Alcott, *The House I Live In*, 13.

82. *Moby Dick* is another text obsessed with consumption, metonymy, and metaphor, which has been extensively treated by Sharon Cameron in *The Corporeal Self: Allegories of the Body in Melville and Hawthorne* (New York: Columbia University Press, 1991). See especially Cameron's interpretation of Ishmael's leaky body as house in chapter 1, "Identity and Disembodiment in Moby Dick," 35. Herman Melville, *Moby Dick* (New York: Norton, 2001).

83. Alcott, *The House I Live In*, 73.

84. Alcott, *The House I Live In*, 166.

85. Ibid., 174, 180.

86. Bruce Burgett, "On the Mormon Question: Race, Sex, and Polygamy in the 1850s and the 1990s," *American Quarterly* 57:1 (March 2005): 79.

87. Graham, *Lecture*, 35.

88. Ibid., 39.

89. Ibid., 9.

90. Ibid., 146.

91. Ibid., 166–167.

92. Ibid., 166–167.

93. For a more extended discussion of the relationship between invisibility, masturbation, and social control, see Neil Hertz's discussion of Freud's analysis of Dora's sexuality in Neil Hertz, *The End of the Line* (New York: Columbia University Press, 1985), chapter 8.

94. Graham, *Lecture*, 169.

95. In *Solitary Sex*, Laqueur argues that masturbation became an issue in the eighteenth century because it symbolized the conjoining of new forms of individuality with discourses of imagination and addiction. Masturbation, he argues, became a lightning rod for medical concern because it drew attention away from other new behaviors that

similarly invoked these three discourses, in particular, novel reading and commodity consumption. Graham's conjoining of consumption with masturbatory behavior is right on point with Laqueur's observations about European medical discourse. The addendum I discuss here points to masturbation's relevance to emerging forms of liberal womanhood.

96. Jeanne Boydston, *Home and Work: Housework, Wages, and the Ideology of Labor in the Early Republic* (New York: Oxford University Press, 1994), 102.

97. Graham, *Lecture*, 168.

98. Maggie Kilgour writes in her work on cannibalism, "One of the most important characteristics of eating is its ambivalence: it is the most material need yet is invested with a great deal of significance, an act that involves both desire and aggression, as it creates a total identity between inside and outside, eater and eaten while insisting on the total control—the literal consumption—of the latter by the former. Like all acts of incorporation, it assumes an absolute distinction between inside and outside, eater and eaten, which, however, breaks down, as the law 'you are what you eat' obscures identity and makes it impossible to say who's who." Maggie Kilgour, *From Communion to Cannibalism: An Anatomy of Metaphors of Incorporation* (Princeton: Princeton University Press, 1990), 7.

99. Graham, *Treatise*, 171.

100. Ibid., 172.

101. Stoler, "Tense and Tender Ties," 52.

102. I am indebted to Rachel Poliquin's work on this issue. See Rachel Poliquin, "Vegetal Prejudice and Healing Territories in Early Modern England," in *Textual Healing: Essays on Medieval and Early Modern Medicine*, ed. Elizabeth Lane Furdell (Leiden, the Netherlands: Brill, 2005).

103. Ann Laura Stoler, *Race and the Education of Desire: Foucault's History of Sexuality and the Colonial Order of Things* (Durham: Duke University Press, 1995), 7.

104. Ibid., 7.

105. A familiar example is the old chestnut "An apple a day keeps the doctor away." As Harvey Levenstein notes in *Revolution at the Table*, by the middle of the nineteenth century it was popularly believed that apples were curative; this idea is inseparable from the story of Johnny Appleseed sowing apples, a European fruit, across America, one of the nation's most popular allegories that, read via the symbolics of empire, is revealed to be at heart about domesticating the national space. Harvey Levenstein, *Revolution at the Table: The Transformation of the American Diet* (Berkeley: University of California Press, 1988).

106. Ibid., 5.

107. The change in editors was announced in the *Graham Journal of Health and Longevity: Devoted to the Practical Illustration of the Science of Human Life, as Taught by Sylvester Graham and Others* 3:21 (1839): 339.

108. Walters, *American Reformers*, 154–155.

NOTES TO CHAPTER 3

1. Suzan-Lori Parks, *Venus: A Play* (New York: Theatre Communications Group, 1997), 105.

2. See Sander Gilman, *Difference and Pathology: Stereotypes of Sexuality, Race, and Madness* (Ithaca: Cornell University Press, 1985). See also Clifton C. Crais and Pamela Scully, *Sara Baartman and the Hottentot Venus: A Ghost Story and a Biography* (Princeton: Princeton University Press, 2009), 148. I engage with Parks's play here because it demonstrates many of the central themes of this chapter, including the use of food to represent racial difference and the problematics of the white desire for the racial other as they are enacted through food metaphors.

3. Although this is a play set in England, and about European colonialism, I am taking the liberty of reading it in terms of its American implications, which would be present for its American author and its first American audiences. Nonetheless I recognize that the history of Saartje Baartman has ramifications that go beyond the American scene, which I will not be exploring here.

4. Although in this chapter I am interested in the literary conjunction of food with historical constructions of blackness, there are many other avenues into this problematic material history. Some scholars have explored the conjunction of race and food in literature and popular culture, while there is a large body of historical work treating the relationships between immigrants, ethnicity, and foodways. Along with Doris Witt's important book—*Black Hunger: Food and the Politics of U.S. Identity* (New York: Oxford University Press, 1999)—I am thinking here of Psyche Williams-Forson, *Building Houses Out of Chicken Legs: Black Women, Food, and Power* (Chapel Hill: University of North Carolina, 2006), as well as Fabio Parasecoli, *Bite Me: Food in Popular Culture* (New York: Berg, 2008). For the literature on food, ethnic identity, and migration, see Hasia R. Diner, *Hungering for America: Italian, Irish, and Jewish Foodways in the Age of Migration* (Cambridge: Harvard University Press, 2003); Donna R. Gabaccia, *We Are What We Eat: Ethnic Food and the Making of Americans* (Cambridge: Harvard University Press, 2000); Krishnendu Ray, *The Migrant's Table: Meals and Memories in Bengali-American Households* (Philadelphia: Temple University Press, 2004); and, more recently, an excellent discussion of Asian American culture and foodways in Anita Mannur, ed., "Meat vs. Rice," special issue, *Amerasia Journal* 32 (2006).

There is also a considerable body of literature on the conjunction between black bodies and food in late nineteenth- and early twentieth-century material culture—with the image of Aunt Jemima operating as a central hieroglyph in this social text. In particular I am thinking of Lauren Berlant's insights into the various incarnations of Fannie Hurst's Delilah Johnson character from Hurst's novel *Imitation of Life*. In her readings of Hurst's 1933 novel, John Stahl's 1934 film, and Douglas Sirk's 1955 film, Berlant explores the relationship between white and black women as hyperembodied subjects exiled from the public sphere of disembodied citizenship. For Berlant the black cook figures in the novel and its two adaptations as, respectively, "part of a white woman's emancipatory strategy, . . . the political place of surplus embodiment and the personal rage of collective suffering," and the "trademark's curtain" covering white women's commodification." Lauren Berlant, "National Brands, National Body: *Imitation of Life*," in *The Female Complaint: The Unfinished Business of Sentimentality in American Culture*, 107–144 (Durham: Duke University Press, 2008), 132. Berlant picks up the figure of Aunt Delilah as a substitution for the Aunt Jemima trademark, using that symbol to explore the various relationships that overembodied subjects occupy in relation to the nation. I am interested here in Berlant's exploration of the homosocial and erotic in relation to commodity culture but want to delve more deeply, as my project suggests, into the body politics constructed and bolstered by discourses of food and eating when the object-cum-person being eaten is so closely tied to the particularly racialized body of the food producer. Berlant's article is also interesting to me in that it explores the various strategies of projection, reembodiment, and invisibility deployed by white women in their hierarchical and uneven relationships with black women. Like Berlant I am interested in the projection of embodiment by white women onto black women; I am also looking for the ways that blackness refuses to be so easily suppressed. See also Marilyn Kern-Foxworth, *Aunt Jemima, Uncle Ben, and Rastus: Blacks in Advertising, Yesterday, Today, and Tomorrow* (Westport, CT: Praeger, 1994); Maurice M. Manring, *Slave in a Box: The Strange Career of Aunt Jemima* (Charlottesville: University of Virginia Press, 1998).

5. For a discussion of cannibalism in Kara Walker's work see Gwendolyn DuBois Shaw, *Seeing the Unspeakable* (Durham: Duke University Press, 2004), 52–53.

6. See Witt, *Black Hunger*, 39. On a certain level this chapter does seek new answers to the puzzling status of an Aunt Jemima or an Uncle Ben in the popular culture. By shifting the focus away from the turn of the twentieth century to the antebellum encoding of black figures in terms of food language I hope to help the reader see a historically oral relationship between whites and blacks which precedes the post–Civil War economic conditions that made the black cook an embodiment of free, abundant labor and to offer a new reading of the commercial representations that followed.

Just as I argue that the formation of a Grahamite temperance movement produced a template for a post–Civil War identification of moral health, nutrition, and the imperial white body, part of the work of this chapter is to ask, are Aunt Jemima and Uncle Ben really meant to be so cute that you could just eat them up? Do these products not only bank on the promise of labor but on the mythical deliciousness of the bodies that made the food product? In the case of Aunt Jemima syrup, notoriously, this racial troping went so far that the syrup was contained in bottles shaped to look like Aunt Jemima's body, using the color of the syrup to mirror the color of her skin and, presumably, the emptying of the bottle to mirror her death and afterlife as a "white," transparent figure.

The endurance of the delicious black body, even today, when ceramic and porcelain Mammy cookie jars are still being produced, the innumerable postcards of black children threatened by alligators are still being sold, and the tiresome advertisements of Rastus, Uncle Sam, and other men and women serving up Cream of Wheat, rice, or pancakes are still in circulation at your nearest neighborhood store, should help us to see the relevance in the work of going back to the roots of this representation. The best place to examine these objects is at the online Jim Crow Museum of Racist Memorabilia, which is hosted by Ferris University: http://www.ferris.edu/JIMCROW/collect/ (accessed June 10, 2011)

7. Or, in hooks's terms, the "commodification of the other." See bell hooks, "Eating the Other: Desire and Resistance," in *Black Looks: Race and Representation*, 21–41 (Cambridge, MA: South End, 1999). In this essay hooks discusses the twentieth-century iteration of the commodification of ethnic difference, or nonwhite cultural practices. Although hooks is largely interested in issues of sexual desire for the racial other, it is interesting that she opens her essay with an alimentary metaphor: "Within commodity culture, ethnicity becomes spice, seasoning that can liven up the dull dish that is mainstream white culture" (21).

8. In doing so I build on the work of a previous generation of feminist scholars such as Shirley Samuels and Karen Sanchez-Eppler who have sought to understand the ways that, in Sanchez-Eppler's words, "The body of the woman and the body of the slave . . . merge through metaphor." Karen Sanchez-Eppler, "Bodily Bonds: The Intersecting Rhetorics of Feminism and Abolition," in *The Culture of Sentiment: Race, Gender, and Sentimentality in Nineteenth-Century America*, ed. Shirley Samuels, 93–107 (New York: Oxford University Press, 1999), 93. Both of these authors have explored the tendency of "feminist-abolitionist" writings (Sanchez-Eppler's term) to conflate the slave body with the body of the white woman, with Samuels looking at the literal conjoining of those bodies in the topsy-turvy doll. Sanchez-Eppler's sensitive exposition of the ways that "such pairings generally tend toward asymmetry and exploitation" and her argument that "sentimental fiction constitutes an intensely bodily genre" are particularly relevant to my work, as is her observation that "forbidden desire constitutes . . . even the most conventional of these stories" (ibid., 93, 99, 107). By looking at the moments when midcentury whiteness is constituted through the metaphoric consumption of blackness I also depart from Eric Lott's foundational work on racial impersonation in order to look at the ways in which whiteness constitutes itself through the internalization, rather than the external wearing, of blackness. See also Shirley Samuels's discussion of the topsy-turvy doll in Shirley Samuels, "The Identity of Slavery," in Samuels, *The Culture of Sentiment*, 157–171. I am also indebted to Eric Lott's insights into the ambivalence of this relationship, what he famously termed a dynamic of "love and theft." See Eric Lott, *Love and Theft: Blackface Minstrelsy and the American Working Class* (New York: Oxford University Press, 1995).

9. Toni Morrison, *Playing in the Dark* (Cambridge: Harvard University Press, 1992), 8, 58. For a discussion of the interconnections between domestic racial ideology and foreign policy see also John Carlos Rowe, *Literary Culture and U.S Imperialism: From the Revolution to World War II* (New York: Oxford University Press, 2000), 8.

10. Charlie Moses, interview by Esther de Sola, in *Born in Slavery: Slave Narratives from the Federal Writers' Project, 1936–1938*, American Memory Project, Library of Congress, http://memory.loc.gov/ammem/snhtml/snhome.html (accessed January 9, 2007).

11. Nathaniel Hawthorne, *The House of the Seven Gables* (London: G. Routledge, 1851). Here I wish to note that my reading is very much in conversation with David Anthony's

essay in which he explores this scene at length: "Class, Culture, and the Trouble with White Skin in Hawthorne's *The House of the Seven Gables*," *Yale Journal of Criticism* 12:2 (1999): 249–269. Anthony's discussion of this scene focuses on the ways that "race acted as a crucial third term in negotiations of class and culture during the antebellum period" (251).As he argues, "what the novel shows is the inextricable relation between representations of white men . . . and the representation, both literal and figurative, of blackness" (251). I admire Anthony's article very much and share his reading of the penny's miscegenating force. However, I diverge from him here in my aim to shift the reading of race from a functionalist signifier of class difference between whites to a signifier on which female whiteness is dependent.

12. Hawthorne, *The House of the Seven Gables*, 45.

13. Ibid., 59.

14. Ibid.

15. Ibid., 43.

16. Peter Hulme, "Introduction: The Cannibal Scene," in *Cannibalism and the Colonial World*, ed. Francis Barker, Peter Hulme, and Margaret Iversen, 1–38 (Cambridge: Cambridge University Press, 1998), in particular Hulme's discussion of Tarzan; Stuart Hall et al., eds., *Modernity: An Introduction to Modern Societies* (Malden, MA: Blackwell, 1996), especially chapter 6, "Discourse and Power: The West and the Rest," 184–228.

17. Maggie Kilgour, *From Communion to Cannibalism: An Anatomy of Metaphors of Incorporation* (Princeton: Princeton University Press, 1990), for instance, 167.

18. In fact most early retail ventures took place in houses and homes. See also Gillian Brown's chapter on Hawthorne, "Women's Work and Bodies in *The House of the Seven Gables*," in Gillian Brown, *Domestic Individualism: Imagining Self in Nineteenth-Century America*, 63–95 (Berkeley: University of California Press, 1990). Although Brown is interested in the energizing qualities of commerce, she sees the staining of Hepzibah's palm as a "soiling" rather than an energizing moment. Paul Gilmore, by contrast, sees this moment as one that "blackens" Hepzibah as a sign of her "descent into the plebian class." Paul Gilmore, *The Genuine Article: Race, Class and American Literary Manhood* (Durham: Duke University Press, 2001), 131.

19. Hawthorne, *The House of the Seven Gables*, 60.

20. Karen Sánchez-Eppler, *Dependent States: The Child's Part in Nineteenth-Century American Culture* (Chicago: University of Chicago Press, 2005), 53. Sánchez-Eppler cites Meredith McGill's *American Literature and the Culture of Reprinting, 1834–1853* (Philadelphia: University of Pennsylvania Press, 2003); and Elizabeth Freeman's "Honeymoon with a Stranger: Pedophiliac Picaresque from Poe to Nabokov," *American Literature* 70 (December 1998): 863–897.

21. Sánchez-Eppler, *Dependent States*, 186.

22. "Gripe: . . . 2b. An intermittent spasmodic pain in the bowels. Usually pl., colic pains." *Oxford English Dictionary*, 2nd ed. (online), s.v. "Gripe," http://www.oed.com (accessed April 28, 2011).

23. Hawthorne, *The House of the Seven Gables*, 60.

24. Ibid., 61.

25. Ibid.

26. Mimi Sheller, *Consuming the Caribbean: From Arawaks to Zombies* (New York: Routledge, 2003), 82. Sheller is quoting Pere Pierre Francois-Xavier de Charlevoix, from *A Voyage to North America; Undertaken by Command of the Present King of France, Containing . . . a Description of the Natural History of the Islands of the West Indies Belonging to the Different Powers of Europe*, 2 vols. (Dublin: John Exshaw and James Potts, 1766), 1:310.

27. Sidney W. Mintz, *Sweetness and Power: The Place of Sugar in Modern History* (New York: Penguin, 1986), 109. The female-led anti-Saccharite movement in England attests to the widespread connection between sugar and slaves in the discourse of the transatlantic antislavery movement, as abolitionist women there led a boycott of all sugar products. In England, as Marcus Wood has shown, that connection also played out in visual culture, where cartoons and pamphlets both supporting and lampooning the sugar boycott consistently portrayed sugar consumption as a form of cannibalism, what Timothy Morton has called the "blood sugar topos," in which sugar-sweetened products such as coffee and tea are "rendered suddenly nauseating by the notion that they are full of the blood of slaves." In this image, as Morton shows, disgust is deployed to powerful political effect. The anti-Saccharite movement was paralleled in the United States in the small free-produce movement, which urged immediate emancipation and the total boycott of all slave-produced products, including sugar and cotton, and whose writers seem to have at least occasionally echoed this cannibalistic imagery. See Marcus Wood's discussion of James Gillray's print *Anti-Saccharites or John Bull and His Brother Leaving Off Sugar* in Marcus Wood, *Blind Memory* (Manchester: Manchester University Press, 2000), 154; Timothy Morton, *The Poetics of Spice* (Cambridge: Cambridge University Press, 2006), 173.

Food boycotts never found widespread support in the U.S. abolitionist movement, although, according to historians, at least fifty free-produce stores opened in at least eight states and some utopian communities. Quakers, for instance, and, as we will see in the next chapter, Bronson Alcott and Charles Lane's Fruitlands project did exclude sugar from their diets on political grounds. Historian Lawrence Glickman writes that "free produce campaigners overlaid, through metonymy, seemingly neutral and even beautiful slave-made products with graphic and disturbing images of suffering, . . . [giving] consumers the tools to take the imaginative leap, to, in effect, defetishize commodities through visualization." Although Glickman does not develop the point, his examples of the free-produce movement's literary strategies are telling and important to this project: "Henry Highland Garnet wrote, 'The sugar with which we sweetened our tea, and the rice which we ate, were actually spread with the sweat of the slaves, sprinkled with their tears, and fanned by their sighs' and a columnist in the non-Slaveholder exclaimed, 'Go to yonder store, and the products of oppression will stare you in the face.'" Lawrence B. Glickman, "'Buy for the Sake of the Slave': Abolitionism and the Origins of American Consumer Activism," *American Quarterly* 56:4 (2004): 889–912; Ruth Ketring Nuermberger, *The Free Produce Movement: A Quaker Protest against Slavery* (Durham: Duke University Press,

1942); see also Carol Faulkner, "The Root of the Evil: Free Produce and Radical Antislavery, 1820–1860," *Journal of the Early Republic* 27:3 (2007): 377–405.

28. Hawthorne, *The House of the Seven Gables*, 43. See also Esther Allen Howland, *The New England Economical Housekeeper, and Family Receipt Book* (Boston: S. A. Howland, 1845), 54–61. The recipe for Gingerbread No. 1 (there are eight) reads, "Rub four and a half pounds of flour with half a pound of lard, and half a pound of butter; a pint of molasses, a gill of milk, two table-spoonfuls of ginger, a tea-spoonful of saleratus, stirred together. All mixed, bake in shallow pans, twenty or thirty minutes" (54).

29. Sheller, *Consuming the Caribbean*, 81.

30. Hawthorne, *The House of the Seven Gables*, 47. On the issue of the photograph, Hawthorne, and modernity, see Alan Trachtenberg, "Seeing and Believing: Hawthorne's Reflections on the Daguerreotype in *The House of the Seven Gables*," *American Literary History* 9:3 (1997): 460. On the topic of the union between heterosexuality and normative futurity see Judith Halberstam, *In a Queer Time and Place: Transgender Bodies, Subcultural Lives* (New York: NYU Press, 2005). See also Elizabeth Freeman, introduction to "Queer Temporalities," special issue, *GLQ: A Journal of Lesbian and Gay Studies* 13:2–3 (2007): 159–176.

31. Jean Fagan Yellin's article "Hawthorne and the American National Sin"—in *The Green American Tradition: Essays and Poems for Sherman Paul*, ed. H. Daniel Peck, 75–97 (Baton Rouge: Louisiana State University Press, 1989)—is the classic essay on Hawthorne's ambivalence toward and avoidance of the issue of slavery.

32. When I speak here of white women's entrance into public discourse and spaces, or the interpenetration of private and public, I am not referring to the separation of spheres as a material fact but rather to the continued relevance of that separation as a discursive regime. The question of the difference between private domestic spaces and the public sphere, in the Habermasian sense, is thus construed as one part of the antebellum political imaginary, closely linked to the hierarchical relationships between middle-class white women and men.

33. Or is it the excursion of market concerns? Conversations with Meredith McGill at the American Antiquarian Society in December 2003 led me to consider that this feminist trope of the penetration of the domestic sphere by the market economy may in fact be historically inaccurate. The original use of the word *market* is in the sense of "going marketing"—that is, going shopping for household goods, usually made in other households. Was the market, then, initially a product of the domestic sphere instead of the opposite?

34. Hawthorne, *The House of the Seven Gables*, 59.

35. Ibid., 310.

36. Ibid., 313.

37. In Chris Castiglia's reading of the novel the disciplining of the self that defines the regime of antebellum interiority is "queered" by the fact that the novel's key characters refuse to be emotionally transparent or to perform socially acceptable affect: "The queer characters of Hawthorne's romance—and almost all of the characters are described, at

some moment, as queer—. . . deviate not by breaking the law . . . but by virtue of their excessive and inscrutable emotions, their melancholic devotion to the past, their antisocial reclusiveness, *even their lack of control over bodily functions*." Christopher Castiglia, "The Marvelous Queer Interiors of *The House of the Seven Gables*," in *The Cambridge Companion to Nathaniel Hawthorne*, ed. Richard H. Millington, 186–206 (New York: Cambridge University Press, 2004), 187.

While one might read Hepzibah and Clifford as the novel's primary queer characters, Judge Pyncheon is also marked by a disobedient gullet, one that connects him to the family sin through the sound of that "miraculous blood [that] might now and then be heard gurgling in [Pyncheon] throats." Hawthorne, *The House of the Seven Gables*, 135. Indeed, as Castiglia notes, when Phoebe Pyncheon meets the judge, she is startled by "a certain noise in Judge Pyncheon's throat, . . . [a] queer and awkward ingurgitation" (ibid., 136). The Pyncheon patriarch, as the local embodiment of the law, does interiorize, but he can barely do so successfully; and his unsuccessful swallowing, it is implied, ultimately kills him.

38. Hawthorne, *The House of the Seven Gables*, 135.

39. See G. Brown, *Domestic Individualism*; Jane Tompkins, *Sensational Designs: The Cultural Work of American Fiction, 1790–1860* (New York: Oxford University Press, 1986); and Haryette Mullen, "Runaway Tongue: Resistant Orality in *Uncle Tom's Cabin, Our Nig, Incidents in the Life of a Slave Girl*, and *Beloved*," in Samuels, *The Culture of Sentiment*, 244–264. As Mullen nicely puts it, "the compartmentalization of the bourgeois home, with its parlor, kitchen, servants quarters, and family living space, . . . tends to reify the existing relations of domination and exploitation between social classes and genders" (254). The classic discussion of the bourgeois home with its distinctive spaces and bodies is Peter Stallybrass and Allon White, *The Politics and Poetics of Transgression* (Ithaca: Cornell University Press, 1986).

40. See Gavin Roger Jones, *Strange Talk: The Politics of Dialect Literature in Gilded Age America* (Berkeley: University of California Press, 1999).

41. Harriet Beecher Stowe, *Uncle Tom's Cabin; or, Life among the Lowly* (1852; repr., New York: Penguin, 1981), 41. Chapter 5 is titled "The Feelings of Living Property." As Lauren Berlant has noted, the issue of "feelings" is significant as part of Stowe's program to "[promote] a way of exploiting apparently reducible social differences to produce a universalism around, especially, modes of suffering or painful feeling." The idea that "this structure has been deployed mainly by the culturally privileged to humanize those very subjects who are also . . . reduced to cliché" structures this chapter: no text, as Berlant notes, has ever so completely exemplified the dominant culture's ambivalence toward those subjects whom it wishes to liberate. See Lauren Berlant, "Poor Eliza," *American Literature* 70:3 (September 1998): 635–668.

42. Stowe, *Uncle Tom's Cabin*, 6.

43. This parallel was first suggested to me by a later echo of the word in chapter 12, in which Haley sells the infant of a young woman he has acquired to a man he meets on the boat south: "'I've got a good place for raisin', and I thought of takin' in a little more stock,' said the man, 'One cook lost a young 'un last week,—got drownded in a washtub, while she

was hangin' out the clothes,—and I reckon well enough to set her to raisin' this yer'" (ibid., 206). The alimentary pun, which I am arguing is implicit in the "raisin'" of the infant by the bereaved cook, is strangely echoed by another pun implicit in the word *stock*. While the first reference is of course to the idea of livestock, inherent to the word *stock* is another image—that of boiled stock, rendered from raw materials, usually the odds and ends left from other meals. That this child is meant to replace another who "drownded" in a tub only underlines the parallel.

44. Ibid., 5.

45. Both P. Gabrielle Foreman and Hortense Spillers have pointed to the subtext of sexual transgression in Stowe's novel, a subtext subtly gestured to in the dovetailing of carnivorous appetite with the desire for forced sexual labor that rests in Haley's later suggestion that Eliza be sold in New Orleans. Foreman has explored the moments in which the various unspeakable forms of sexual torture that underwrite slavery's racial hierarchies peek through the text, either in the form of white men's homoerotic, nonconsensual desire for black men or in the subtextual gestures to the various forms of prostitution and concubinage (male and female) enabled by the slave economy; Spillers has looked at the erotics of the relationship between Uncle Tom and Little Eva, arguing that their deaths are not, perhaps, part of Stowe's Christian eschatology, as Jane Tompkins suggests, but rather punishment for their transgressively intimate relationship. P. Gabrielle Foreman, "'This Promiscuous Housekeeping': Death, Transgression, and Homoeroticism in *Uncle Tom's Cabin*," *Representations* 43 (1993): 51–72; Hortense J. Spillers, "Changing the Letter: The Yokes, the Jokes of Discourse, or, Mrs. Stowe, Mr. Reed," in *Slavery and the Literary Imagination*, ed. Deborah E. McDowell and Arnold Rampersad, 25–61 (Baltimore: Johns Hopkins University Press, 1989).

46. Ann Douglas, introduction to *Uncle Tom's Cabin*.

47. Stowe, *Uncle Tom's Cabin*, 1.

48. Gillian Brown, "Getting in the Kitchen with Dinah: Domestic Politics in *Uncle Tom's Cabin*," *American Quarterly* 36 (Fall 1984): 503–523. As I state elsewhere, many feminist critics have taken up the kitchen in *Uncle Tom's Cabin*, including Gillian Brown, who argues that the kitchen is a site where Stowe most vividly depicts the morally disastrous interpenetration of private and public sphere, as well as Jane Tompkins's argument that the kitchen is where Stowe stages her vision of a female-dominated public sphere. Tompkins writes, "Stowe relocates the center of power in American life, placing it not in the government, nor in courts of law, nor in the factories, nor in the marketplace, but in the kitchen. . . . The image of the home created by Stowe and Beecher in their treatise on domestic science is in no sense a shelter from the stormy blast of economic and political life." Tompkins, *Sensational Designs*, 143. In this way, and throughout her essay on Stowe's novel, Tompkins folds the one space into the other, when in fact, as I argue here and in chapter 1, these are very different spaces in the home. As such, while Tompkins sees within the novel's kitchens various stages on which Stowe can rehearse different relationships to masculine economy, my own reading builds on her work but explores the kitchen's historical relationship to alimentarity, orality, and bodily discourses of difference, as making it a

highly specific space within which the political tensions between white and black women can play out. For a discussion of the separate spaces within the middle-class home see also Millette Shamir's *Inexpressible Privacy: The Interior Life of Antebellum American Literature* (Philadelphia: University of Pennsylvania Press, 2006).

49. Stowe, *Uncle Tom's Cabin*, 32–33.

50. The OED notes that the first use of *stump* as a verb is in Robert Montgomery Bird's *Peter Pilgrim; or, A Rambler's Recollections* (Philadelphia: Lea & Blanchard, 1838). It is picked up by John Camden Hotten's *Slang Dictionary* (London: Chatto and Windus, 1874) to mean "to go about speechmaking on politics or other subjects." Stump speeches, full of malapropisms, were a popular form of minstrel skit.

51. Stowe, *Uncle Tom's Cabin*, 27.

52. "Not a chicken or turkey or duck in the barn-yard but looked grave when they saw her approaching, and seemed evidently to be reflecting on their latter end." Ibid.

53. Ibid., 36.

54. Ibid., 31.

55. See Sigmund Freud, *Jokes and Their Relation to the Unconscious* (New York: Norton, 1960), 115–116.

56. James C. Scott, *Domination and the Arts of Resistance: Hidden Transcripts* (New Haven: Yale University Press, 1992), 9.

57. Stowe, *Uncle Tom's Cabin*, 31.

58. Saidiya V. Hartman, *Scenes of Subjection: Terror, Slavery, and Self-Making in Nineteenth-Century America* (New York: Oxford University Press, 1997), 5, italics added.

59. Karen Sánchez-Eppler writes, "The human body has always served as an emblem for conceptions of the body politic. The bodily biases of the state are evident in the white male privilege that has pertained within American society. Feminist political theorists are reappraising the constitutional rhetoric of disembodied, naturally equal and interchangeable 'persons.' . . . The feminist and abolitionist [agenda] . . . reveals the bodily basis of women's and blacks' exclusion from political power and uncovers the physical attributes of whiteness and maleness implicit in such power." Karen Sánchez-Eppler, *Touching Liberty: Abolition, Feminism, and the Politics of the Body* (Berkeley: University of California Press, 1993), 3.

60. As such, food metaphors lend themselves nicely to the politics of sentimentality; as Lauren Berlant has written, "When sentimentality meets politics, it uses personal stories to tell of structural effects, but in so doing it risks thwarting its very attempt to perform rhetorically a scene of pain that must be soothed politically. . . . The political as a place of acts oriented toward publicness becomes replaced by a world of private thoughts, leanings, and gestures." Berlant, "Poor Eliza," 641.

61. Mikhail Mikhailovich Bakhtin, *Rabelais and His World* (Bloomington: Indiana University Press, 1984), especially chapter 6, "Images of the Material Bodily Lower Stratum."

62. Stowe, *Uncle Tom's Cabin*, 451.

63. Ibid., 454.

64. Achille Mbembe, "Necropolitics," trans. Libby Meintjes, *Public Culture* 15:1 (2003): 21.

65. Stowe, *Uncle Tom's Cabin*, 445.

66. Ibid., 447.

67. See Mbembe, "Necropolitics," 21, 14. See also Karen Halttunen, "Gothic Imagination and Social Reform: The Haunted Houses of Lyman Beecher, Henry Ward Beecher, and Harriet Beecher Stowe," in *New Essays on* Uncle Tom's Cabin, ed. Eric J. Sundquist, 107–134 (Cambridge: Cambridge University Press, 1986).

68. See William Andrus Alcott, *The House I Live In; or, The Human Body* (Boston: Light & Stearns, 1837); William Andrus Alcott, *The Laws of Health; or, Sequel to "The House I Live In"* (Boston: Jewett, 1859); William Andrus Alcott, *Forty Years in the Wilderness of Pills and Powders* (Boston: Jewett, 1859). Also see John Locke, *Some Thoughts Concerning Education* (Cambridge: Cambridge University Press, 1902), 19.

69. See Robert M. Durling, "Deceit and Digestion in the Belly of Hell," in *Allegory and Interpretation: Selected Papers from the English Institute, 1979–80*, ed. Stephen J. Greenblatt, 61–93 (Baltimore: Johns Hopkins Press, 1981). This idea of the *Inferno* as structured by an excremental logic was, however, developed at length by Jeffrey Schnapp in a "Food and Literature" seminar during the fall of 1998 at Stanford University.

70. Harriet Beecher Stowe, *Agnes of Sorrento* (Boston: Ticknor and Fields, 1862).

71. Halttunen, "Gothic Imagination and Social Reform." Jane Tompkins famously underlined the importance of eschatology in the novel's evangelical imaginary. For Tompkins, Stowe's evangelism, which allows a heaven in the end for Tom, has a secular and political meaning; however, both Hortense Spillers and Gabrielle Foreman persuasively point to the internal limits within Christian eschatology that ultimately make it a faulty vehicle for transcending the politics of race or sexuality. Tompkins, *Sensational Designs*, 139; Foreman, "This Promiscuous Housekeeping," 51; Spillers, "Changing the Letter," 39.

72. Leo Bersani, *Is the Rectum a Grave? And Other Essays* (Chicago: University of Chicago Press, 2009).

73. Foreman, "This Promiscuous Housekeeping"; Leslie Fiedler, *Love and Death in the American Novel* (New York: Criterion Books, 1960).

74. See Joan D. Hedrick, *Harriet Beecher Stowe, a Life* (New York: Oxford University Press, 1994), 190.

75. Teresa A. Goddu, *Gothic America: Narrative, History, Nation* (New York: Columbia University Press, 1997).

76. Audre Lorde, "Eye to Eye: Black Women, Hatred, and Anger," in *Sister Outsider: Essays and Speeches*, 145–175 (Berkeley, CA: Crossing, 1984), 145.

77. Julia Stern, "Excavating Genre in *Our Nig*," *American Literature* 67:3 (September 1995): 441–442.

78. Ibid., 454.

79. In Wilson's preface she refers to her readership as "the public" and writes, "I have purposely omitted what would most provoke shame in our good anti-slavery friends at home," implying that abolitionists may read or hear of her book; she then concludes with

an "appeal to my colored brethren universally." See Harriet Wilson, *Our Nig; Sketches from the Life of a Free Black, in a Two-Story White House, North: Showing That Slavery's Shadows Fall Even There*, 2nd ed., ed. Henry Louis Gates, Jr. (New York: Viking, 1983), preface.

80. I refer here to the scenes in which Frado cavorts for the field hands, tempting a sheep to chase her down to the river and fall in. Ibid., 54–55.

81. Ibid., 66.

82. Ibid., 35.

83. Ibid., 36.

84. Ibid., 90.

85. Ibid., 82–83.

86. Elaine Scarry writes, "Whatever pain achieves, it achieves in part through its unsharability, and it ensures this unsharability through its resistance to language. . . . Physical pain does not simply resist language but actively destroys it, bringing about an immediate reversion to a state anterior to language, to the sounds and cries a human being makes before language is learned." Elaine Scarry, *The Body in Pain: The Making and Unmaking of the World* (New York: Oxford University Press, 1985), 4.

87. Marjorie Spiegel, *The Dreaded Comparison: Human and Animal Slavery* (New York: Mirror Books, 1996).

88. Wilson, *Our Nig*, 3.

NOTES TO CHAPTER 4

1. Louisa May Alcott, *Work: A Story of Experience* (Boston: Roberts Brothers, 1873), 1.

2. Louisa May Alcott, *Little Women* (1868; repr., New York: Signet, 2004), 355. Elizabeth Young discusses this passage in *Disarming the Nation* (Chicago: University of Chicago Press, 1999), 101.

3. For a more focused discussion of *Work* as a sentimental novel that pushes at the boundaries of the genre see Glenn Hendler, *Public Sentiments: Structures of Feeling in Nineteenth-Century Literature* (Chapel Hill: University of North Carolina Press, 2001), particularly chapter 4. I depart from Hendler's analysis only very slightly in my reading of the relevance of food imagery in the opening to Alcott's novel *Work*. Although I agree with Hendler that Alcott's model of sentimentality seeks to invoke a particularly gendered public, in part by beginning her novel with her heroine's departure from the domestic sphere, I build on his argument that the language of food in this opening chapter is entirely about "the complete domestication of Aunt Betsey" (ibid., 123) by pointing out that Alcott also describes Christie with food language. The difference between the two uses of food language, I argue, is that while Aunt Betsey (who "curiously interlarded her speech with audible directions to herself"; Alcott, *Work*, 3) is humorously described as a meat dish (*interlarding* meaning the lacing of a dish with bacon fat) that is as-yet uncooked, the food imagery attached to Christie is about making an old-fashioned food item that was increasingly being factory produced and therefore is about having the kinds of skills

that would liberate her from dependence on market goods; as I will show, for antebellum reformers breadmaking is indeed a domestic-sphere skill, but it is nonetheless about a certain kind of female economic independence as well. This is the irony of the nostalgia inherent to domestic manuals and food reform movements; while backward looking and therefore irrevocably traditionalist, they are nonetheless antimodern and anticapitalist. As the inheritor of the Alcott relationship to Grahamite foodways, Louisa May would have been well aware of the critique of industrial bread, on which more later. For more on the revaluation of women's labor in the early nineteenth century see Mary P. Ryan, *Cradle of the Middle Class: The Family in Oneida County, New York, 1790–1865* (New York: Cambridge University Press, 1981); Nancy F. Cott, *The Bonds of Womanhood: "Woman's Sphere" in New England, 1780–1835* (New Haven: Yale University Press, 1977).

4. Alcott, *Work*, 5.

5. Ibid., 6.

6. For the imagery of yeast fermentation is indeed imagery of aliveness.

7. Although I do not deal with it here, there is a fascinating scene in *Eight Cousins* in which Dr. Alec teaches Rose and her cousins anatomy by showing them a real skeleton. Obviously meant to address the issue of women's access to medical education, the chapter, called "Brother Bones," quotes directly from William Alcott's *The House I Live In*.

8. Michael Warner, "Whitman Drunk," in *Publics and Counterpublics*, 269–289 (New York: Zone Books, 2005). Warner writes, "The temperance movement *invented* addiction. . . . Addiction had been a legal term, describing the performative act of bondage, before it was metaphorized to describe a person's self-relation" (272).

9. Louisa May Alcott, *Eight Cousins* (New York: Little, Brown, 1922), 71.

10. Ibid., 288.

11. Ibid., 284, 285.

12. Ibid., 27.

13. Ibid., 244.

14. Ibid., 45.

15. Ibid., 2.

16. Ibid.

17. Ibid.

18. Ibid., 4.

19. The literature on lesbian, proto-lesbian, and queer representations in Alcott's work is, of course, quite extensive. See for instance Michael Moon's "Nineteenth-Century Discourses on Childhood Gender Training: The Case of Louisa May Alcott's *Little Men* and *Jo's Boys*," in *Queer Representations*, ed. Martin B. Duberman and City University of New York, Center for Lesbian and Gay Studies, 209–215 (New York: NYU Press, 1997).

20. *Oxford English Dictionary*, 2nd ed. (online), s.v. "Closet, n.," definition 3a, http://www.oed.com (accessed May 7, 2011).

21. According to the *Oxford English Dictionary*, which also lists "quassia cup" as a medicinal cup popular in the mid- to late nineteenth century, quassia is a tree found in Surinam and Jamaica that was thought to impart medicinal qualities to that which it held.

In particular, quassia was held to be antiparasitic, and therefore of benefit to the stomach, and antipyretic, or able to cool fevers. *Oxford English Dictionary*, 2nd ed. (online), s.v. "Quassia," http://www.oed.com (accessed May 7, 2011).

22. Alcott, *Eight Cousins*, 54.

23. See Lorinda B. Cohoon's "'A Highly Satisfactory Chinaman': Orientalism and American Girlhood in Louisa May Alcott's *Eight Cousins*," *Children's Literature* 36 (2008): 49–68.

24. See for instance John Kuo-Wei Chen, *New York before Chinatown* (Baltimore: Johns Hopkins University Press, 2001); and Yen-p'ing Hao, *The Commercial Revolution in Nineteenth-Century China* (Berkeley: University of California Press, 1986).

25. For at least the first four decades of the nineteenth century commerce with China and diplomatic relations with China were inextricable: for years key diplomatic positions were held by businessmen also working for companies invested in the Canton trade. See Charles Clarkson Stelle, *Americans and the China Opium Trade in the Nineteenth Century* (New York: Arno, 1981).

26. Ibid., 144.

27. Alcott, *Eight Cousins*, 44.

28. Ibid., 182.

29. In a classic Alcott-ish statement of this nostalgia the preface to *An Old-Fashioned Girl* reads, "The 'Old-Fashioned Girl' is not intended as a perfect model, but as a possible improvement upon the Girl of the Period, who seems sorrowfully ignorant or ashamed of the good old fashions which make woman truly beautiful and honored, and through her, render home what it should be,—a happy place, where parents, and children, brothers and sisters, learn to love and know and help one another." The "good old fashions" thus improve the modern "girl of the period." The passage also argues that one might pick out the "good" selectively: the girl that Alcott dreams of is both an improvement—a new girl—and a grouping of characteristics from the past. Louisa May Alcott, preface to *An Old-Fashioned Girl* (Boston: Roberts Brothers, 1870), xii.

30. Hendler, *Public Sentiments*, 114.

31. Alcott, *Work*, 14.

32. Alcott, *Eight Cousins*, 184.

33. Ibid., 185, italics added.

34. Ibid., 179–180.

35. For a discussion of Fruitlands see Clara Endicott Sears and Louisa May Alcott, *Bronson Alcott's Fruitlands* (Boston: Houghton Mifflin, 1915). The volume also includes transcripts of Louisa May's diary from Fruitlands and her short novella *Transcendental Wild Oats*.

36. Ibid., 157.

37. William Andrus Alcott, *Lectures on Life and Health; or, The Laws and Means of Physical Culture* (Boston: Phillips, Sampson, 1853), 326.

38. Louisa May Alcott, *Rose in Bloom* (Boston: A. L. Burt, 1918), 5.

39. Alcott, *Eight Cousins*, 32.

40. Ibid., 33.

41. Ibid., 32.

42. "Oats, n.: A grain, which in England is generally given to horses, but in Scotland supports the people." Samuel Johnson, *A Dictionary of the English Language: In Which the Words Are Deduced from Their Originals, and Illustrated in Their Different Significations by Examples from the Best Writers, to Which Are Prefixed, a History of the Language, and an English Grammar*, 2 vols., 2nd ed. (London, 1755–56), s.v. "Oats," available at Eighteenth Century Collections Online, http://gdc.gale.com/products/eighteenth-century-collections-online/ (accessed May 24, 2011).

43. Alcott, *Eight Cousins*, 188.

44. Alcott, *Rose in Bloom*, 54.

45. On this geopolitical trope Eve Sedgwick writes, "From the Opium Wars of the mid-nineteenth century up to the current details of U.S. relations with Turkey, Colombia, Mexico, and Peru, the drama of 'foreign substances' and the drama of the new imperialisms and the new nationalisms have been quite inextricable. The integrity of (new and contested) borders, the reifications of national will and vitality, were readily organized around these narratives of introjection." Eve Kosofsky Sedgwick, *Tendencies* (Durham: Duke University Press, 1993), 135.

46. Edward W. Said, *Culture and Imperialism* (New York: Vintage Books, 1994), 54.

47. Ibid., 59–60.

48. Alcott, *Eight Cousins*, 76.

49. An image of Fun See in the first edition of *Eight Cousins* shows him facing the twinned teapot in almost identical dress. The caption quotes the text: "Fun signified in pantomime that they were hers." The only other mention of the word *pantomime* is during a scene in which the family engages in theatrical parlor games. Ibid., 78, 155. For a discussion of the history of Chinese representations in U.S. theater and popular culture see James S. Moy, *Marginal Sights: Staging the Chinese in America* (Des Moines: University of Iowa Press, 1994); and Ronald Takaki, *Iron Cages: Race and Culture in 19th-Century America*, 2nd ed. (New York: Oxford University Press, 2000), especially chapter 10, "The 'Heathen Chinee' and American Technology." Robert G. Lee writes a very useful account of images of the Chinese in the nineteenth century in *Orientals: Asian Americans in Popular Culture* (Philadelphia: Temple University Press, 1999), particularly chapter 1, "The 'Heathen Chinee' on God's Free Soil."

50. Alcott, *Eight Cousins*, 77. Mari Yoshihara discusses the relationship between white women, commodity culture, and Orientalism in *Embracing the East: White Women and American Orientalism* (New York: Oxford University Press, 2002). In particular, she discusses Alcott and the "Trip to China" chapter on pages 14–18.

51. For a developed discussion of this twinning motif see Cynthia Wu, "The Siamese Twins in Late-Nineteenth-Century Narratives of Conflict and Reconciliation," *American Literature* 80:1 (2008): 29.

52. Indeed, by the time that Alcott was writing in the 1870s Chinese labor, contained within Chinese male bodies, was one of China's primary exports.

53. Alcott, *Eight Cousins*, 76.

54. Ibid., 40.

55. Close to the end of the first novel, Alcott describes Fun See as "in American costume now, with a cropped head, and [speaking] remarkably good English after six months at school; but for all that, his yellow face and beady eyes made a curious contrast to the blonde Campbells around him." Ibid., 230. My thanks to Cynthia Wu for pointing this out.

56. See Hugh McElaney, "Alcott's Freaking of Boyhood: The Perplex of Gender and Disability in *Under the Lilacs*," *Children's Literature* 34 (2006): 139–160. The canonical Asian American feminist writer Maxine Hong Kingston sees her encounter with the character Fun See in Alcott's fiction as a seminal moment in which she understood her invisibility in the face of racist stereotypes. Cited in Leslie Bow, "'For Every Gesture of Loyalty, There Doesn't Have to Be a Betrayal': Asian American Criticism and the Politics of Locality," in *Who Can Speak? Authority and Critical Identity*, ed. Judith Roof and Robyn Wiegman, 30–55 (Urbana: University of Illinois Press, 1995), 39.

57. For extended discussions of yellowface see John Kuo Wei Tchen, *New York before Chinatown: Orientalism and the Shaping of American Culture, 1776–1882* (Baltimore: Johns Hopkins University Press, 2001); and Krystyn R. Moon, *Yellowface* (New Brunswick: Rutgers University Press, 2005).

58. Bret Harte, *The Writings of Bret Harte* (New York: Houghton Mifflin, 1914), 129–131.

59. It hardly needs mentioning that Fun See's irrelevance to any kind of realism or documentary impulse is nicely encapsulated by his last name being the capital city of Japan.

60. Alcott, *Rose in Bloom*, 236.

61. Ibid., 181.

62. Ibid., 182.

63. Typically, Alcott does take a moment to write in defense of the spinster and the bachelor, for, as she writes, "in this queer world of ours, fatherly and motherly hearts often beat warm and wise in the breasts of bachelor uncles and maiden aunts; and it is my private opinion that these worthy creatures are a beautiful provision of nature for the cherishing of other people's children. They certainly get great comfort out of it, and receive much innocent affection that would otherwise be lost." Ibid., 221.

64. Alcott, *Eight Cousins*, 154.

65. Ibid., 79. Andrew Coe notes the first appearance of the widespread idea that puppies are a common Chinese delicacy in the eighteenth century: "In nearly every western description of Chinese food from the late eighteenth and the early nineteenth centuries, this information is repeated: the Chinese dine on dogs, cats, and rats. . . . If readers of the time remembered anything about Chinese culinary habits, it was that they extended their eating habits to include beloved pets." Coe points out that U.S. missionary Elijah Coleman Bridgman, who in 1837 published "a long account of his voyage that is filled with virulent xenophobia," had an office facing the dog and cat market in Guangzhou. One enjoyable fact from Coe's book is that after twenty years Bridgman had failed to convert a single Chinese "barbarian." Andrew Coe, *Chop Suey: A Cultural History of Chinese Food in the United States* (New York: Oxford University Press. 2009), 24.

66. Alcott, *Rose in Bloom*, 200.

67. Alcott, *Eight Cousins*, 91.

68. *Oxford English Dictionary*, 2nd ed. (online), s.v. "Mac, n. 1," http://www.oed.com (accessed May 9, 2011).

69. Alcott, *Rose in Bloom*, 344.

70. Christopher Castiglia, *Interior States: Institutional Consciousness and the Inner Life of Democracy in the Antebellum United States* (Durham: Duke University Press, 2008), 259.

NOTES TO CHAPTER 5

1. As Suzanne Freidberg demonstrates, ice harvested and/or produced for domestic ice boxes gained popularity in the 1830s and '40s, when Eliza Leslie suggested that each family should "buy two iceboxes, one for dairy products and another for meat. . . . New York City's annual consumption increased from 12,000 tons in 1843 to . . . 100,000 tons in 1856. Boston's consumption leapt from 6,000 to . . . 85,000 tons during the same period." Consumption really exploded, however, in the second half of the country: "Between 1879 and 1919, sales of iceboxes rose from less than $1.8 million to more than $26 million." Suzanne Freidberg, *Fresh: A Perishable History* (Cambridge: Belknap Press of Harvard University Press, 2009), 23, 28–29. Mark William Wilde demonstrates that while Gail Borden "began experimenting with canned milk in the 1850s," the pressures of the Civil War accelerated the demand for canned goods: "spurred by the War, the industry had been placed on solid footing." Drawing on census bureau data, Wilde shows that between 1870 and 1910 the number of canning factories in the United States rose from 97 to 2789. Mark William Wilde, "Industrialization of Food Processing in the United States, 1860–1960" (Ph.D. diss., University of Delaware, 1988). Famously, Upton Sinclair's novel *The Jungle*, which outlined conditions in the canned beef factories, was published in 1906. Upton Sinclair, *The Jungle* (1906; repr., New York: Penguin, 2006).

2. Jack Goody, "Industrial Food," in *Food and Culture: A Reader*, ed. Carole Counihan and Penny Van Esterik, 338–356 (New York: Routledge, 1997), 344.

3. Freidberg, *Fresh*, 25.

4. Harvey Levenstein, *Revolution at the Table: The Transformation of the American Diet* (Berkeley: University of California Press, 1988), 185–186.

5. Ibid., 12.

6. Nathaniel Hawthorne, *The House of the Seven Gables* (London: G. Routledge, 1851), 309.

7. Thorstein Veblen, *The Theory of the Leisure Class* (New York: B. W. Huebsch, 1912), 112.

8. For more on this new culture of poetry see Mike Chasar, "The Business of Rhyming: Burma Shave Poetry and Popular Culture," *PMLA* 125:1 (January 2010): 29–47.

9. Pamela Walker Laird, *Advertising Progress: American Business and the Rise of Consumer Marketing* (Baltimore: Johns Hopkins University Press, 1998) 75.

10. Robert Jay writes that prominent trade card printer Louis Prang brought over three hundred different designs for illustrated business, advertising, and visiting cards, all of which was of course advertised on its own trading card. Robert Jay, *The Trade Card in Nineteenth-Century America* (Columbia: University of Missouri Press, 1987), 30.

11. Jackson Lears, *Fables of Abundance: A Cultural History of Advertising in America* (New York: Basic Books, 1994), 102–103.

12. Daphne Brooks, *Bodies in Dissent: Spectacular Performances of Race and Freedom, 1850–1910* (Durham: Duke University Press, 2007), 5.

13. Here my understanding of disgust is in conversation with William Ian Miller's, when he writes, "Some emotions, among which disgust and its close cousin contempt are the most prominent, have intensely political significance. They work to hierarchize our political order: in some settings they do the work of maintaining hierarchy. . . . Disgust evaluates negatively what it touches, proclaims the meanness and inferiority of its object. And by doing so it presents a nervous claim of right to be free of the dangers imposed by the proximity of the inferior. It is thus an assertion of a claim to superiority that at the same time recognizes the vulnerability of that superiority to the defiling powers of the low." William Ian Miller, *The Anatomy of Disgust* (Cambridge: Harvard University Press, 1998), 8–9.

14. Eric Lott, *Love and Theft: Blackface Minstrelsy and the American Working Class* (New York: Oxford University Press, 1995).

15. In an antiques store in Half Moon Bay, California, near to where I lived while writing this book, there is a shelf of "racial kitsch," but it is accompanied by a sign apologizing for the racism of the objects and claiming that the objects are being collected by "our African American clientele." The issue of who collects racial kitsch and who should be allowed to display has been explored in public debates over curatorial practice.

16. Roderigo Lazo, "Migrant Archives: New Routes in and out of American Studies," in *States of Emergency: The Object of American Studies*, ed. Russ Castronovo and Susan Gillman, 36–54 (Chapel Hill: University of North Carolina Press, 2009), 38.

17. See Tavia Nyong'o, "Racial Kitsch and Black Performance," *Yale Journal of Criticism* 15:2 (2002): 371–391; and Manthia Diawara, "Afro-Kitsch," in *Black Popular Culture: A Project*, ed. Gina Dent and Michele Wallace, 287–289 (Seattle: Bay, 1992).

18. Lazo, "Migrant Archives," 36. Although the largely free-floating early twenty-first-century market in trade cards echoes its original circulation in the total community of consumers, there are some differences that need to be taken account of. First, trade cards are no longer free of cost but, as objects of historical interest, range in price from the very cheap to the very expensive, depending on the image, type, and condition. This affects the material conditions of their circulation, availability, and cost, which has in turn affected my own collection. Second, as I have noted, trade cards originally circulated in a period in which racially problematic imagery was far more socially permissible, and therefore the number of cards depicting a variety of nonwhite stereotypes and grotesques—which are generally offensive to a contemporary audience that is still racially divided—that are still available may be far less due to their suppression or destruction. Both of these factors affect my archive and my reading practices.

19. Laird, *Advertising Progress*, 140–142. Given the anonymity of Internet auctions, at present we have almost no way of knowing who collects these cards today. We do know that the audience for which they were originally intended lived approximately between 1873—when Louis Prang "hit upon the idea of issuing relatively simple chromolithographed trade cards onto which the name of the advertiser could be stamped or overprinted later" (Jay, *The Trade Card in Nineteenth-Century America*, 29)—and the turn of the twentieth century—when lowered postal rates for magazines and the congruent rise in magazine advertising, as well as the rise of the postcard, directed advertising dollars to other genres. Additionally, largely unchecked monopolistic practices put many small producers and manufacturers, who had been the advertisers who used the trade card the most, out of business in droves. The majority of chromolithographic cards that were still being printed after approximately 1900 were to advertise products that often could not be advertised in magazines, such as patent remedies. Otherwise, we can only deduce the dating from events depicted on or referred to by the cards themselves.

20. Ellen Gruber Garvey, "Dreaming in Commerce: Advertising Trade Card Scrapbooks," in *Acts of Possession: Collecting in America*, ed. Leah Dilworth, 66–88 (New Brunswick: Rutgers University Press, 2003), 68.

21. Ellen Gruber Garvey discusses this card, and the association of trade card scrapbooks with girls, at length in ibid.

22. Yuko Matsukawa, "Representing the Oriental in Nineteenth-Century Trade Cards," in *Re/collecting Early Asian America: Essays in Cultural History*, ed. Josephine Lee, Imogene L. Lim, and Yuko Matsukawa, 200–217 (Philadelphia: Temple University Press, 2002); M. M. Manring, *Slave in a Box* (Charlottesville: University of Virginia Press, 1998); Marilyn Kern-Foxworth, *Aunt Jemima, Uncle Ben, and Rastus: Blacks in Advertising, Yesterday, Today, and Tomorrow* (Westport, CT: Praeger, 1994). I include in this first category Marlon Riggs's important documentary, which first screened on PBS in 1987: Marlon Riggs, *Ethnic Notions*, DVD (California Newsreel, 1986).

23. Feminist work that looks at the "consumer citizen" began with Ellen Gruber Garvey's important book *The Adman in the Parlor: Magazines and the Gendering of Consumer Culture, 1880s to 1910s* (New York: Oxford University Press, 1996); Marilyn Mehaffy sees the dyad of white mistress–black servant as modeling consumer citizenship for women on the basis of "her juxtaposition with an ethnic other." Marilyn Maness Mehaffy, "Advertising Race/Raceing Advertising: The Feminine Consumer(-Nation), 1876–1900," *Signs: Journal of Women in Culture and Society* 23:1 (1997): 141.

24. Anne McClintock, *Imperial Leather: Race, Gender, and Sexuality in the Colonial Contest* (New York: Routledge, 1995); Lori Merish, *Sentimental Materialism: Gender, Commodity Culture, and Nineteenth-Century American Literature* (Durham: Duke University Press, 2000).

25. Primarily Lears, *Fables of Abundance*; and Jay, *The Trade Card in Nineteenth-Century America*.

26. See Rachel Shteir, "Ethnic Theatre in America," in *A Companion to Twentieth-Century American Drama*, ed. David Krasner, 18–33 (Malden, MA: Blackwell, 2007);

and Annemarie Bean, "Playwrights and Plays of the Harlem Renaissance," in Krasner, *A Companion to Twentieth-Century American Drama*, 91–105. See also Gavin Roger Jones, *Strange Talk: The Politics of Dialect Literature in Gilded Age America* (Berkeley: University of California Press, 1999), particularly chapter 6.

27. Timothy E. Scheurer, *American Popular Music: The Nineteenth Century and Tin Pan Alley* (Bowling Green, OH: Bowling Green State University Press, 1989), 121.

28. "Freud's corsets"! Who could resist a quick foray into this advertisement's unconscious?

29. The term *yum* for "delicious" is traced back by the OED to the 1870s. *Yum-yum girls* are prostitutes—a term that may have its origin in sailor slang. Gilbert claimed that the girls were based on the "tea-house" Japanese girls who performed in an exhibit in London. The tea-house girl was quickly assimilated to a new term in English, the *geisha*. See *Oxford English Dictionary*, 2nd ed. (online), s.v. "yum-yum, n."; and John K. Walton, *Histories of Tourism: Representation, Identity, and Conflict* (Bristol, UK: Channel View, 2005), 104.

30. See Gary Y. Okihiro, *The Columbia Guide to Asian American History* (New York: Columbia University Press, 2001), 19–20; and Jean Yu-wen Shen Wu and Min Song, *Asian American Studies: A Reader* (New Brunswick: Rutgers University Press, 2000), 57–58.

31. Anne Friedberg documents the "instrumentalization of flânerie into 'commodity-experiences'"; more specifically, she argues that, even before cinema, "the speculative gaze of the shopper was an instrumentalization of the *mobilized* (but not *virtual*) gaze to a consumer end." Anne Friedberg, *Window Shopping: Cinema and the Postmodern* (Berkeley: University of California Press, 1993), 38, 58. Because one medium is largely stationary and the other counts on what Friedberg calls "virtual mobility," one cannot entirely conflate early motion pictures and the trade card. Nonetheless, both mediums exist on a continuum as products and makers of the enormous shift in visual regimes at the end of the nineteenth century. As the sanctions limiting bourgeois female mobility fell, "consumer contemplation" centering on the peripatetic female consumer found its correlative in images and fantasies (68). Friedberg writes, "New desires were created *for her* by advertising and consumer culture; desires elaborated in a system of selling and consumption which depended on the relation between *looking* and *buying*, and the indirect desire to possess and incorporate through the eye" (37). Trade cards offer an elaboration of Friedberg's theory: some were marketed to women and girls to be collected and displayed in scrapbooks, although undoubtedly some women might have been considered too old or adult for this hobby; they brought the new public culture of female consumption right back into the home, even as they rehearsed encounters with commodities that could only be purchased by leaving the home.

32. Friedberg connects this shift in visuality to "a mobilized gaze that conducts a *flânerie* through an imaginary other place and time. . . . During the mid nineteenth century, the coincident introduction of department-store shopping, packaged tourism, and protocinematic entertainment began to transform this gaze into a commodity, sold to a consumer-spectator." Anne Friedberg, "Les Flâneurs du Mal(l): Cinema and the Postmodern Condition," *PMLA 106:3 (May 1991):* 420.

33. Roland Marchand, "Advertisements as Social Tableaux," in *Advertising the American Dream: Making Way for Modernity, 1920–1940*, 164–205 (Berkeley: University of California Press, 1986), 166.

34. Signifying the return, perhaps, of the species-inversion trope of earlier hearth-centered chapbooks and children's books.

35. Although my observations indicate a different number, based on an oral interview, Marilyn Mehaffy writes, "According to historian Faith Ruffins, archivist of the Warshaw Collection [at the Smithsonian Institute], 30 to 40 percent of the collection's nineteenth-century illustrated artifacts invoke familiar ethnic stereotypes—Asian, Middle Eastern, Irish, British, Dutch, and French, as well as the most common, African and Native American—as a means for establishing a link between the potential consumer and the product." Mehaffy, "Advertising Race/Raceing Advertising," 141.

36. See Cheryl Harris, "Whiteness as Property," *Harvard Law Review* 106:8 (1993): 1707–1791.

37. The connection between stove blacking and black skin is less obvious here: as Ann McClintock writes of Pear soaps, black skin is variously shown to be either indelible, or erasable, using the proper products. McClintock, *Imperial Leather*, 32.

38. Carl Kelsey, "Some Causes of Negro Emigration: The Men," in *The Negro in the Cities of the North* (New York: Charity Organization Society, 1905), 15–17. The journal that originally published this essay, *Charities*, listed Jane Addams and Jacob Riis as members of the editorial board and published articles by W. E. B. Du Bois and Booker T. Washington. Interestingly, and rather jarringly, in the same essay Kelsey speculates that one reason that "the Negro male" might wish to move to the North is that he may have heard he could walk into a restaurant and be waited on by a white waitress, a move that presages the intensely overdetermined segregation of the lunch counter. In the civil rights era, of course, these same lunch counters became a lightning rod for nonviolent actions. Here again sexual and alimentary threats overlap.

39. Tom Gunning, "The Cinema of Attractions: Early Film, Its Spectator and the Avant-Garde," in *Early Film: Space, Frame, Narrative*, ed. Thomas Elsaesser and Adam Barker, 56–62 (London: British Film Institute, 1989).

40. For instance, Miriam Hansen summons up the trade card only to disavow its importance immediately. She argues that the deployment of the female gaze in the service of consumption, specifically in "modern advertising and the department store," undermined the historic hegemony of the male gaze in art and in the public sphere generally, thus provoking "a profound ambivalence toward the female spectator." Miriam Hansen, *Babel and Babylon: Spectatorship in American Silent Film* (Cambridge: Harvard University Press, 1991), 122. She connects the Orientalist turn in silent film to a long history of exotic imagery that includes trade cards when she writes, "[In] the primitivist iconography of nineteenth-century advertising and trade cards . . . images of ethnic and racial otherness were evoked only to be disavowed, transfigured into an exotic spectacle for the purpose of—primarily female—consumption" (255–256). While Hansen argues that white female spectators are meant to finally disavow trade card exoticism, she also argues that the

silent-film period saw the brief emergence of a female gaze invested in a singularly exotic male actor, Valentino. In her reading of *The Son of the Sheik* (1926) Hansen argues that the overdeterminedly Orientalized Valentino assumes the position of masochistic object to the female gaze, allowing female spectators to identify with both his passivity and his aggressive sexuality, that is, both to look at him and to imagine themselves as him, to wish to be him, to enter him, and to consume him. My reading argues, however, that the racial mobility of the female gaze that Hansen reads in the Valentino films is clearly anticipated by these nineteenth-century trade cards.

41. Brooks McNamara, *Step Right Up* (Jackson: University Press of Mississippi, 1995), 11.

42. One primary source that Richard Butsch cites in his article on the subject, the *New York Clipper*, notes, "Matinees are on the increase. On Saturday last, matinees were given at the Olympic Theatre, Niblo's Garden, Broadway, New Bowery, Hippotheatron, Wood's Minstrels." The list goes on, but the mention of Wood's Minstrels seems noteworthy. Richard Butsch, "Bowery B'Hoys and Matinee Ladies: The Re-gendering of Nineteenth-Century American Theatre Audiences," *American Quarterly* 46:3 (September 1994): 390. For a discussion of the presence of minstrel sheet music in middle-class parlors see also Stephanie Dunson, "The Minstrel in the Parlor: Nineteenth-Century Sheet Music and the Domestication of Blackface Minstrelsy," *ATQ: The American Transcendental Quarterly* 16 (December 2002).

43. Ellen Gruber Garvey, book forthcoming from Oxford University Press, 2012.

44. Jacqueline Najuma Stewart, *Migrating to the Movies* (Berkeley: University of California Press, 2005), 4.

45. "Niblo's Garden," *New York Times*, March 24, 1885, 5. The article charmingly mourns the decline of "the palmy days of the old Bowery" during which "the delighted shrieks of the gallery boys made dents in the ceiling." *The Bandit King* must have shown to what the article calls the "new generation" of theatergoers, who were likely much more attentive than were their apparently rowdy Bowery predecessors.

46. "Struggling with 'Othello'; Second Rehearsal of the Colored Theatrical Troupe," *New York Times*, April 18, 1884, 2.

47. Brooks, *Bodies in Dissent*, 8.

48. Ibid., 8. Brooks's critical frame can be put into conversation with Marjorie Garber's work on transvestism, in which she argues that to look *through* the transvestite instead of looking *at* her is to capitulate to a mode of binary thinking that underlies conservative ideas of gender formation. Garber writes, "This tendency to erase the third term, to appropriate the cross-dresser 'as' one of the two sexes, is emblematic of a fairly consistent critical desire to look away from the transvestite as transvestite, not to see cross-dressing except as male or female manqué, whether motivated by social, cultural or aesthetic designs. And this tendency might be called an *underestimation* of the object." Marjorie Garber, *Vested Interests: Cross-Dressing and Cultural Anxiety* (New York: Routledge, 1997), 10.

49. Lears, *Fables of Abundance*, 18.

50. Ethnic conflicts spilled over into the city in the form of gangs, feuds between neighborhoods, and workplace mayhem, particularly as the pace of immigration picked

up in the twenty years between 1890 and 1910. In addition, the Protestant white establishment was subject to periodic scares about the propensity of "people from sections of southern and eastern Europe" who were "noted for their high murder rate." Samuel Sidney McClure, "The Tammanyizing of a Civilization," *McClure's Magazine* 34 (1909): 125. In the 1890s Irish immigrants from Flatbush and Russian Jews from the Brownsville area of New York engaged in low-level conflicts. See Wendell E. Pritchet, *Brownsville, Brooklyn: Blacks, Jews, and the Changing Face of the Ghetto* (Chicago: University of Chicago Press, 2002), 14.

51. The term *metamorphic* is used by trade card collectors to describe cards that open and close or that change when a paper lever is pulled. In my mind these are some of the most fascinating cards: they make the cards into toys but also point to the joyous and carnivalesque figuring of the body that seems to have dominated the visual culture of late nineteenth-century commodity culture.

52. Paul R. Mullins, *Race and Affluence: An Archaeology of African-American and Consumer Culture* (New York: Springer, 1999), 22. Mullins writes a superb account of the ways that consumer spaces were policed and monitored to limit black participation, but my sense is that his thesis limits an understanding of the creative and oppositional ways that African Americans negotiated these images. His point that there were no images of these consumers seems easily disproven by my archive. Regarding immigrant populations, some cards were in fact bilingual: one trade card album that I bought in 2008 featured quite a few trade cards written in German and printed in the United States. It was apparently owned by a young and apparently bilingual person named Margaret Meyer. I deduce the "young" from an award of merit given her by her teacher.

53. See Elizabeth Ewen, *Immigrant Women in the Land of Dollars: Life and Culture on the Lower East Side, 1890–1925* (New York: Monthly Review Press, 1985); Lary May, *Screening Out the Past: The Birth of Mass Culture and the Motion Picture Industry* (Chicago: University of Chicago Press, 1983); Kathy Peiss, *Cheap Amusements: Working Women and Leisure in Turn-of-the-Century New York* (Philadelphia: Temple University Press, 1986); Roy Rosenzweig, *Eight Hours for What We Will: Workers and Leisure in an Industrial City, 1870–1920* (New York: Cambridge University Press, 1985).

54. Karl Marx, *Capital: A Critique of Political Economy,* vol. 1 (New York: Penguin, 1992), 290.

55. Hartman, *Scenes of Subjection.*

56. Ibid., 51.

57. Interestingly, in the cards pictured in plates 30 and 31 the commodity that is advertised—fruit vinegar or children's clothing—has little to do with the image. And yet the disconnect between product and image that appears in many of these cards only points to the shared culture of commodities, in which the image maker—be it advertiser or artisan printer—can rely on the spectator to supply the associative links that bind the image to the product. In the case of the children's clothing outlet these associations are with childhood "fun," and in the case of the fruit vinegar, with rural pastoralia.

58. W. E. B. Du Bois and Isabel Eaton, *The Philadelphia Negro* (Philadelphia: University of Pennsylvania, 1899), 33.

59. Oyster houses were so popular in the United States in the nineteenth century that Alan Davidson estimates that 170 million pounds of oysters were harvested in 1895. Oysters were popular across classes. Alan Davidson and Tom Jaine, *The Oxford Companion to Food* (New York: Oxford University Press, 2006), 565.

60. Dandy Jim chewing tobacco is a product of the Lorillard Tobacco Company, which is today the oldest U.S. tobacco company in existence. It was founded in 1760.

61. Hartman, *Scenes of Subjection*, 22.

62. See Paul Mullins, "'A Bold and Gorgeous Front': The Contradictions of African America and Consumer Culture," in *Historical Archaeologies of Capitalism*, ed. Mark P. Leone and Parker B. Potter, Jr., 169–193 (New York: Kluwer/Plenum, 1999); Paul Mullins, "Race and the Genteel Consumer: Class and African-American Consumption, 1850–1930," in "The Historical Archaeology of Class," ed. Lou Ann Wurst and Robert Fitts, special issue, *Historical Archaeology* 33:1 (1999): 22–38; Paul Mullins, "Expanding Archaeological Discourse: Ideology, Metaphor, and Critical Theory in Historical Archaeology," in *Annapolis Pasts: Historical Archaeology in Annapolis, Maryland*, ed. Paul A. Shackel, Paul R. Mullins, and Mark S. Warner, 7–34 (Knoxville: University of Tennessee Press, 1999).

63. Stewart, *Migrating to the Movies*, 93. See especially chapter 3, "'Negroes Laughing at Themselves'? Black Spectatorship and the Performance of Urban Modernity."

64. The question of how many black-owned printing businesses created advertising is one that needs exploring. According to *The Negro Artisan: Report of a Social Study Made under the Direction of Atlanta University* (1902), in 1890 there were twenty-eight black printers in Philadelphia, sixty-four in Washington, D.C., and twenty-nine in New York. Of the Philadelphia and New York printers, four were women; in Washington, D.C., seventeen were women. See W. E. B. Du Bois, *The Negro Artisan* (Atlanta: Atlanta University Press, 1902), 70, 72.

65. S. S. L. Jain, "'Come Up to the Kool Taste': African American Upward Mobility and the Semiotics of Smoking Menthols," *Public Culture* 15:2 (2003): 295.

66. Sianne Ngai, *Ugly Feelings* (Cambridge: Harvard University Press, 2005), 95.

67. Tara McPherson, *Reconstructing Dixie: Race, Gender, and Nostalgia in the Imagined South* (Durham: Duke University Press, 2003), 7.

68. Because of the metamorphic card's obvious investment in representing the mouth, it deserves a closer look. And while I simply cannot do justice to the genre here, I am going to briefly discuss two cards which are not pictured in the book. As discussed earlier, the metamorphic card is usually a half-folded card on which one or two bodies are depicted in a "before" relationship to a commodity. Upon unfolding the card the bottom halves of the faces change, and the happy "after" of commodity consumption is portrayed. The Chase and Sanborn window-shutter card is thus the exception that proves the rule, as most metaphoric cards follow the before/after structure. Recall the Allen's Jewel Ten Cent Plug from the earlier discussion of orality and ethnicity. What the Allen's Jewel advertisement points to is that the mouth is a central bodily site through which selfhood is, if not negotiated, then represented: in the metamorphic advertisement transformation takes place at the site of the mouth, as for instance in a truly bizarre (by today's standards) advertisement for

Duke of Durham tobacco, which depicts two crying babies, mouths wide open, with heads of hair that look suspiciously similar to male pattern balding. When the card is unfolded, the babies have rejected the "candy, cakes and pie" given them to keep them quiet and are happy with their tins of tobacco. Like the Libby's Cooked Corned Beef ad, what is celebrated here is the packaging, the industrial process by which the product is delivered, rather than the product itself. In other words, one's mediate connection to the commodity is, itself, commodified. Of course, it may be that the advertisement is really about letting children play with containers: we never see them smoking. Nonetheless, the card's gag rests on the unfolding of the lower half of the children's faces, which serves to depict the mouth as the seat of affective change or, more precisely, of individual subjectivity.

Another revealing opening is a card for Blackwell's Durham Smoke tobacco, which cites the presidential race of 1876. The ad compares presidential contender Samuel J. Tilden to Ulysses S. Grant by using the same top half of a face to signify both men and then flipping open the card to reveal Grant's bearded lower face and much-pinker cheeks. In other words, the figures' lower faces mark their difference from each other. More than that, the lower half of the face and in particular the mouth is encoded as a central physical site through which to read others. In each of these cards difference or conflict is ultimately overcome through shared commodity consumption: whatever your party, the Tilden/ Grant card claims, we may all "coincide when we remark / the choicest brand to smoke / is Blackwell's Durham Smoke." Commodity culture thus works here to suppress political difference, bringing the viewer back into his or her apolitical everyday. That everyday is definitively oral. (Grant in fact never ran against Tilden, and thus the card is something of a mystery. It implies that Grant has yet to win the nomination but asserts that Tilden is the Democratic nominee. This means that the card refers to the election of 1876, which ultimately went to Rutherford B. Hayes as part of the Compromise of 1877. One of the great contested U.S. presidential elections until Bush versus Gore, the Tilden defeat marked the end of Reconstruction. All of this leaves unclear why the card posits Grant as a potential nominee.)

69. Publisher unknown; image available at http://www.tradecards.com/scrapbook/ethnic/013.28.html (accessed May 16, 2011).

70. Lloyd Pratt, "Dialect Writing and Simultaneity in the American Historical Romance," *differences: A Journal of Feminist Cultural Studies* 13:3 (2002): 128.

71. Quoted in Susan Buck-Morss, *The Dialectics of Seeing: Walter Benjamin and the Arcades Project* (Cambridge: MIT Press, 1991), 114.

72. Marilyn Kern-Foxworth has demonstrated that the earliest representations of African Americans in advertising are the advertisements of slaves for sale and the posters for runaway slaves. Kern-Foxworth, *Aunt Jemima, Uncle Ben, and Rastus*. Clearly the entry of the African American body into European/North American consciousness is inextricably linked to the extreme pole of the commodity culture, with that body represented as a commodity on the market. The next step to objectification and transformation of blackness into material object is not a large one.

NOTES TO THE CONCLUSION

1. Leo Bersani, "Is the Rectum a Grave," in *Is the Rectum a Grave? And Other Essays* (Chicago: University of Chicago Press, 2009); originally published in *October* 43 (Winter 1987): 197–222.

2. See for instance Lisa Heldke, *Culinary Tourism* (Lexington: University of Kentucky Press, 2003).

3. Richard Lea, "Penguin Cookbook Calls for 'Freshly Ground Black People,'" *Guardian* (UK), April 19, 2010, http://guardian.co.uk/books/2010/apr/19/penguin-cook-book (accessed April 29, 2010).

4. Ibid.

5. Alison Flood, "Cookbook's 'Freshly Ground Black People' Gaffe Boosts Sales," *Guardian* (UK), May 5, 2010, http://www.guardian.co.uk/books/2010/may/05/cookbook-freshly-ground-black-people-gaffe-sales (accessed June 9, 2011).

6. And then again, just a few days before I sat down to write this conclusion, a few friends sent me a news item about the model Naomi Campbell, who was suing Cadbury's chocolate for running an advertisement for a new chocolate bar with the tagline "Move Over Naomi, There's a New Diva in Town." Cadbury, reported all the gossip blogs and more reputable news sites, offered an apology after Naomi Campbell issued a statement in which she said, "It's upsetting to be described as chocolate, not just for me but for all black women and black people. I do not find any humour in this. It is insulting and hurtful." Mark Sweeney, "Cadbury Apologises to Naomi Campbell over 'Racist' Ad," *Guardian* (UK), June 3, 2011, http://www.guardian.co.uk/media/2011/jun/03/cadbury-naomi-campbell-ad (accessed June 3, 2011). See also Alan Duke, "Chocolate 'Diva' Ad Hurts, Supermodel Naomi Campbell Complains," CNN.com, May 31, 2011, http://articles.cnn.com/2011-05-31/entertainment/naomi.campbell.cadbury_1_chocolate-naomi-campbell-supermodel?_s=PM:SHOWBIZ (accessed June 3, 2011). My thanks to Dana Luciano and Andrew Ragni for bringing this article to my attention.

7. See Fabio Parasecoli, *Bite Me: Food in Popular Culture* (New York: Berg, 2008).

Bibliography

Ahmed, Sara. *The Cultural Politics of Emotion*. New York: Routledge, 2004.

Alcott, Louisa May. *Eight Cousins*. New York: Little, Brown, 1922.

———. *Little Women*. 1868; repr., New York: Signet, 2004.

———. *An Old-Fashioned Girl*. Boston: Roberts Brothers, 1870.

———. *Rose in Bloom*. Boston: A. L. Burt, 1918.

———. *Work: A Story of Experience*. Boston: Roberts Brothers, 1873.

Alcott, Louisa May, and Sarah Elbert. *Louisa May Alcott on Race, Sex, and Slavery*. Hanover, NH: University Press of New England, 1997.

Alcott, William Andrus. *Forty Years in the Wilderness of Pills and Powders*. Boston: Jewett, 1859.

———. *The House I Live In; or, The Human Body*. Boston: Light and Stearns, 1837.

———. *The Laws of Health; or, Sequel to "The House I Live In."* Boston: Jewett, 1859.

———. *Lectures on Life and Health; or, The Laws and Means of Physical Culture*. Boston: Phillips, Sampson, 1853.

Ameri, Amir H. "Housing Ideologies in the New England and Chesapeake Bay Colonies, c. 1650–1700." *Journal of the Society of Architectural Historians* 56:1 (March 1997): 6–15.

"Amusements: General Mention." *New York Times*, November 28, 1879.

Anderson, Benedict. *Imagined Communities: Reflections on the Origin and Spread of Nationalism*. New York: Verso, 1991.

Anthony, David. "Class, Culture, and the Trouble with White Skin in Hawthorne's *The House of the Seven Gables*." *Yale Journal of Criticism* 12:2 (1999): 249–269.

Appadurai, Arjun, ed. *The Social Life of Things: Commodities in Cultural Perspective*. New York: Cambridge University Press, 1988.

Ardener, Shirley. "Male Dames and Female Boys: Cross-Dressing in the English Pantomime." In *Changing Sex and Bending Gender*, edited by Alison Shaw and Shirley Ardener, 119–137. New York: Berghahn Books, 2005.

Aristotle. *Poetics*. Translated by Malcolm Heath. New York: Penguin, 1996.

"Art of Making a Delicate Bread without Yeast." *Weekly Magazine of Original Essays, Fugitive Pieces, and Interesting Intelligence*, June 2, 1798. In *American Periodicals Series Online, 1740–1900*, 151.

Ashley, Bob, Joanne Hollows, Steve Jones, and Ben Taylor. *Food and Cultural Studies*. New York: Routledge, 2004.

Atkins, Robert C. *Dr. Atkins' Diet Revolution*. New York: Bantam, 1972.

Ayers, Edward L., Patricia Nelson Limerick, Stephen Nissenbaum, and Peter S. Onuf. *All Over the Map: Rethinking American Regions*. Baltimore: Johns Hopkins University Press, 1995.

Bakhtin, Mikhail Mikhailovich. *Rabelais and His World*. Bloomington: Indiana University Press, 1984.

Banting, William. *Letter on Corpulence Addressed to the Public*. London: Harrison, 1863.

Bean, Annemarie. "Playwrights and Plays of the Harlem Renaissance." In *A Companion to Twentieth-Century American Drama*, edited by David Krasner, 91–105. Malden, MA: Blackwell, 2007.

Beecher, Catharine Esther. *A Treatise on Domestic Economy*. Boston: Thomas H. Webb, 1841.

Beecher, Catharine Esther, and Harriet Beecher Stowe. *The American Woman's Home; or, Principles of Domestic Science; Being a Guide to the Formation and Maintenance of Economical, Healthful, Beautiful, and Christian Homes*. New York: J. B. Ford, 1869.

Benfield, Ben Barker. "The Spermatic Economy: A Nineteenth-Century View of Sexuality." *Feminist Studies* 1 (Summer 1972): 45–74.

Berlant, Lauren. "National Brands, National Body: *Imitation of Life*." In *The Female Complaint: The Unfinished Business of Sentimentality in American Culture*, 107–144. Durham: Duke University Press, 2008.

———. "Poor Eliza." *American Literature* 70:3 (September 1998): 635–668.

Bersani, Leo. *Is the Rectum a Grave? And Other Essays*. Chicago: University of Chicago Press, 2009.

Bertolini, Vincent J. "Fireside Chastity: The Erotics of Sentimental Bachelorhood in the 1850s." *American Literature* 68:4 (December 1996): 707–737.

Bird, Robert Montgomery. *Peter Pilgrim; or, A Rambler's Recollections*. Philadelphia: Lea & Blanchard, 1838.

Blumin, Stuart. *The Emergence of the Middle Class*. New York: Cambridge University Press, 1989.

Bordo, Susan. *Unbearable Weight: Feminism, Western Culture, and the Body*. Berkeley: University of California Press, 1993.

Bourdieu, Pierre. *Distinction: A Social Critique of the Judgement of Taste*. Cambridge: Harvard University Press, 1984.

Bow, Leslie. "'For Every Gesture of Loyalty, There Doesn't Have to Be a Betrayal': Asian American Criticism and the Politics of Locality." In *Who Can Speak? Authority and Critical Identity*, edited by Judith Roof and Robyn Wiegman, 30–55. Urbana: University of Illinois Press, 1995.

Boydston, Jeanne. *Home and Work: Housework, Wages, and the Ideology of Labor in the Early Republic*. New York: Oxford University Press, 1994.

Brewer, Priscilla J. *From Fireplace to Cookstove: Technology and the Domestic Ideal in America*. Syracuse: Syracuse University Press, 2000.

Bridgeman, T. "Pumpkin Bread." *Workingman's Advocate*, January 2, 1836. In *American Periodicals Series Online, 1740–1900*, 151.

Brillat-Savarin, Anthelme. *The Physiology of Taste; or, Meditations on Transcendental Gastronomy.* Translated by M. F. K. Fisher. New York: Everyman's Library, 2009.

Brooks, Daphne. *Bodies in Dissent: Spectacular Performances of Race and Freedom, 1850–1910.* Durham: Duke University Press, 2007.

Brown, Bill. "Reification, Reanimation, and the American Uncanny." *Critical Inquiry* 32:2 (2006): 207.

———. *A Sense of Things: The Object Matter of American Literature.* Chicago: University of Chicago Press, 2004.

Brown, Gillian. *Domestic Individualism: Imagining Self in Nineteenth-Century America.* Berkeley: University of California Press, 1990.

———. "Getting in the Kitchen with Dinah: Domestic Politics in *Uncle Tom's Cabin.*" *American Quarterly* 36 (Fall 1984): 503–523.

Buck-Morss, Susan. *The Dialectics of Seeing: Walter Benjamin and the Arcades Project.* Cambridge: MIT Press, 1991.

Burgett, Bruce. "Between Speculation and Population: The Problem of 'Sex' in Our Long Eighteenth Century." *Early American Literature* 37:1 (2002): 119–153.

———. "On the Mormon Question: Race, Sex, and Polygamy in the 1850s and the 1990s." *American Quarterly* 57:1 (March 2005): 75–102.

Bushman, Richard Lyman. "Markets and Composite Farms in Early America." *William and Mary Quarterly* 55:3 (1998): 351–374.

———. *The Refinement of America: Persons, Houses, Cities.* New York: Vintage, 1993.

Butler, Judith. *Bodies That Matter: On the Discursive Limits of Sex.* New York: Routledge, 1993.

Butsch, Richard. "Bowery B'Hoys and Matinee Ladies: The Re-gendering of Nineteenth-Century American Theatre Audiences." *American Quarterly* 46:3 (September 1994): 374–405.

Cadbury, Deborah. *Chocolate Wars: The 150-Year Rivalry between the World's Greatest Chocolate Makers.* New York: Public Affairs, 2010.

Cakeling, Christopher. "Whimsical Distresses of an Attempt to Make Bread." *Literary Museum, or, Monthly Magazine*, March 1797. In *American Periodicals Series Online, 1740–1900*, 155.

Cameron, Sharon. *The Corporeal Self: Allegories of the Body in Melville and Hawthorne.* New York: Columbia University Press, 1991.

Campos, Paul. *The Obesity Myth: Why America's Obsession with Weight Is Hazardous to Your Health.* New York: Gotham, 2004.

Carter, Susannah. *The Frugal Housewife; or, Complete Woman Cook: Wherein the Art of Dressing All Sorts of Viands with Cleanliness, Decency and Elegance, Is Explained in Five Hundred Approved Receipts . . . to Which Are Added Twelve New Prints, Exhibiting a Proper Arrangement of Dinners, Two Courses for Every Month in the Year.* New York: G. & R. Waite, 1765; reprinted 1803.

Castiglia, Christopher. *Interior States: Institutional Consciousness and the Inner Life of Democracy in the Antebellum United States*. Durham: Duke University Press, 2008.

———. "The Marvelous Queer Interiors of *The House of the Seven Gables*." In *The Cambridge Companion to Nathaniel Hawthorne*, edited by Richard H. Millington, 186–206. New York: Cambridge University Press, 2004.

Chasar, Mike. "The Business of Rhyming: Burma Shave Poetry and Popular Culture." *PMLA* 125:1 (January 2010): 29–47.

Chen, John Kuo-Wei. *New York before Chinatown*. Baltimore: Johns Hopkins University Press, 2001.

Child, Lydia Maria Francis. *The American Frugal Housewife*. Boston: Carter and Hendee, 1830.

Clarence-Smith, William Gervase. *Cocoa and Chocolate, 1765–1914*. New York: Routledge, 2000.

Coe, Andrew. *Chop Suey: A Cultural History of Chinese Food in the United States*. New York: Oxford University Press, 2009.

Coe, Sophie D., and Michael D. Coe. *The True History of Chocolate*. 2nd ed. London: Thames & Hudson, 2007.

Cohoon, Lorinda B. "'A Highly Satisfactory Chinaman': Orientalism and American Girlhood in Louisa May Alcott's *Eight Cousins*." *Children's Literature* 36 (2008): 49–68.

Cott, Nancy F. *The Bonds of Womanhood: "Woman's Sphere" in New England, 1780–1835*. New Haven: Yale University Press, 1977.

Cowan, Ruth Schwartz. *More Work for Mother: The Ironies of Household Technology from the Open Hearth to the Microwave*. New York: Basic Books, 1983.

Crais, Clifton C., and Pamela Scully. *Sara Baartman and the Hottentot Venus: A Ghost Story and a Biography*. Princeton: Princeton University Press, 2009.

Crowley, John E.. *The Invention of Comfort: Sensibilities and Design in Early Modern Britain and Early America*. Baltimore: Johns Hopkins University Press, 2001.

Dame Trot and Her Comical Cat: Illustrated with Sixteen Elegant Engravings. Philadelphia: Wm. Charles, American Antiquarian Society, 1809.

Davidson, Alan. *The Penguin Companion to Food*. New York: Penguin, 2002.

Davidson, Alan, and Tom Jaine. *The Oxford Companion to Food*. 2nd ed. Oxford: Oxford University Press, 2006.

Davidson, Cathy, and Jessmyn Hatcher, eds. *No More Separate Spheres! A Next Wave American Studies Reader*. Durham: Duke University Press, 2002.

de Certeau, Michel. *The Practice of Everyday Life*. Translated by Steven Rendall. Berkeley: University of California Press, 1988.

de Charlevoix, Pere Pierre Francois-Xavier. *A Voyage to North America; Undertaken by Command of the Present King of France, Containing . . . a Description of the Natural History of the Islands of the West Indies Belonging to the Different Powers of Europe*. 2 vols. Dublin: John Exshaw and James Potts, 1766.

Derrida, Jacques, "'Eating Well,' or the Calculation of the Subject: An Interview with Jacques Derrida." In *Who Comes after the Subject?*, edited by Eduardo Cadava, Jean-Luc Nancy, and Peter Connor, 96–119. New York: Routledge, 1991.

Diawara, Manthia. "Afro-Kitsch." In *Black Popular Culture: A Project*, edited by Gina Dent and Michele Wallace, 287–289. Seattle: Bay, 1992.

Diner, Hasia R. *Hungering for America: Italian, Irish, and Jewish Foodways in the Age of Migration*. Cambridge: Harvard University Press, 2003.

"The Domestic Guide." *New York Weekly Museum*, December 7, 1816. In *American Periodicals Series Online, 1740–1900*, 96.

Douglas, Ann. Introduction to *Uncle Tom's Cabin*, by Harriet Beecher Stowe. New York: Penguin, 1981.

Douglas, Mary. *Purity and Danger: An Analysis of the Concepts of Pollution and Taboo.* New York: Routledge, 2000.

Drayton, John. "To Make Rice Bread." *Archives of Useful Knowledge*, January 1813. In *American Periodicals Series Online, 1740–1900*, 272.

Dreiss, Meredith L., and Sharon Edgar Greenhill. *Chocolate: Pathway to the Gods*. Tucson: University of Arizona Press, 2008.

Du Bois, W. E. B. *The Negro Artisan: Report of a Social Study Made under the Direction of Atlanta University*. Atlanta: Atlanta University Press, 1902.

Du Bois, W. E. B., and Isabel Eaton. *The Philadelphia Negro*. Philadelphia: University of Pennsylvania, 1899.

Dudden, Faye. *Serving Women: Household Service in Nineteenth-Century America*. New York: Harper and Row, 1983.

Duke, Alan. "Chocolate 'Diva' Ad Hurts, Supermodel Naomi Campbell Complains." CNN.com, May 31, 2011. http://articles.cnn.com/2011-05-31/entertainment/naomi.campbell.cadbury_1_chocolate-naomi-campbell-supermodel?_s=PM:SHOWBIZ (accessed June 3, 2011).

Dunson, Stephanie. "The Minstrel in the Parlor: Nineteenth-Century Sheet Music and the Domestication of Blackface Minstrelsy." *ATQ: The American Transcendental Quarterly* 16 (December 2002): 241–256.

DuPuis, Melanie. *Nature's Perfect Food: How Milk Became America's Drink*. New York: NYU Press, 2002.

DuPuis, E. Melanie, and David Goodman. "Should We Go 'Home' to Eat? Toward a Reflexive Politics of Localism." *Journal of Rural Studies* 21:3 (July 2005): 359–371.

Durling, Richard M. "Deceit and Digestion in the Belly of Hell." In *Allegory and Interpretation: Selected Papers from the English Institute, 1970–80*, edited by Stephen J. Greenblatt, 61–93. Baltimore: Johns Hopkins Press, 1981.

Egerton, John, with Ann Bleidt Egerton. *Southern Food: At Home, on the Road, in History.* New York: Knopf, 1987.

Emerson, Ralph Waldo. *Journals of Ralph Waldo Emerson with Annotations*. New York: Houghton Mifflin, 1911.

———. "New England Reformers: A Lecture Read Before the Society in Amory Hall on Sunday, 3 March, 1844." In *Essays and Lectures*, 589–614. New York: Library of America, 1983.

Ewen, Elizabeth. *Immigrant Women in the Land of Dollars: Life and Culture on the Lower East Side, 1890–1925*. New York: Monthly Review Press, 1985.

Farmer, Fannie Merritt. *The Boston Cooking-School Cook Book*. Boston: Little, Brown, 1896.

Farrar, Mrs. John. *The Young Lady's Friend*. Boston: American Stationers' Company, 1837.

Faulkner, Carol. "The Root of the Evil: Free Produce and Radical Antislavery, 1820–1860." *Journal of the Early Republic* 27:3 (2007): 377–405.

Fiedler, Leslie. *Love and Death in the American Novel*. New York: Criterion Books, 1960.

Fliegelman, Jay. *Prodigals and Pilgrims: The American Revolution against Patriarchal Authority, 1750–1800*. New York: Cambridge University Press, 1985.

Flood, Allison. "Cookbook's 'Freshly Ground Black People' Gaffe Boosts Sales." *Guardian* (UK), May 5, 2010. http://www.guardian.co.uk/books/2010/may/05/cookbook-freshly-ground-black-people-gaffe-sales.

Folster, David. *Ganong: A Sweet History of Chocolate*. Fredericton, NB: Goose Lane, 2006.

Foreman, P. Gabrielle. "'This Promiscuous Housekeeping': Death, Transgression, and Homoeroticism in *Uncle Tom's Cabin*." *Representations* 44 (1993): 51–72.

Foucault, Michel. *The History of Sexuality, Volume 1: An Introduction*. New York: Vintage Books, 1990.

Franklin, Benjamin, Lewis Evans, and James Turner. *An Account of the New Invented Pennsylvanian Fire-Places: Wherein Their Construction and Manner of Operation Is Particularly Explained; Their Advantages above Every Other Method of Warming Rooms Demonstrated; and All Objections That Have Been Raised against the Use of Them, Answered and Obviated; with Directions for Putting Them Up, and for Using Them to the Best Advantage; and a Copper-Plate, in Which the Several Parts of the Machine Are Exactly Laid Down, from a Scale of Equal Parts*. Philadelphia: B. Franklin, 1744.

Freeman, Elizabeth. "Honeymoon with a Stranger: Pedophiliac Picaresque from Poe to Nabokov." *American Literature* 70 (December 1998): 863–897.

———. Introduction to "Queer Temporalities." Special issue. *GLQ: A Journal of Lesbian and Gay Studies* 13:2–3 (2007): 159–176.

Freidberg, Suzanne. *Fresh: A Perishable History*. Cambridge: Belknap Press of Harvard University Press, 2009.

Freud, Sigmund. *Jokes and Their Relation to the Unconscious*. New York: Norton, 1960.

———. *Three Essays on the History of Sexuality*. New York: Basic Books, 1975.

Friedberg, Anne. "Les Flâneurs du Mal(l): Cinema and the Postmodern Condition." *PMLA* 106:3 (May 1991): 419–431.

———. *Window Shopping: Cinema and the Postmodern*. Berkeley: University of California Press, 1993.

Gabaccia, Donna R. *We Are What We Eat: Ethnic Food and the Making of Americans*. Cambridge: Harvard University Press, 2000.

Garber, Marjorie. *Vested Interests: Cross-Dressing and Cultural Anxiety*. New York: Routledge, 1997.

Garvey, Ellen Gruber. *The Adman in the Parlor: Magazines and the Gendering of Consumer Culture, 1880s to 1910s*. New York: Oxford University Press, 1996.

———. "Dreaming in Commerce: Advertising Trade Card Scrapbooks." In *Acts of Possession: Collecting in America*, edited by Leah Dilworth, 66–88. New Brunswick: Rutgers University Press, 2003.

Garvey, T. Gregory. *Creating the Culture of Reform in Antebellum America*. Athens: University of Georgia Press, 2006.

Gigante, Denise. *Taste: A Literary History*. New Haven: Yale University Press, 2005.

Gilman, Caroline. *Recollections of a Southern Matron*. New York: Harper and Brothers, 1838.

Gilman, Charlotte Perkins. "The Kitchen Fly" (1910). In *The Forerunner, Volume 1 (1909–1910): A Monthly Magazine*, 459–462. Middlesex, UK: Echo Library, 2007.

Gilman, Sander. *Difference and Pathology: Stereotypes of Sexuality, Race, and Madness*. Ithaca: Cornell University Press, 1985.

———. *Fat: A Cultural History of Obesity*. Malden, MA: Polity, 2008.

———. *Fat Boys: A Slim Book*. Lincoln: University of Nebraska Press, 2004.

Gilmore, Paul. *The Genuine Article: Race, Class and American Literary Manhood*. Durham: Duke University Press, 2001.

Glickman, Lawrence B. "'Buy for the Sake of the Slave': Abolitionism and the Origins of American Consumer Activism." *American Quarterly* 56:4 (2004): 889–912.

Goddu, Teresa A. *Gothic America: Narrative, History, Nation*. New York: Columbia University Press, 1997.

Goodman, David, and E. Melanie DuPuis. "Knowing Food and Growing Food: Beyond the Production-Consumption Debate in the Sociology of Agriculture." *Sociologia Ruralis* 42 (January 2002): 5–22.

Goody, Jack. "Industrial Food." In *Food and Culture: A Reader*, edited by Carole Counihan and Penny Van Esterik, 338–356. New York: Routledge, 1997.

Graham, Sylvester. *A Lecture to Young Men on Chastity*. Boston: Light and Stearns, 1838.

———. *Lectures on the Science of Human Life*. Boston: Marsh, Capen, Lyon and Webb, 1839.

———. *Thy Kingdom Come: A Discourse on the Importance of Infant and Sunday Schools, Delivered at the Crown St. Church, Philadelphia, December 13th, 1829*. Philadelphia: Wm. F. Geddes, 1831.

———. *A Treatise on Bread and Breadmaking*. Boston: Light and Stearns, 1837.

Greenbaum, Florence Kreisler. *The International Jewish Cookbook: 1600 Recipes According to the Jewish Dietary Laws with the Rules for Kashering; The Favorite Recipes of America, Austria, Germany, Russia, France, Poland, Roumania, Etc., Etc*. New York: Bloch, 1919.

Grivetti, Louis E., and Howard-Yana Shapiro. *Chocolate: History, Culture, and Heritage*. London: Wiley, 2009.

Gunning, Tom. "The Cinema of Attractions: Early Film, Its Spectator and the Avant-Garde." In *Early Film: Space, Frame, Narrative*, edited by Thomas Elsaesser and Adam Barker, 56–62. London: British Film Institute, 1989.

Halberstam, Judith. *In a Queer Time and Place: Transgender Bodies, Subcultural Lives*. New York: NYU Press, 2005.

Hale, Sarah Josepha Buell. *The Good Housekeeper; or, The Way to Live Well and to Be Well While We Live: Containing Directions for Choosing and Preparing Food, in Regard to Health, Economy and Taste.* Boston: Weeks, Jordan, 1839.

Hall, Stuart. "For Allon White: Metaphors of Transformation." In *Stuart Hall: Critical Dialogues in Cultural Studies,* edited by David Morley and Kuan-Hsing Chen, 287–306. New York: Routledge, 1996.

Hall, Stuart, David Held, Don Hubert, and Kenneth Thompson, eds. *Modernity: An Introduction to Modern Societies.* Malden, MA: Blackwell, 1996.

Halttunen, Karen. *Confidence Men and Painted Women: A Study of Middle-Class Culture in America, 1830–1870.* New Haven: Yale University Press, 1986.

———. "Gothic Imagination and Social Reform: The Haunted Houses of Lyman Beecher, Henry Ward Beecher, and Harriet Beecher Stowe." In *New Essays on* Uncle Tom's Cabin, edited by Eric J. Sundquist, 107–134. Cambridge: Cambridge University Press, 1986.

Hansen, Miriam. *Babel and Babylon: Spectatorship in American Silent Film.* Cambridge: Harvard University Press, 1991.

Hao, Yen-p'ing. *The Commercial Revolution in Nineteenth-Century China.* Berkeley: University of California Press, 1986.

Harris, Cheryl. "Whiteness as Property." *Harvard Law Review* 106:8 (1993): 1707–1791.

Harte, Bret. *The Writings of Bret Harte.* New York: Houghton Mifflin, 1914.

Hartman, Saidiya V. *Scenes of Subjection: Terror, Slavery, and Self-Making in Nineteenth-Century America.* New York: Oxford University Press, 1997.

Hauck-Lawson, Annie. "Introduction." *Food, Culture and Society: An International Journal of Multidisciplinary Research* 7 (Spring 2004): 24–25.

———. "When Food Is the Voice: A Case Study of a Polish-American Woman." *Journal for the Study of Food and Society* 2:1 (1998): 21–28.

Hawthorne, Nathaniel. "Fire Worship." In *Mosses from an Old Manse.* New York: Modern Library, 2003.

———. *The House of the Seven Gables.* London: G. Routledge, 1851.

Hayden, Dolores. *The Grand Domestic Revolution: A History of Feminist Designs for American Homes, Neighborhoods, and Cities.* Cambridge: MIT Press, 1982.

Hearn, Lafcadio. *La Cuisine Creole: A Collection of Culinary Recipes, from Leading Chefs and Noted Creole Housewives, Who Have Made New Orleans Famous for Its Cuisine.* New Orleans: F. F. Hansell, 1885.

Hedrick, Joan D. *Harriet Beecher Stowe, a Life.* New York: Oxford University Press, 1994.

Heldke, Lisa. *Culinary Tourism.* Lexington: University of Kentucky Press, 2003.

Hendler, Glenn. *Public Sentiments: Structures of Feeling in Nineteenth-Century Literature.* Chapel Hill: University of North Carolina Press, 2001.

Herbst, Sharon Tyler, and Ron Herbst. *The New Food Lover's Companion.* 4th ed. Hauppauge, NY: Barron's Educational Series, 2007.

Hertz, Neil. *The End of the Line.* New York: Columbia University Press, 1985.

Higginson, Francis. "A Letter Sent Home." In *The Life of Francis Higginson, First Minister in the Massachusetts Bay Colony, and Author of "New England's Plantation,"* by Thomas Wentworth Higginson, 75. New York: Dodd, Mead, 1891.

———. *New England's Plantation: With Sea Journal and Other Writings*. Salem, MA: Essex Book and Print Club, 1908.

Hinrichs, C. Clare. "The Practice and Politics of Food System Localization." *Journal of Rural Studies* 19:1 (January 2003): 33–45.

Ho, Jennifer A. *Consumption and Identity in Asian American Coming-of-Age Novels*. New York: Routledge, 2005.

hooks, bell. "Eating the Other: Desire and Resistance." In *Black Looks: Race and Representation*, 21–41. Cambridge, MA: South End, 1999.

Horowitz, Helen Lefkowitz. *Rereading Sex: Battles over Sexual Knowledge and Suppression in Nineteenth-Century America*. New York: Knopf, 2002.

Hotten, John Camden. *Slang Dictionary*. London: Chatto and Windus, 1874.

Howland, Esther Allen. *The New England Economical Housekeeper, and Family Receipt Book*. Boston: S. A. Howland, 1845.

Hulme, Peter. "Introduction: The Cannibal Scene." In *Cannibalism and the Colonial World*, edited by Francis Barker, Peter Hulme, and Margaret Iversen, 1–38. Cambridge: Cambridge University Press, 1998.

ICON Group International. *Chocolate: Webster's Timeline History, 1585–2007*. New York: ICON, 2009.

Jain, S. S. L. "'Come Up to the Kool Taste': African American Upward Mobility and the Semiotics of Smoking Menthols." *Public Culture* 15:2 (2003): 295.

Jay, Robert. *The Trade Card in Nineteenth-Century America*. Columbia: University of Missouri Press, 1987.

Jeanneret, Michel. *A Feast of Words: Banquets and Table Talk in the Renaissance*. Chicago: Chicago University Press, 1991.

Johnson, Samuel. *A Dictionary of the English Language: In Which the Words Are Deduced from Their Originals, and Illustrated in Their Different Significations by Examples from the Best Writers, to Which Are Prefixed, a History of the Language, and an English Grammar*. 2 vols. 2nd ed. London, 1755–56. Available at Eighteenth Century Collections Online, http://gdc.gale.com/products/eighteenth-century-collections-online/ (accessed November 25, 2011).

Jones, Gavin Roger. *Strange Talk: The Politics of Dialect Literature in Gilded Age America*. Berkeley: University of California Press, 1999.

Kamp, David. *The United States of Arugula: How We Became a Gourmet Nation*. New York: Broadway Books, 2006.

Kaplan, Amy. "Manifest Domesticity." In *No More Separate Spheres! A Next Wave American Studies Reader*, edited by Cathy N. Davidson and Jessamyn Hatcher, 183–208. Durham: Duke University Press, 2002.

Kelsey, Carl. "Some Causes of Negro Emigration: The Men." In *The Negro in the Cities of the North*, 15–17. New York: Charity Organization Society, 1905.

Kern-Foxworth, Marilyn. *Aunt Jemima, Uncle Ben, and Rastus: Blacks in Advertising, Yesterday, Today, and Tomorrow.* Westport, CT: Praeger, 1994.

Kilgour, Maggie. *From Communion to Cannibalism: An Anatomy of Metaphors of Incorporation.* Princeton: Princeton University Press, 1990.

Kitchiner, William. *The Cook's Oracle: Containing Receipts for Plain Cookery, on the Most Economical Plan for Private Families: Also, the Art of Composing the Most Simple, and Most Highly Finished Broths, Gravies, Soups, Sauces, Store Sauces, and Flavouring Essences: The Quantity of Each Article Is Accurately Stated by Weight and Measure; the Whole Being the Result of Actual Experiments Instituted in the Kitchen of a Physician.* Edinburgh: A. Constable; Cheapside: Hurst, Robinson, 1822.

Kleiman, Jordan. "Local Food and the Problem of Public Authority." *Technology and Culture* 50:2 (2009): 399–417.

Klosterman, Chuck. *Sex, Drugs, and Cocoa Puffs: A Low Culture Manifesto.* New York: Scribner, 2003.

Knapp, Arthur William. *Cocoa and Chocolate: Their History from Plantation to Consumer.* Charleston, SC: Nabu, 2010.

Knopf, Henry Adolf. *Changes in Wheat Production in the United States, 1607–1960.* Ithaca: Cornell University Press, 1967.

Kolodny, Annette. *The Lay of the Land: Metaphor as Experience and History in American Life and Letters.* Chapel Hill: University of North Carolina Press, 1984.

Kopytoff, Igor. "The Cultural Biography of Things: Commoditization as Process." In *The Social Life of Things,* edited by Arjun Appadurai, 64–94. New York: Cambridge University Press, 1988.

Laird, Pamela Walker. *Advertising Progress: American Business and the Rise of Consumer Marketing.* Baltimore: Johns Hopkins University Press, 1998.

Laqueur, Thomas W. *Solitary Sex: A Cultural History of Masturbation.* New York: Zone Books, 2003.

Lawless, Cecelia. "Cooking, Community, Culture: A Reading of *Like Water for Chocolate.*" In *Recipes for Reading: Community Cookbooks, Stories, Histories,* edited by Anne Bower. Amherst: University of Massachusetts Press, 1997.

Lazo, Roderigo. "Migrant Archives: New Routes in and out of American Studies." In *States of Emergency: The Object of American Studies,* edited by Russ Castronovo and Susan Gillman, 36–54. Chapel Hill: University of North Carolina Press, 2009.

Lea, Richard. "Penguin Cookbook Calls for 'Freshly Ground Black People.'" *Guardian* (UK), April 19, 2010. http://www.guardian.co.uk/books/2010/april/19/penguin-cook-book.

Lears, Jackson. *Fables of Abundance: A Cultural History of Advertising in America.* New York: Basic Books, 1994.

Lee, Robert G. *Orientals: Asian Americans in Popular Culture.* Philadelphia: Temple University Press, 1999.

Leslie, Eliza. *Directions for Cookery, in Its Various Branches.* Philadelphia: E. L. Carey & Hart, 1840.

Levenstein, Harvey. *Revolution at the Table: The Transformation of the American Diet.* Berkeley: University of California Press, 1988.

Lévi-Strauss, Claude. *The Raw and the Cooked: Mythologiques, Volume 1.* Chicago: University of Chicago Press, 1983.

Locke, John. *Some Thoughts Concerning Education.* Cambridge: Cambridge University Press, 1902.

Lorde, Audre. "Eye to Eye: Black Women, Hatred, and Anger." In *Sister Outsider: Essays and Speeches*, 145–175. Berkeley, CA: Crossing, 1984.

Lott, Eric. *Love and Theft: Blackface Minstrelsy and the American Working Class.* New York: Oxford University Press, 1995.

Manning, M. M. *Slave in a Box.* Charlottesville: University of Virginia Press, 1998.

Mannur, Anita, ed. "Meat vs. Rice." Special issue, *Amerasia Journal* 32 (2006).

Manring, Maurice M. *Slave in a Box: The Strange Career of Aunt Jemima.* Charlottesville: University of Virginia Press, 1998.

Marchand, Roland. "Advertisements as Social Tableaux." In *Advertising the American Dream: Making Way for Modernity, 1920–1940*, 164–205. Berkeley: University of California Press, 1986.

Marx, Karl. *Capital: A Critique of Political Economy.* Vol. 1. New York: Penguin, 1992.

Mather, Cotton. *The Diary of Cotton Mather, 1621–1724.* Worcester: Massachusetts Historical Society, 1911.

Matsukawa, Yuko. "Representing the Oriental in Nineteenth-Century Trade Cards." In *Re/collecting Early Asian America: Essays in Cultural History*, edited by Josephine Lee, Imogene L. Lim, and Yuko Matsukawa, 200–217. Philadelphia: Temple University Press, 2002.

May, Lary. *Screening Out the Past: The Birth of Mass Culture and the Motion Picture Industry.* Chicago: University of Chicago Press, 1983.

Mbembe, Achille. "Necropolitics." Translated by Libby Meintjes. *Public Culture* 15:1 (2003): 11–40.

McClintock, Anne. *Imperial Leather: Race, Gender, and Sexuality in the Colonial Contest.* New York: Routledge, 1995.

McClure, Samuel Sydney. "The Tammanyizing of a Civilization." *McClure's Magazine* 34 (1909): 125.

McElaney, Hugh. "Alcott's Freaking of Boyhood: The Perplex of Gender and Disability in *Under the Lilacs*." *Children's Literature* 34 (2006): 139–160.

McGill, Meredith. *American Literature and the Culture of Reprinting, 1834–1853.* Philadelphia: University of Pennsylvania Press, 2003.

McNamara, Brooks. *Step Right Up.* Jackson: University Press of Mississippi, 1995.

McNeil, Cameron L. *Chocolate in Mesoamerica: A Cultural History of Cacao.* Gainesville: University Press of Florida, 2009.

McPherson, Tara. *Reconstructing Dixie: Race, Gender, and Nostalgia in the Imagined South.* Durham: Duke University Press, 2003.

Mehaffy, Marilyn Maness. "Advertising Race/Raceing Advertising: The Feminine Consumer(-Nation), 1876–1900." *Signs: Journal of Women in Culture and Society* 23:1 (1997): 141.

Melville, Herman. "I and My Chimney." In *Tales, Poems, and Other Writings*, 264–290. New York: Modern Library, 2002.

———. *Moby Dick*. New York: Norton, 2001.

Merish, Lori. *Sentimental Materialism: Gender, Commodity Culture, and Nineteenth-Century American Literature*. Durham: Duke University Press, 2000.

Miller, William Ian. *The Anatomy of Disgust*. Cambridge: Harvard University Press, 1998.

Mintz, Sidney. "Eating American." In *Food in the USA*, edited by Carole Counihan. New York: Routledge, 2002.

———. *Sweetness and Power: The Place of Sugar in Modern History*. New York: Penguin, 1986.

Moon, Krystyn R. *Yellowface*. New Brunswick: Rutgers University Press, 2005.

Moon, Michael. "Nineteenth-Century Discourses on Childhood Gender Training: The Case of Louisa May Alcott's *Little Men* and *Jo's Boys*." In *Queer Representations*, edited by Martin B. Duberman and City University of New York, Center for Lesbian and Gay Studies, 209–215. New York: NYU Press, 1997.

Morrison, Toni. *Playing in the Dark*. Cambridge: Harvard University Press, 1992.

Morton, Timothy. *Cultures of Taste/Theories of Appetite: Eating Romanticism*. New York: Palgrave Macmillan, 2004.

———. *The Poetics of Spice*. New York: Cambridge University Press, 2006.

———. *Shelley and the Revolution in Taste: The Body and the Natural World*. New York: Cambridge University Press, 1995.

Moses, Charles. Interview by Esther de Sola. In *Born in Slavery: Slave Narratives from the Federal Writers' Project, 1936–1938*. American Memory Project, Library of Congress. http://memory.loc.gov/ammem/snhtml/snhome.html.

Moy, James S. *Marginal Sights: Staging the Chinese in America*. Des Moines: University of Iowa Press, 1994.

Mullen, Haryette. "Runaway Tongue: Resistant Orality in *Uncle Tom's Cabin*, *Our Nig*, *Incidents in the Life of a Slave Girl*, and *Beloved*." In *The Culture of Sentiment: Race, Gender, and Sentimentality in Nineteenth-Century America*, edited by Shirley Samuels, 244–264. New York: Oxford University Press, 1999.

Mullins, Paul R. "'A Bold and Gorgeous Front': The Contradictions of African America and Consumer Culture." In *Historical Archaeologies of Capitalism*, edited by Mark P. Leone and Parker B. Potter, Jr., 169–193. New York: Kluwer/Plenum, 1999.

———. "Expanding Archaeological Discourse: Ideology, Metaphor, and Critical Theory in Historical Archaeology." In *Annapolis Past: Historical Archaeology in Annapolis, Maryland*, edited by Paul A. Shackel, Paul R. Mullins, and Mark S. Warner, 7–34. Knoxville: University of Tennessee Press, 1999.

———. *Race and Affluence: An Archaeology of African-American and Consumer Culture*. New York: Springer, 1999.

———. "Race and the Genteel Consumer: Class and African-American Consumption, 1850–1930." In "The Historical Archaeology of Class," edited by Lou Ann Wurst and Robert Fitts, special issue, *Historical Archaeology* 33:1 (1999): 22–38.

Newman, Lea Bertani Vozar. *A Reader's Guide to the Short Stories of Herman Melville.* New York: G. K. Hall, 1986.

Ngai, Sianne. *Ugly Feelings.* Cambridge: Harvard University Press, 2005.

"Niblo's Garden." *New York Times,* March 24, 1885.

Nissenbaum, Stephen. *Sex, Diet, and Debility in Jacksonian America: Sylvester Graham and Health Reform.* Westport, CT: Greenwood, 1980.

Norton, Marcy. *Sacred Gifts, Profane Pleasures: A History of Tobacco and Chocolate in the Atlantic World.* Ithaca: Cornell University Press, 2010.

Nuermberger, Ruth Ketring. *The Free Produce Movement: A Quaker Protest against Slavery.* Durham: Duke University Press, 1942.

Nylander, Jane C. *Our Own Snug Fireside: Images of the New England Home, 1760–1860.* New Haven: Yale University Press, 1994.

Nyong'o, Tavia. "Racial Kitsch and Black Performance." *Yale Journal of Criticism* 15:2 (2002): 371–391.

Obenzinger, Hilton. *American Palestine: Melville, Twain, and the Holy Land Mania.* Princeton: Princeton University Press, 1999.

Okihiro, Gary Y. *The Columbia Guide to Asian American History.* New York: Columbia University Press, 2001.

Olaya, Clara. *Frutas de América: Tropical y subtropical: Historia y usos.* Barcelona: Grupo Editorial Norma, 1991.

"On the Means of Making Bread from Rice." *South-Carolina Weekly Museum and Complete Magazine of Entertainment and Intelligence,* February 25, 1797. In *American Periodicals Series Online, 1740–1900,* 230.

Opie, Iona Archibald, and Peter Opie. *The Oxford Dictionary of Nursery Rhymes.* New York: Oxford University Press, 1977.

Panagia, Davide. *The Political Life of Sensation.* Durham: Duke University Press, 2009.

Parasecoli, Fabio. *Bite Me: Food in Popular Culture.* New York: Berg, 2008.

Parker, Emma. "You Are What You Eat: The Politics of Eating in the Novels of Margaret Atwood." *Twentieth-Century Literature* 41:3 (1995): 349–369.

Parks, Suzan-Lori. *Venus: A Play.* New York: Theatre Communications Group, 1997.

Peiss, Kathy. *Cheap Amusements: Working Women and Leisure in Turn-of-the-Century New York.* Philadelphia: Temple University Press, 1986.

Pender, John. "Manufacturing Oats into Bread Stuffs." *Fessenden's Silk Manual and Practical Farmer,* December 1836. In *American Periodicals Series Online, 1740–1900,* 118.

Philanthropos. "On the Regulation of the Price of Bread." *Columbian Magazine,* December 1789. In *American Periodicals Series Online, 1740–1900,* 714.

Plante, Ellen M. *The American Kitchen, 1700 to the Present: From Hearth to Highrise.* New York: Facts on File Press, 1995.

Poliquin, Rachel. "Vegetal Prejudice and Healing Territories in Early Modern England." In *Textual Healing: Essays on Medieval and Early Modern Medicine*, edited by Elizabeth Lane Furdell. Leiden, the Netherlands: Brill, 2005.

Pollan, Michael. *In Defense of Food: An Eater's Manifesto*. New York: Penguin, 2008.

———. *The Omnivore's Dilemma*. New York: Penguin, 2006.

Pratt, Lloyd. "Dialect Writing and Simultaneity in the American Historical Romance." *differences: A Journal of Feminist Cultural Studies* 13:3 (2002): 121–142.

Pritchet, Wendell E. *Brownsville, Brooklyn: Blacks, Jews, and the Changing Face of the Ghetto*. Chicago: University of Chicago Press, 2002.

Probyn, Elspeth. *Carnal Appetites: Foodsexidentities*. London: Routledge, 2000.

Rabelais, François. *Gargantua and Pantagruel*. New York: Penguin, 2006.

Randolph, Mary. *The Virginia Housewife; or, Methodical Cook: A Facsimile of an Authentic Early American Cookbook*. Baltimore: Plaskitt, Fite, 1838.

Ray, Krishnendu. *The Migrant's Table: Meals and Memories in Bengali-American Households*. Philadelphia: Temple University Press, 2004.

"Remarks on Bread." *Christian's, Scholar's, and Farmer's Magazine*, April–May 1790. In *American Periodicals Series Online, 1740–1900*, 118.

"Remarks on Carrots, as an Ingredient of Bread." *New York Magazine, or Literary Repository*, August 1796. In *American Periodicals Series Online, 1740–1900*, 424.

"Review of an Account of Experiments Tried by the Board of Agriculture, in the Composition of Various Sorts of Bread." *Weekly Magazine of Original Essays, Fugitive Pieces, and Interesting Intelligence*, August 4, 1798. In *American Periodicals Series Online, 1740–1900*, 20.

Reynolds, David S. *Beneath the American Renaissance: The Subversive Imagination in the Age of Emerson and Melville*. Cambridge: Harvard University Press, 1989.

Riggs, Marlon. *Ethnic Notions*. DVD. California Newsreel, 1986.

Roberts, Robert. *The House Servant's Dictionary; or, A Monitor for Private Families: Comprising Hints on the Arrangement and Performance of Servants' Work*. Boston: Munroe and Francis, 1827.

Robertson, Emma. *Chocolate, Women and Empire: A Social and Cultural History*. Manchester: Manchester University Press, 2010.

Romero, Lora. *Home Fronts: Domesticity and Its Critics in the Antebellum United States*. Durham: Duke University Press, 1997.

Rosenzweig, Roy. *Eight Hours for What We Will: Workers and Leisure in an Industrial City, 1870–1920*. New York: Cambridge University Press, 1985.

Rowe, John Carlos. *Literary Culture and U.S. Imperialism: From the Revolution to World War II*. New York: Oxford University Press, 2000.

Roy, Parama. *Alimentary Tracts: Appetites, Aversions, and the Postcolonial*. Durham: Duke University Press. 2010.

Ruark, Jennifer K. "More Scholars Focus on Historical, Social, and Cultural Meanings of Food, but Some Critics Say It's Scholarship-Lite: Selected Books in Food Studies." *Chronicle of Higher Education*, July 9, 1999. http://chronicle.com/article/More-Scholars-Focus-on-Hist/15471/.

Rubin, Gayle. "Thinking Sex: Notes for a Radical Theory of the Politics of Sexuality." In *Pleasure and Danger: Exploring Female Sexuality*, edited by Carole S. Vance, 267–293. London: Pandora, 1992.

Ryan, Barbara. "Kitchen Testimony: Ex-Slaves' Narratives in New Company." *Callaloo* 22:1 (1999): 141–156.

Ryan, Mary P. *Cradle of the Middle Class: The Family in Oneida County, New York, 1790–1865*. New York: Cambridge University Press, 1981.

Said, Edward W. *Culture and Imperialism*. New York: Vintage Books, 1994.

Samuels, Shirley. "The Identity of Slavery." In *The Culture of Sentiment: Race, Gender, and Sentimentality in Nineteenth-Century America*, edited by Shirley Samuels, 157–171. New York: Oxford University Press, 1999.

Sánchez-Eppler, Karen. "Bodily Bonds: The Intersecting Rhetorics of Feminism and Abolition." In *The Culture of Sentiment: Race, Gender, and Sentimentality in Nineteenth-Century America*, edited by Shirley Samuels, 93–107. New York: Oxford University Press, 1999.

———. *Dependent States: The Child's Part in Nineteenth-Century American Culture*. Chicago: University of Chicago Press, 2005.

———. *Touching Liberty: Abolition, Feminism, and the Politics of the Body*. Berkeley: University of California Press, 1993.

Satre, Lowell J. *Chocolate on Trial: Slavery, Politics, and the Ethics of Business*. Athens: Ohio University Press, 2005.

Scarry, Elaine. *The Body in Pain: The Making and Unmaking of the World*. New York: Oxford University Press, 1985.

Scheurer, Timothy E. *American Popular Music: The Nineteenth Century and Tin Pan Alley*. Bowling Green, OH: Bowling Green State University Press, 1989.

Schlosser, Eric. *Fast Food Nation: The Dark Side of the All-American Meal*. New York: Houghton Mifflin, 2001.

Scott, James C. *Domination and the Arts of Resistance: Hidden Transcripts*. New Haven: Yale University Press, 1992.

Sears, Clara Endicott, and Louisa May Alcott. *Bronson Alcott's Fruitlands*. Boston: Houghton Mifflin, 1915.

Sedgwick, Eve Kosofsky. "Jane Austen and the Masturbating Girl." In *Solitary Pleasures: The Historical, Literary, and Artistic Discourses of Autoeroticism*, edited by Paula Bennett and Vernon A. Rosario, 133–155. New York: Routledge, 1995.

———. *Tendencies*. Durham: Duke University Press, 1993.

Shamir, Millette. *Inexpressible Privacy: The Interior Life of Antebellum American Literature*. Philadelphia: University of Pennsylvania Press, 2006.

Shaw, Gwendolyn DuBois. *Seeing the Unspeakable*. Durham: Duke University Press, 2004.

Sheller, Mimi. *Consuming the Caribbean: From Arawaks to Zombies*. London: Routledge, 2003.

Shteir, Rachel. "Ethnic Theatre in America." In *A Companion to Twentieth-Century American Drama*, edited by David Krasner, 18–33. Malden, MA: Blackwell, 2007.

Simmons, Amelia. *American Cookery; or The Art of Dressing Viands, Fish, Poultry, and Vegetables, and the Best Modes of Making Pastes, Puffs, Pies, Tarts, Puddings, Custards, and Preserves, and All Kinds of Cakes, from the Imperial Plum to Plain Cake: Adapted to This Country, and All Grades of Life*. Albany, NY: C. R. Webster, 1796. Reprinted as *The First American Cookbook: A Facsimile of "American Cookery."* New York: Dover, 1984.

Sinclair, Upton. *The Jungle*. 1906; repr., New York: Penguin, 2006.

Sklar, Kathryn Kish. *Catharine Beecher: A Study in American Domesticity*. New York: Norton, 1976.

Spiegel, Marjorie. *The Dreaded Comparison: Human and Animal Slavery*. New York: Mirror Books, 1996.

Spillers, Hortense J. "Changing the Letter: The Yokes, the Jokes of Discourse, or, Mrs. Stowe, Mr. Reed." In *Slavery and the Literary Imagination*, edited by Deborah E. McDowell and Arnold Rampersad, 25–61. Baltimore: Johns Hopkins University Press, 1989.

———. "Mama's Baby, Papa's Maybe: An American Grammar Book." In *Black, White, and in Color: Essays on American Literature and Culture*. Chicago: University of Chicago Press, 2003.

Stallybrass, Peter, and Allon White. *The Politics and Poetics of Transgression*. Ithaca: Cornell University Press, 1986.

Stein, Jordan Alexander. "Mary Rowlandson's Hunger and the Historiography of Sexuality." *American Literature* 81 (2009): 469–495.

Stelle, Charles Clarkson. *Americans and the China Opium Trade in the Nineteenth Century*. New York: Arno, 1981.

Stern, Julia. "Excavating Genre in *Our Nig*." *American Literature* 67:3 (September 1995): 439–466.

Stewart, Jacqueline Najuma. *Migrating to the Movies*. Berkeley: University of California Press, 2005.

Stoler, Ann Laura. "Matters of Intimacy as Matters of State: A Response." *Journal of American History* 88:3 (December 2001): 893–897.

———. *Race and the Education of Desire: Foucault's History of Sexuality and the Colonial Order of Things*. Durham: Duke University Press, 1995.

———. "Tense and Tender Ties: The Politics of Comparison in North American and (Post) Colonial Studies." *Journal of American History* 88:3 (December 2001): 829–865.

Stowe, Harriet Beecher. *Agnes of Sorrento*. Boston: Ticknor and Fields, 1862.

——— [Christopher Crowfield, pseud.]. "Chapter IX: Service," from the *House and Home Papers*. *Atlantic Monthly*, January 1864, 442.

———. "Our Second Girl." *Atlantic Monthly*, January 1868, 442–463.

———. *Uncle Tom's Cabin; or, Life among the Lowly*. 1852; repr., New York: Penguin, 1981.

Strasser, Susan. *Never Done: A History of American Housework*. New York: Holt, 2000.

"Struggling with 'Othello'; Second Rehearsal of the Colored Theatrical Troupe." *New York Times*, April 18, 1884.

Sweeney, Mark. "Cadbury Apologises to Naomi Campbell over 'Racist' Ad." *Guardian* (UK), June 3, 2011. http://www.guardian.co.uk/media/2011/jun/03/cadbury-naomi-campbell-ad (accessed June 3, 2011).

Tadman, Michael. *Speculators and Slaves: Masters, Traders, and Slaves in the Old South.* Madison: University of Wisconsin Press, 1996.

Takaki, Ronald. *Iron Cages: Race and Culture in 19th-Century America.* 2nd ed. New York: Oxford University Press, 2000.

Tchen, John Kuo Wei. *New York before Chinatown: Orientalism and the Shaping of American Culture, 1776–1882.* Baltimore: Johns Hopkins University Press, 2001.

Terrio, Susan J. *Crafting the Culture and History of French Chocolate.* Berkeley: University of California Press, 2000.

Tompkins, Jane. *Sensational Designs: The Cultural Work of American Fiction, 1790–1860.* New York: Oxford University Press, 1986.

———. "Sentimental Power: *Uncle Tom's Cabin* and the Politics of Literary History." In *Sensational Designs: The Cultural Work of American Fiction, 1790–1860*, 122–146. New York: Oxford University Press, 1985.

Trachtenberg, Alan. "Seeing and Believing: Hawthorne's Reflections on the Daguerreotype in *The House of Seven Gables.*" *American Literary History* 9:3 (1997): 460.

Turgeon, Laurier, and Madeleine Pastinelli. "'Eat the World': Postcolonial Encounters in Quebec City's Ethnic Restaurants." *Journal of American Folklore* 115:456 (Spring 2002): 247–268.

Turner Dorset, Catharine Ann. *Think Before You Speak; or, The Three Wishes: A Tale.* Philadelphia: Johnson and Warner, 1809.

Veblen, Thorstein. *The Theory of the Leisure Class.* New York: B. W. Huebsch, 1912.

Walters, Ronald. *American Reformers, 1815–1860.* Rev. ed. New York: Hill and Wang, 1997.

Walton, John K. *Histories of Tourism: Representation, Identity, and Conflict.* Bristol, UK: Channel View, 2005.

Warner, Michael. "Whitman Drunk." In *Publics and Counterpublics*, 269–289. New York: Zone Books, 2005.

Weiner, Juli. "Accidentally Cannibalistic Cookbook Suggest Using 'Freshly Ground Black People,' Not 'Black Pepper.'" *Vanity Fair* (*VF Daily Online*), April 19, 2010. http://www.vanityfair.com/online/daily/2010/04/accidentally-cannibalistic-cookbook-suggests-using-freshly-ground-black-people-not-black-pepper.html (accessed November 25, 2011).

"'Whatcha Gonna Do?': Revisiting 'Mama's Baby, Papa's Maybe: An American Grammar Book': A Conversation with Hortense Spillers, Saidiya Hartman, Farah Jasmine Griffin, Shelly Eversley and Jennifer L. Morgan." *Women's Studies Quarterly* 35:1–2 (Spring–Summer 2007): 299–309.

"Wholesome and Nutritious Bread from Saw-Dust." *Journal of Health*, November 9, 1831. In *American Periodicals Series Online, 1740–1900*, 70.

Wilde, Mark William. "Industrialization of Food Processing in the United States, 1860–1960." Ph.D. diss., University of Delaware, 1988.

Williams-Forson, Psyche A. *Building Houses Out of Chicken Legs: Black Women, Food, and Power.* Chapel Hill: University of North Carolina Press, 2006.

Wilson, Harriet. *Our Nig; Sketches from the Life of a Free Black, in a Two-Story White House, North: Showing That Slavery's Shadows Fall Even There.* 2nd ed. Edited by Henry Louis Gates, Jr. New York: Viking, 1983.

Wilson, Sarah. "Melville and the Architecture of Antebellum Masculinity." *American Literature* 76:1 (2004): 59–87.

Witt, Doris. *Black Hunger: Food and the Politics of U.S. Identity.* New York: Oxford University Press, 1999.

Wolfe, Cary. *Animal Rites: American Culture, the Discourse of Species, and Posthumanist Culture.* Chicago: University of Chicago Press, 2003.

Wood, Marcus. *Blind Memory.* Manchester: Manchester University Press, 2000.

The World Turned Upside Down; or The Comical Metamorphoses: A Work Entirely Calculated to Excite Laughter in Grown Persons and Promote Morality in the Young Ones of Both Sexes: Decorated with 34 Copper Plates Curiously Drawn and Engraved. Boston: I. Norman, 1794.

Wu, Cynthia. "The Siamese Twins in Late-Nineteenth-Century Narratives of Conflict and Reconciliation." *American Literature* 80:1 (2008): 29.

Wu, Jean Yu-wen Shen, and Min Song. *Asian American Studies: A Reader.* New Brunswick: Rutgers University Press, 2000.

Xu, Wenying. *Eating Identities: Reading Food in Asian American Literature.* Honolulu: University of Hawaiʻi Press, 2008.

Yellin, Jean Fagan. "Hawthorne and the American National Sin." In *The Green American Tradition: Essays and Poems for Sherman Paul,* edited by H. Daniel Peck, 75–97. Baton Rouge: University of Louisiana Press, 1989.

Yoshihara, Mari. *Embracing the East: White Women and American Orientalism.* New York: Oxford University Press, 2002.

Young, Allen M. *The Chocolate Tree: A Natural History of Cacao.* 2nd ed. Gainesville: University Press of Florida, 2007.

Young, Elizabeth. *Disarming the Nation.* Chicago: University of Chicago Press, 1999.

Yue, Gang. *The Mouth That Begs: Hunger, Cannibalism, and the Politics of Eating in Modern China.* Durham: Duke University Press, 1999.

Zafar, Rafia. "The Proof of the Pudding: Of Haggis, Hasty Pudding, and Transatlantic Influence." *Early American Literature* 31:2 (1996): 133–149.

Index

Illustrations are denoted by page numbers in italics, or by reference to the numbered Color Plate section.

About the Author

Kyla Wazana Tompkins is Associate Professor of English and Gender and Women's Studies at Pomona College. She is a former journalist and restaurant critic and has published in *Callaloo*, the *Journal of Food, Culture and Society*, and *Gastronomica*, as well as the *Globe and Mail*, *Xtra!* Magazine and the *San Francisco Chronicle*.